D0018615

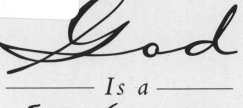

# God Is a Verb

KABBALAH AND

THE PRACTICE OF

MYSTICAL JUDAISM

*Rabbi David A. Cooper*

RIVERHEAD BOOKS, NEW YORK

Most Riverhead Books are available at special quantity discounts for bulk purchases for sales promotions, premiums, fund-raising or educational use. Special books, or book excerpts, can also be created to fit specific needs.

For details, write: Special Markets, The Berkley Publishing Group, 375 Hudson Street, New York, New York 10014.

Riverhead Books
Published by The Berkley Publishing Group
A division of Penguin Putnam Inc.
375 Hudson Street
New York, New York 10014

Copyright © 1997 by Rabbi David A. Cooper
Book design by Judith Stagnitto Abbate
Interior illustrations by Ark Lemal
Cover design copyright © 1997 by Marc J. Cohen
Back cover photograph of the author by John Liskin

All rights reserved. This book, or parts thereof, may not be reproduced in any form without permission.

First Riverhead hardcover edition: August 1997
First Riverhead trade paperback edition: September 1998
Riverhead trade paperback ISBN: 1-57322-694-7

The Library of Congress has catalogued the Riverhead hardcover edition as follows:

Cooper, David A.
God is a verb : Kabbalah and the practice of mystical Judaism /
by David A. Cooper.
p.     cm.
Includes bibliographical references and index.
ISBN 1-57322-055-8
1. Spiritual life—Judaism.  2. Cabala.  3. Judaism—Essence,
genius, nature.  I. Title.
BM723.C66   1997
296.7'12—DC21            97-12353   CIP

Printed in the United States of America

30 29 28 27 26 25 24 23

This book is dedicated to my parents, Helene Markens and Sampson D. Cooper, who now dwell in realms beyond this reality but nonetheless frequently visit me in dreams and dozens of other ways to *kvetch* and *kvell* about how I am living my life.

# PREFACE

*J*EWISH MYSTICS have always been reticent to reveal the esoteric teachings of Kabbalah. The Talmud says that these secret teachings are to be carefully controlled. As a result, mainstream Jewish scholars prior to the twentieth century rarely explored this segment of hidden knowledge. More important, as the mystical insight of kabbalistic wisdom was reserved for only a handful of practitioners, most people involved in Judaism never had the opportunity to experience the wealth of this treasure within the tradition.

During the last half of this century, great strides have been taken to investigate and make available heretofore inaccessible kabbalistic material. Many texts have been translated and considerable research has been undertaken at institutes of higher learning. However, a gap still stands between the intellectual appreciation of these esoteric teachings and their integration into everyday Jewish practice.

Prior to fifty years ago, anyone saying the things that are addressed in this book might have been ostracized by the rabbinic community. Some readers would have been outraged to see esoteric discussions meant to be read by only a selected few. A large number would have been ill at ease with Torah interpretations from an egalitarian perspective. Still others would have found the mystical teachings of the *Zohar* quite strange, and in some ways a little too close for comfort to Eastern belief.

Thus, I resonate deeply with the feelings expressed by Rabbi Aryeh Kaplan, the most prolific modern commentator on Jewish mysticism, who opens one of his books, *Meditation and Kabbalah,* with the following statement: "It is with great trepidation that one begins to write a work such as this. . . ."

I often encounter objections to elementary mystical Jewish teachings by fellow Jews who are unfamiliar with the scope and breadth of their own tradition. Typically, they are in denial. I have been told that meditation is not Jewish; belief in reincarnation is not Jewish; praying alone is not the Jewish way. These people are mistaken. Indeed, Jewish mysticism is a profoundly sensual, nature-connected spiritual practice that openly discusses angels and demons, souls' journeys after death, reincarnation, resurrection, and the goal of achieving messianic consciousness. This often is a source of considerable embarrassment for some Jewish teachers. They don't like to talk about such things.

Yet one of the biggest complaints of people in the West, Jews in particular, is that our religious traditions are not spiritual enough. We want to feel a connection with the great unknown; we want to experience the secrets of other realities and the meaning of life. We want spiritual practices that touch the heart and nourish the soul. We want a place of sanctuary where we can get a respite from the busy world around us.

Our yearning to reconnect with our essential nature transcends the limits of the intellect. It comes from a place of inner knowing that there is far more to life than material wealth. We know deeply within that the mysteries of creation speak in a language that can be absorbed only through "being" rather than by doing or thinking.

Western religious tradition and mythology are built upon the foundation of the teachings of the Old Testament. Many of these teachings became ossified long ago in fixed beliefs; to challenge them meant to be excommunicated. Now spiritual leaders in the West have had the courage to suggest different possibilities for understanding ancient tales. This new way of looking at things opens the gates for the potential of a paradigm shift that will change our very thought process and our relationship with the Divine.

This book contains many ancient ideas expressed in modern language. It suggests ways of interpreting biblical stories that confront traditional perspectives. All of the material presented has been thoroughly researched and cited for anyone interested who would like to inquire into the sources.

The purpose of this book is to provide insight into the foundation of Western mysticism. The reader does not need a background in traditional religious study to appreciate the ideas discussed herein. Although the base of information is from a Jewish point of view, the insights overflow into Christian and Muslim traditions, for the teachings are universal. This book is also written for people who are drawn to Eastern practices—Buddhism, Hinduism, Taoism—to add to the dialogue and cross-fertilization of mystical insight between East and West.

If you are among the many people in the West who seek a richer spiritual life in the tradition of your heritage, you will discover within this book a new world of almost endless possibilities. This is not a book simply to be read, but to be experienced. It uses hasidic tales to amplify teachings, and offers exercises for those who would like to integrate practice into everyday life. This is a guide for the person who really wants to nurture the soul and come closer to God. If you are such a person, welcome to the hidden treasures of Jewish mysticism.

# AUTHOR'S NOTE

ESTERN LANGUAGE persists in referring to God in masculine terminology, despite thousand-year-old teachings of mystics that emphasize the fact that God does not have a gender. Is it not time to stop this practice?

Throughout this book, whenever I needed a pronoun for God or the Divine, I used the neutral "It." The truth is that God should not even be called It, because this suggests a "thing." God is not a thing. But the limits of language compel some kind of pronoun, and It is far superior to He.

Along these lines, I have taken the liberty to adjust translations in a way that neutralizes the subject. An example of this is the following quotation offered in the first section of the thirteenth-century Jewish sage Abraham Abulafia: "Now we are no longer separated from our source, and behold we *are* the source and the source is us. We are so intimately united with It, we cannot by any means be separated from It, for we are It."

In this case, the original read: "Now he is no longer separated from his Master, and behold he is his Master, and his Master is he: for he is so intimately united with Him, he cannot by any means be separated from Him, for he is He." As the thrust of my writing is to find a new relationship with the Divine—in which It is definitely not "Master"—I see no point in continuing to perpetuate references that imply God is a He and that all spiritual aspirants are men.

In addition to changing gender references, I have more freely translated text to bring concepts up to date. The *Zohar* uses archaic and obscure language that does not include words for awareness and levels of consciousness, but the intent is there. Rather than staying with literal translations that would only serve to confuse the issue, I have offered interpretive translations with the full knowledge that some linguists would disagree. This is a risk I am willing to take. I would rather initiate an open debate than continue to hide these wonderful ideas in the camouflage of puzzling language.

The transliteration of Hebrew or Aramaic terms also has been simplified. Many methods are available, but each has its deficiencies. For example, the guttural sound of *ch*, as in the name *Bach*, is common in Hebrew. Rather than introduce confusing diacritical marks, such as a dot under an *h*, I simply spell the word as it sounds: *chesed, chayah, chochma*, or *chutzpah*. However, in some instances where the *ch* might be confusing, I use *kh*, as in *malkhut* rather than *malchut*. In all instances, I have attempted to write the word as it sounds rather than adhere to a convention. Easy readability takes precedence over arbitrary consistency.

Although Sephardic pronunciation is the standard in Israel, Ashkenazic pronunciation is often heard, particularly in religious neighborhoods. Almost all of the words in this book are transliterated in the Sephardic manner. However, the word for the Sabbath has been offered both ways: Shabbat and Shabbos. Each has its own flavor and both are important.

The world of mysticism lends itself to a multitude of interpretations. Each of us has filters; we select what comes in and what goes out. Although I have carefully researched a wide variety of esoteric material, the ideas expressed in this book are the result of my own perceptions and understanding, and they do not represent any particular school or teacher. Any errors in translations are my own; I take full responsibility for the level of scholarship presented herein.

# ACKNOWLEDGMENTS

*T*HE MYSTIC KNOWS THAT an untold number of variables interact to influence how our days will flow in the dance we call life. The way things happen, opportunities that present themselves, how we react, our very thoughts are inextricably interwoven with our relationships, families, friends, associates, and the unknown forces that surround us. Thus, while it is important to acknowledge the help and love we receive, whatever we say always seems to fall somewhat short. For, more than we realize, our lives hinge on little things: one telephone call, a letter, a thoughtful gesture, even a nod or smile at just the right moment.

With this in mind, I am thankful to all of those, known and unknown, in this world and in others, who have played a role in the writing of this book. I do not feel that it is my book; the ideas in it do not belong to anyone. These are universal teachings, hopefully said in a way that brings them home to a larger number of people.

In the process of putting the words to paper, I found that many casual conversations or teaching situations added a new dimension to the writing. It was as if we were all engaged in a collaborative effort, without it being named as such. Mysteriously, subjects were brought up and insights offered at precisely the right moments to be included in the manuscript; the spirit of universal guidance made its presence known.

My wife, Shoshana, played a major role in this process. During the writing of this book, we spent a great deal of time teaching and learning from each other. We discussed esoteric material throughout the day and particularly on Shabbat. Many times we discovered a new idea; neither her thought nor mine, alone, but ours. As we are continuously together on the path of spiritual inquiry, she is not only my helpmate, friend, lover, and advisor, she is a co-creator of this book. Although I have been blessed with some writing skills and a talent for expression, without Shoshana this book never could have been written.

As a rabbi, I am privileged to work with many wise people who are my teachers as well as my students. I am particularly indebted to the members of my Kabbalah and Torah classes, for many have raised questions or offered insights that have opened new gateways for me. Of course, I would not have any of my rabbinic skills if it were not for the many teachers who have transmitted the wisdom of mystical Judaism. Most of these spiritual guides speak to me from other realms, but I have been most fortunate to have been taught by two outstanding teachers of this century, Rabbi Zalman Schacter-Shalomi and Rabbi Shlomo Carlebach, may his memory be a blessing for all beings.

A number of people read parts of the manuscript in the early stages. I wish to thank them all, including Marty and Min Kantrowitz, Elie Spitz, Reuben Weinzveg, and Tom Hast. I especially want to thank my friend Eliezer Sobel, who carefully read the entire final draft. His suggestions were invaluable.

This book was indirectly conceived in the fertile mind of Tami Simon, the owner of Sounds True Catalogue, who first suggested that I record a taped series on Kabbalah. Many thanks, as well, to the entire Sounds True staff for the quality of their work and their enthusiasm. Another friend who indirectly played a role in the development of this book was Joel Fotinos, the publisher of Jeremy Tarcher Books, who has always been a great fan.

The single most important driving force behind this book, however, has been my editor, Amy Hertz. Amy had the initial vision for a comprehensive work on Jewish mysticism, and has continuously improved this manuscript throughout its development. It would not resemble its final shape without her tireless efforts all along the way.

Of course, my agent, Ned Leavitt, handled this project with great timing and the right frame of mind to keep things on track. Ned makes sure that lines of communication remain open. His efforts were of enormous value to the health and well-being of this book.

My thanks to all of you. I hope and pray that our joint efforts will touch some souls and that this book will help heighten awareness and bring the world closer to the peace and harmony that is our destiny.

# CONTENTS

# INTRODUCTION

*The wisdom of philosophy ends with the physical world.*
*Beyond the stars, it can only imagine God's Essence. There are*
*actually many levels of universes beyond this, but this truth is*
*only found in the Kabbalah. It is written, "God's*
*understanding cannot be grasped" (Isaiah 40:28). One who*
*knows the truth of Kabbalah perceives this well, for there is*
*level above level . . .*

—REBBE NACHMAN OF BRESLOV[1]

ODAY IS THE first day of the Counting of the Omer, a day that encompasses the mystical heart of lovingkindness, the second day of Passover in the Hebrew calendar year 5755 (1995).[2] According to Jewish mysticism, five thousand seven hundred fifty-five years ago, a new paradigm of human consciousness was born. It was a paradigm shift in the world, for it was a level of awareness that could consciously merge with its own origin. The beginning and continuation of this merging make up what we call the process of enlightenment. Kabbalists say that we are rapidly approaching another major paradigm shift in awareness. It will be called messianic consciousness, and we will understand everything in an entirely new light.

Today is one week after my fifty-sixth birthday. The Kabbalah teaches that each year in a person's life, a particular quality is accentuated. The fifty-sixth year of one's life is a period in which one is immersed in the loving side of one's strength, a domain of enormous forgiveness in the cosmic flow and a fresh opportunity to raise holy sparks within and around oneself to higher levels of awareness.[3]

Thus, today is an auspicious time for me to begin writing a book. It is a book about the mysteries of life and death, a search into the mystical teachings of creation and creator, and an exploration into realms of consciousness that transcend the boundaries of our minds.

My spiritual quest was initiated more than forty years ago, during my teens, when I began to understand that we, as human beings, at one time or another in our lives, have unusual experiences, connections with other realities, moments of deep insight into the nature of things, inexplicable dreams that transcend the imagination, and inner voices that direct us along peculiar paths. Most important, everyone seems to have perplexing relationships with family, friends, lovers, and even strangers which constantly touch a mysterious inner essence that in the West we call the soul.

During the era of the 1960s, when I was in my twenties, Eastern spiritual traditions gained extraordinary popularity among many people of my generation. Some of those followers were called flower children, an interesting name for the blossoming of a new era. Indeed, it was often called the birthing of the Age of Aquarius. It became a subculture, the New Age. Today the New Age seems somewhat worn out, but then it was a youthful, exhilarating time.

In the sixties, Zen Buddhism flourished in San Francisco, as did an American version of Sufism, the mystical lineage of the Islamic tradition. Hinduism permeated the streets of the Haight-Ashbury district, and the chants of *aum* could be heard in many parts of Golden Gate Park. Hari Krishna drummers and dancers often swooned in ecstasy on the busy corners of Montgomery Street, in the financial district, as bemused working people walked briskly to their offices. I was one of those in suit and tie, puzzled and intrigued by the energy and vitality of this new outlook on life.

I became a student of Eastern traditions, reading about the ideologies, experiencing many of the practices. The world of gray suits and business transactions soon became dull in comparison with the glitter of exotic spiritual exercises and the wisdom of ancient teachings—not to speak of the fact that it was cool and hip to be a renegade. In my late-twenties, after having developed an upwardly mobile career in San Francisco and New York, I quit my job and began traveling, all my worldly possessions in a small pack.

I traveled for many years, reading every book I could find on Buddhism and Hinduism, searching for the secret of existence and the purpose of life. It was a noble pilgrimage, one that has been taken by untold numbers of spiritual seekers, and it left me with far more questions than I had when I began.

In my mid-thirties I met my wife-to-be, Susan, who later became Shoshana, and the direction of my spiritual inquiry changed. Within the first couple of years of our relationship, we began to explore the practice of taking solitary, silent retreats.

Our first group retreat was with Sufis, and we were initiated as members of the Sufi Order of the West. After this, I frequently undertook personal meditation retreats, spending days and sometimes weeks in silence. During this period I used Sufi techniques, particularly *wazifas* (a type of mantra), a process in which one repeats a name connected with attributes of the Divine. I also took on the practice of *dhikr,* which means remembrance, a chant that repeats the Arabic words *La illa-ha il Allah-Hu,* which means "There is no God but God."

Something extraordinary began to occur during these retreats. I started to let go of intellectual inquiry as I discovered a deeper sense of knowing that transcended the mind. An undefinable perception floated in shadow realms that exist between the conscious and unconscious mind. I could not discern the nature of these hidden teachings, but I knew without a doubt that a profound awareness was within my reach.

As my retreats became longer and more penetrating, I realized that I wanted to intensify all aspects of my spiritual quest. During a forty-day retreat when I was forty-one years old, I decided to immerse myself in Jewish mysticism. This was not a logical decision, for although I had been born of Jewish parents, I knew hardly anything about Judaism.

## Meditation and Insight

We moved to Jerusalem and lived in the fortress of the Old City, less than a five-minute walk to the Western Wall. Although I was primarily interested in mystical teachings, I had to do a great deal of catch-up as a late bloomer to learn the elementary aspects of Jewish practice. This took a number of years.

Judaism, in general, is a rich and diverse tradition. It is filled with ritual and observance. The study of Torah and Talmud is extraordinary. The daily life of a practicing Jew is quite demanding, requiring close attention to details in every matter: how and what we eat, when to pray, how to relate to others, the ethics of business, moral codes of behavior, and, of course, how we relate to God.

The mystical component of Judaism, often called Kabbalah, is more interested in the esoteric nature of creation. What is God? How did creation occur? What are the hidden meanings of the teachings of the Torah? What is the architecture of the cosmos? What is ultimate truth? This is not an easy field of study. Much of it is veiled behind technical language, arcane concepts, and intentionally obscure codes. Only a handful of Kabbalists wrote about their experiences. Most, however, chose to remain hidden in anonymity.

In addition, virtually all of the commentary in Jewish religious literature is from the male perspective. Almost everything written about the Kabbalah tends to be intellectual and abstract, more theoretical metaphysics than practical wisdom. I was seeking meaning in life, not a system of abstruse concepts, and the first couple of years were quite challenging.

I turned back to my meditative practice, which I knew held the key to deep spiritual wisdom. All of the major religious traditions use meditation in one form or another. In silence, when I allowed my cognitive function to rest, a deeper understanding invariably arose.

It is important to note that sitting quietly is precisely the opposite approach to that of normative Jewish learning, which engages the mind in complex problems and analyzes every facet of an argument in extraordinary detail. I had experienced this process of *pilpul* (dialectics and debate) in *yeshiva* (an institution of Jewish higher learning) for a number of years, but it had not taken me to the wisdom level I was seeking. This kind of learning nurtured my hunger for information, and working with the Talmud is a highly satisfying experience, but I wanted to be more in communion with God; I needed to feel surrounded by the presence of the Divine at all times. This longing seemed to arise primarily during contemplative practices, so my need for silent meditation became more urgent.

At this time I encountered *vipassana,* insight meditation, a school of Buddhism that utilizes an intense practice of silence for extended periods. While on a retreat, it is not unusual for a student to sit in meditation for nine or ten hours a day, in forty-five- to sixty-minute segments. During the periods between sitting, walking meditation is performed, which adds up to another six to seven hours of meditation each day. The goal of the practice is for the student to maintain a meditative state throughout all of the waking hours, including during mealtimes.

Although this schedule may seem severe, most students of *vipassana* discover that after an initial adjustment of three or four days of practice, the rhythm of constant meditation quickly leads one to an altered state of consciousness that opens gates of penetrating insight—precisely what I wanted.

Westerners who experience Buddhism, Hinduism, Sufism, or other contemplative traditions often are transformed by the state of mind that can be induced through serious meditative practice. At times this transformation is so overwhelming, the meditator chooses to "convert" to a new religion. However, many have found that their contemplative experiences actually open new gateways into their original spiritual heritages. This was my experience. Suddenly I discovered new depths in Judaism: the commentaries to the Torah became alive, and my study of Kabbalah took an entirely different turn.

I had not fully appreciated the difference between learning Kabbalah as an intellectual exercise and experiencing Kabbalah through mystical insight. Some of the writings of Jewish mystics clearly indicate that much of their Kabbalah came through contemplative experience. For example, in the sixteenth century, Eleazar Azikri, a member of the kabbalistic circle of Moses Cordovero in Safed, stated that *hitbodedut* (isolation) was "helpful to the soul seven times more than study, and according to one's strength and ability, he or she should concentrate and meditate one [entire] day a week."[4]

Concerning one's practice, Azikri gave the following advice: "At every moment one should try to unite names [of God] with joy and trembling. One should flee from society as much as is possible and be completely silent, in a brilliant flame, alone, fearful and trembling. The light which is above your head make always into your teacher."[5] There are dozens of writings similar those of Azikri, but finding a living teacher in our day who exemplifies these teachings is not easy to do.[6]

Quite simply, Kabbalah cannot be comprehended solely through the intellect. Rather, Kabbalah is a way of life and a way of looking at things. One becomes a Kabbalist by bringing a new level of awareness to every act, every word that flows out of one's mouth, and every thought that arises in the mind. We do not gain kabbalistic insight simply through the intellect; we gain it by the way we live our lives, which includes integrating study, daily practice, and contemplative exercises. We immerse ourselves in different aspects of kabbalistic teachings, and from this, mystical awareness arises.

The mystery of life is and always has been the central focus of the contemplative mind. Almost everyone spends his or her early years as a natural mystic, wondering about how things work. What holds us to the earth while birds seem free from all restraints? Where does the wind come from, and why are all those stars in the sky? As we grow older, many explanations are given, but new questions arise that ultimately lead to a shrug of the shoulders from our parents and teachers, and eventually even from philosophers.

Somewhere along the way, as we mature sexually, our focus of attention shifts dramatically. We become absorbed in the mysteries of love, relationship, and individuality, and the eternal questions of life are buried within. We are embarrassed to tell others about what is happening inside of us, and often we struggle with these secrets of life in silence.

As adults, most of us are so preoccupied with financial and family issues that we spend little, if any, time contemplating life's predicaments. Nonetheless they present themselves, suddenly and overwhelmingly, throughout our lives. Often this happens as the result of highly stressful and traumatic events: violent accidents, severe illness, or death.

Kabbalistic teachings are quite clear on one matter: Things are more than we think they are. This world is a reflection of, and is in symbiotic relationship with, other realms of reality. Each event that we experience has a deeper message if we have the eyes to see and the ears to hear. Everything has mystical meaning and significance. Life is enormously rich and purposeful once we are able to penetrate its mysteries.

## THE BOOK OF ADAM

In the eighteenth century, the Baal Shem Tov dramatically changed the character of Judaism by proposing that joy, prayer, and an ecstatic connection with God through physical action were as important, if not more so, than simply living an observant life as a Jew. He is viewed as one of the key leaders in the movement that was built on these ideas, which is called Hasidism. According to scholars, the hasidic movement is based on kabbalistic principles.[7]

Legend teaches that the Baal Shem Tov received his secret wisdom from a mysterious source called the *Book of Adam*. It is said that there is only one copy of this book in existence. It is designed with an essential, mysterious ingredient that cannot be reproduced. The letters themselves, their shapes and shadings, all contain a spark of the Divine.

Not only is this book unique, the reader herself or himself must know how to interpret its coded messages. The secrets are hidden behind veils within veils, so that those who are ignorant of the power of truth cannot misuse these teachings. You see, the *Book of Adam* reveals the definitive explanation of the meaning and purpose of life and death, love and relationship, souls, angels, and other realms of reality.

The original text of the *Book of Adam* was given to the primordial beings, Adam and Eve, who passed it, along with the methods needed for interpretation, on to their successors. If the book fell into the hands of one who had not attained spiritual maturity, his or her misunderstanding inevitably would bring about this person's own downfall. Thus the mysterious book was passed from teacher to student for more than five thousand years, until it came into the possession a few hundred years ago of someone called Rabbi Adam.

Rabbi Adam's son Yitzhak was a learned person, but he lacked the inner fire and yearning that one needs to be successful in the search for ultimate truth. Rabbi Adam knew that his son could never learn from this book on his own. In the hour of Rabbi Adam's death, he instructed Yitzhak to take the book to the town of Okup. There he was to search for a boy named Israel the son of Eliezer. For it was young Israel ben Eliezer, and only he among all the learned people in the world, who could glean the deeper meanings hidden in this holy book.

Reb Yitzhak traveled to Okup, a difficult journey in those days. He searched for Israel ben Eliezer and was told not to waste his time with this lazy boy. Indeed, the people of the town could not understand why the boy spent most of his time wandering alone in the woods. They did not realize that he was learning the language of the winds, the dance of the bees, and the deepest wisdom-teachings of the forest.

Reb Yitzhak hired the boy to run errands, and waited until he was certain that the boy actually merited seeing the book. As part of his wages, the boy was given a place to sleep in the stable behind the house. One dark night, Reb Yitzhak noticed a light glowing from beneath the barn door. He hurried out, concerned lest a candle had set the hay ablaze. Before reaching the door, Reb Yitzhak glanced through a window and saw young Israel absorbed in the study of a book. Behold! The boy was aglow in the rapture of his contemplation. There were no candles burning that night.

The next morning, Reb Yitzhak gave the *Book of Adam* to Israel ben Eliezer. The boy quickly became engrossed and studied this magical text day and night. Once again, whenever the boy was hunched over the book, a glowing light emanated throughout the room as if it were filled with lamps. With each line Israel read, he experienced a continuous flow of wondrous thoughts, as if the book's author were able to whisper directly into his mind.

Grasping the meaning of this experience required a special intuition, a place of inner knowing necessary for learning teachings that transcend the intellect. Reb Yitzhak lacked this insight. Unfortunately, Israel was unsuccessful in his attempts to teach Rabbi Adam's son. After many frustrating experiences, Reb Yitzhak begged Israel to use kabbalistic means to invoke the prophet Elijah, who is known to all as the Prince of Teaching. Israel urged Reb Yitzhak to wait; it was a dangerous experience to undertake. But Reb Yitzhak insisted.

They fasted and purified themselves for six days. Then they began the ritual to summon the Prince of Teaching. However, just as Israel intoned one of the names of God, Reb Yitzhak could not maintain his concentration. He lost focus and his mind wandered. This lapse occurred at a critical instant and had terrible consequences. Rather than invoking the Prince of Teaching, they inadvertently invoked the Prince of Fire. As everyone knows, the Prince of Fire consumes everything in its path unless one instantly builds a shield of faith for protection.

They both immediately built this shield in their imaginations. They knew that their only chance for survival was to remain awake until sunrise, when the Prince of Fire would lose its power. All was fine until, just before dawn, Reb Yitzhak could stay awake no longer. He dozed off for a mere few seconds, and in a flash, the Prince of Fire took him away.

From this time on, Israel ben Eliezer studied the *Book of Adam* by himself. He learned how to invoke the different names of God, all of which, when pronounced correctly, have power to heal the world. With this knowledge he was able to keep the world in good repair, and it is because of this that he is called the Baal Shem Tov, which means Master of the Holy Name.

## THE MYSTERIES OF
## LIFE AND DEATH

Is there really meaning and purpose in life and death? Are there wisdom-teachings that reveal universal truths? What is the connection between Adam and Eve and the *Book of Adam*? How are wisdom-teachings encoded, and what is needed to break the codes? What does it mean to invoke divine protection, and how does one do this? What was lacking in Rabbi Adam's son? What do we need in order to gain access to profound wisdom-teachings?

These questions, and others that intrigue Kabbalists, are asked by everyone. What is God? What is the purpose of creation? What is a soul? Are there really soul mates? What happens after death? Is there reincarnation? What is holiness? What is truth? What is wisdom? What is the basis of faith? Are there angels? What is heaven all about, and what is hell? Does prayer really accomplish anything? What is the basis of forgiveness? Can suffering in this world ever end? If we have a soul, does it suffer after death? What does it mean to sin? What is true freedom? Finally, which spiritual practices can we use to attain higher wisdom and greater awareness?

These were the issues discussed in the *Book of Adam,* and they are the questions we address in *God Is a Verb.*

Is it not curious that although we have great libraries in which virtually all of the world's wisdom-teachings are readily available, although we have access to more information than the greatest scholars and monarchs of the past, we have not been able to use this knowledge sufficiently to actually raise our levels of awareness much higher than others could a few thousand years ago? Indeed, many would say that we have regressed. Great teachers have taught what they know, but somehow great students are extraordinarily rare.

The world has grown in the knowledge of some fields of inquiry. We have increased our scientific information; we have improved our technology; we have made gains in the social sciences and in the field of economics. Our philosophical and spiritual wisdom, however, seems to be at a standstill; we seem not to learn the lessons of the past. We know nothing more about creation today than was known by the Greeks. Concepts of heaven and hell remain mysterious. The efficacy of prayer for healing has been documented, but we have not the slightest idea how it works.[8] The interconnectedness of all things is a truism of current spiritual and scientific wisdom, but it seems more theoretical than a working reality.

## ENLIGHTENMENT

One of the primary texts of the Kabbalah, the *Zohar,* cries out to humankind, saying, "You beings on earth who are in deep slumber, awaken! Who among you has labored to turn darkness into light and bitterness into sweetness?"[9] It pleads with us, "Stop sleeping! Wake up! What are you waiting for?"

In my readings and wanderings throughout the years, I have gathered wisdom-teachings from around the world. In truth, if I were able to collate and distill all that I collected, it could be summed up entirely in the three admonishments of this kabbalistic teaching: Awaken! Enlighten! Transform darkness into light!

Spiritual teachers ultimately agree that true wisdom does not come from outside of us, but from within. And it does not come from within simply because we want it. It comes when we live in a way that invites wisdom. It comes through direct experience.

Here is a good example of direct experience: Consider the fragrance of a rose. If we try to describe this scent to someone who has never before smelled a flower, we fail. It is impossible to accurately relate this aroma through language. We may come close by referring to similar experiences, but we can never be successful using only the intellect. Yet, place a rose into the hand of a person, and in the briefest instant the communication will be completed without words.

So it is with the greatest wisdom-teachings. Until they become part of our daily experience, they remain abstract. Many people who are serious spiritual explorers have learned a great deal of information but have integrated very little. We can learn about the spiritual experiences of others, or we can bring meaningful practice into our own daily lives. We can learn about mysticism, or we can practice being mystics.

Most of us experience deep pleasure when in a garden. We encounter sensory delights: colors, shapes, and odors. Intellectually we may appreciate the process of preparing the land, planting the seed, caring for the sprouts, fertilizing, watering, and all of the work that a well-tended garden requires. Emotionally we may be touched by the vibration of blossoming life, the tenderness of fragile plants, the calmness and serenity of the garden during some moments, and the busyness and vitality during others.

A mystic in the garden experiences all this, but is drawn to other contemplations as well. He or she attempts to connect with the soul of each plant, the other beings that live in this garden, the angels that hover everywhere, and the interactions of plants with one another. A mystic contemplates the sparks of holiness that reside within every plant and insect, knowing that these sparks are raised to new levels of consciousness when the fruits or vegetables are ingested by beings with higher consciousness. In the mystic's holistic view, every garden—every aspect of creation, for that matter—is a microcosm of the Garden of Eden and a reflection of everything happening in the cosmos.

# WHAT IS KABBALAH?

Kabbalah has intrigued Western scholars and theologians for many centuries. Cloaked in mystery, concealed by secret societies, buried under layers of arcane symbols and impenetrable language, it has been a source of fascination for seekers of spiritual truth in every generation of the last thousand years. Even today it continues to have a strange charisma. Yet when asked what Kabbalah is, who invented it, or how it originated, even the most accomplished student is hard pressed to provide an answer.

Kabbalah does not lend itself to a straightforward definition or even a clear-cut history. Although Kabbalists agree on some essential points, it is impossible to present a single systematic approach that includes the entire spectrum of kabbalistic perspective. Kabbalah is not a system, as some suppose. Rather, it is an outlook, a way of perceiving the nature of reality. In essence, Kabbalah is founded upon mystical conceptions regarding life, death, creation, and creator. It teaches us about the mysteries of life, how the creation works, where we are going, and how we get there.

Judaism derived the term "Kabbalah." The word comes from the Hebrew root *kbl,* which means to receive. The natural questions that arise are, What is it that Kabbalists receive? and From whom do they receive it?

There are two viewpoints regarding the transmission of Kabbalah. One perspective, held by the theosophical school, suggests that mystical teachings must be transmitted from teacher to student. This is the most popular school in Jewish Kabbalah, and its teachings tend to be abstract, impossible to understand without guidance. These teachings cannot be learned from books because the presumption is that the subtle mysteries of Kabbalah require interpretation by a qualified teacher.

The other school is oriented to one's direct experience. This is called the school of Ecstatic Kabbalah.[10] Through the use of meditative techniques, the student enters into a state of altered consciousness and receives insight from the Unknown and Unknowable. This does not require a teacher, for the transmission comes via a main channel between the student and the center of creation.[11]

As a result the school of Ecstatic Kabbalah assumes that *anyone* can receive the teaching of universal truth by way of a personal connection with the Divine. Although a flesh-and-blood teacher can greatly accelerate a student's progress, the ultimate teacher is the source of life. Quite often this teacher is represented as the prophet Eliahu, Elijah, who comes to the student through dreams or deep meditative states.

Traditional Kabbalists were always religiously observant; they shared a wide variety of exclusive spiritual practices. Every action, feeling, or thought was measured against a meticulous code of law that described, in extraordinary detail, all aspects of acceptable human behavior. In addition, they studied the same texts, were intimate with the same complex talmudic arguments, and closely followed an identical calendar of events. Their lives centered on prayer, the study of Torah, the Sabbath, and celebration of the holy days.

They "lived" their Kabbalah. It permeated every activity of their lives. This does not mean that one must be religious to fully appreciate Jewish mysticism. Many kabbalistic teachings are universal and hold wisdom for us all. But it does mean that Kabbalah will be useful only if we learn how to live it, to bring it into our day-to-day relationship with the Divine. If we are able to do so, we will be able to open up an entirely new world of meaning in our lives, as well as gain a clear sense of direction of the flow of humankind, for kabbalistic insight reveals the principles of creation.

Ecstatic Kabbalists are far more interested in the experience of merging with the Divine than in any theoretical application or magical use of kabbalistic techniques. Thus, whereas the theosophical approach intellectually appreciates the intricate interplay of the cosmic rhythms, those in the kabbalistic school of direct experience choose to actively engage in practice that not only facilitates our ability to hear celestial music, but inspires us to dance with it as well.

## My Teachers

My long-term teachers, both of whom are quite well known, are Reb Shlomo Carlebach and Reb Zalman Schachter-Shalomi. These two rebbes, each in his own way, have dramatically influenced modern Judaism. They were friends and soul mates for forty years. Reb Shlomo died in 1994; Reb Zalman continues to transform the Jewish world with messages that speak to the soul.

Reb Zalman and Reb Shlomo realized many years ago that something radically different was needed in post-Holocaust Jewish life. Whereas the external form of Judaism continued to stand in place, the spiritual substance of the tradition had been seriously crippled when the six million vanished.

A third of world Jewry died in the early 1940s; this was a tragedy of enormous proportions. An even greater catastrophe for Judaism was the number lost of people who carefully practiced every detail of the tradition. It is estimated that well more than 50 percent of religiously observant Jews were killed in the Holocaust; some say the number is as high as 80 percent. As a result, most of the great teachers were wiped out, and many lineages of hasidic and kabbalistic transmission were completely destroyed.

After the Holocaust, most surviving Jews remained culturally identified, but only a small percentage was comfortable with the spiritual practices of the tradition. Observance of the Sabbath, keeping kosher, and relating to the annual cycle of the holy days simply did not fit into the lives of a majority of Jews. For many people, Jewish spirituality seemed to be a thing of the past. The soul of Judaism was in exile.

Obviously, different leaders in Judaism have responded to this challenge in various ways. Some believe that traditional learning in *yeshiva* is the way to revitalize spirituality. Others emphasize ancient rituals. One of the more recent approaches is referred to as Jewish renewal. Its goal is to bring a sense of vitality to Judaism: to nurture its soul, deepen its spiritual content, open its heart to the needs of humanity, be relevant in the modern world.

The primary leader and mystic-visionary of Jewish renewal has been Reb Zalman. Reb Shlomo was the poet-minstrel for people involved in this movement. He transformed the way the Jewish world sings and prays; while Reb Zalman has dramatically influenced, and continues to do so, the way many Jews live their lives.

## PARADIGM SHIFT

During the past few decades, religious traditions have been strongly affected by innovative thinking. As one of the leaders in Judaism for building a new paradigm, Reb Zalman has found ways to open gates of awareness that have been jammed shut for hundreds of years. In so doing, he has helped thousands of people develop a new relationship with Judaism.

He says, "At one time, religions used to talk about a product. The product was virtuous behavior; the product was faith, hope and charity. People had a notion that there was something to *get*—a pot of gold at the end of the rainbow. That fit the old paradigm of the Middle Ages. But there's been a switch now. People are interested in the process. It's alive."[12]

The world is an integrated whole, not a collection of parts. We can no longer think as individuals, but rather as integral members of a global community. As Reb Zalman says, "The flag does not wave in the wind; the wind does not wave the flag. The flag and the wind are interwaving."[13] That is to say, individuals and nations are not separate; everyone and everything is interconnected.

The concept of what it means to be kosher must be reframed into what Reb Zalman calls eco-kosher. The traditional idea of kosherness is based upon ancient laws of what is fit to eat for an observant Jew. The law comes from biblical injunctions. It says animals must be slaughtered in certain ways; meat that contains any residual blood cannot be eaten; certain sea life and animals are forbidden; and meat and milk products cannot be mixed, based on the injunction that a young animal cannot be cooked in its mother's milk. But these laws do not speak about chemical additives, types of packaging, the depletion of species, or the ruination of forests. How can we say something is kosher if it carries seeds of destruction for humankind? How can we eat something if it means the loss of a species? How can we use a product if it means others must suffer? These are questions of enormous significance in our day and cannot be separated from the essential meaning of our religious beliefs.

Reb Zalman asks, "Is electricity from a nuclear reactor kosher?" and "Is something that is bottled in a one-way bottle more or less kosher than something bottled in a recyclable one?"[14] This approach to kosherness seeks the spirit of the tradition rather than the letter of the law.

Reb Zalman's views of religious law fit the new paradigm. "We must give up the notion of legislation and take on the notion of discovering the laws of nature. . . . In this context, our old relationship as the child of a God-father, the subject of a God-king, or the defendant under the power of a God-judge would change to 'friend-friend, lover-lover, partner-partner.' "[15] He says further, "Not only are we God's partners—God is our partner too!"[16]

The word "peace," he says, is self-contradictory, for normally it is treated as a product, something to have, a noun. Rather, it must be viewed as an ongoing process, an interactive and mutual relationship that is constantly attended, adjusted, and nurtured. This approach, of course, must be applied to every relationship. Relationship, by definition, is a process that needs careful, ongoing attention. The universe is eternally in dynamic interaction and requires continuous awareness.

Reb Zalman is famous for his diverse interests in many fields of inquiry and all spiritual traditions. He says, "I see myself as a Jewish practitioner of generic religion."[17] As an empiricist, Reb Zalman searches for truth. We have learned many things about what is true and what is not. His teaching is that we must be prepared to move ahead in the spirit of truth, even if it means leaving some things behind.

He sees himself as postdenominational. Labels and definitions suggest a static belief, while these days we need to be flexible. The issues of modern life demand penetrating insight and adaptation. Nonetheless, he feels strongly that tradition has a great deal to teach. Ritual is often encoded with messages that ancient sages wanted to transmit but could not do so with words. Thus, the move toward renewal does not mean the wholesale elimination of the "old way," but the appraisal of everything from a fresh, honest perspective. Considerable wisdom and insight are required.

## DEFINITIONS: TORAH, TALMUD, MISHNAH, AND MIDRASH

There are a number of definitions for the word "Torah." Normally, the Torah refers to the actual document of the five books of Moses: Genesis, Exodus, Leviticus, Numbers, and Deuteronomy. In a looser definition, some expand Torah to include the books of the Prophets and the Holy Writings. The books of the Prophets are Joshua, Judges, Samuel, Kings, Isaiah, Jeremiah, Ezekiel, and others. The Holy Writings include Psalms, Proverbs, Job, Song of Songs, Ruth, Lamentations, Ecclesiastes, Esther, Daniel, and so forth. All of this is commonly referred to as the Old Testament. More precisely, these collected writings are called the Tanakh, which comes from the Hebrew letters *tnkh*, representing Torah, *Nevi'im* (Prophets), and *Ketuvim* (Holy Writings).

The Torah is viewed as the written law. However, a careful reading of the Written Torah reveals a number of sections that seem to contradict one another or are ambiguous. These inconsistencies suggest that more information is required for us to understand the true meaning of the law. Thus, it is said that Moses explained the meanings of the written law through oral communication. This Oral Law is the basis for resolving many difficulties in the written text. Indeed, the most intricate questions regarding the law are often settled by responding, "It comes directly from Moses on Sinai."

In addition to difficulties in the meaning of the written text itself, there is another problem. The five books of Moses were originally written in Hebrew, without vowels, as are all Torah scrolls written today. The Hebrew language is constructed in a way that vowel substitutions can dramatically change the meaning of a word. It is like seeing the letters PN as a word, which could be pin, pan, pane, pain, pen, peon, pine, or pun. Usually we can derive the meaning of a word in the Written Torah through the context in which it is used, but some sentences could leave us wondering. For example, imagine reading a sentence that says, "If you know how to properly work with a PN, you will qualify for a million-dollar reward."

Understanding the meaning of the sentence could become even more challenging if the letters P and N were codes symbolizing other letters. For example, the letter P resembles and sounds like the letter B. The letter N looks like the letter Z turned on its side. Thus PN could be a code for bin, ban, bun, or buzz. This is what Kabbalists do because they always look beyond the obvious. Everything is viewed as a metaphor for hidden wisdom-teachings. For a Jewish mystic, a million-dollar reward is of little value compared to the experience of decoding a message from God.

Many meanings of the Written Torah, decoded and explained on various levels, were included in the body of collected wisdom known as the Oral Law. This is also viewed as Torah. Talmudic sages Shammai and Hillel, when asked the question, "How many Torahs do you have?" both responded, "Two: one written and one oral."[18]

The Oral Torah was passed down for a thousand years by word of mouth from teacher to student. The way to remember oral teachings is to repeat them over and over again. The verb in Hebrew that means "to repeat" is *shanah;* thus the primary Oral Law came to be called the Mishnah.

In ancient days, twenty-five hundred years ago, memories were prodigious. Memorizing the entire Written Torah, including Prophets and the Holy Writings, word for word, was child's play. It is said that the memories of sages were so precise, they were tested by driving a pin through many pages of a book. The sage was told which word the pin went through on the first page and then was required to say which word it touched on every page thereafter for dozens of pages.

The sages memorized as well a vast amount of law *(halacha)* and teaching stories *(aggadah)* that augmented the collection of written material. In essence, they memorized, in detail, hundreds of books.

Around two thousand years ago, however, students began to lose these skills. The Holy Land was conquered under Pompey, and the Roman Empire brought a new level of commerce to the land, which in turn brought along changes in the culture and new ways of perceiving things. Higher learning deteriorated under these conditions, and the Oral Torah was in jeopardy of being lost forever. As a result, in the beginning of the third century, the Mishnah was committed to writing by Judah ha-Nasi.

Because the Mishnah is a body of law that was intended for memorization, it is highly cryptic. Each phrase elicits a set of associations. When we see the words "Four score," we do not need to read further to assume that it is followed by "and seven years ago, our forefathers," for we presume that this is the beginning of the Gettysburg Address. But as time goes by, we may not be certain of the specific wording or even the intention of a phrase, for it may have been referring to something entirely different.

By the time of Judah ha-Nasi, more than a thousand years had passed since the giving of the Written Torah. Much confusion arose regarding associations and meanings of pithy sayings in the Oral Law. Differences of opinion arose about how to interpret a particular statement in the Mishnah. Separate schools were founded, each having its own view on how to read the text. Discussions and debates regarding these diverse interpretations took place in various academies, and a great body of new commentary arose. This collection of commentary was written down in the sixth century and is what we call the Babylonian Talmud, which is the primary Talmud used today. A less-popular, earlier version, the Jerusalem Talmud, was compiled some time in the third or fourth century.[19] So, the Talmud is the accumulation of commentaries to explain the Mishnah—the Oral Law.

The Talmud is encyclopedic in sweep. It inquires into the meanings of words, analyzes why some words are physically close to others, why some are spelled in certain ways, why some are repeated, why events take place in a specific order, what various names of people and places really represent, what the true meanings and intentions of the laws were, and on and on. Two thirds of the Babylonian Talmud relates to the meaning of the Jewish law; one third tells stories and homilies that themselves are material for further investigation.

Most of the logic used in talmudic reasoning is not Aristotelian, the kind of logic we normally use in our ordinary thinking. Aristotelian logic is made up of syllogisms. If A is bigger than B, and B is bigger than C, then is A bigger, or smaller, than C? Of course, we would say bigger. Our minds are conditioned to think this way.

But talmudic reasoning uses a form of logic called hermeneutics, a complicated set of principles that considers things like placement, repetition, or meanings of words. If black refers to white in one place, and black refers to a house in another place, there must be a connection between white and house. This is not logical by the rules of Aristotle, but it is a common method of hermeneutic reasoning. According to Rabbi Adin Steinsaltz, who has undertaken the mammoth task of translating the Talmud, which is written mainly in Aramaic, into Hebrew and English, there are hundreds of rules for this type of reasoning.[20]

Thus, the Talmud carries the student into other mind-states, different ways of looking at things. Kabbalah goes even further, often using intuitive methodology that transcends even hermeneutic logic. Therefore, every avenue of exploration is open to students of the Torah, presenting a vast potential for mystical understanding. For this reason, many people study Torah and Talmud, often going over the same text year after year, without ever coming close to exhausting the wealth of material available.

In addition, a unique genre of rabbinic literature developed as the result of intense examination of biblical writings. This literature is called Midrash, from the Hebrew root *drsh,* which means "to search" or "to investigate." Because these explorations followed different avenues of inquiry, many midrashic teachings contradict one another. The point, however, was not to develop a consistent perspective of the hidden meanings of Torah, but to extend to the widest magnitude possible the variety of conceivable interpretations for a teaching.

Jewish mysticism relies on all of these sources. The Tanakh, the Mishnah, the Talmud, and the Midrash are the main materials out of which kabbalistic writings were developed. The Kabbalah brought a fresh perspective, different methods for understanding this literature, and thus became a new genre of Jewish literature in itself.

Because the available material for the study of Jewish mysticism is enormous, a coherent approach must, by necessity, be selective. Almost every idea in Kabbalah can lead the student to an inquiry involving many areas that diverge from the primary objective. Although virtually every aspect of Jewish thinking has opposing perspectives, many teachings of Jewish mysticism are particularly relevant for today's world.

I have selected among these to help interested readers penetrate the mysteries of Kabbalah. I hope this overview will serve its purpose: to provide a pool of Jewish wisdom-teachings through which we can bathe in ancient mystical knowledge about who we are, where we come from, where we are going, and how we get to our destiny. When we gain insight into these teachings, we never again see the world through the same eyes.

The goal of this book is to help the reader use Kabbalah to delve into the mysteries of life and find a practical application through which he or she can develop new connections and heart-openings with the Divine Source of existence. By balancing practice with theory, the reader will not only learn about mystical principles, but actually begin to integrate kabbalistic methods into his or her own life. The book is designed to provide a series of experiences, each of which is a segment of a circle. The picture becomes clear when the circle is complete; each part complements and is necessary to the whole. The exercises and meditations are as important as the theoretical information; the hasidic tales are as illuminating as the illustrations.

Jewish mysticism has been hidden for thousands of years from Jews and non-Jews alike. It is time to open this rich world for all to appreciate. May we be blessed to grow together in increasing awareness, to bring a new consciousness to the world, and to experience true peace in our times.

# Part One

## THE PAST

*MA'ASEY BERESHIT*

(The Work of Creation)

# RAISING

# HOLY SPARKS

*R*abbi Shlomo Carlebach was one of the great Jewish teachers of this century. His music can be heard in synagogues and at Shabbat tables all over the world. These melodies are so much a part of Jewish tradition today, they have already become classics. He was adored by hundreds of thousands of fans worldwide. Indeed, he was a phenomenon that changed the face of modern Judaism.

When Reb Shlomo died, thousands of mourners attended his burial in Jerusalem. His followers were incredibly diverse, from the most Orthodox, all in black with fur-lined *striemels* (top hats), to the most flamboyant, who wore tie-dyed T-shirts and psychedelic, Rastafarian berets. Shlomo had touched each and every one of them with his music and his enormous heart.

Reb Shlomo always arrived late. He lived in his own time zone. This zone would expand or contract depending upon what was happening at the moment. Whenever he was on his way to a teaching or a concert, he could be distracted by anyone who seemed to be in need. He was like a motorist who could never pass a car pulled off to the side of the road without offering assistance. Thus a normal fifteen-minute trip could take hours. He would stop for every beggar: "Holy sister, times are hard!" or "Holy brother, what can I do to help you?"

Moreover, he would not simply give money, like the rest of us, and then pass by. No, Reb Shlomo would stop for a short conversation because each *neshama* (soul) called to him. Each person was treated as if he or she were a saint. A mystic, Reb Shlomo believed that the world was balanced on our ability to help one another. Should someone fail to assist another person, the world could be destroyed. He really believed this.

When Shlomo entered a room, no matter how crowded, he would try to physically touch every person there. Sometimes a handshake but usually a hug would accompany his wide-eyed look of pleasure in every greeting. Whenever he saw me, it did not matter if it had been a day or a year since we had last been together; each time we met, he seemed overjoyed to re-connect. Usually his greeting was a characteristic Shlomoism that mixed Hebrew, Yiddish, and hip English. It was usually something like, *"Mamash! Heligeh bra-the!"* (Wow! Holy brother!)[1] I often did not understand what he was saying, but who cared? The smile and hug could melt diamonds.

On one occasion I remember in the late-1980s, Reb Shlomo arrived at a Jerusalem Old City apartment at 10:00 P.M., even though it had been rumored that he would be there two hours earlier. The living room of the apartment was filled to capacity. Word had been spreading since three in the afternoon that he would be teaching that night. This is the way he usually arrived in Jerusalem: no flyers, no posters, no formal announcements. The grapevine was extraordinary when Reb Shlomo was in town. On only a few hours' notice, he would invariably teach to a packed audience.

That night he told the group a story that has become one of my favorites.

## The Snuffbox

"Everybody knows that holy beggars hold the world together. Never, never pass a holy beggar. Walk across the street, go out of your way. Many times it is Eliahu ha-Navi (Elijah the prophet), and, oh, if you only knew, if you only knew . . .

"Our holy teachers tell us—Did you know this?—that we must give to a beggar according to his or her previous station. A person who was rich should be given more than someone who was poor. The secrets of the universe are hidden in that teaching. Think about it as I tell you the story of the snuffbox.

"One day a beggar came to see the Baal Shem Tov. You should have heard him. He yelled, he moaned, he complained loudly to the Baal Shem, saying, 'What kind of a God is It, anyway? I used to be rich, I helped many people, I never turned anyone away, and now, look at me. I am in rags. I have nothing. This is my reward?'

"The holy Besht (Baal Shem Tov) looked at this man closely. Everybody knows that the Besht could see into the future and into the past. He said to the beggar, 'Moshe—You see, he knew his name just by looking at him—Moshe, why do you rail at the Holy One? All you need do is look carefully at your life, and you will understand.'

"The Besht continued, 'Do you remember Yom Kippur two years ago?' He stopped and looked at Moshe now that he had his attention. How could the Baal Shem Tov know what Moshe did two years earlier? Do you believe this? But he knew, he knew. He said to Moshe, 'Two years ago, when you were the wealthiest man in town, you went to *shul* (synagogue) on Yom Kippur with your snuffbox.'

"Many of you know," Shlomo said, "that although we must fast on Yom Kippur, we can nourish the soul by bringing a fragrance into the body. So in the old country, they used to carry snuff into the *shul,* and every so often they would pass the snuffbox around so that people could be revived, especially in the afternoon when the fast gets the hardest."

Shlomo did not mention that these days, some people at the Western Wall on Friday night pass snuff around just after the evening service. Some of these snuffs have pungent, fruity fragrances. One in particular is noted for its ripe banana odor, another smells like passion fruit, yet another like mango. On many occasions, I carried a pinch home for Shoshana and our guests to smell.

Shlomo continued with the story: "So the holy Baal Shem Tov said to Moshe, 'You went around the *shul* that day giving snuff to everyone. Do you remember? And there was a *shlepper* (someone heavily burdened) in the back of the *shul,* lying on a bench. You said to yourself, *Why should I walk back there for him when he could come to me for his snuff?* So he did not get any. Do you remember?'

"Moshe nodded his head. He did remember! The Besht continued, 'That *shlepper* had been fasting for three days. If you only knew how much he needed some snuff! He was so deep, so deep in his prayers that the heavens were wide open for him. When the heavenly angels saw that you did not walk over and give him a pinch of your snuff, they closed the judgment book on you. Do you know what they wrote into that book? They wrote that you should lose all of your money and that the *shlepper* should become wealthy in your stead.'

"Moshe jumped up, outraged, saying, 'You mean to tell me that that *shlepper* has all of my money! What *chutzpah* (audacity)! How do I get it back?'

"The Baal Shem Tov said to him, 'If you can find a time, any time at all, when you ask him and he refuses to give you a pinch of snuff, all of your wealth will be returned.'

"Can you imagine what went through Moshe's mind? He searched out the richest man in town, and when he saw him, he knew it was the *shlepper*. He began to follow him around. Moshe learned everything about the man, when he left in the morning and when he returned at night; when he went to the *shul* and where he bought flowers for his wife. Moshe sought to discover the times when the man would be most rushed, most harried, and most irritable.

"He planned for the perfect time. It was just before Shabbos and the wealthy man was loaded with packages, hurrying home because his wife was anxious to finish her cooking. Moshe waited in the bushes, and as the wealthy man came past, Moshe jumped in front of him and asked, 'Could you spare a pinch of snuff?'

"The wealthy man stopped abruptly, hesitated a few seconds, and began to put down his packages one by one. It took a minute. Then he reached into his pocket and pulled out his snuffbox. Moshe, terribly disappointed, took a pinch and walked off, not even helping to load the man up again with his packages.

"Moshe tried again a few times in the next couple of months. Once he caught the wealthy man in a downpour of rain, when everyone around was running for cover, but the wealthy man had stopped and, although his snuff was ruined by the rain, he still offered it.

"Moshe approached the wealthy man on the way to an important business meeting, loaded with papers, but he offered his snuff nonetheless. Moshe encountered him in *shul,* in the middle of prayers; he found him in the bank, making a deposit; he even snared him in a public building on his way to the bathroom, and, of course, the snuff was always offered without delay.

"Finally Moshe thought of a foolproof idea. He waited one Friday morning in the *mikveh*,[2] the community pool of water in which men traditionally immerse themselves to prepare for Shabbos. After the wealthy man had removed all of his clothes and was dripping from the shower, as he was about to enter the *mikveh* for his submersion in the pool of water, Moshe approached him and asked for a pinch of snuff. Believe it or not, the most amazing thing happened. The wealthy man stopped what he was doing, toweled himself off, and went back to the dressing room to get his snuffbox.

"Disheartened, Moshe almost gave up. But he had one more opportunity. In two weeks the wealthy man's daughter was going to be married, and Moshe figured that he could trap him at his daughter's wedding.

"On the special day, Moshe walked to the wedding. You know, my friends," Shlomo added, "it is always important to bring poor people into a wedding. In those days, people would go out looking for a stranger they could invite. They knew it would bring the married couple good luck. We do not think about things like this these days, but maybe we should. Anyway, Moshe stood there in his dirty clothes, waiting for an opportunity to trap his opponent. When the music started, he saw the wealthy man begin to dance with his daughter, the new bride, and Moshe knew this was the perfect time to interrupt. So he walked onto the dance floor, tapped the wealthy man's shoulder, and asked him for a pinch of snuff.

"Yes, this was the perfect time. But it did not matter. The wealthy man stopped dancing with his beloved daughter, reached into his pocket, and offered Moshe a pinch of snuff. Moshe was overwhelmed. Awed by this man's incredible spirit of generosity, he got dizzier and dizzier; then he fainted right there on the dance floor.

"When he was revived, Moshe told the wealthy man the whole story. He told about the Baal Shem Tov and how he had learned about his own failure to offer snuff on Yom Kippur. The man said to him, 'You know, Moshe, I never doubted for a minute that everything that happened to me, especially during the last few years, was a message from the Master of the Universe. But now I see that you have suffered so much, I must tell you I will equally share with you all of the wealth I have.'

"It came to pass that this town became famous for its two wealthiest men who gave more and more *tzeddakah* (charity) throughout the years. The spirit of generosity grew to unknown heights in those days. And by the way, there was more snuff given away in that city than ever before or ever after."

WHEN SHLOMO FINISHED telling his tale, he sang a beautiful *niggun* (wordless melody). This story contains a number of key kabbalistic teachings. One's actions, particularly deeds of lovingkindness, profoundly impact upon the universe. Minor actions can have significant consequences; one's fame and fortune can pivot on a single twist of fate; everything happening to us is connected with a complex weave of variables. Moreover, angelic forces are associated with our thoughts, words, and deeds.

Finally, deep spiritual work can open the gates of heaven; a spiritual master can be profoundly attuned to one's destiny; and holy sparks can be raised by an act as simple as offering a pinch of snuff. All this in one hasidic tale.

## SPARKS OF THE DIVINE

One of the most influential Kabbalists in the history of Jewish mysticism was Isaac Luria, known as the Ari (the lion), who lived in the sixteenth century. It is said that Luria lived in Egypt in semiretreat for more than ten years, returning from his isolation on an river island only one day each week—Shabbat. In his late twenties he traveled to the city of Safed, not far from Jerusalem, where he met with and taught many of the well-known Kabbalists who lived in Safed at that time. Luria had an entirely new vision. In a matter of a few years, his mystical insights were so captivating, he dramatically changed the course of Judaism.

A great deal of today's Kabbalah refers to the raising of holy sparks. This comes from the teaching of Luria, who said, "There is no sphere of existence, including organic and inorganic nature, that is not full of holy sparks which are mixed in with the *kelippot* (husks) and need to be separated from them and lifted up."[3]

Imagine that you are an artisan with a fixed amount of liquid gold that is to be poured into a mold to make a perfect work of art. This work of art will cast a magical light that will permeate the world and produce the highest awareness possible in all creation. However, when you pour the gold into the mold, something terrible happens: the mold cracks, and many flecks of gold leak out and float away.

The only way the work of art can be completed is for you to gather all of the missing gold in one place so that the mold can be cast again. As the gold spreads, however, the flecks themselves split apart until untold numbers of gold atoms are scattered across creation, each one surrounded by a shell of dust that hides it. The gold drifts everywhere, and the only way you can get the job done of casting your completed work of art is to employ the help of many others to collect the gold.

The gold represents the light of divine consciousness, and each atom a spark of holiness. If gathered together into one place—not a physical place, but symbolically the center of the universe—all the sparks combined would radiate ultimate awareness. But when scattered, the sparks drop to denser and denser levels of consciousness, represented by shells or husks *(kelippot)* that surround them.

The artisan and the lost gold is a simple metaphor used to illustrate Isaac Luria's cosmology known as the Shattering of the Vessels. This cosmology was developed from the opening lines of Genesis that say: "And the earth was without form *(tohu)* and empty *(bohu)*; and darkness was on the face of the deep *(tohum)*."[4]

The word *"tohu"* means chaos, astonishment,[5] or confoundedness.[6] This primordial chaos was viewed by Luria as a situation in which vessels that were supposed to contain the light of creation shattered, and the light was thereby concealed in "the deep." The deep is an allusion to death.[7] The gold is thus lost.

However, along with chaos there was emptiness *(bohu)*, which implies that there were other vessels ready to receive the light.[8] *Bohu* therefore represents the potential of creation, and is called in Kabbalah, the Universe of *Tikkun* (Rectification).[9] This Universe of *Tikkun* is a container for the collection of all the missing gold. In kabbalistic language, the gold of our story is called *nitzotzot*: sparks.[10]

Every particle in our physical universe, every structure and every being, is a shell that contains sparks of holiness. Our task, according to Luria, is to release each spark from the shell and raise it up, ultimately to return it to its original state. The way these sparks are raised is through acts of lovingkindness, of being in harmony with the universe, and through higher awareness.

The ramifications of this teaching are enormous. In each moment of existence we have the potential to raise holy sparks. If we are unaware of this ability and are spiritually asleep, then we do not accomplish much, for the medium through which sparks are raised is consciousness itself.

Our opportunities to raise sparks are boundless. The choices we make for our activities, the interactions we have with our family, friends, neighbors, business associates, and even strangers, the way we spend our leisure time, the books we read, the television we watch, the way we relate to food, everything in daily life presents sparks locked in husks awaiting release.

# AWARENESS

*A*t the turn of the nineteenth century, in the city of Lublin, Poland, lived a hasidic rebbe, Jacob Isaac Ha-Hozeh, otherwise known as the Seer of Lublin. He is the subject of many hasidic tales. It is said that he had the power to determine whether someone was guilty or innocent of an act simply by looking at his or her face. But even more, he could see into a person's soul and reveal what task it had to do at each stage of its reincarnation. This task is often referred to as a *tikkun*—meaning to mend or fix—which in mystical terms refers to the spiritual work we have an opportunity to do in this lifetime to repair our souls, the souls of others, and the world as a whole.

The congregation the Seer of Lublin served needed to raise a huge sum of money one particular year to establish a special security fund. Life was always dangerous for Jews in Poland; pogroms occurred frequently. Those days, however, were especially unsettled because a young general named Napoleon was building an empire in Europe, and rumor was that he would invade Poland and Russia in the not-too-distant future. So an emergency fund was needed for any contingency.

The fund-raisers went to Shmuel, the wealthiest man in town, and he told them, "I will give you six million rubles (an enormous sum of money) on one condition. I want to have permanent rights to occupy the seat next to the rebbe. Otherwise, I will not contribute as much as a kopek."

In their wildest dreams they had not expected to raise even one million rubles from the entire community. Shmuel was willing to give six million. But the problem was that Heshel, the merchant, usually sat in the seat next to the rebbe.

They went to Heshel and told him the story. He said, "The only way that I will give up that seat is if the rebbe asks me to do so."

They went to the rebbe and told him what Heshel had said. The Seer of Lublin knew the money was needed, but he knew also that each soul is enormously important. So he called Heshel, the merchant, for a conference.

The two of them talked for a long time. The rebbe told Heshel that he could not promise him anything, that the only way the seat could be given up was through free will. The rebbe did not want to coerce him in any way. Heshel looked closely at the rebbe's face; it did not reveal that he was going to get a special share in the world to come by doing this. Yet he thought he saw a twinkle and he felt certain that he would be rewarded in some way for giving up his seat. So he agreed.

Shmuel gave his six million, and from that time on he had the privilege of occupying the seat next to the great Seer of Lublin. He was there for every prayer service and every holy day. He often sat there just to be close to the rebbe when petitioners came and asked for things. He heard every word that the rebbe spoke in public. Whenever he was close to the rebbe like this, he felt a radiation of light pouring through his own body.

In fact, this seat was so important to Shmuel, he stopped worrying about everything else in his life. He rarely went home; he hardly ever went to work. After a couple of years, his business failed completely, but Shmuel was oblivious because the seat next to the rebbe was more important than life itself.

He borrowed money to pay the bills at home. His biggest creditor, in fact, was Heshel, the merchant. Indeed, during the years that Shmuel was in decline, Heshel was on the ascendant. He had incredibly good luck in the marketplace, always buying merchandise at the lowest price and selling it at the highest. He could do no wrong, and he became enormously wealthy.

One day, Heshel thought to himself, *I have enough money to retire and enough to buy back my seat for twice the money that Shmuel paid.* Besides, Shmuel now owed him tens of thousands of rubles, and there was not much chance of it ever being paid. He would buy back the seat, clear the debt, and have his retirement as well.

Heshel offered to do just that. But Shmuel refused, saying that he would never give up the seat. This argument went on for a few months. The entire congregation got into the act. Some said that they could use the money. Others said that the seat rightfully belonged to Shmuel.

Then came the High Holy Days. On Rosh Hashana, the rebbe carried the Torah to the *bimah* (platform), where the reading would take place. Shmuel naturally followed close to the rebbe. After the Torah reading, he returned to his seat. But sitting in it was Heshel, the merchant.

They argued. *Oy voi voi,* it was Rosh Hashana and they were arguing. The entire congregation was in an uproar. It went on for a while, and finally it was put to the rebbe to decide.

Heshel said, "Rebbe, it has been a long time. I was the original holder of the seat. I left it voluntarily, but only because the congregation would benefit from a six-million-ruble contribution. Now this person owes me money. Moreover, I am willing to make a twelve-million-ruble contribution. It seems only fair that I should have my seat back."

It was a strong argument. When he said twelve million rubles, there was an audible gasp in the congregation. An astronomical sum! If they had voted on the spot, he would have won with a huge majority. But the rebbe himself was going to decide.

Shmuel stood up and was silent for a while. What could he say? For two minutes, everyone waited. And then he spoke. "Rebbe," he said, "please give me back my seat." His voice cracked, almost sobbed, as he cried out, *"It is the only thing I have in this world!"*

That is all he said; it was all he needed to say. After a moment the rebbe replied, "Heshel, you traded that seat for wealth. It was a fair trade. You are the wealthiest man in the whole area. But Shmuel traded that seat for his soul. The seat belongs to Shmuel. I did not decide this, it was decided in heaven. For when Shmuel said that it was the only thing that he had in this world, the angels in heaven cried out, "Give it back to Shmuel!"

OUR MOST
PRECIOUS GIFT

*W*e all have priceless things in our lives. Have you ever stopped to consider what is the most precious thing you have in the world? What is the one thing you have that if it were taken away, you would never be the same again? Think about it. Take a minute; close your eyes.

You may answer that a particular relationship you have is the most precious thing in the world to you. You may answer that your health and the health of those around you is the most precious. Perhaps you have a different answer. In the end, though, when you consider this question very carefully, is there not something that takes priority over it all?

I would suggest that our awareness is our most priceless gift. We usually take it for granted. But what would a relationship be if our minds did not function? What would our excellent physical health be worth if we could not appreciate the finer things of life? What would anything be worth, for that matter, if we could not be fully aware of its presence? Indeed, the only reason anything is precious to us is because we are aware of its value.

Some traditional spiritual teachings seem to imply that the mind is the enemy. Our thoughts keep us lost in the illusion of duality. If we stop the mind, we will attain the highest level of enlightenment. This idea can be misleading. It is true that the vast majority of our thinking process leads nowhere. But the mind adds a dimension to our natural awareness that differentiates us from the awareness of animal life.

Did you ever closely watch deer in the wild? Every few moments they stop what they are doing, lift their heads, and listen, smell, watch. Every few moments they are acutely alert for possible danger. Most wild animals have fine-tuned awareness like this. Yet our potential for higher awareness far exceeds that of any animal, because we have unique minds.

We must take the reins of the mind in hand, and at the same time we must realize that the mind is not the enemy. It is all that we have that allows us to appreciate everything we consider precious in life. Without the awareness of the human mind, we could never experience our own process, and, more important, the connection with the Divine could never be made.

## LIVING WITHOUT
## HIGHER AWARENESS

I cannot help but think of a man we met in Jerusalem. His nickname was Jochito, and he was cared for by his younger sister. They used to live in Germany in the 1930s. Early in the morning of November 10, 1938, Germans went on a rampage in retaliation for the assassination of a German-embassy employee in Paris. He was killed by a Jew. Hitler youth responded by smashing windows, burning buildings, and beating people. It is known as Kristallnacht, the Night of Broken Glass. Almost two hundred synagogues were destroyed. Three dozen Jews were killed, and another three dozen severely injured.

Unfortunately, Jochito was one of those injured. He was caught in the street, beaten, and stomped on the head with jackboots. He never was the same again. Fifty years later, his physical body was completely healthy. In fact, he was so healthy that his sister worried he would outlive her. This would be a problem, for each day since that night fifty years earlier, he had to be fed by someone, and the only words he could say were "da, da, da."

The price paid by Jochito saved most of his family. They were so horrified, they moved to Argentina before the mass murders began. So something "good" came of it. But the cost was dear, beyond calculation, as his mind had been utterly destroyed. We cannot take our awareness for granted, and nothing comes close to its value in our lives.

The story of the seat next to the rebbe is about awareness. As Shmuel's mind became more aligned with the Seer of Lublin's, he linked himself with other levels of reality. In this state, what did it matter that he lost his fortune? He had the only thing that counted in his life: the continuous opportunity to be carried to higher realms. He knew the angels would support him, and he knew the rebbe would see this.

Our awareness is not a fixed commodity. It can fluctuate on a fairly wide spectrum. Shmuel was not content with ordinary, daily awareness. He sought another degree, a new opening that ensued when he rubbed shoulders with the rebbe. Whereas awareness in general is our most important possession, we can do things to heighten or lower it.

## The Continuum
## of Awareness

The *Zohar* discusses the universe, as a whole, in far broader terms than merely the physical universe. Indeed, the physical universe, as vast as it may be, is dwarfed in comparison with the mystical universe that embraces angelic and demonic realms. Whereas the physical universe is measured in time and distance, the mystical universe is measured in terms of levels of awareness. These levels should not be viewed as separate boundaries, for awareness is a continuum.

The sound of a musical note is a good metaphor for this kind of continuum. If we sharply hit one key on a piano, the note instantly sounds at its densest, strongest level. Then it slowly fades. We can hear from one moment to the next that it is softer, but there are no obvious dividing lines. Also, when we hit a note, other stringed instruments in the room will vibrate at that same frequency. Thus, when we hit one string, others are affected.

The worlds of awareness integrate along a continuum. Each has parts of the others that cannot be separated. Just as a musical note has a common vibratory frequency no matter how loud or soft, the kabbalistic universes share the common medium of awareness.

As the central feature of creation, awareness is like a magnet that draws everything to it. Our yearning, our efforts on the spiritual path, our desire for knowledge, and our fascination with finding ultimate truth are our responses to the inexorable attraction of this magnet. Just as a water molecule in a raindrop is ultimately drawn to the ocean, one way or another, no matter how long it takes and how many incarnations it must go through, so too is awareness drawn to its source.

Kabbalists say that love operates in the same way. Love is based on a yearning for completion: to be whole, to be in harmony, to be connected, and to be free. Although initially our hormonal impulses may be the source of our sexual urges, as love matures it ultimately moves the partners closer to the light of awareness, one way or another. We seek partners that complement us in some way, that help us become complete. We seek to awaken their higher self so that they may experience our higher self.

The *Zohar* says, "To create the world, It (*Ein Sof,* Infinite Nothingness) emanated a secret spark (awareness) from which emerged and radiated all light. The upper world was constituted of this light. Then a [different dimension of] light, a light without brightness (lower consciousness), was fashioned into the lower world. As it is composed of unilluminated light, the lower world is attracted to the upper world."[11]

The erotic imagery of the merging of lovers is a common theme in the *Zohar.* Jewish mystics generally agree that the Song of Songs, with its allusions to love and sexuality, holds more secrets of the universe than any other scriptural work. For example, concerning the verse "I am my beloved's and his desire is towards me,"[12] the *Zohar* says, "The inner meaning of this verse is that the stirring below is accompanied by a stirring above, for there is no stirring above until there is a stirring below."[13]

This mystical description suggests that everything above and below is interconnected. We cannot separate heaven and earth, the spiritual realms and our material world, or anything else that gives the appearance of opposition. The interconnectness of all realms is one of the fundamental teachings of Kabbalah. When fully appreciated, it has significant impact upon the way we live our lives.

## AS ABOVE, SO BELOW;
## AS BELOW, SO ABOVE

Throughout the *Zohar*, the theme of higher and lower worlds repeats itself dozens of times: "The Holy One has disposed all things in such a way that everything in this world should be a replica of something in the world above"[14]; "There is a realm above in supernal holiness, and a realm below"[15]; "When the Holy One puts on Its 'crowns,' It receives them from above and below."[16]

The language of "above" and "below" should not be understood literally in a linear fashion. It is referring to realms of consciousness. Higher and lower realms of consciousness are not separated by space; rather, they are dimensions that represent a proximity of relationship to ultimate truth. The higher the consciousness, the less there is an illusion of separateness.

Earth represents a level of consciousness. Everything on this level has its likeness in higher consciousness. There is no object, however small, that does not have its counterpart in other realms. So when the thing below bestirs itself, the result is a simultaneous stimulation of its likeness above. The two realms form one interconnected whole.[17]

It is as if everything in the universe were reflected by a heavenly counterpart. This companion is more than a twin; it is multifaceted as a composite of all of our elements. Assuming each individual is a composite of many subpersonalities, each time we express a part of ourselves in reality as we know it, our counterpart is being activated in other realities. The lover is there, the conniver, the little child, the judge, our inner strengths, and our inner weaknesses. Whatever mode we happen to be in, this is the character that we energize in the other realms.

When we are consistently thoughtful, for example, our higher thoughtful essence is aroused. When we are erratic, our "angel" of erratic behavior is animated. When we enter into a state of lovingkindness, our higher self of lovingkindness is activated. Moreover, just as all of our actions, words, or thoughts reverberate in this world, so too does the arousal of our higher beings reverberate in the heavens.

This ancient kabbalistic idea is a holistic, energetic model of the universe. It cuts across layers of reality and includes every possible dimension of creation, angels, demons, thoughts, feelings, past, future, this incarnation, and all others. According to this Jewish mystical viewpoint, everything and every "non-thing" that ever was or will be in creation is interconnected.

The idea of interconnectedness initially was described in detail by a twelfth-century Jewish mystic, Isaac the Blind, who also was the first to use the word "Kabbalah" to designate a variety of mystical teachings and practices. Prior to Isaac the Blind, these teachings were referred to more obliquely, such as the work of the chariot, the work of creation, the way of truth, and other phrases that hinted at hidden mysteries. People who followed the mystical path had many names as well: masters of knowledge, the wise-hearted, those who know measures, and other enigmatic labels.[18]

It is not known whether this teacher Isaac was really blind, or if this was an appellation intimating that he did not see things the way other people saw them. Indeed, it was said that he had phenomenal mystical powers, being able to sense a "feeling in the air" whether a person would die in the near future, and whether a person's soul was newly formed or was an older, reincarnated soul.[19]

He described the medium of interconnectedness as *tzippiyah,* which could be translated as "contemplative observation." *Tzippiyah* is mystical awareness, what we experience when the sense of past and future dissolves and we are fully present, totally in the moment. This, I believe, was Isaac the Blind's personal experience and the basis for his powerful insights into the mystical nature of the universe.

*Tzippiyah,* when we ponder it, lures us into a new way of relating to the universe. Each time we move our arms, our supernal arms are being moved. Each time we write a word, a word in the heavens is being inscribed. We interact with the world and all along are simultaneously stimulating the upper worlds. Not only are we never alone, everything we do, say, or think moves universes beyond our imagination.

This is a highly provocative contemplation. It is compelling. How am I living my life? To what extent is the world balanced on my next action? If everything reverberates in the universe, how do my actions, words, and thoughts affect who I am, who I have been, and who I will be? It is imperative to ask ourselves these questions. Kabbalah is quite clear on the answers.

# SPHERES OF
## CONSCIOUSNESS

*O*ur sense of reality directly reflects our level of consciousness. Each of us has a perspective of reality that is but a razor-thin slice of a pie. The pie itself reaches to the limits of the universe. If we change our consciousness, we can get another slice of the pie. Moreover, we can switch our perceptions more rapidly than most people realize.

It is said, "The Holy One found it necessary to create all the things in the world so that there should be a central light of awareness with many vessels encircling it."[20] All of creation is constructed on this principle; that is to say, creation is made up of spheres of consciousness. If we could describe it from God's perspective, so to speak, we would see that everything in creation is connected to a center: the source of creation.

The story of creation in Genesis describes the unfolding of consciousness. The first day: light. The second day: cosmic fluid and separation of upper and lower fluids. The third day: earth, land, sea, plants, fruits, seeds. The fourth day: heavenly bodies, stars, sun, and moon. The fifth day: sea life and birds and great sea creatures. The sixth day: land creatures. At the end of the sixth day: humankind. This final aspect of creation was distinguished by the language *na-aseh adam betzelmaynu kidmutaynu,* meaning, "Let us make a creature called Adam in our shadow, resembling us."[21]

Of course, the ancient sages wondered why this was stated in the plural. The Divine is a unity. Who or what else in addition was referred to as "*our* shadow"? The words imply that God was communicating with something that could communicate with It. The logical conclusion we draw from this, at the very least, is that one of the aspects of the resemblance *must* be that Adam would be able to communicate with the Divine.

The essential paradox of creation is the issue of how unity becomes multiplicity. How does the one, all-perfect source create something less than itself? How does a total oneness that encompasses everything make room for otherness? Even if we drop the idea of "creator," as is done in Eastern traditions, we are still left with an incongruity of the coexistence of unity and multiplicity.

Spiritual teachers in Eastern traditions refer to our view of reality as *maya,* or illusion. We are trapped behind a series of veils that "distort" reality. These teachers suggest a theology of non-duality, a monistic system of total unity:

there is only one reality, and all multiplicity is imaginary. The world *seems* pluralistic only because our awareness has limitations.

The Kabbalist, on the other hand, does not say that our view of reality is distorted; rather, that it is merely the reality of human consciousness. For example, we might hypothesize that a mosquito has a different level of consciousness in that its universe is made up of elementary components such as heat, cold, softness, hardness, light, dark, and so forth. Assuming this is so, we cannot say that it has a distorted perception. Rather, it has a perfect "mosquito perception" of reality, whatever that may be.

From the perspective of higher planes of consciousness, human awareness is comparable to the mosquito. The greater our awareness, the more our perception of multiplicity dissolves. This is a universal wisdom-teaching, with one essential difference emphasized in Kabbalah. Whereas many traditions accentuate the illusory nature of the world in a way that debases our reality, Kabbalah goes in the opposite direction. It emphasizes the holistic nature of all levels of awareness and suggests that each is a reflection of all the others.

Thus, the kabbalistic approach is to suggest that through our reality, however limited it may be, we have access to all others. When we add to this perspective that human life is based on conscious free will, as opposed to most other aspects of creation, the importance of our potential impact on the unfolding of the universe is enormous. So, whereas in many traditions we can hardly wait to get out of our bodies, in Kabbalah we try to maximize the precious time we have in this body. From the kabbalistic perspective, multiplicity is a purposeful aspect in the totality of creation.

We can utilize this idea of the holistic nature of creation in order to work with paradox. We can be a unity and pluralistic simultaneously. Each cell in a person's body does its own task, yet each has a set of chromosomes identical to every other cell in the body. We can choose to focus on the separateness or on the unity. One is rational; the other requires fuzzy logic—it is here, it is not here.

People who dwell in the realms of intuition have no difficulty discussing souls, where they come from, where they go, death, angels, demons, heaven, or hell. Those who are drawn more to rational, analytical foundations of reality are more challenged by these ideas. But there is no right or wrong way to explore the mysteries of life and death. If the holistic model is correct, each of us is connected to the center of creation in her or his own way. We need simply to discover the inner language that helps us communicate with the hidden parts of the soul.

Clearly, human consciousness is different from that of other forms of life. Certain types of symbolic thinking, imagination, reflection, projection, planning, and humor are, in general, unique activities of human consciousness. But if in fact human consciousness is equated to mosquito consciousness relative to the universe, we must ask a key question: What happens to human reality as we continue to expand our consciousness?

E X P A N D E D

C O N S C I O U S N E S S

n Kabbalah, expanded consciousness is called *mochin de gadlut,* which literally means "mind of bigness." Many techniques are used to achieve this state. We can get a hint of it by doing a simple exercise. If you are willing, allow your vision to expand peripherally. You do not have to turn your head away from these words to look around. Just notice that you can look at this book, read these words, and still take in more visual information about what is happening around you at this moment.

Now, notice how it feels to widen your visual awareness. You will discover immediately a sense of more alertness and greater presence. At first it may take an effort for you to sustain this alertness, but soon it becomes natural. Although you may occasionally slip away out of habit and simply see the words before you without noticing much else, with a simple reminder you will find that you can rapidly expand your sense of visual awareness.

You can do the same by paying more attention to sounds that are occurring around you at this moment. Normally there are sounds that we ignore while we are concentrating on something. But suddenly you will notice that a sound has been present all this time and has gone unnoticed. You do not have to stop reading to intensify your listening. This too gives us a sense of a higher state of awareness.

One more thing: Notice your body. You can feel pressure of something under your buttocks if you are sitting; you can feel how your feet touch the ground; you can be aware of the position of your torso and arms; you can notice your neck, head, and eye movements. All of these details are constantly furnishing us with a steady flow of information. The more we become conscious and pay attention to this, the more we feel a sense of alertness. We become sharper, more present, more attuned to each moment. All this is the process of enhancing our natural awareness.

Most of us develop rote patterns through repetition, and we become unaware of the nuances in each situation. With so much happening around us and so little time in our lives, we go on automatic. As long as the routine remains familiar, we cope. Unfortunately, when we live for years in this automatic state of mind, the mirror of life tends to become foggy and our spirit lags. It is no surprise that today, in the extraordinary busyness of the world, the feelings of apathy, frustration, futility, and despair have reached almost epidemic proportions.

We have far more awareness potential than we normally actualize. Usually we are daydreaming, our minds are busily reviewing things that have already happened or fantasizing about future events that will rarely come to pass as we envision them. As we are busy with all of this mind activity, we are missing what is happening right here and right now.

We can expand our minds far wider without much effort. All we need is a reminder, an inner clock that rings an alarm to awaken us each time we slip into our more contracted state of awareness. Every time this inner alarm rings, we learn to instantly invite in bigness of mind, *mochin de gadlut*.

# THE GARDEN
# OF EDEN

The Garden of Eden is one of the best known and least understood tales in biblical literature. This story has been interpreted in dozens of ways, many of which suggest that it is the prototype for understanding the nature of good and evil, the relationship between men and women, or the purpose of humankind. Unfortunately, however, the insight of Jewish mysticism on this subject rarely has been made available to the general public, and thus a major component for understanding the deeper wisdom-teachings of this story has remained virtually unknown.

The story of Adam and Eve is buried deeply in the Western psyche, and in many ways it continues to influence the ways in which we relate to one another. The literal reading of the story suggests that Adam and Eve were the first humans and that Eve was an easy object of seduction. She quickly succumbed to the wily serpent. Not only did she eat the forbidden fruit, but she rushed off to get her partner to do the same. For this act of "disobedience," she has been reviled throughout the centuries. All of women's suffering during childbirth is blamed on Eve's ignorance. Worse, the entire downfall and degradation of humankind is said to be her fault.

A woman rabbi once said to me, "The story of Adam and Eve is perhaps the most obvious instance in the entire Torah in which the relationship between male and female has been contaminated by absurd implications. Any assumption that Adam and Eve represent a relationship of gender as the first man and woman of creation is ludicrous. Rather, the mystics treat these— and all major biblical characters—as divine principles. Adam and Eve represent the principle of duality, each a polar opposite of the other."

One of the ways Eastern tradition discusses polarity of this type is through the image of *yin* and *yang*. In exactly the same way, the language of Adam and Eve is of expansion and contraction, outward and inward, light and dark, hard and soft. Neither is better than the other; both are required for balance and harmony.

In addition to the duality of Adam and Eve, a third element is required for creation. This is the serpent, which represents a force of fragmentation. One of the more ancient midrashic texts, written by Rabbi Eliezer, suggests that the serpent who seduced Eve had the appearance of a camel.[22] Most people have never heard this idea. The Jewish oral tradition goes on to say that the angel Samael, otherwise known as Satan, rode this camel. Many say that the serpent itself was Satan.[23]

The word "camel" in Hebrew is *gamal,* which is the same word for the Hebrew letter *gimel.*[24] *Gimel,* in the Hebrew alphabet, represents the number three. Thus, when Rabbi Eliezer says that the serpent represented a camel, he is alluding to the number three. Mathematically, the number three is necessary for the physical world, which is three-dimensional—composed of three lines of direction: north-south, east-west, and up-down.[25]

In Kabbalah, Satan is said to represent the physical universe. Indeed, the universe as we know it is referred to in mystical writings as "the skin of the serpent." In the mystical cosmology of the Garden of Eden, the archetype of the serpent merges with the life-force, the form and substance represented by Adam and Eve. Once the serpent is able to merge with this life-force, the mystical formula is complete for the metaphysics of creation.[26]

The kabbalistic teaching is that Satan, the force of fragmentation, is the crucial element required for creation, because without it everything would unite with God—everything would become one. This does not mean that the splintering force of Satan is separate from the unity of God, but, paradoxically, that it is contained within the oneness of the Divine.

In this kabbalistic approach, we clearly see that the story of the Garden of Eden is a cosmology that far transcends the more commonly accepted versions. Obviously, a new perception of the Western creation story not only would dramatically affect our images of Adam, Eve, and the serpent, but also would permeate our collective consciousness in a way that could profoundly impact how we view ourselves as human beings, how we relate to one another, and how we relate to God.

## SEEDS OF SIN
## AND GUILT

*L*et us take a closer look at the more traditional reading of the creation story to gain insight into how it developed in the consciousness of Western thought. The biblical story tells of a garden "planted by God" on the eastern side of Eden, which had in it every tree that was good for food. In the center of this garden were two special trees: the Tree of Life and the Tree of Knowledge of good and evil.

A river ran from Eden into the garden, where it split into four rivers that ran out of the garden. God made a man from the dust of the four corners of the earth and placed him in this garden to tend and maintain it. The man was told that he could eat from every tree except the Tree of Knowledge of good and evil. Moreover, the man was warned that "on the day you eat of that tree, you will surely die."[27]

After God brought all the animals and birds to the man so that the man could give each one its name, God caused him to fall into a deep sleep, and from the man's side, a woman was made. At this point both the man and the woman were naked and they knew no shame. Almost immediately in the story, a serpent approached the woman and told her that she would not die if she ate the fruit of the Tree of Knowledge. Rather, her eyes would be opened and she would be like a god because she would know about good and evil. So she ate some of the fruit and gave some to her man to eat. Sure enough, their eyes were opened to the extent that they now recognized their nakedness. They immediately sewed fig leaves together so they could cover themselves with loincloths.

Then they "heard the voice of the Lord God walking in the garden in the breeze of the day." So they hid themselves in the trees. God called out, "Where are you?" and the man responded that he heard a voice and hid because he knew he was naked and was afraid. "How did you know you were naked?" asked God. "Did you eat from the tree from which I told you not to eat?"

The scene is set. In the standard interpretation that has been passed down from generation to generation, Adam and Eve, confronted by God, caught in an infraction of the single rule established for this garden, tried to push the blame away from themselves. Adam said, "The woman gave it to me." Eve said, "The serpent enticed me."

Thus, according to common thinking, the serpent was the first to be punished by God. It was cursed forever to live on its belly and eat dust. Next God turned to Eve and said that her pain in childbirth would be greatly multiplied and that her husband would rule over her. Finally God turned to Adam and told him that from now on he would have to work and sweat to get his food, and that the ground would give forth "thorns and thistles" for his labors. At this point God gave them clothes made of skin.

Then it appears that God said to Itself, almost as an afterthought, "Man has become like one of us, knowing good and evil. What if he eats from the Tree of Life and lives forever?" So God cast Adam and Eve out of the Garden of Eden. Cherubic guards were positioned there so that Adam and Eve could not return; a revolving sword was set in motion so that they could not approach the Tree of Life.[28]

This story, interpreted literally, is the archetype of sin, even though the word "sin" is never mentioned. This original sin was disobeying God, and it resulted in the fall of humankind from God's grace. The story also includes the archetype of evil, the serpent, and of purity and innocence, because Adam and Eve did not know that they were naked. It has in it the archetype of guilt, which instantly breeds the first denial, and it includes the first curse made by God, giving us an initial glimpse, theoretically, of the kind of punishment that awaits disobedience.

When we read this story through the filters of twentieth-century awareness, we cannot help but wonder what was so captivating that it became the principal creation story for Western spiritual tradition. A modern editor would have rejected this manuscript after reading the first few pages. Not only is it politically incorrect to treat women as vassals, but the nature of the act of eating something forbidden leads to unbelievable consequences.

The way it reads, God makes the promise that anyone eating this fruit is going to die that very day. But it does not happen that way. Adam and Eve do not die on that day. Rather, they are punished for eternity. God never said anything about eternal punishment. A modern editor would point out that the story is inconsistent. Moreover, the editor would note that the story's treatment of sexuality is untenable, as if nakedness were something awful. Who would relate to that?

There are too many holes in the logic. The biggest one is that only the Tree of Knowledge was forbidden; Adam could have eaten from the Tree of

Life all along. In that case, he would never die. Why would God take the chance that Adam might eat from the Tree of Life first, thereby attaining eternal life, and then from the Tree of Knowledge?

In addition, why would the serpent set itself up to be the recipient of God's wrath? What did it have to gain? Why bring death upon itself? It could have eaten from the Tree of Life and become eternal. Then it could have eaten from the Tree of Knowledge itself and would have become like God. As clever as it was, its behavior is totally illogical.

Worst of all, the story demeans God, which our editor might think would offend readers. It makes God out to be less than Almighty. God has to instruct Adam not to eat the fruit of this special tree rather than making it too hard to reach or impossible to find or any one of thousands of scenarios. Would we put a candy on the coffee table and tell an innocent two-year-old never to eat it?

The voice of God "walks" in the garden. What does that mean? God calls out to Adam, "Where are you?" Does this mean God does not know where Adam is? God does not know the nature of serpents? God does not know in advance that Adam and Eve will eat the fruit? God "wonders" whether they will eat from the Tree of Life? God has to send them out of the garden to keep them from eating other fruits? God has to set up cherubs to guard the garden, and a revolving blade to guard the Tree of Life? This will not work. Modern readers would definitely reject the presentation of a God that lacks foresight, strength, wisdom, understanding, and compassion. "No," a modern editor would say, "this manuscript will never get past the critics."

## The Art of
## Torah Study

*T*he literal account of the five books of Moses is almost impossible to appreciate without assistance. Hundreds of commentaries exist, and, as we might imagine, many offer interpretations that contradict others. Nobody agrees that there is a definitively "correct" way to read the Torah. In fact the oral tradition suggests that there are at least 600,000 different interpretations, representing the number of those who received the Torah through Moses at Mt. Sinai.

This is what makes the study of Torah so interesting. If we simply accept the literal meaning of what it says, then it is merely a book with many unusual stories. If we engage it, however, work with it and use a variety of methods to analyze the text, it yields hidden clues that lead us on to further investigation. Study like this, a continuous give and take, becomes a mystical relationship between the text and the one studying it.

Many experiences with inanimate objects involve mystical interactions. A mechanic who fine-tunes an engine often relates to it as if the engine were communicating with him or her. A pilot or boat skipper interacts with the "personality" of an airplane or boat. Clay and potter become one as a bowl rises on the wheel; oils, canvas, and a painter merge into a relationship that carries the work to a different reality. Art transcends the objective world and enters a mystical realm that is inexplicable.

Students of Torah have always had an artistic-spiritual engagement with the scriptural text. Engagement is a good word because the experience is almost like a betrothal. The student becomes intimate with a set of words, commentaries, commentaries on the commentaries, and a brand-new world opens.

This is the world that has kept Torah alive and well in Judaism for more than two thousand years. The questions raised in the mind of our imaginary editor were obvious to readers thousands of years ago. A great deal of oral tradition speaks to these issues. Many other questions, not easy for modern readers to see, were addressed as well.

## PARDES: THE ORCHARD OF TORAH

The Torah is studied on four different levels, known by the acronym P–R–D–S. A *pardes* is an orchard or garden. In Hebrew it is spelled with the consonants *peh, resh, dalet,* and *samekh.* In the context of studying Torah, the *peh* represents *p'shat,* which means the simple or literal interpretation. *Resh* represents *remez,* which means the interpretation of what is being hinted at in the text: the metaphors, allegories, and parables. *Dalet* represents *drosh,* which is an examination of the text by bringing in additional material. Finally, *samekh* represents the *sod* of the material, the secret, hidden meanings that offer insights into the structure of the universe.

Let us look at a few elements of the Garden of Eden story, the trees, the rivers, the forming of man, and see how this is viewed from the four different perspectives of interpretation.

## P'shat *(Literal)*

There was a place called Eden and it had a garden. The word "Eden" comes from the Akkadian word *"edinu,"* derived from the Sumerian word "eden," which means "plain," as in prairie or plateau. This, in addition to the mention of the rivers that run through it, suggests that Eden is a geographical location.[29] Commentators generally agree that two of the four rivers running out of Eden are the Tigris and the Euphrates. Regarding the other two rivers,[30] some say one could be the Nile, with the fourth being the Indus or Ganges; but most would agree that the common meeting point was the Persian Gulf, which may be the undivided "river" running into the garden.[31]

Although the Garden of Eden has never been seen by a living human being, Resh Lakish, a talmudic sage, said, "If it is in the land of Israel, its gate is Bet Shean (a fertile area near Tiberias); if it is in Arabia, its gate is Bet Gerem (possibly a highly fertile area facing Bet Shean on the other side of the Jordan); and if it is between the rivers (unknown), its gate is Damascus."[32]

An anecdote recorded in the Talmud says that Alexander of Macedonia found the Garden of Eden in the middle of Africa.[33] On his journey he encountered women warriors who warned him not to make war with them, for he would lose either way: If he killed them, it would be said that he took advantage of women, and if they killed him, he would be called the King Who Was Killed by Women.

When asked for bread, these women served him loaves of gold. He asked them if they ate gold, and they replied, "If you wanted bread, did you not have enough bread in your own home to eat that you had to travel all the way here?" When he left this place, he wrote on the gate of the city, "I, Alexander of Macedonia, was a fool until I came to this city of women in Africa and learned wisdom."[34]

Farther on, he ate some salted fish washed by water from a local well. The fish gave off a sweet odor. He recognized by this scent that the water had come from the Garden of Eden. He found the garden and cried out that the gate should be opened. The guards said it was the gate of the Lord and would be opened only for the righteous. He said that he was a king and wanted something. So they gave him an eyeball. Here the story moves from literal to metaphoric.

## Remez *(Hints, Metaphor, Parable)*

Alexander took this eyeball and weighed it against the gold and silver he was carrying, a significant amount. The eyeball was heavier than all his wealth combined. He asked the wise ones traveling with him, "How could this be?" They replied that this was a human eyeball, which represents desire that can never be satisfied. The desire of human beings is immeasurably weightier than all the gold and silver in the world. He asked them to prove it, and they sprinkled some dust over the eyeball so that it could not see. Immediately it lost it weightiness.[35]

Here's the creation story on the *remez* level:

*T*HE FIRST MAN was created from dust taken from the four corners of the world. Humankind was created in this way so that if a person born in the East should happen to die in the West, the earth would not refuse to receive the dead. Thus, wherever anyone happens to die, the body will be returned to the earth.[36] Also the dust taken was of various colors: red, for blood; black, for bowels; white, for bones; and green, for pale skin.[37]

Rabbi Yehuda said that Adam is so named because he was taken from the ground *(adamah)*. Rabbi Joshua the son of Korhah said Adam was so named because he was made of flesh and blood *(dam)*.[38]

Rabbi Eliezer wondered what kind of work the first man was supposed to do in the garden. There were no fields to plow, and the trees grew on their own. There was no need for watering, for a river ran through it. Therefore, the instruction God gave to Adam to "tend and maintain it" must not refer to tending the garden. Rather, it must mean to follow the teachings of the Torah. Rabbi Eliezer said, "The Tree of Life signifies only the Torah; for it says in Proverbs (3:18), 'She is a tree of life to those that hold her, and happy are those that hold her tightly.' "[39]

At another point, Rabbi Eliezer described a different metaphor. He said that the tree refers to a man because it says in Deuteronomy that "man is a tree of the field."[40] The garden refers to woman because it says in Song of Songs, "An enclosed garden is my sister, my bride."[41] Therefore the midst of the garden suggests the center of the woman, and the taking of forbidden fruit refers to inappropriate sexual intercourse.[42]

# Drosh *(Searching, Examining)*

Rabbi Meir said the fruit of the Tree of Knowledge of good and evil was wheat. (The word for wheat, *hita,* is similar to the word for sin, *het.*) Rabbi Judah said the fruit was grapes. (Grapes were known to be the fruits of gods.) Rabbi Abba of Acco said it was a citron. (Fruit like a lemon—from a play of words related to desire.) Rabbi Jose said that it was figs. (Adam and Eve covered themselves with fig leaves.) Rabbi Azariah and Rabbi Judah the son of Rabbi Simon said, "Heaven forbid [we should be guessing at the fruit of the tree]. The Holy One purposely did not reveal the type of tree or its fruit so that we would never accuse [this fruit] of bringing sin to the world."[43] (It is interesting to note that not a single commentary in the Talmud or the *Midrash Rabbah* says that the Tree of Knowledge was an apple tree. This idea comes from non-Jewish sources.)

The words "man" and "woman" each are composed of an element of fire and God. The Hebrew name for man is *ish,* and for woman *isha.* Both include in their spelling the letters for fire *(aish),* which are *aleph* and *shin.* In addition to the letters for fire, man is spelled with a *yod,* and woman is spelled with a *hey.* The new letters *yod* and *hey* are the first two letters of the four-letter name for God: *yod-hey-vav-hey.* Thus it is taught that God says, "If you follow my ways, my name will be with you; but if you do not, I will take away my name and you will become fire."[44]

The four streams that flow through the Garden of Eden come from the roots of the Tree of Life. They separate the lower (earth) region from the upper (heavenly) region. The lower waters, associated with the earth, are equated with the feminine principle. The upper waters represent the masculine principle.[45] Water is used as the symbol because it spontaneously merges with itself, suggesting that the separation of heaven and earth is temporary and all will be one in the world to come.

# Sod *(Hidden, Secret)*

The hidden teachings of the Torah are derived through kabbalistic techniques. They are mysterious and very difficult to understand without considerable background. This is why so few of these teachings are available to a more general readership, and it is why the mystical approach to the Garden of Eden story is rarely heard.

In the *sod* reading, there are actually two gardens of Eden, one below and one above. Saintly beings stay for a while in the lower Garden of Eden after they die, and then rise to the celestial academy, which is the upper garden. There is yet a realm higher than the upper garden, for these righteous beings eventually rise to bathe "in dewy rivers of pure balsam."[46]

The river that goes forth from the Garden of Eden represents the central one of three columns on the kabbalistic Tree of Life. Eden is viewed in Kabbalah as the principle of the Supernal Mother, and the central column represents the presence of the Divine on earth, called the *Shekhina*. The *Shekhina* (water) is the nurturing force for the entire earth (garden).

The four rivers coming out of the one river represent four major emanations of the Divine: lovingkindness *(chesed),* which is the personification of the archangel Michael; strength *(gevorah),* the archangel Gabriel; triumph *(netzach),* the archangel Uriel; and grandeur *(hod),* the archangel Raphael.[47]

The mystery of saying the *Shema* prayer (*Shema Yisrael, Adonoy Elohaynu, Adonoy Ehad*—Hear, O Israel, the Lord is Our God, the Lord is One) is that it draws a beam of light from a hidden supernal world and divides it into seventy lights, representing the seventy nations of creation. Those lights become luminous branches of the Tree of Life. When the seventy branches are illuminated, this Tree and all other trees in the Garden of Eden emit sweet odors and perfumes, preparing all the polarities to unite into the Divine Oneness.[48] In Kabbalah, the urge for this union, bringing the upper and lower together, is the driving force of the process of creation, the process of our lives.

## KABBALISTIC
## TECHNIQUES

*K*abbalistic insights constantly challenge our sense of reality. They urge us on, presenting new entryways into the mysteries of creation. The eyeball that Alexander was given was a subtle slap on the wrist that he did not recognize. The sages told him about the bottomless pit of human desire, but he did not recognize this eyeball as a symbol of his own acquisitiveness. Had he understood the message from the beginning, he might have gained entrance to the garden.

# Gematria: Value of the Hebrew Letters

| Form | Sounded as | Pronunciation | Numerical Value |
|---|---|---|---|
| א | Aleph | Silent | 1 |
| ב | Bet | B or V | 2 |
| ג | Gimel | G | 3 |
| ד | Dalet | D | 4 |
| ה | Hey | H | 5 |
| ו | Vav | V | 6 |
| ז | Zayin | Z | 7 |
| ח | Chet | CH | 8 |
| ט | Tet | T | 9 |
| י | Yod | Y | 10 |
| כ | Kaf | K or KH | 20 |
| ל | Lamed | L | 30 |
| מ | Mem | M | 40 |
| נ | Nun | N | 50 |
| ס | Samekh | S | 60 |
| ע | Ayin | Gutteral | 70 |
| פ | Peh | P or F | 80 |
| צ | Tzadi | Tz | 90 |
| ק | Kuf | K | 100 |
| ר | Resh | R | 200 |
| ש | Shin | SH or S | 300 |
| ת | Tav | T | 400 |

Kabbalah assumes that there are hidden secrets in everything. We must see things without our eyes, hear without our ears, know without our intellect. If we are able to penetrate the surface of appearances, we will discover the mysteries of creation. This is particularly true of Torah. It is often viewed by Kabbalists as the mind of God. All we need is to learn how to decode it.

Kabbalists use a wide variety of tools in their search for hidden codes. One tool is the analytical method of gematria, in which each letter of the Hebrew alphabet has a numeric value. The first letter, *aleph,* has the value of one; the second letter, *bet,* the value of two; and so on. After *yod,* which equals ten, the numbers climb by tens until they reach *kuf,* one hundred. Then they climb by hundreds to the last letter, *tav,* four hundred.

There are a number of variations in the gematria method of decoding the Torah. Certain letters are shaped differently when they are the final letters of words. In their new contours they can receive different numerical values. Another variation is to exchange the first letter of the alphabet, *aleph,* with the last, *tav;* then the second, *bet,* with the second-to-last, *shin;* and so forth. This is called the *atbash* method *(aleph-tav-bet-shin),* and any letter can be switched with its corresponding pair.[49] Obviously, these substitutions completely alter words and meanings of statements.

Most important, every word itself is a code for something else. As we saw above, garden can mean earth, water can mean the Divine Presence, Eden can mean mother. Kabbalists are enormously creative in their attempts to break the mystical codes. They feel that each teaching is drawn from another level of reality.

Thus, it is understood that the Torah contains all of the wisdom of creation. Every time a new code is broken, we discover something we had not known before. Therefore, many complex methods have been used in this process to give us a magnifying glass so that we can explore the cosmic fabric fiber by fiber.

## The *Atbash* Code

א ב ג ר ה ו ה ז ו ה ט י כ ל מ נ ס ע פ צ ק ד ש ת
ת ש ר ק צ פ ע ס נ מ ל כ י ט חַ ז ו ה ד ג ב א

The Atbash Cipher

|  |  |  |
|---|---|---|
| Aleph (1) | = | Tav (22) |
| Bet (2) | = | Shin (21) |
| Gimel (3) | = | Resh (20) |
| Dalet (4) | = | Kuf (19) |
| Hey (5) | = | Tzadi (18) |
| Vav (6) | = | Peh (17) |
| Zayin (7) | = | Ayin (16) |
| Chet (8) | = | Samekh (15) |
| Tet (9) | = | Nun (14) |
| Yod (10) | = | Mem (13) |
| Kaf (11) | = | Lamed (12) |

# ADAM AND EVE WERE
## SIAMESE TWINS

*T*he first Adam/Eve is called by Kabbalists *Adam ha-Rishon* (primeval human consciousness). This in no way resembled the human form as we know it. The Jewish sages spoke of it in hyperbole. It had stupendous proportions, reaching from earth to heaven; it stood astride earth from one end to the other.[50] It could see to the far reaches of the universe, for the light at that time was called *Ohr Ein Sof*, the Limitless Light, a metaphor for pure awareness.

*Adam ha-Rishon* did not see with eyes; it saw with an immeasurable "knowing."[51] Because each and every mortal being is a spark from the original *Adam ha-Rishon*, we all have the potential to perceive everything knowable in this universe.

Adam and Eve were born simultaneously, side-by-side or back-to-back, attached like Siamese twins.[52] It says in Genesis, "Male and female It created *them*." In biblical language it says that to separate them, God took one of Adam's "sides"; in zoharic language, it says, "God sawed Eve off from him."[53] (For those who say Adam and Eve were attached back-to-back, this sawing is viewed as the cause of the bumps all humans have along the back of the spine.)

The *Midrash Rabbah* says, "When the Holy One created *Adam [ha-Rishon]*, it was androgynous. God created *Adam ha-Rishon* double-faced, and split him/her so there were two backs, one on this side and one on the other."[54] The idea that Adam and Eve were co-equal at birth is not a kabbalistic secret; it was openly discussed in ancient midrashic literature. Moreover, it was known two thousand years ago that the idea that Eve came from Adam's rib was a common misunderstanding. The Torah is unambiguous on this point. It repeats a second time, "Male and female It created *them*," and goes on to say, "and blessed *them,* and called *their* name Adam on the day *they* were created."[55] Whenever the Torah repeats something, the emphasis always suggests deeper implications. Here, it is impossible to ignore that the creation of male and female was simultaneous.

It was only *after* the "sin" that *Adam ha-Rishon* was diminished in size.[56] This means that Eve and Adam became separate entities while both were still of gigantic proportions, that is, when both could see to the ends of the universe. The Garden of Eden, of course, was also viewed as enormous. The

Tree of Life, at the center of the garden, was more than twelve thousand miles high and approximately fifty thousand miles in diameter.[57] Some midrashic sources suggest that it would take a person five hundred years to walk its diameter; this would make it millions of miles across.[58]

This enormous size is described to suggest that the Tree of Life is all-inclusive; it shelters under its branches every living thing, plant or animal. Even though today we know that the universe is significantly larger than a few million miles, ancient astronomers may have assumed that the entire universe could be enclosed in a space of such magnitude.

Exaggeration in size and numbers is used purposefully in wisdom-teachings to shatter the boundaries of our minds. Mystically oriented traditions, such as Buddhism and Hinduism, often use the device of overstatement in their primary texts. In Buddhism it is said: "Buddha shall have a thousand-millionfold worlds equal in number to sands of the Ganges. There should be a *boddhisatva* multitude numbering incalculable . . . thousands of myriads of millions."[59] In the Hindu tales, King Nagnajit provides his daughter, Satya, the following dowry for her marriage to Krishna: "Ten thousand cows, nine thousand elephants, nine hundred thousand chariots, ninety million horses, [and] nine billion slaves."[60] And this was only one of many thousands of wives taken by Krishna!

The sheer magnitude of ideas such as these bursts the limits of our reality. We immediately appreciate the fact that mystical teachings transcend normal thought processes. In many ways, the literal translation of the biblical stories of Adam, Eve, and the Garden of Eden in human proportions is a major disservice, for this invites comparisons, projections, and simplistic interpretations that frequently put us on a track of distorted images and wrong-headed deductions. The mystical perspective, however, imposes an altered frame of reference upon us from the start.

## TWO CREATION STORIES

When we read the Adam and Eve story literally, fundamental questions arise: Was the serpent under instructions from God to seduce Eve? If so, God's punishment would seem hypocritical, or worse, downright diabolical. If the serpent was not under God's instructions, was it simply a troublemaker? A troublemaker in the Garden of Eden? This is an oxymoron. The Garden of Eden is another name for paradise. Paradise does not have troublemakers.

So the serpent must benefit in some way from a connection with Eve. In the mystical scenario described above, the serpent benefits by gaining vitality. Eve's name, Chava, means life, because she was "the mother of all living."[61] She holds the power of life; the entire physical universe is dependent upon her. If the serpent is able to merge with her, then physical creation is possible; if not, then physicality, as we know it, could never occur.

The intrinsic nature of Eve as the Supernal Mother is to give life. The serpent says to her, 'You will be like gods,'[62] meaning, you will be able to create life. Later on, God agrees that the serpent was not lying, for God says that Adam and Eve "have become like one of us."[63] That is to say, Adam and Eve were God-like, for they now had the ability to create life.

The *Zohar* says clearly that the forbidden fruit was sexuality. Eve and the serpent had sexual intercourse. In other words, they merged. Matter was now vitalized. Adam merged as well and added form. And this is the story of the physical creation as we know it.

One who reads the Torah literally might challenge this mystical interpretation with the more popular belief that this is a teaching story regarding sin and punishment. Indeed, the association of Eve and the serpent with sin and punishment is automatic in Western mythology. How would the Kabbalist respond to this objection?

When we carefully reread the text at the opening of the Torah, we find that there are two creation stories. In the first, male and female are created and are told to "be fruitful and multiply."[64] In this opening chapter, which goes all the way through the seventh day, everything is fine and beautiful. The creation is perfect, no problems appear on the horizon, and the whole story could come to an end after one page.

So this is one way for creation to unfold: perfect, untroubled, utopic. But this level of perfection is a two-dimensional flatland. It has no depth in the sense that there is no real free will. If the universe were entirely pre-conditioned, there would be no potential for creativity. This is one of the meanings of the idea that human consciousness was created in the image of God—that is to say, we can create. The proof of this creativity is in confronting God by eating the fruit. This is the expression of free will and the source of an imperfect, but vital, creation.

Thus the Torah retells the story. It returns to the sixth day and provides a new rendition. In this retelling, the Garden of Eden is introduced, and God instructs *Adam ha-Rishon* not to eat from the Tree of Knowledge because it will surely bring death. This is a statement of fact. Up to this point, there is no death in the Garden of Eden. Death does not exist at all. In fact, the physical universe does not exist. All of the lovely creations in the garden are nonphysical. This might seem confusing because we read about earth, plants, seas, birds, creatures, and so forth. It seems to resemble earth as we know it. But from the mystical perspective, the Garden of Eden is beyond any reality we can relate to at our current level of consciousness.[65]

The Garden of Eden story describes a situation in which there is no separation, no sense of identity. The body of Adam and Eve combined initially does not look like anything familiar. Even the concept of Siamese twins is misleading, because Adam/Eve was not in a human form when it was first divided into two entities. Nothing is familiar in the way that we see things.

But once a physical universe is formed, we read a metaphor that the voice of God "walks" in the garden in the breeze of day. This is mystical poetic imagery to indicate that a new materiality has come into the creation.

God asks of Adam and Eve, "Where are you!" This is not a question. It is rhetorical: "Look at where you are! You are in bodies, you are physical beings. I told you this would be the result. Now you will surely die." Then what happens? God gives Adam and Eve clothing made of skin. That is to say, now they have a sense of separation. This was the "punishment" of discriminating thought. Things became separate; they saw themselves as separate beings. Prior to the serpent, the sense of nakedness did not exist. It comes only when one has an identity, a sense of individuality.

As a sexual metaphor, the eating from the Tree of Knowledge is not a singular act, like eating fruit. It is relational; it takes two to eat from this tree. When we read this section carefully, we find that Adam does not say that Eve forced him to eat, rather that she offered the fruit and he freely took it.[66] This is an acknowledgment of relationship rather than the placing of blame.

There is a different way to read the traditional translation in which Eve says "The serpent beguiled (seduced) me and I did eat."[67] The word used here for seduction, *hishiani,* can be translated in a way to mean "to elevate," or "lift up."[68] Thus, one could translate this same sentence as: "He elevated me [to a higher state] and we ate (had sexual relations)." This interpretation adds an entirely new dimension to the story. A higher state of consciousness was aroused. That is to say, creation brought about a new potential for awareness. Standard commentaries to the Torah never mention this possible reading of Eve and the serpent.

At this point in the story, God curses the serpent. The reading is, "You are cursed above all cattle and above all beasts of the field."[69] Is that not curious? Does this mean that all cattle and other beasts are cursed? Why are they cursed? If they are not cursed, what is the big deal about the curse on the serpent? It would have been much stronger for God simply to say to the serpent that it is cursed forever.

This is an issue that bothered many of the commentators. Some talmudic scholars suggested that this curse referred to procreation, and that the period of gestation for a serpent would be longer than that of other beasts.[70] Others disputed this line of reasoning. Everybody agreed, however, that the curse does not make sense the way it is written; indeed, the language of comparison mitigates the power of the curse.

The other part of the curse is that the serpent would go on its belly and eat dust. There are thousands of creatures that go on their bellies, and many of them live under the surface of the earth. Are they cursed as well? In the end, there are serious questions regarding the true meaning and intention of the curse; some say that it is not really a curse at all.

The Torah says that there will be enmity between humans and serpents; humans will crush serpents' heads, and serpents will bite the heels of humans. In the Kabbalah, head and heel are code words for epochs in the unfolding of creation. The head represents the earliest part of an era, while the heel represents the end of an era.

According to this way of looking at things, we are currently in the heel phase of a six-thousand-year cycle. When it ends, a messianic era begins. Crushing and biting suggest points of transition. The serpent biting at our heels indicates that we are moving closer to the realization of messianic consciousness. When we step on its head, we will finally enter the new era.[71] The Hebrew word for serpent *(nahash)* is equal in value to the word for messiah *(meshiach)*.[72] From this kabbalistic perspective, the serpent is the vehicle for messianic consciousness. Thus the serpent represents far more in mystical Judaism than is commonly known, and a deeper understanding of these teachings changes entirely our appreciation of the story of creation. Without the serpent, without the energizing of creation, we would never have the opportunity to follow a path returning us to our Divine Source.

# MYSTICAL
# CREATION

In September 1981, not long after our wedding, Shoshana and I made an exploratory trip to Israel to decide if it was a place we would want to live and study. We arrived just before Rosh Hashana and were invited to more than two dozen homes of religiously observant families for festive Holy Day and Sabbath meals during that month. It was a marvelous experience in almost every way, but a single theme pervaded throughout our visit that deeply bothered us and almost discouraged us from returning.

Rosh Hashana is viewed as the day marking the creation of the world. It is Adam and Eve's birthday, so to speak.[73] On an esoteric level it is a day of judgment,[74] when each person's name is inscribed in a heavenly book for life or death in the coming year.[75] My curiosity was piqued at one of the first households we visited when Elisha, our host, held firm to a fundamentalist belief that Adam and Eve were real people and that creation had occurred 5,742 years earlier. According to Elisha, nothing had existed prior to this.

I found this idea somewhat amusing and said, "But science clearly proves otherwise. Archeology, geology, biology, and astronomy all have methods to show that the world is hundreds of millions of years old."

Elisha said, "None of these scientific hypotheses can be proven. They all are dependent upon observation. But consider this: What if the creation were done in a way that artifacts were created in place? Every bone of so-called prehistoric animals was created at the same time as Adam and Eve, and every one was created in a way that a carbon test would show it to be millions of years old."

"You mean to say," I responded, "that God played a cosmic joke on science, and everything is really a fake, put there to fool people into thinking that the universe is billions of years old when in fact it is only a few thousand years old?"

"Yes, that is precisely what I am saying. Moreover, there is nothing a scientist can do to absolutely prove me wrong."

Arguing this point with Elisha would be like arguing whether a falling tree makes a sound if nobody hears it. Clearly, an omniscient and omnipotent prankster could set up almost any mirage. If this were so, there would be no reason to believe that anything happened *one minute* ago, much less billions of years.

Nonetheless, I had difficulty with Elisha's approach in that it was founded upon a God that used an elaborate scheme of deceit. Although it is true that a belief system that questions the physicality of the material world could be helpful in opening us to mystical awareness, there are many ways to suggest the illusory nature of our reality without proposing a willful trick. Unfortunately, God as a trickster would have a creation that by its nature would be missing true faith as an essential quality, because nothing could be believed in a universe built upon deception.

Elisha is not alone in his position. He represents a small but significant fraction of Jewry that maintains fundamentalist beliefs. Interestingly, many fundamentalists live at the core of what some people believe is "authentic" Judaism, and their interpretations or opinions concerning laws, customs, and rituals are highly respected. Thus I was greatly disturbed because these were not the kind of people I could turn to for spiritual guidance.

Kabbalah, however, teaches differently. It says that creation is not something that happened at some point in time; creation is happening at all times. It is happening right now. About fifty-seven hundred years ago, according to the Hebrew calendar, human consciousness became a new reality in this part of the universe. This is what is referred to in the Torah as Adam and Eve in the Garden of Eden. It is the story of the inception of a new level of awareness. But we should never refer to creation as a thing of the past because it is ongoing and constant, an unceasing phenomenon. This does not preclude the fact that the physical universe—from our point of view—had a point of conception. In fact, according to kabbalistic calculations, the beginning of the physical universe extends more than fifteen billion years.[76] But Kabbalah also teaches that even fifteen billion years is not sufficient because this universe, as we know it, is not the first. There have been others.[77] The important point, however, is that creation itself is an ongoing process. Therefore, to set it into a time frame is absurd—whether one is a scientist or a religious fundamentalist.

Scientists have argued with theologians for hundreds of years about evolution and the timing of creation. But Kabbalah is far more radical than science, for it proposes a string of creations. The *Sefer Yetzirah,* one of the earlier kabbalistic texts, says that seven specific letters of the Hebrew alphabet symbolize seven universes and seven firmaments.[78] These are universes that were created and destroyed, but there are differences of opinion as to which universe we currently inhabit. As Aryeh Kaplan points out, "According to some Kabbalists, the present creation is the second, while others state that it is the sixth or seventh."[79] From another perspective, many universes can run concurrently, for once we transcend the universe as we know it, time shifts in meaning. These kabbalistic concepts of multiple universes, whether linear or concurrent, encompass essentially all scientific theory, including evolution, and extend beyond it.

## Continuous Creation

The principle of continuous creation, without beginning or end, is based upon the idea that there is a source of life that eternally emanates the energy required for all existence. If this source of life were to withhold itself for but a split second, everything would vanish. That is to say, all humanity, all nature, all of creation is constantly being sustained each and every moment. It is as if creation were a lightbulb that stays illuminated as long as the electricity is flowing. The instant we shut off the power, the light fades out.

If we walk into a room with a light shining, we do not know when that light was turned on. It may have been turned on the instant before we walked in. As with a refrigerator, perhaps the door itself to this room has a switch built into it that turns on the light when it is opened. Without additional information, however, we cannot deduce anything from the fact that the light is on when we open the door to this room. No matter how fast we open the door to catch the darkness, the light is always on when the door is open.

Imagine that creation works the same way. If we go into a dark, sound-proof room, we have no idea what is going on in the world, or if there even is a world. In fact, we so quickly lose our sense of reality in that situation that we have no way of knowing if the world even exists. Indeed, we could be in our own coffins, we could be dying or dead, for in a void without any stimuli we have no basis for assessing reality. If we were able to exit from the darkness and open our eyes, we would quickly reconstitute our reality base. During that instant when we reformulated our world, it would be as if creation were brand new.

Now imagine that each time we blink our eyes we fall into a mind-state of being in an isolated room. Each time we open our eyes, we experience creation anew. Assuming we could blink thousands of times a second, creation would always seem to be beginning.[80]

This is actually the way it is. Look around you. As you look at something, try to imagine that from one second to the next it is receiving its form and substance from the center of the universe. If that source were shut off, everything would be gone in a blink. Everything we see, everything we know, could evaporate at any instant in time.

Modern theoretical science postulates this idea in the Heisenberg Uncertainty Principle. It suggests that we never know if the existence of a certain form will persist, or if something will instantaneously take on a completely new form.[81] Indeed, although there are few absolute truths in this creation, one of them is that things are constantly changing. This means that we never have certainty from one moment to the next if the sustained flow of creation will persevere.

This idea of the continuous flow of creation completely alters the way we view things. When we have a sense of substance and solidity, we are inclined to have more faith in the past and future. History has an important dimension in our reality, and we base our lives on our own experiences and those of others. The theory of continuous creation, however, leads us to a relationship with life that mystics around the world suggest is the ultimate reality: there is only Now.

The added dimension in Judaism, of course, is that the Now rests upon the palm of God's hand, so to speak. The dimension of this moment is supported in its entirety by the nature of the Divine. Thus there is a vital relationship between God and every aspect of creation. Each breath I draw is initiated, sustained, and nourished by the power of creation. Each event is permeated by the magic of the Divine Presence.

# KABBALAH AND
## THE BIG BANG THEORY

*T*he kabbalistic view of a continuous creation is in variance with modern theoretical physics, which currently is pursuing the Big Bang theory. The Big Bang concept is that something happened many billions of years ago that instantaneously expanded into a primordial universe. Following this theory, our universe continues to expand from an initial impulse.

The idea that creation occurred in the past leads to the assumption of a time distance between the creative act and our present experience. It implies a physical distance between our location in space and the creative force. Thus, the reality in which we live, as long as we surrender to the limits of time and space, leads us to our erroneous belief in the separation between ourselves and the source of life.

The belief in separateness often leads us to the loss of hope and feelings of isolation, which can manifest as alienation and despair. Almost all of the difficulties experienced in the spiritual quest are related to the sense of feeling isolated, different from other people, disconnected from the source of life.

Jewish mysticism approaches the issue of feeling alone in the cosmos by questioning our essential assumptions regarding creation. Once we realize and experience our intimate relationship with God, which is continuous and fills each moment, we can never again feel alone. The mystical perspective suggests that this relationship is indispensable for both sides, for Creator and creation unfold simultaneously. For example, a parent is defined by his or her child. Without a child, one is not a parent, and vice versa. There can be no giver without a receiver, and one cannot receive without something being given. Nothing is separate, except for the "sense" of separateness, a feeling which is readily disproven. Indeed, if we were separated from the source of life at any moment, we could not exist.

The problem with the Big Bang theory is that it suggests something happened in the past, a burst of energy that continues on its own momentum for billions of years. But in the realm of the Divine, there is no past or future as we know it. Moreover, the momentum of the Big Bang theory would be predictable, while Jewish mystics believe that creation is always uncertain.

Rather, the Big Bang is an ongoing creative emanation. The universe is constantly balanced upon a symbiotic relationship of Creator and creation, each integral to the continuation of the universe. If either part of the relationship fails to nourish the other, the whole thing comes to a screeching halt. On the other hand, the ongoing interaction between Creator and creation defines and nurtures each moment—and each moment is another Big Bang impulse.

One of the great hasidic masters of the eighteenth century, Rebbe Levi Yitzhak of Berdichev, wrote, "The Creator's continuous radiation of creative force never ceases from the world; in every instant these [vital] emanations radiate to Its creations, to all the worlds, to all the palaces (realms of higher consciousness) and to all the angels."[82]

# THE NATURE
# OF GOD

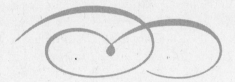

What is God? In a way, there is no God. Our perception of God usually leads to a misunderstanding that seriously undermines our spiritual development.

God is not what we think It is. God is not a thing, a being, a noun. It does not exist, as existence is defined, for It takes up no space and is not bound by time. Jewish mystics often refer to It as *Ein Sof,* which means Endlessness.

*Ein Sof* should never be conceptualized in any way. It should not be called Creator, Almighty, Father, Mother, Infinite, the One, Brahma, Buddhamind, Allah, *Adonoy, Elohim, El,* or *Shaddai;* and It should never, never be called He. It is none of these names, and It has no gender.

When we call It God, what are we talking about? If we say that It is compassionate, full of lovingkindness, the source of love, we may be talking about our image of what we think the divine nature *ought* to be, but we are not talking about *Ein Sof.* In the same way, if we say that the God portrayed in the Bible is vindictive, jealous, angry, cruel, uncaring, or punitive, we cannot be referring to *Ein Sof. Ein Sof* includes every attribute but cannot be defined by any of them individually or all of them combined.

The mystery of the origin of the universe has fascinated human consciousness from the beginning of recorded history. In all cultures of the world we find the timeless inquiries: Is there a creator, and if so, what is its nature? If not, how did creation begin, and what is its purpose?

Mystics teach that there is a universal connection among all things; modern science offers the same message. This connection has various names. Some say it is a soul force, others call it love; the ancients called it ether, science often names it energy. Yet although there is general agreement that there seems to be a fundamental nature in the continuous unfolding of the universe, our relationship to the core of this nature has been a matter of considerable debate.

Jewish mystics are particularly concerned about naming the universal connection. People confuse names with identities. Many primitive cultures have name-secrets. They will not tell you their names for fear that you will have power over them. Similarly, at times they will not allow you to take pictures of them. In the primitive mind, the essence of a person can be captured and imprisoned if one has control over a name or an image.

Giving a name to the nameless creates a stumbling block that trips most people. We think that if something has a name, it has an identity. An identity comes with attributes. So we think we know something about it. This is a mistake.

For thousands of years this mistake has become ingrained in the human psyche. The word "God" suggests an embodiment of something that can be grasped. We have given a name to the Unknown and Unknowable and then have spent endless time trying to know It. We try because It has a name; but we must always fail because It is unknowable. Judaism is so concerned about this misunderstanding that it goes to great lengths to avoid naming God. Yet various names seep through because our minds cannot work without symbols.

What, then, is the God that is written about in the Bible? Kabbalists teach that the very first line of Genesis has been mistranslated. Most people think it says: "In the beginning, God created the heavens and the earth." But the actual words in Hebrew can be read another way. A Kabbalist could say: "With a beginning, [It] created God *(Elohim),* the heavens and the earth."[83] That is to say, out of Nothingness the potential to begin was created—Beginningness. Once there was a beginning, God (in a plural form) was created—a God to which the rest of creation could relate. Then the heavens and the earth were created.[84]

The implication of this interpretation profoundly affects our entire relationship with God and creation, for it says that all the names we have for

God and all the ways in which we relate to God are a few degrees removed from the source of creation that precedes even Nothingness. This is called *Ein Sof,* which is not the name of a thing, but is an ongoing process.

## EIN SOF

*T*he idea of *Ein Sof* was first described by the twelfth-century Kabbalist, Isaac the Blind. He taught that *Ein Sof* precedes thought *(machshavah),* and it even precedes the Nothingness *(ayin)* out of which thought is born. Nothingness is viewed as a level of awareness that is the result of the "annihilation of thought."[85]

The idea of the annihilation of thought, of course, is paradoxical. Can we imagine a void without beginning or end? Can we, limited by minds that are finite, imagine infinity? The answer is no, we cannot think of Nothing.[86] Anything that we can imagine has some kind of boundary—Kabbalists call it garment or vessel—and boundaries are containers. All thoughts, including all imagination, are garments or vessels.

By definition, a boundary sets limits. We may be able to put a name to infinity, we can draw a symbol of a figure eight on its side and say that this represents infinity, but no matter how much we may believe that our imagination is limitless, we remain confined by the boundaries of our own reality. If it can be imagined, it is not infinite.

As infinity is beyond the imagination, what about that which transcends infinity—that which created it? *Ein Sof* is not "restricted" by infinity. Indeed, we have suddenly run out of words because the idea of "trans-infinite" is a logical absurdity. What can go beyond infinity? Moreover, what can go beyond the Nothingness that surrounds infinity? This is *Ein Sof.*

Although we are informed that *Ein Sof* is inaccessible through any intellectual endeavor, we may still ask if there is a "knowing" that surpasses the intellect. Did Isaac the Blind have access to a level of awareness through which he could sense, somehow, the imperceivable?

The answer is yes. Jewish mysticism teaches that we can know *Ein Sof* in ways that transcend thought. This aspect of developing a relationship with Endlessness, the source of creation, is the key to all Kabbalah and the lifeblood of all Jewish practice. The secret teaching in developing this relationship with the Unknowable is hidden in the mystical foundation of the nature of relationship itself.

The word "God," and each of Its various names in Judaism, such as *El, Elohim, Adonoy, Shaddai,* and so forth, represent aspects of *Ein Sof.* The exploration of these aspects gives us insight into the nature of *Ein Sof.* Thus, whenever God is discussed in this book, we are not talking about a thing in itself, but a representation of a far deeper mystery.

## THE DIVINE KISS

In the Song of Songs, the mystic whispers about the kiss of its lover: "Let him kiss me with the kisses of his mouth; for your love is better than wine."[87] We can feel the aching heart of the lover: "I am sick with love, his left hand is under my head and his right embraces me."[88] We experience the thrill of anticipation: "My beloved put his hand by the latch of the door and my heart was thrilled; I rose to open to my beloved."[89]

"Ah," we say, "the passion of young love!" But this is not a poem about young lovers. It is about us, about every human being, and it describes our potential relationship with the Divine. Perhaps you do not believe this; perhaps you feel that having an intimate relationship with the Divine is beyond you, reserved for others or another lifetime. This is not so. It is part of our heritage; it is yours and mine to have. All we need do is learn how to let go of our fear, for fear maintains the barriers of separation.

In many traditions, the mystical expression of our relationship with the Divine is through Eros, the flame of a burning heart. Why? Because when we awaken to the realization that the presence of the Divine is revealed in the fullness of each moment, our hearts melt and the floodgates of our inner yearning open wide.

This is a mystical epiphany. It cannot be rationally explained. Although we cannot cross the barrier between us and that which lies beyond infinity, we can experience in the depths of our beings the realization that for each step we take, the Divine steps with us; each breath we draw is connected with the breath of the universe; and that lover, beloved, and the essence of love itself *all are reflections of exactly the same thing.* In each of these moments we "know" the presence of the Divine, and there is no separation.

One of the great Jewish mystics of the thirteenth century, Abraham Abulafia, said about one who has achieved this level of spiritual awareness: "Now we are no longer separated from our source, and behold we *are* the source and the source is us. We are so intimately united with It, we cannot by any means be separated from It, for we are It."[90]

There is a lovely Sufi story of a man who constantly cried out to God but received no response. After a while the devil whispered to this man, "How long will you wait for God to respond 'Here I am' to all of your entreaties?" This broke the man's spirit, and he stopped calling out to God. In a dream, however, he envisioned an image of the Divine,[91] who asked him why he had stopped. The man said that God had never answered his call. The wise dream-image, representing God, then said, "Did you not realize that every calling of yours IS itself my response?"[92]

The urge to call out to God is *always* answered simultaneously as it is spoken, for ultimately there is no difference between the caller and that to which it calls.

The Kotzker rebbe, Menachem Mendel, a famous hasidic teacher in the nineteenth century who lived his last twenty years in voluntary seclusion, asked one of his students, "Where does God dwell?" As the student stumbled in his attempt to respond, the Kotzker rebbe answered his own question: "God resides wherever we let God in!"[93]

Mystics throughout time, in all traditions, have said the same thing. We do not have to search for God, because the presence of the Divine permeates all things. If there is a search at all, it is God searching for Itself, so to speak.

## GOD IS A VERB

The closest we can come to thinking about God is as a process rather than a being. We can think of it as "be-ing," as verb rather than noun. Perhaps we would understand this concept better if we renamed God. We might call It God-ing, a process, rather than God, which suggests a noun.

This idea was developed by Rabbi Zalman Schachter-Shalomi, who explains that the kind of verb that represents God-ing is different from the ones we have in our ordinary language. Most of our verbs are considered transitive, which require a direct object, or intransitive, which do not. He suggests that God-ing is a mutually interactive verb, one which entails an interdependency between two subjects, each being the object for the other.[94]

For example, "communicating" could be such a verb. If I were speaking to an audience, I might not be communicating. I would be engaged in the act of communication, but if the audience were not attentive and were thinking about other things, I would not be communicating no matter how much I talked. My verbal communication is dependent upon a listener; it cannot be a one-way street. Other obvious verbs that fit into this category are loving, sharing, dancing, kissing, hugging, and so forth.

We can relate to God as an interactive verb. It is God-ing. Moreover, from this perspective, creation should not be treated as a noun. It too is an interactive verb; it is constantly creation-ing. And, dear reader, you should not treat yourself as a noun—as Joan, or Bill, or Barbara, or John. With regard to God as an interactive verb, you are also verbs; you are Joan-ing, Bill-ing, Barbara-ing, or John-ing in relation to God-ing, just as I am David-ing.

Each part in the universe is in dynamic relationship with every other part. In human interactions, such as marriage, one partner is husband-ing while the other is wife-ing. The two, in this sense, are one. We normally experience relationships in terms of their component parts; we are mistaken, however, when we assume the parts are separate.

It is important for us to remember that the concept of God-ing is a way for us to have a relationship with the Divine, not to be misunderstood as having a relationship with *Ein Sof.* Many names of God are included in *Ein Sof;* God-ing is one name—a name that happens to be a verb rather than a noun.

The true discovery of the intimacy of our ongoing relationship with the Divine can dramatically change our lives. It often happens spontaneously, without a reason. Some call this experience "grace." It arises out of nowhere. You could be sitting on the beach, walking in the woods, caring for someone who is dying, even driving on the freeway, and suddenly you are overwhelmed by a strange light that penetrates your consciousness and you are never again the same. We read accounts of such transformations and conversion experiences that have changed the world.

Occasionally individuals devote themselves to spiritual lives because of such experiences. However, most people who commit to inner paths do so because they yearn to connect with truth and meaning. This commitment usually involves undertaking a variety of practices that become part of one's daily life. They may include meditation, prayer, movement, diet, self-restraint, periods of seclusion, mantras, service, acts of loving-kindness, and other time-tested techniques to alter consciousness. Eventually, when the practitioner's priorities are clear, the inner light of aware-ness slowly becomes illuminated, and her or his perception of reality steadily changes.

On the spiritual path, either through a brilliant flash of insight or in the slow, steady progress of continuous practice, we gain wisdom. It is not in-tellectual knowledge, but wisdom—a deep knowing—inexplicable, inde-scribable, and exquisite beyond imagination. This wisdom is the fountain of true mystical experience, the driving force of all spiritual inquiry. It is what sustains us when we are faced with doubts, nourishes us when the world seems bleak, and comforts us when we face the death of loved ones. With-out it, where would we turn? What would we be without the awesomeness of the unknowable God?

There is no answer to this question; we cannot prove anything about *Ein Sof.* Rather, it is a self-reflecting inquiry. Yet when viewed from the per-spective of our dynamic relationship with the Divine, it is a self-fulfilling question, for paradoxically the source of the question is the answer it seeks. "What would I be without God?"

Consider this question from your inner awareness. Not you the noun, the person you may think you are, but you the verb, the process of being in full relationship, continuously, with its creator. When a question arises within you, who is asking the question, and to whom is the question addressed? As-sume that there is no "me" to ask the question, and there is no God out there to answer it. The question is part of the process of David-ing and God-ing in a mutual unfolding.

Try to do this in a way that melts all barriers of separation. No subject and no object. Simply an ever-opening process. No past, no future; only the Now. Each moment is a fresh opening. Each breath we draw, each move we make, is only Now. This is my dance with God-ing. It is an awesome expe-rience.

Awe leads to wisdom. The opening of the Jewish morning prayers quotes a line from Psalms that says: "The beginning of wisdom is the awe of the Y-H-V-H (the tetragrammaton, one of the key nameless names of God)."[95] This Y-H-V-H is often referred to as *Hashem,* the Name. We don't want to give It a name, so we call It *the* Name. It is too awesome to name. Yet we can experience awe.

Perhaps you will take a few moments to close your eyes and allow your-self to sink into this idea. Meditate on this thought: The teaching of the mys-tery of *Ein Sof* is that the center of our being, out of which awe arises, is that about which we are awed. It is It! When we contemplate our continuous process of opening, right here, right now, we realize that God-ing is *always* with us.

$T$HE ZOHAR SAYS: "Before shape and form were created, It *(Ein Sof)* was without form or appearance. Therefore, it is forbidden to perceive It in any way, not even by the letters of Its holy name or by any symbol. However, had Its brightness and glory not been radiated over the whole of creation, how could It have been discerned, even by the wise? Therefore, It descended on a [mystical] chariot to be known by the letters Y-H-V-H, in order that It could be inferred, and for this reason It allows Itself to be called by various names, such as *El, Elohim, Shaddai, Zevaoth,* and *Y-H-V-H* [among others, such as God], each being a symbol of divine attributes. However, woe to anyone who presumes to compare *Ein Sof* with any attributes. For it is limitless, and there are no means to comprehend It."[96]

Another zoharic teaching says: "That which is within the thought [of *Ein Sof*] is inconceivable. Much less can anyone know about *Ein Sof,* of which no trace can be found and which cannot be reached by any means of thought. Yet from the midst of this impenetrable mystery, the first descent of *Ein Sof* (whatever gives us insight regarding It) glimmers like a faint, undiscernible light just like the point of a needle, a hidden recess of thought which is not knowable until a light extends from it where there is an imprint of letters."[97]

The Unknowable can be discerned. Beginning at an indefinable point as sharp as a needle, It radiates in various ways which can be perceived—only in the context of process and interaction. We are not an audience watching the God-ing process onstage. We are onstage, ourselves. We mysteriously begin to get a glimmer of God-ing when we succeed in merging with the continuous process of unfolding creation.

Our own experience of God-ing is not like anything we read about. It is a different kind of revelation than that described by ancient prophets. Perhaps some people still are able to hear a voice that booms out of the heavens. But this is rare, indeed, and even the Talmud has serious questions about its veracity.

However, we do not have to be prophets to experience God-ing. It is everywhere around us and an aspect of everything we do. It arises when we repeatedly encounter the magical quality of life, the incredible blend and variety of experience, the exquisite unfolding of nature, the intricacies of our minds, and more than anything, the awe, the profound awe we experience when we sense the enormity of this universe. Somehow the awe itself draws us into the center of creation. At some point we merge with it.

## COPARTNERSHIP WITH GOD-ING

*A*s long as we relate to God as Father and we as children, we sustain the dysfunctional paternalistic model in which Father knows best. We not only remain alienated with a sense of abandonment, we relinquish our personal sense of responsibility. We think Father will take care of everything.

The Talmud records a wonderful story of a debate over an esoteric point of law in which one sage, Rabbi Eliezer, stood alone against dozens of other sages.[98] He tried every conceivable argument to convince his peers, to no avail. Finally, exasperated, he said, "If the Law (God) agrees with me, let this carob tree prove that I am right." At that moment, the carob tree flew out of the ground. Some say it moved 150 feet, others say 600 feet. But the sages were not convinced, and they responded, "You cannot prove anything from a carob tree."

So Rabbi Eliezer said, "If the Law agrees with me, let this stream of water prove that I am right," whereupon the stream reversed itself and began to flow uphill. The sages once again replied, "Proof cannot be brought from a stream of water."

Rabbi Eliezer persisted. "If the Law agrees with me, let the schoolhouse walls prove that I am right." It is said that the walls of the schoolhouse began to lean inward, but before they could fall, another sage, Rabbi Joshua, yelled at the walls, saying, "When scholars are involved in a dispute about the Law, what right do you have to interfere?" At this the walls stopped leaning inward. It is said that in honor of Rabbi Eliezer, they never went completely upright. But in honor of Rabbi Joshua, they did not fall. Rather, they remained on a permanent slant.

The story does not end here. Rabbi Eliezer stubbornly called out, "If the Law agrees with me, let heaven prove that I am right!" At this, a *bat kol,* a heavenly voice, thundered against all the scholars: "Why do you argue with Rabbi Eliezer? Do you not know that the Law *always* agrees with him!"

One would think that this would be sufficient for the sages to change their minds, but not so. At this point, Rabbi Joshua stood up and quoted a verse from Deuteronomy: "The commandment which I command you is not hidden from you, nor is it far. It is not in heaven that you should say, 'Who will go up to heaven and bring it to us that we can hear it and do it?' Nor is it beyond the sea that you should say, 'Who will cross the sea and bring it to us that we can hear it and do it?' But the word is very near you, in your mouth and in your heart that you may do it."[99]

Rabbi Joshua's position was that the Torah was given at Mt. Sinai so that earthly matters were now mankind's domain, and heaven should not interfere. This astounding talmudic assertion indicates that human reason carries precedence over heavenly mandates. It strongly declares complete independence in interpreting the laws of Moses. In many ways it is definitive evidence in support of total free will. The sages voted, and defeated Rabbi Eliezer, despite the fact that God was clearly on his side!

The Talmud goes on to record a conversation between Rabbi Nathan and the prophet Elijah, who spoke with him from heaven. Elijah frequently conversed with sages when they were dreaming or in various trans-states. In this exchange, Rabbi Nathan asked out of curiosity what the Holy One did at the time of this debate between Rabbi Eliezer and the sages. Elijah responded that the Holy One had laughed and had said to all of the angelic hosts (with obvious pleasure), "My children have defeated me!"[100]

Judaism is noted for its *chutzpah* in its relationship with the creative force. The Torah describes a number of biblical events in which Abraham and Moses repeatedly argue with God until their points are made; that is to say, until God changes Its mind, so to speak. Moreover, biblical commentators depreciate Noah because he did not argue with God about the destruction of the world but meekly built the ark when told to do so. Clearly the word of God in Judaism has never been viewed as a final decree but as divine intention that can be debated and in some instances reversed.

According to Kabbalah, the linchpin of our relationship with God is founded on the belief that human beings have creative capability to intervene in the "normal" course of events. One word, one gesture, or even one thought can change the direction of the creative process. This being so, we are led to conclude that human beings play a cocreative role.

## FREE WILL

The essential issue upon which all is balanced for creation to be creation-ing is that of free will. Throughout the ages, theologians have debated whether or not human beings have the ability to choose freely. It has been a key issue because free will imputes that God does not control the universe. If God is in control, then we are not really free to choose; God always "knows" what we are going to do. If we really have choice and God does not "know," then God is missing essential information.

The Torah is built upon the foundation of free choice for humankind. The story of Adam and Eve in the Garden of Eden is a description of free choice. From that point forward, every biblical story involves free choice.

We have human consciousness. We are informed that acts of lovingkindness, over the long run, will bring a higher level of consciousness to everyone in the world. We have the choice to do them or not. We are informed that an unkind word can set things in motion that may cause great harm and pain in the world. We have the choice of how we will speak. Even more, when the mystic suggests that our prayers can sway the outcome of events, our behavior can influence the degree to which there is peace in the world, or that our observance of ancient ritual can bring a healing to souls in other realms, imagine how this weighs on us as responsible, conscious beings.

Nothing is inconsequential. Each grain of sand holds amazing secrets. Each event contains mysterious messages. Every encounter with another being is a point of contact upon which the universe pivots. When we enter into this frame of mind, reality as we see it becomes a vast opportunity to experience the interconnectedness of all creation. From this perspective, we come to the realization that every piece is integral in the unfolding of creation, including us.

Free will and process go hand in hand. If we are caught in the illusion of separation, trapped in the sense of our "selves," we do not experience the interactive process. We cannot realize this because "self" and "other" are distinct. If, however, we are able to mediate this "self-consciousness," we can enter the realm of Now, in which everything is connected to and in process with everything else.

When we pull all of these ideas together, the paradigm of relationship between Creator and creation dramatically shifts. God is God-ing, creation is creation-ing, every aspect of creation is in process and continuously unfolding like an infinite flower opening its petals. In this reality, "knowing" is a moment-to-moment phenomenon, past and future are only in our minds, we are copartners with God-ing in the cosmic process, and each person has the full freedom of choice to change the universe. Nothing we do, say, or think is inconsequential; every action affects not only this reality but also other realities, and all of creation is interconnected. We should never assign attributes to our partner in process (God-ing), but we can "know" this partner through the direct experience of all that we encounter and every thought that arises in our minds.

## CREATION IS
## A THOUGHT IN
## THE MIND OF GOD

The intrinsic definition of Limitlessness is that It lacks nothing and can receive nothing, for It is everything. As It is everything, theoretically It is the potential to be an infinite source of giving.

The question arises, however, that there is nothing for It to give to because It is everything. It would have to give to Itself. This has been a major conundrum in philosophy and theology for thousands of years.

Kabbalah suggests one way of dealing with this issue. It says that as long as the infinite source of giving has no "will" to give, nothing happens. However, the instant It has the will to give, this will initiates a "thought." Kabbalah says, "Will, which is [primordial] thought, is the beginning of all things, and the expression [of this thought] is the completion."[101]

That is, the entire creation is nothing more than a thought in the "mind" of *Ein Sof,* so to speak. Another way to express this idea is that the will to give instantly creates a will to receive. The idea that an infinite giver can create receptivity in Itself is what Kabbalists call *tzimtzum* (contraction). It has to make an opening within Itself for receiving.

That which is given is called light. That which receives is called vessel. Light and vessel are always in balance, because light comes from an infinite source and thus will fill a vessel to its capacity. If we put a bucket under Niagara Falls, it instantly fills. If we put a freight train there, it also instantly fills. Imagine that the entire universe rests under a Niagara Falls of light, continuously being filled.

According to Kabbalah, the interaction between vessel and light is what makes the world go around. Everything in the universe is a vessel that "wills" to receive the light of the infinite bestower. Each molecule, plant, animal, rock, and human is a vessel; each has the "will" to be exactly what it is.

Human consciousness is unique in that it has the quality of being "in the image of God." This quality is expressed by what we call free will, and free will at its core is nothing more than the ability to bestow light. That is to say, human consciousness has an inherent will to give. *This human capability of acting like God in being a bestower is the fulcrum upon which the entire universe is balanced.*

The reason this is so important is that if there were a will only to receive, as described above, the universe would be completely predictable. Everything would be predetermined, all receptivity would find shape in its implicit design, and every aspect of the unfolding of creation could be anticipated. The wild card introduced here is the premise that human consciousness is informed by a soul force that gives it the capacity to emulate the infinite Bestower.

Thus human beings have an extraordinary capacity to influence the direction of creation. Each time we make use of our free will by giving, we are in copartnership with the infinite Bestower. When this is accomplished, with clear awareness of what we are doing, we raise the consciousness of creation.

## CONSTANTLY
## PERFECTING CREATION

Kabbalists say that *Ein Sof* is perfect, by definition, and this universe is constantly in the process of perfecting itself. Indeed, Judaism says that the very purpose of existence is the continuous perfecting of the universe.

Imagine an advanced computer program in an "intelligent" computer that is designed to learn as it goes. Each time it does a function, it learns by its mistakes and does the function more efficiently the next time. As long as it is learning, constantly improving, it is fulfilling its purpose.

However, if the computer functions in a way that it ceases to improve itself, it is programed to self-destruct. Why? Because its purpose is to continuously perfect itself. If it achieves perfection, it no longer has anything to do. Thus it enters a stalemate with no place to go.

God represents perfection. This universe represents the potential for perfecting. Can we ever expect to make the universe perfect? The kabbalistic answer is no, because our purpose is to continuously perfect ourselves and the universe. If we achieve perfection, we are finished and the universe would cease to exist.

Perfection is an absurd goal for the Kabbalist because an essential aspect of God's perfection is the creation. You see, perfection cannot be perfect without the potential for perfecting! The Baal Shem Tov has said, "The book of the *Zohar* has, each and every day, a different meaning."[102] This is a crucial understanding.

Some teachings say that everything is perfect, everyone is perfect, everything happens as it is supposed to, and there are no accidents. The only reason that we do not appreciate this perfection is due to our limited perspective. They say that once we become more enlightened, we will see that everything is perfect.

This may be true from a different point of reference, but from where we stand life is the process of being constantly urged this way and that; we are never satisfied with what is. We rarely attain a sense of perfection, and if we ever do it only lasts for a moment. We live in paradox. We rarely want what we can have, and we often desire what is out of our reach. Because the nature of duality is imperfect, we never meet the perfect friend, the perfect spouse, or the perfect teacher. And if we follow the belief that perfection is within our reach, we assuredly will become frustrated, unhappy, and unfulfilled, or even worse, bored, constantly tired, and indifferent.

This view of our continuous perfecting is of great importance. Once we fully appreciate that our purpose is not to achieve some transcendental level but to deal with the imperfect world as a partner in creation, we gain the very thing we turn away from. That is to say, once we surrender to the fact that we will constantly be repairing our own souls and those of others around us, we gain a new sense of the fullness of each moment.

The myth of perfection is one in which we constantly are dissatisfied with what is currently happening. We are never "here" because we are always trying to be "there," wherever that is. But understand this important teaching: *When we accept each moment as a new opportunity for fulfilling our purpose, we are always present, always succeeding, always changing the world for the better. And we are always "here."*

One of my teachers, a woman Sufi, taught me this idea about here and there. She said simply, "Forget about there; it does not exist. We only have here. This is it." Whenever you use the word "there," check yourselves carefully to see if the word "here" could be more correct. Nine out of ten times it will be.

When we fully realize that life is here, right now, we do not fall asleep, and we don't get bored. We don't seek the perfect mate or the perfect teacher. We make the best choices we can and work with what we have. With perfecting as our model, we do not need to look beyond what we have because this idea of continuous perfecting is in itself perfect.

The Jewish sages asked, "Who is rich?"[103] The answer: "One who is happy with his or her lot." And, "This person is praiseworthy in this world, and all will be well in the world to come." May we all be blessed to find comfort in being less than perfect, and to find peace in the eternal chaos of life. Remember, we are always here.

# Part Two

## THE PRESENT

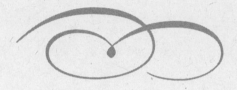

### OLAM HA-ZEH
(This World)

# TEMPLATE OF
# CREATION

*T*he best-known symbol in Kabbalah is the Tree of Life. It is said
to represent the essential foundation of creation.

In all, the Tree of Life has ten primordial elements. These ten are based
on the opening to the Torah, in which there are ten statements that use the
words *va-omer elohim,* "And *Elohim* (God) said . . ."[1] These ten statements are
considered to be divine emanations out of which the world was created. Each
emanation is an archetype, which in combination with other emanations provides the mystical elements necessary to form everything in creation, whether
physical, emotional, intellectual, or spiritual. The emanations are referred to
as *sefirot* (numbers), because every possible number in creation is a combination of the ten basic numbers from zero to nine.

Kabbalists believe that every time the number ten is written in the
Torah, it is related in some way to the Tree of Life. Ten plagues in the story
of Exodus, ten commandments, ten days of judgment from Rosh Hashana
to Yom Kippur. Even the fact that we have ten fingers and ten toes is related
to the Tree of Life.

Virtually everything in creation can be associated with the Tree of Life.
Commentators often do not agree on the definitions or characteristics for

the various *sefirot*. Nonetheless, Kabbalists tend to catalog the biblical patriarchs and matriarchs, archangels, parts of the human body, names of God, directions, planets, vowels, colors, and a wide variety of associated qualities with various *sefirot*.

The Tree of Life is viewed as a graphic representation of the blueprint of creation. Because each emanation is an archetype, each represents a wide spectrum of categories. The system is complex because the archetypes are not easily defined. The *Sefer Yetzirah* uses language like "These are the ten *sefirot* of nothingness: the breath of the living God; breath from breath; water from breath; fire from water; up, down, east, west, north, south."[2]

Read literally, the first *sefirah* is the breath of God; the second is breath caused by this breath; the third is water; and the fourth is fire, followed by six directions—ten *sefirot* in all. The Hebrew names usually given to the ten sefirot are *keter* (crown), *chochma* (wisdom), *binah* (understanding), *chesed* (lovingkindness), *gevorah* (strength), *tiferet* (beauty), *netzach* (triumph/dominance), *hod* (grandeur/empathy), *yesod* (foundation), and *malkhut* (sovereignty).[3] Since *keter* is ineffable and inaccessible, an additional *sefirah* called *daat* (knowledge) is often added to the list so that there are ten working attributes.

The Tree of Life is commonly represented by an illustration of ten (sometimes eleven) drawings of circles. Schematically, the *sefirot* are drawn in three vertical lines. The center is the trunk, representing four (or five) *sefirot*. Two vertical branches, one on either side of the trunk, represent three *sefirot* each. (See illustration page 87).

## DNA AND
### THE TREE OF LIFE

*D*NA researchers have discovered that four amino acids—adenine, thymine, guanine, and cytosine—form themselves in various combinations that are sequenced into patterns upon which all life is built. Each pattern holds within it a genetic code that determines all of our genetic characteristics.

Each amino acid always works in a pair, and each always pairs with the same partner: adenine pairs with thymine (A-T), and guanine pairs with cytosine (G-C). We can imagine these pairs like coins with heads and tails. If we line up coins on a sheet of glass, whatever they read on top would be opposite from the way they would read from under the glass. Similarly, for amino-acid pairs, if we had a sequence such as A, A, A, G, G, G, there would be a parallel track that would read T, T, T, C, C, C.

It is said that the code for a human being contains billions of pairs. Can you imagine how many variations on a theme we could have by stringing out a billion coins and then turning them one at a time to form new combinations? The number is enormous.

The sequence in which pairs of amino acids are combined is the determining factor of heredity. Microbiologists describe these extended strands as parallel tracks that curve into a spiral, called a double helix, in order to fit into a small space.

Today we have DNA testing to determine many things. Microbiologists must find the precise location along this thin thread of a double helix where the encoded combination for a particular gene resides. When they zero in on this location, they can determine whether or not the code matches another sample.

Thus only four amino acids, coupled into two pairs, offer an almost unlimited prospect for variation. This is precisely the same model that Kabbalists have used for a thousand years. Rather than amino acids, the Kabbalists have described four key elements of creation: expansion *(chesed)*, which always pairs with contraction *(gevorah)*; and giving *(netzach)*, which always pairs with receiving *(hod)*.

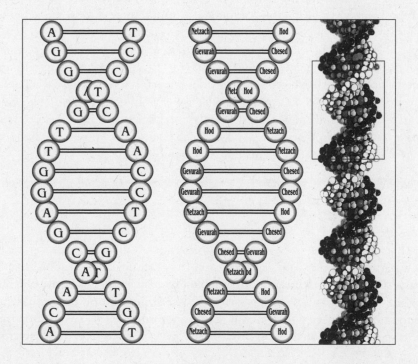

However, these are only four of ten primordial elements that compose the Tree of Life. Whereas the physical universe can be described in terms of four elements gathered together in an infinite number of combinations, the kabbalistic model is far more extensive when we add in all ten dimensions of the Tree of Life.

## THIRTY-TWO PATHS

The ten *sefirot* are connected by a series of twenty-two vertical, horizontal, and diagonal lines. There are twelve diagonal lines, said to represent the twelve tribes, as well as other characteristics such as twelve months, twelve signs of the zodiac, twelve permutations of the tetragrammaton (the four-letter holy name of God), and twelve primary qualities of human expression—speech, thought, action, sight, hearing, motion, coition, smell, sleep, anger, taste, and laughter.[4]

Each of the twenty-two connectors also represents one letter of the Hebrew alphabet. These twenty-two letters plus the ten are referred to as the thirty-two paths of wisdom.[5] Because each of the *sefirot* represents a vowel, and every connecting link is a consonant, we can readily see that every word in the Hebrew language is a combination of different paths in this scheme. This opens up a huge potential for analyzing words.

The Kabbalah is holistic in many dimensions. All thirty-two paths are connected with one another, either directly or indirectly. A change in any one affects them all. Moreover, each individual *sefirah* represents layers upon layers of inner *sefirot*. Thus each *sefirah* alone has an entire Tree of Life with thirty-two paths in it. We must view it as spheres within spheres within spheres. Like a stack of chinese boxes, each time we open one, we discover a new one inside that looks just like the outer box.

## PERSONALITY AND
## THE TREE OF LIFE

Each aspect of creation, and each individual person, is a miniature Tree of Life. Each of us represents a physical, emotional, intellectual, and spiritual shape based upon the way we harmonize our inner tree. Some parts of us pull more strongly than other parts. We have dominant traits, person-

# 32 Mystical Paths
## (According to the Ari)

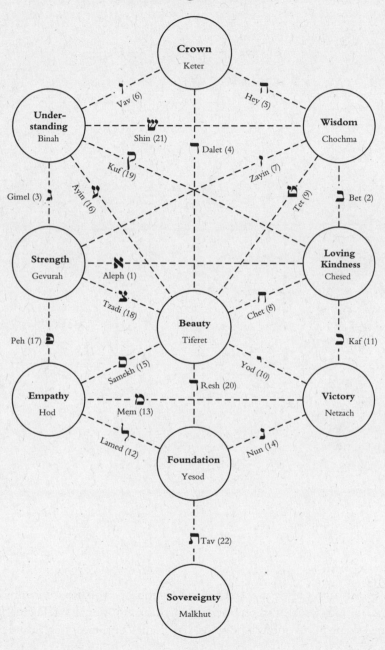

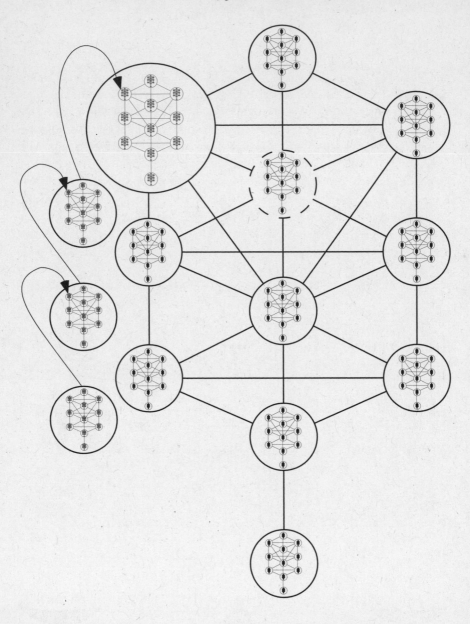

ality quirks, physical strengths and weaknesses, emotional idiosyncrasies, neuroses, patterns of social behavior, and so on.

If we had tools to measure all of the energies represented in the Tree of Life, we could find patterns, just like the microbiologist does with amino acids. However, because the kabbalistic system is extraordinarily diverse, expanding well beyond the field of genetics, our task is far more complicated than that of a scientist measuring the spectrograph of DNA results.

A currently popular system used for personality classification, called the Enneagram, suggests that there are nine personality archetypes. Some commentators have shown the parallels between this system and the Tree of Life. But the kabbalistic approach is somewhat more subtle than the descriptions of personalities in the Enneagram. The Tree of Life is modeled in triads; two aspects work in opposition to each other, with a third on a moving equilibrium point between the two. Here is how it works.

*Chesed* is the quality of expansiveness and generosity, the part of us that yields even though another part says no. It operates best when there is no self-consciousness holding it back. The tendency of *chesed* is to be extremely liberal, willing to try anything. Uncontrolled, however, it has the potential to smother the recipient. It has no self-limitation; it knows only how to be-

*Sefirot* Triplets

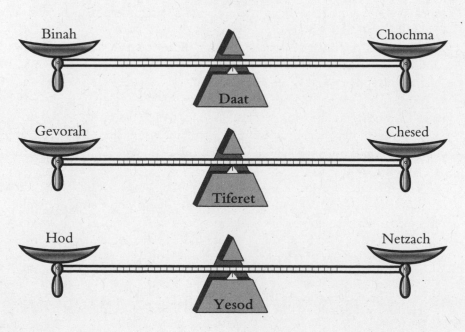

stow things. Pure generosity will keep piling the food high on the plate; it will spin cotton candy until it fills the circus tent; it will give away the family jewels.

*Gevorah* is the quality of contraction and restraint. It stands in opposition to generosity. Restraint is the ability to say no even when social pressure is brought to bear. *Gevorah* represents universal justice as well; it understands that everything impacts and has repercussions. The tendency of *gevorah* is to be excessively conservative, preferring things just as they are. Uncontrolled, *gevorah* is stifling. It does not allow for any movement. It is strictly conformist, unspontaneous, rigid, and hypercritical.

These two poles work and interact with each other. At times we are drawn more by our generous spirit; other times we withdraw. The system is dynamic and continuously fluid. We all have tendencies to lean one way or the other. Yet we are under the influence of many variables. Thus, nobody is ever 100-percent predictable.

Because the poles of generosity and restraint constantly tug or push against each other, a pendulum, or balance point *(tiferet),* is needed to mediate between the two. *Tiferet* represents compassion and beauty. In many ways it is the middle path, neither too self-indulgent nor too self-restrictive. It is important to note that *tiferet* has its own impact on the triad; it is not merely the passive consequence of the two opposing forces. It brings to bear a third component, which is drawn from the trunk of the tree itself: reflection to generosity, and consideration to restraint. Thus one can see that the entire triad is dynamic and mobile.

The next triad includes *netzach,* which represents parent, domination, confidence, and self-centeredness. Its opposite is *hod,* which represents child, yielding, receptivity, and acceptance. We can immediately see positive and negative aspects in this dichotomy. Parenting, which is a force of protection as well as one of domination, versus childing, which has purity and innocence as well as dependency. In simple terms, this is the dance between our inner parent and our inner child, between self-confidence and yielding to that which is outside of the self.

The mediator for this is *yesod,* normally translated as foundation, but often called harmony. Without a balance in the drama between inner child and inner parent, we do not have a solid foundation. Once again, however, this system is dynamic. Sometimes we are more self-confident; other times we are quite insecure. We have various degrees of acceptance, depending upon the strength of our inner voice of doubt. We sometimes push harder to get our way, while at other times we yield to a situation.

Harmony slides along this line and brings to bear an additional force. It pressures the inner child to be more assertive; it pushes against our ego-centeredness to lighten up. It invites a balance between individual confidence and the potential of yielding to reason.

Finally, *malkhut,* at the bottom of the tree, is the result of everything happening in these other six *sefirot.* It is our reality. Things happen to us in life that cause ripples upward. *Malkhut* is the receiver from both ends. We are the accumulation of a set of archetypes that interact with the world drama that enfolds us.

## CHOCHMA AND BINAH CONSCIOUSNESS

The lower seven *sefirot* represent ordinary consciousness. All the things that normally go on in our minds could be defined by combinations of the lower seven *sefirot.* They represent the physical universe. This is the level at which ordinary consciousness operates.

However, we have access to higher realms of consciousness. Various names are attributed to the experience of these higher levels, such as *satori* or cosmic consciousness. In Kabbalah, we call it *chochma* and *binah* consciousness.

Kabbalah says that thought is born out of the realm of Nothingness. This Nothingness is called *chochma,* which translated literally means "wisdom." Obviously, it does not mean wisdom in the ordinary way. Rather, it is an archetype of wisdom out of which the mold of thought can first form.

If somebody offers a mathematical formula, such as $A^2 + B^2 = C^2$, it is meaningless unless we know how to apply it. We must know what A and B represent. Without this understanding, a formula is pure *chochma* consciousness. It is an empty mold. It may have great wisdom, it may represent a universal truth, but without the element of *binah* (understanding), it does not help us in any way.

*Binah* would be the realization that there is a relationship between the two sides and the hypotenuse in every right triangle. This is interesting and good information, but it is not of too much use until we know how the relationship works. Once we put *chochma* together with *binah,* the formula with the understanding, we have knowledge *(daat).* This is the model of consciousness suggested in the Tree of Life. It is the conscious process for almost everything we do in life.

At first, we go through each level, up to *daat,* at lightning speeds. But if we are able to closely investigate our thought processes, we will usually be able to spot most, if not all, of these elements.

The meditative practice of attaining *binah* consciousness and *chochma* consciousness is described in detail later in the Path of Selflessness (page 211).

## FORTY-NINE DAYS
## TO MEND THE SOUL

*T*he holy day of Shavuot comes fifty days after Passover. The number fifty represents the gateway to a new level of awareness. It is sometimes called the "mysterious gate," because we do not know exactly how to access it.[6] The Talmud tells us that "fifty gates of understanding were created in the world and all were given to Moses but one."[7]

The forty-nine days between Passover and Shavuot are called the Counting of the Omer. During this period, Jews count the days and weeks as part of the conventional prayer service, preparing for the time of Shavuot, which was also known as the day of the first fruits, a time when the barley harvest was completed and the wheat would be planted. Each week of the seven weeks represents a different *sefirah* on the Tree of Life, beginning with *chesed* and ending with *malkhut*. Each day of the week also represents its own *sefirah*.

Traditionally, Shavuot is celebrated as the day when the Torah was given to Moses on Mt. Sinai. Because the Torah is viewed as a gift to help us attain higher consciousness, and by kabbalists as the blueprint of creation, the mystics explain the forty-nine-day count of the Omer as a period in which we can prepare ourselves to be ready to receive the light of Torah.

To the extent that we can, during these forty-nine days of counting we try to examine characteristics within ourselves in great detail. The practice of counting the Omer is really a *musar* practice (developing one's ethics and morals) to investigate our inner process.[8] By spending a half hour in contemplation each day for forty-nine days, we can significantly alter our lives. Even busy people can do this.

The first day of the first week of our practice is called *chesed* of *chesed*. If we think of *chesed* as generosity, this day would represent the heart of lovingkindness. We would explore the source of generosity. Which part of me is giving? How does it feel when I give? How does it feel when I do not give? Where is my inner giver connected to my higher self? We spend ten to fifteen minutes contemplating these questions. Throughout the day we allow ourselves a few minutes at various times to reflect on them.

The second day is *gevorah* of *chesed*. It represents our restraint within our generosity. Where is my inner giver cramped? What part says no? What part is really the self-protector as distinct from the selfish part?

The third day is *tiferet* of *chesed*: the compassion within generosity. What part of me is connected to my center when I am giving? Do I have compassion regarding myself when I give and when I do not give? Is my giving balanced; too much, too little? How do I best determine a balanced, generous perspective?

The fourth day is *netzach* of *chesed*: self-confidence when generous. Do I have regrets when I give things away? Do I have strings attached? Do I remember my generosity for long periods? Am I attached to being a generous person? Do I crave to be identified as a great giver?

This process continues for the forty-nine days as we go through the permutations of the characteristics and explore ourselves in exhausting detail. It is a good idea to keep a journal during this practice. Each evening we write down any insights we have learned about ourselves during that day. Even one or two sentences is sufficient. More examples are included in the endnotes.[9]

As might be imagined, we learn a great deal about ourselves by spending considerable time in introspection. We become our own therapists, and we put into action any new self-discovery.

## CYCLES WITHIN CYCLES

Kabbalists believe that every chronological process parallels the Tree of Life. The first seven years of life are viewed as an era of *chesed*. The first year is *chesed* of *chesed* (the essence of expansion), the second *gevorah* of *chesed* (the restraint of expansion), the third *tiferet* of *chesed* (the beauty of expansion), and so on. The second seven years of life, leading up to adolescence, is viewed as an era of *gevorah* (restraint or justice), with each year representing a different *sefirah* within *gevorah*. Ages fourteen to twenty-one are viewed as a time of *tiferet* (balancing lovingkindness and restraint), and so on. At age forty-nine, we complete a cycle.

Jewish mystics say that every seventh year should be a year of reflection. The forty-ninth year should lead into a Jubilee, where we free ourselves from as many old habits as we can and take a deep look at our lives. We can participate in this Jubilee in many ways. We do not have to give up our jobs and wander the world. Rather, we can celebrate our sevens and forty-nines by bringing a wealth of different experiences into our daily lives. We try new things, give ourselves more personal time, eliminate many time-consuming distractions, try to develop new aspects to relationships we already have, reflect on who we are and what we have done with our lives. We can do all this in the course of regular daily activity.

Marriages and relationships also go through cycles. Some say that each of these cycles lasts seven years as well. Whatever the numbers, the cyclic nature of life is crucial for us to understand. Our tendency is to view things as if they will never change. The stock market is going down, so we sell; it goes up, we buy. Things are rough in our relationships, we want to bail out; things are great, we want to make commitments forever.

When we work with the kabbalistic techniques, we learn not only about ourselves, but also about the permutations of life. We gain insight into the ebbs and flows of the universe and of our own rhythms. Just as we have biorhythms throughout various periods in our lives, we have emotional rhythms, mental rhythms, and, on the mystical level, spiritual rhythms.

There are times when things just seem to go better than others in our relationships, our financial situations, our well-being, our moods, our luck, and just about everything else. It is not as important for us to explain the differences in our rhythms as to become aware of them. This awareness helps us understand the cyclic nature of everything in creation. When we fully comprehend these cycles, our choices and decisions are far better informed. We do not get caught in the roller coaster of events or whipsawed by our emotions. Understanding cycles is a key to success in all areas of life.

# FIVE WORLDS, FIVE SOUL DIMENSIONS

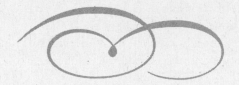

Cccording to Kabbalah, creation is composed of five major categories of consciousness, called worlds or universes.[10] Although
we give different names to the worlds, they are not separate universes, but
are concentric, one within the other. *Assiyah* is the world of physicality; *yetzirah,* the world of emotions; *beriyah,* the world of the intellect; *atzilut,* the
world of the spirit; and *adam kadmon,* the primordial source.

Each of these worlds is a lens through which we gain a unique perspective of reality. Thus, the Kabbalah teaches that the soul has five levels,
five dimensions of awareness. Each soul dimension has a unique relationship
with its world, and each relationship is the vehicle through which we mysteriously connect with that world. Some aspects of soul relate more to our
physicality, while others dwell, so to speak, in different realms of awareness.
One aspect of the soul is always joined with the center of creation, and this
is our eternal link with truth.

Briefly, the soul dimensions are as follows:

---

# NEFESH: THE WORLD
## OF ACTION

*T*he *nefesh* is the level of the soul most connected with physicality. In essence, *nefesh* is the soul of atomic structure. Every particle of matter has a *nefesh,* every rock, every plant, every celestial body.

In human terms, the *nefesh* is associated with body awareness. It is the part of us most linked with the physical world around us. After death, it is the aspect of the soul that lingers around the deceased for the longest period. It is also the part of the soul that is most involved with the process of purification after death.

The *nefesh* is sometimes called the animal soul. The *Zohar* has a beautiful description of it: "*Nefesh* is the lowest stirring to which the body cleaves, like the dark light at the bottom of the candle-flame which clings to the wick (body) and exists only through it. When the candle is fully kindled, this dark light becomes a throne for the white light above it (the next higher soul level: *ruach*). When both are fully kindled, the white light becomes a throne for a light which cannot be fully discerned (still a higher level of the soul: *neshama*). So there is formed a complete light."[11]

Thus, although the *nefesh* is the densest part of the soul, the least connected with its Divine Source, it is the foundation of all the soul levels and the most directly associated with the body. This aspect of the soul is integral to life itself, and virtually any Jewish law can be overridden for the single most important commandment, that of the *mitzvah* of saving life, called *pikuach nefesh*.

Many forms of physical matter, such as elementary atoms, neutrons, protons, and electrons are primarily composed of the *nefesh* soul level. However, just as physical matter can be organized in increasingly complex forms, from single-celled organisms to the human being, so too can the essential soul develop aspects, higher levels of the soul, that are more closely united with the central source of creation. This process distinguishes human life.

# RUACH: THE WORLD
## OF FORMATION

*R*uach means "wind" or "spirit." It is associated with elementary consciousness and information that moves through the senses. In humans, *ruach* is related to speech and emotions, both of which are constantly moving within the body. Whereas *nefesh* is associated with body awareness, *ruach* is more correlated with emotional awareness.

Our "spirituality" is founded upon the *ruach* level of soul. It inexpressibly *moves* us to tears when we are touched by a poem, a glance, a work of art, or a simple moment in nature. Love on this level is more real to us and longer lasting. Our senses of purpose and meaning in life depend a great deal upon the extent to which our *ruach* is nourished.

This nourishment is the result of how we live our lives, where we spend our time, and the raw materials we ingest through our senses. Just as a body is sustained by food, the soul is supported by experiences. In many traditions, foods are classified by qualities, such as agitating, soothing, stimulating, disturbing, calming, strengthening, and so forth. In the same way, experiences affect the spirit.

When the *ruach* is raised to its highest elevation, we attain a state of awareness that is described as *ruach ha-kodesh,* literally translated as holy spirit. It is a state of being that transcends ordinary awareness. With *ruach ha-kodesh,* we dwell in other dimensions of reality and gain a clear sense of the way life will unfold. All of the biblical prophets had *ruach ha-kodesh;* this level of prophesy is one of the aspirations of intense contemplative work in Judaism.

# NESHAMA: THE WORLD
## OF CREATION

*T*he word *"neshama"* has the same root in Hebrew *(nshm)* as the word for breath. This soul level is associated with higher awareness and angelic realms. It is a defining quality of human consciousness.

The *Zohar* describes the *neshama* as follows: "The *nefesh* and the *ruach* intertwine together, while the *neshama* resides in a person's character. This is an abode which cannot be discovered or located. Should a person strive towards purity in life, he or she is aided by a holy *neshama*. But should the person not strive for righteousness and purity of life, this person is animated only by two grades: *nefesh* and *ruach*."[12]

Although we all have the power to develop the *neshama* aspect of our souls, there is no assurance that we will do so. For instance, consider a potter's kiln. Some glazes require baking at a specific temperature for a fixed length of time. If this temperature is not reached, the glaze will not set.

From a spiritual perspective, our lives are fired by conscious action (fuel) and clean living (oxygen). We need a good mix of the two to get the temperature high enough to vitalize our higher soul potential. Once this is accomplished, we have access to expanded realms of awareness.

Even though our power to nurture our highest soul level is not guaranteed, it is assumed that the purpose of human existence is to parent this lofty objective. The *Zohar* says: "At first a person has a *nefesh*. Then she or he is crowned by the grade that rests upon the *nefesh,* which is the *ruach*. After this, a superior grade that dominates the others, the *neshama,* takes up its abode, and the person becomes worthy of the world to come. *Nefesh* cannot exist without the help of *ruach,* and *ruach* in turn is sustained by *neshama*. The three form a unity."[13] Simply said, human life is not complete without the *neshama*.

The *neshama* emanates from an elevated source, while the *ruach* emanates from a somewhat lower origin. When these two sources unite, they shine with a celestial light and are called the "lamp." As stated in Proverbs, "The lamp of God is the *neshama* of humankind."[14] In many ways, the *neshama* is an essential aspect of creation. Because the *neshama* is an aspect of soul that is directly connected with the Divine Source of life, it is via the *neshama* and the higher levels of soul that we copartner with God in the continuous unfolding of creation.

The *neshama* is pure in its essence. It cannot be blemished. When we die, it immediately returns to its Divine Source.

## CHAYAH: THE WORLD OF EMANATION

There are two additional, much more highly refined levels of soul. The *chayah,* or living essence, is so etheric that it has little connection with the body and dwells mostly in other realms. It is too subtle for our consciousness, and we gain awareness of this level only when we enter altered states. In those rare moments when we experience oceanic unity and a bright light of pure oneness, we are tapping into *chayah* consciousness.

Nothing can be said about this soul level except that it represents the highest degree of awareness accessible to human beings. This is the kabbalistic realm of wisdom *(chochma)*, which is the source of all understanding *(binah)*.

The experience of Jewish enlightenment or merging with God, *devekut*, dwells in the soul dimension of *chayah*.[15] It is too subtle to describe, too bright to be contained by concept.

## YEHIDAH:
## THE WORLD OF WILL

The soul level most connected with the source of awareness is called *yehidah*, which means "unity." It is the center point of the soul, and as such it disappears into the infinitude of creation. Some would say that this is the aspect of the soul that is hardwired directly into the essence of the Divine. It is not "with" us, but we are never apart from it.

This is where duality dissolves. It is far too subtle for human consciousness. *Yehidah* is our ultimate link with God-ing, the part of us that can never be separated from the Divine. When all else fails, the awareness of our *yehidah* endowment may be sufficient to carry us through our more difficult times, for it is the aspect of each person eternally connected with perfection.

## PURITY OF SOUL

The kabbalistic perspective of the soul is that upper levels— *neshama, chayah,* and *yehidah*—always remain pure. This is a difficult teaching for people who equate the soul with the actions of a person. How could someone who murders, rapes, or commits other heinous crimes have a pure soul? On the other hand, we might ask how the level of soul in union with the Divine could possibly be impure.

One of the better-known stories about the Baal Shem Tov is based on the theme of the purity of the soul. It is a wonderful tale about a storyteller who forgot his stories. It begins the day of the Baal Shem Tov's death, when he called his students to his bedside and gave each an assignment. Some were sent to other masters, some were given leadership roles, and some were sent home. But one of his more cherished students was given a strange commission. Reb Yakov Yosef was told by the master to live as a wanderer and to make his living as a storyteller.

Although Reb Yakov was a devoted student of the Baal Shem Tov, he was extremely disturbed when he was told about a future that seemed bleak to him. He inquired of his dying master, "Rebbe, I have done all in my power to achieve humility and acceptance, but I must say that I am terrified of living my life as a wanderer, never having a home."

The rebbe carefully scrutinized his student and finally said, "Yakov, my beloved, this you must do to heal yourself and to bring about a great healing in the world. But it will not be for the rest of your life, and I am confident that you will have a home and family, for that is your destiny."

Yakov was relieved, but still he was uncertain. "Rebbe, I will do as you ask. Yet, as I have so much resistance, I fear that perhaps I will not perform my task to its fullest. How will I know when I am finished?"

The Baal Shem Tov smiled and said gently, "You will receive a clear sign and you will have absolutely no doubt that your wandering days are over."

After the death of his master, Reb Yakov began his life as a wanderer and storyteller. He seemed to have an almost infinite reservoir of stories: stories that the Baal Shem had told, stories about the life of the Baal Shem, and other stories that he had learned in his studies of Talmud and Midrash.

In a short time, he became famous. He was known in every synagogue and every tavern, where storytelling was an important pastime. He was given plenty of food and lodging wherever he went. Indeed, in many ways he reached more people with these stories and was better known to the general community than teachers who had their own congregations. As a result of Reb Yakov's traveling, constantly meeting new people, and seeing the conditions of life in many different situations, his heart began to soften. His master clearly had known the importance of this assignment.

Reb Yakov's work went on for a few years, and he was transformed. It no longer mattered to him where he was and with whom he dined. He realized that every person he met offered him another opportunity to help a soul or fix the world. He stopped wondering how long he would be on the road and learned to take life one day at a time, moment to moment.

One day Reb Yakov was told about a nobleman, a baron in Rome, who paid gold pieces for every new story he heard about the Baal Shem Tov. Reb Yakov knew that his own huge repertoire of such stories was probably the most extensive in the world, so he decided to take a trip to Rome. He would have to deplete his meager resources to get there, but he was certain to earn enough to make his life more comfortable in the years ahead.

He arrived the day before Shabbat. He was invited to stay at the baron's mansion and to join the table for Friday-night dinner. Indeed, Reb Yakov's reputation was well known to the baron, and his arrival was received with great enthusiasm.

It was the baron's custom after the meal to have his guests tell stories. Sometimes these storytelling sessions would last most of the night. When the meal ended this Shabbat evening, the guests began to relate story after story. But each time it was Reb Yakov's turn, his mind went completely blank. No matter how much he tried, he could not remember a single story. This was most peculiar. He knew every story that was told that night but could not come up with any of his own. The baron seemed disappointed, the guests were astonished, but Reb Yakov had nothing to say.

He went to bed quite confused. In all the time he had been storytelling, he had never experienced a void like this. While in bed, he could not sleep. One story after another arose in his mind! Dozens upon dozens of stories. Wonderful stories, powerful stories, transformative stories. He prepared himself to tell some of them the next day, when there would be another festive meal in celebration of Shabbat.

In the late morning, seated at the table with the same group as had been there the previous night, he had the weirdest experience. Once again he could not recall a single story, or a line from a story, or even a word for that matter.

When the third festive Shabbat meal arrived, he joined the others at the table. Alas, even if his life had depended upon just one story, he would have failed. This was the most miserable experience since the death of his master. Now what would he do? The stories were gone, seemingly forever.

Meanwhile, throughout all this time, the baron seemed to have infinite patience. He listened to all of the other stories and never pushed or cajoled Reb Yakov. In fact, when the third meal ended, he asked Yakov Yosef to stay on as his guest for a while. Reb Yakov was able to persist a few days longer, but still nothing could be remembered. Saddened and somewhat ashamed, feeling that he had failed his master after all these years, he told the baron that he would have to leave.

He was completely broke, having spent everything he had to travel to Italy. Where would he would go? What would he do, now that he could no longer tell stories?

When the time came for Reb Yakov's departure, the kindly baron gave him a small purse with money, enough to get him home, and told Yakov Yosef that if he ever remembered a good story, he should return.

When the carriage pulled out, an odd story arose in Reb Yakov's mind. Almost out of sight of the mansion, he suddenly called out, "Wait! I thought of a story!" The team was stopped and the carriage returned to the gate, where the baron was still standing.

Reb Yakov stepped down and said, "For some reason I just remembered an event that happened when I was with the rebbe. It was so long ago, it seems like a dream to me. But I was there, it happened, and I am confident that you have never heard this story before." The baron clearly was delighted, and he invited Reb Yakov to sit in the shade.

Reb Yakov now began his story: "Once, when I was quite young and had first joined the rebbe, I remember that just after midnight during the week of Passover he called to me and a few others and said that we should join him on a journey. We hitched up the horses, climbed in the wagon, and, with the Baal Shem Tov at the reins, we took off.

"That was one of my first experiences with *kefitzat ha-derekh,* the shortening of the way. Somehow the rebbe was able to travel great distances in impossibly short periods of time. I do not know how he did it. Dozens of times we traveled hundreds of miles in only a few hours. Since the horses could normally cover only five to ten miles in an hour, we never understood how the master was able to accomplish such a feat. But he did it so many times, we stopped questioning.[16]

"That night we entered a particular town that was more than three hundred miles from where we lived. I do not think any of us had ever visited that town because the people there were notoriously anti-Semitic.

"It was early in the morning when we arrived, and the city was decorated for Easter. As we entered the Jewish section, everywhere we looked the windows were boarded and the doors were locked. The rebbe walked up to one of these houses and, even though it seemed to be abandoned, he persistently knocked on the door. After a few minutes, the door opened a crack and a frightened person said that nobody was home. The rebbe, however, insisted that they let him in, saying that he was Israel the son of Eliezer. That seemed to do the trick; the Baal Shem was a legendary figure even while he was alive.

"When the door was opened, we saw more than a dozen people huddled in the dim, heavily curtained room. Once inside, we spoke with the terrified group. We learned that the non-Jewish residents of this town believed a blood libel about the Jews."

I must pause for a moment in this story to let the reader know that only a couple hundred years ago, it was sometimes rumored that Jews would steal babies and use their blood for secret rituals. Jews were one of many minorities that suffered the kind of atrocities that come out of bigotry and hatred. Sadly, even today in some parts of the world, this kind of ignorance continues. May it be God's will that this should come to an end in our day.

This story has a fascinating twist, however. . . .

Reb Yakov continued: "In that town, around the time of Passover and Easter, the townspeople would catch a hapless Jew and string him up in the town center as a punishment for drinking human blood. Of course, in their recklessness, they had no idea that Jewish law forbids tasting blood of any sort. Even an animal or bird must be salted to draw out all remnants of blood before cooking the meat. But they would not have believed this.

"Most of the time the unfortunate Jew was mocked in the town center, but he would survive. Sometimes, however, especially if there had been a recent accidental death in the community, the Jew would be put to death, as if he and all Jews were at fault for any and every misfortune. Naturally, all of the people in the room were petrified that they would be found and that one of them would be dragged off to the town square.

"My master, the Baal Shem Tov, listened carefully to the fears expressed by these anxious Jews. In fact, at that very moment we could see from the front window that a half block away, the townspeople were gathered in the square to hear their mayor speak. It was the mayor's job to incite the mob into a frenzy. Suddenly the rebbe looked at me and in a booming voice said, 'Reb Yakov, I want you to go into the town square and tell the mayor that I want to see him!'

"I was shocked. I was dressed as a Jew. I had a long black coat and our traditionally shaped hat. I had a beard and side curls. They would spot me immediately. I would be the one to be strung up. But my master just looked at me, and I knew that I had no choice.

"My legs were shaking so much when I walked into that crowded square that I could hardly stand up. The people could not believe their eyes. A Jew walking up to the mayor! I ascended the stairs to the platform; the mayor himself was horrified to have me confront him. I said to him, 'The Baal Shem Tov, Israel the son of Eliezer, has asked that you come to see him.'

"The mayor's face turned white, then purple, then gray. I thought I was a dead man. Then he looked me in the eye and said, 'Tell him that I will come when I am finished here.'

"Somehow, the crowd let me out. I returned to the apartment and told the rebbe what had happened. He became so stern, I hardly recognized him.

He said to me, 'Reb Yakov, return at once and tell the mayor that I demand to see him immediately!'

"I had no choice but to return. Once again the crowd was astounded that a crazy Jew would walk into their midst. I climbed the stairs and noticed that the mayor was trying to hide behind someone. I walked up to him and said, 'The Baal Shem Tov, Israel the son of Eliezer, demands that you come before him immediately.'

"I thought that he would slit my throat. But just the opposite happened. He took my arm, descended the stairs, and followed me to the apartment. Once inside, the Baal Shem Tov guided him into a back room, and the two of them were there alone for more than an hour. When the two returned, the mayor's face had changed completely. He went back to the square, told the people to go home, and put out a proclamation to end the blood libel punishments forever. I heard that a few months later he left the city and did not return. The Baal Shem Tov never told us what had occurred when he was alone with the mayor in that room."

## The Story Within the Story

When Reb Yakov completed his story, the baron was deeply thoughtful for a few moments, and then he grabbed the storyteller and hugged him and kissed him on the cheek. He said with a bright smile, "I know what the Baal Shem Tov said to the mayor! You see," he said, "I was that mayor!"

Reb Yakov looked more closely at the baron. It had been many years. But, yes, something did look familiar about this man.

The baron said, "I recognized you the minute you entered my house. I have been waiting for you many years. I knew you would come. When you could not tell any stories during Shabbat, I was worried. Nevertheless, I never gave up hope. I must say, however, when you pulled away in that carriage, I felt lost. At that moment I called out to your master, the Baal Shem Tov, and I am certain he came back to inspire you. Listen to my story.

"I was born a Jew. My father was a rabbi, his father was a rabbi, and a long ancestry of holy rabbis in our family extended as far back as our records went. When I was young and in university, I turned away from the family tradition. I felt that the ancient laws were ridiculous, the old ways were simplistic. There was a better way, I believed, and so I became a free spirit.

"It did not bother me to be chosen as the mayor of an anti-Semitic town. I felt that the sooner we could be finished with the old ways, the better for everyone. But one night, about a month before you and the Baal Shem Tov arrived in the town, I had an eerie dream. I saw a group of ancient sages sitting around a table that had on it a shriveled, starving soul awaiting judgment. A great *tzaddik* sat at the head of the table.

"The sages seemed to agree that this soul was entirely worthless, nothing good was left of it, and that it should be eternally dammed. But the *tzaddik* said that every soul is pure, every soul has merit, and if this soul could see the truth, the gates of heaven would open to it. This *tzaddik* extended his finger and touched the withered soul. An iridescent, glowing spot appeared where he touched it. Then the dream ended with a voice repeating over and over again: 'This *tzaddik* is the Baal Shem Tov, Israel the son of Eliezer, the Baal Shem Tov.'

"After this dream I did not have the heart to continue with the blood libel, but I was the mayor. What was I to do? And then you showed up and said that the Baal Shem Tov wanted to see me! At first I was stunned, so I sent you away. But the second time I knew that this rebbe would save my life.

"In that room he told me many things. We talked of souls, heaven, hell, and the destiny of humankind. We talked of a new awareness, a change in the way people will look at things—he called it the messiah—and we talked of truth and peace. Then, knowing I was quite wealthy, he told me to sell everything I owned and divide it into thirds. One third I was to give to the poor; one third I was to use to buy my freedom; and the last third I was to use to retire in a faraway land. For the rest of my life I was to do good deeds and make my peace with God. Finally, he said that when someone came and told me my own story, I would know that I had been absolved. Thank you for coming, my friend."

In the end, both Reb Yakov and the baron were liberated in this moment. It is said that the baron gave Reb Yakov one half of his fortune. They both became widely known for their wonderful stories, their warm hearts, and their good deeds. Thus the Baal Shem Tov continued in his work even after he had passed into another reality.

Many hasidic tales suggest that a rebbe can know exactly what is needed to fix one's soul. In this story it was much more complex. As in an epic Russian novel, the rebbe had weaved lives together in a way that was not discovered until many years had passed. The Baal Shem Tov's invitation to Reb Yakov to meet the mayor, and the rebbe's insistence on sending the student into a crowd of angry people were simply scenes in a much bigger play. This hasidic story brings home the message that each event is a nexus point for a multitude of time lines that converge in that moment.

One of the most important teachings of this story is the idea that every human being has a pure soul. No matter how far we have fallen into the depths, we can be redeemed. From a Jewish point of view, the mayor could hardly have been more degenerate, for he condoned the torture and death of Jews in the era of blood libels. Yet the story teaches that the Baal Shem Tov went out of his way to redeem the mayor's holy soul.

## SOUL LEVELS
### AND AWARENESS

*a*s we have seen, the various levels of soul are associated with levels of awareness. Awareness is viewed as if on a continuum; so too the soul. The higher levels of soul are figuratively closer to their source, while the denser levels of soul—*ruach* and *nefesh*—are much closer to the range of human consciousness and can be affected by the way we live our lives. If our actions or words result in harming others, if our minds become contracted, narrow, or rigid, the *ruach* and *nefesh* are affected by the density of human consciousness. It is as if they swim in water that becomes mud. This is how they are "defiled." As such, after death, the *nefesh* and *ruach* must go through a process of purification to regain their fluidity of awareness.

The imagery of the *Zohar* suggests that each level of soul is dependent upon the others, yet all are attuned to the same frequency. We can imagine this like a violin string. If anything interferes with the freedom of movement, the string cannot vibrate properly and thus cannot make its proper sound. At certain levels along the string, we can press down on it, allowing one end of the string to be played. But as long as something encumbers the string, it is never fully operative.

The process of redeeming the *nefesh* and *ruach* is virtually assured after death. This will be discussed in considerable detail later in this book. The point here, however, is that the dimensions of soul that include the *neshama, chayah,* and *yehidah* are always pure. They cannot be blemished, stained, or spoiled in any way. Some traditions suggest that souls can be corrupted. Such teachings completely distort the concept of soul as described in Jewish mysticism and can be harmful.

The Jewish morning prayers include a sentence that says, "My God, the soul *(neshama)* you placed within me, she is pure."[17] One can meditate upon this idea to develop self-esteem and to deepen one's sense of interconnectedness with all beings. It is a simple exercise.

Imagine you have a pure light shining within. If you close your eyes, you can get a hint of this light glowing deep inside your being. Then say to yourself, *No matter what I may feel about myself, I know that I have a pure soul.* When we contemplate this affirmation for a while, we begin to feel a spark of inner peace.

The next step in this practice is to gently acknowledge that every person we encounter has a pure soul. Every time we see someone, we say quietly to ourselves, *There is a pure soul; there is another pure soul.* Notice that the person could be sweet and amenable, or could have an abrasive personality. It does not matter. The soul of every being is pure.[18] If we continue this practice for everyone we meet, including those in whose presence we have negative feelings, the ways we relate to ourselves and to others will be dramatically affected. As simple as it may seem, this exercise opens our hearts.

## SOUL MATES

The *Zohar* teaches that before God sends souls into the world, they are formed into male and female pairs. Then they are placed in the hands of an emissary named Night, who has charge of conception. The pair is separated, and each person is born in his or her time. The *Zohar* goes on to say that these souls are rejoined by God at the right time into one body and one soul.[19]

This teaching raises many questions. For example, is it really suggesting that there is only one person in the world destined to be the soul mate of another? If this were the case, what happens if one does something to cause his or her own early demise? What happens if one makes the free-will choice to be with a person who is not her or his soul mate?

Moreover, does it mean that brothers and sisters cannot be soul mates? Who said that soul mates have to be of opposite genders? How does reincarnation fit into the picture?

In Lurianic Kabbalah, there is only one primordial soul in the world. This is the soul of *adam kadmon.* From this one soul, sparks were disseminated throughout the universe. Everyone carries fallen sparks from the original Adam and Eve, and in this way we all are related, soul to soul.

The goal of Adam and Eve in the garden was to make a rectification that would bring the universe to a new level of consciousness. The so-called failure to do this caused the fall of the great, universal soul.

The original soul is described as having contained 613 "limbs," representing 613 specific missions that Adam and Eve had to accomplish to bring about the rectification of the creation.[20] Each limb was itself a root which contained 600,000 smaller roots.[21] So, when we multiply the 613 limbs, with each having 600,000 smaller roots, we derive that there are more than 3.5 billion soul roots in total.

Each of these billions of smaller roots is called a "great soul." All these great souls themselves are composed of 600,000 individual souls, each represented by a spark. When we calculate this, the number of sparks adds up to more than 2,000 trillion. Despite the enormous number of soul sparks in this accounting, all souls are still of the one family of Adam and Eve, composed of 613 primary limbs.

According to Isaac Luria, there are fundamental divisions of soul types, such as between Cain and Abel. Whereas the simple reading of the story in Genesis is that Cain murders Abel, the esoteric reading is that each represents a primordial force. Abel represents *chesed,* the force of expansion; Cain represents *gevorah,* the force of contraction.

The unfolding of creation is the process of a continuous struggle between opposite poles: light and dark, give and take, up and down, right and left, life and death. The contention between Cain and Abel is the first of many descriptions in the Bible of the ongoing strain between opposing forces. In the same respect, each soul is connected to a root that is associated with forces that may be in harmony with or opposed to the root source of other souls.

The Kabbalah of Luria says clearly that the goal for all of creation continues to be the fulfillment of Adam and Eve's original task. First we must reinstate the awareness of the Garden of Eden, and then our charge is to redeem fallen sparks so that the universe rises to the next level: messianic consciousness.

This idea changes our relationship to the soul. Each soul is composed of many sparks, not just one. The sparks are connected with various roots of the original 613.[22] We can see from this arrangement that the soul has broad diversity and can readily connect with a multitude of other souls. In fact, the number of other souls we can encounter as potential mates is enormous.

Imagine a giant jigsaw puzzle with billions of pieces, but only 613 variations in the way things fit together. This means that each piece will match many others. If this puzzle had only one solution, we might never be able to solve it. However, this puzzle is dynamic and can be solved in almost an infinite number of ways. This is the process of God-ing and creation-ing.

We may not recognize a particular soul-connection we have with another person, because it may not be romantic. Moreover, if it is romantic, it may not look like our dreams. "God constantly mates couples of opposing natures—hard with gentle, talkative with quiet, outgoing with ingoing—so that the world can preserve its balance."[23] The very complaint you have about your mate could well be the essential quality that has drawn you together.

Therefore, the *Zohar*'s primary advice is that every time you are looking for a soul mate, you must bless the Almighty and pray with all your heart,[24] because the entire purpose of connecting with a soul mate, and the purpose for existence, is to elevate the consciousness of the world. Obviously, there are many potential soul mates for all of us.

Indeed, from the Lurianic perspective, we could say that virtually any long-term relationship we have is, by definition, a connection of soul mates. Some last until the death of one of the partners; some do not. Either way, even after the most romantic beginning, almost all committed couples agree that relationship is a challenge, a continuous process of give and take. This is an important aspect of the mystical side of soul mates, which is to raise awareness, and is somewhat different from the idealistic approach, which suggests a perfect blending and harmony between two beings.

The way we work with any of our potential soul mates to help elevate the consciousness of the world is one of the great mysteries of creation. So we pray not only to find a soul mate, but to gain enough understanding to appreciate the nuances of our relationship so that we can distinguish the parts that are unnecessary baggage from those that truly lift us and the world to a new state of awareness.

May we all be blessed to gain such insight.

# SOULS

*A* number of years ago at our Shabbat dinner table in Jerusalem, a Catholic woman named Mary sat quietly, listening to the stories and teachings that were going around. On a couple of occasions, I noticed that she was gently weeping. We were not discussing sad events, but her soul was being touched in a mysterious way. Many tears spill in Jerusalem.

During a lull in the conversation, Mary got the courage to speak. She said, "I know this sounds strange, but when I was eleven years old I was fascinated with *The Diary of Anne Frank.* I must have read it fifty times. I dreamed about it.

"Later, when I was seventeen, something happened that I will never forget. I was taking a trip and had decided to go by train. I had always flown with my parents, and this was the first experience I ever had overnight on a train. After the sun went down, I stared out at the darkness. I don't know what happened, but suddenly I was in a crowded space, packed with people. Someone was crying. It was stiflingly hot. The smell of body odor, excrement, and vomit was awful. I noticed that we were swaying, and I heard the clacking of wheels moving on a track.

"It was like a dream, but I was wide awake. I was frightened. I had relatives close by me. They were not relatives I have now, but from another time. My grandmother was there, my mother and father as well. My sister sat next to me, and I knew that my two brothers were somewhere else. I heard a woman moan and cry out on the other side of the boxcar; I knew that someone had just died. I knew as well that we were heading toward our own death, and I was strangely calm about it."

The guests at our Shabbat table were spellbound by Mary's story. Shoshana and I have heard similar stories, but this was one of the more vivid accounts I can recall.

Mary took a sip of water. I could see that her hand was trembling as she relived this haunting story perhaps for the thousandth time.

"Eventually the train came to its destination. When it stopped, after three days and nights, screaming guards with heavy sticks herded us through fences of barbed wire. Then we stood in a long line, waiting. Slowly we moved toward a room where people were separated to the right and to the left.

"My grandmother, father, and mother stood just in front of my sister and me. I could see ahead that most of the people were sent to the left side. My grandmother was guided to the left, as were my father and mother. I remember exactly how they looked when the guard pulled me to the right. I was seventeen years old. My sister, only eight, was sent to the left. My mother was wailing, and I was punching at the guard, but I had no strength and they dragged me away. I never saw my family again."

Mary began to sob. The rest of us were silent and teary. We sat for many minutes. Then Mary said, "I cannot even begin to tell you of the unspeakable horrors. I lasted only six months, but it was an eternity. I know the faces of my murderers.

"And I want you to know that I am certain this really happened. I just know it. I am not sure what I am supposed to do about it, but the memories are so clear. This is as real for me as anything I have experienced in this lifetime."

MARY'S STORY IS not at all unusual. We have encountered dozens of people, Jews and non-Jews, who have amazing memories of Holocaust experiences yet were too young to have been there. Some do not remember specific events but have a deep sense of having been victims. A few have expressed the belief that they were Nazis who have returned to work on an emptiness in the core of their being.

Stories of the Holocaust wrench the heart. They lead to many questions without answers. All those who died, what happened to their souls?

Yet people like Mary add a new dimension. Something continues to overflow from the Holocaust that fills the memories of a remarkable number of people. Many are embarrassed even to speak about it. This is not simply a phenomenon of fantasy or collective guilt. Something much deeper is happening. The memories are too powerful and in some instances actually have been verified.

This is real. Souls of victims and guards are quite present, here and now. It is a difficult issue, but it gives us hope. It has to do with the mysteries of creation, souls, life, purpose, and death.

What is the soul? This question has plagued theologians for thousands of years. It is not an easy subject to discuss. Where does the soul come from? Where does it go? What is its purpose?

## SOUL GRAVITY

According to Western science, the physical universe is held together by electromagnetic forces. It is hypothesized that the same gravity that keeps the solar system operating also binds the protons, neutrons, and electrons of atoms. Various forces may have different strengths and peculiar nuances, but the general principle remains the same. Physicists continue to search for a universal formula by which to describe this process.

Electromagnetic force is clearly the most dominant feature of the human body, even though we cannot see it. If we could somehow eliminate the space between the nucleus of the atoms that compose our body, all of the physical matter of the body would compact into something smaller than a grain of sand.[25] That is to say, we are a grain of matter scattered through five or six feet of space, held together by electromagnetic forces that nobody has been able to measure.

As has been pointed out in recent years, theoretical physics and esoteric metaphysics frequently share common touch points. The mysteries of electromagnetic forces are to science as the soul is to Western theology. It does not exist as an entity, but the universe is dependent upon it. We cannot taste, smell, see, hear, or touch it, but everything we sense, and our senses themselves, are functional only because of the soul.

The soul in Jewish mysticism is one of the more essential aspects of creation itself. Just as the physical universe could not exist without energy, the spiritual dimension is based upon "soul-matter." The kabbalistic viewpoint, of course, is that we could not have a universe without the spiritual realm, and thus we could say that one of the key pillars upon which creation rests is the soul.

Kabbalah describes the soul as a kind of spiritual magnetic field. This field is not spacial and does not have boundaries, but it is associated with matter. In describing this association, the *Zohar* suggests that souls are "patterned" like bodies. It says: "As the body is formed in this world from the combination of four elements, the spirit is formed in the Garden [of Eden] from the combination of the four winds. The spirit is enveloped there in the impress of the body's shape. If it were not for the four winds, which are the airs of the Garden, the spirit would not have been clothed (given shape) at all."[26]

The "impress of the body's shape" is a primordial pattern that could be described as a mirror image of us in another dimension. The mirror is not like one that reflects our physical shape. Rather, it is like an unusual X-ray mirror that shows our spiritual substance. The pattern of this substance is not only with us, it is simultaneously in other dimensions of reality.

When we think about the soul, we have a tendency to embody it in some way. We give it an identity: my soul, your soul. We view it as an entity that is somehow connected to the body. Some say that it arrives at birth; others say it arrives during gestation or at the moment of conception. Everyone agrees that the soul departs at death. During life it is with us; but perhaps sometimes it is other places as well. We are not sure where it goes after we die, but some say that they know.

Linking the soul to an identity is a mistake because it requires a sense of separation. This is like saying that the electricity needed to power a home is distinct from its source at the generator plant. When we see an electrical appliance working, should we assume that the electricity belongs to it? Is the electricity in one toaster distinct from the electricity in the toaster in the adjacent home? Obviously, the electricity does not belong to any of the homes in question, for when the power at the main plant shuts down, every home in the neighborhood turns off.

However, if I live next to a neighbor whose house is off the grid and who has a different source of electricity, we have a new situation. The electricity in one house is not from the same immediate source as another. Yet it is electricity nonetheless, and it operates on exactly the same principles in both houses regardless of the source.

So too with souls. There is a soul principle, a "great soul," that embodies all souls. Then there are lineages that connect souls with different archetypes.

A survey of religious and philosophical literature in Judaism shows that there are widely divergent points of view concerning the soul. The soul cannot be explored without delving into the mysteries of the purpose of life, reward, punishment, death, heaven, and hell. This may be why the soul is a subject that seems to cause an intellectual rash. One has the sense that a great deal of itching is going on when a philosopher or theologian discusses the soul.

Mystics, however, discuss the soul with disregard for logic, consistency, or concern about agreement with any accepted system. This is because a mystic "experiences" other realities and therefore has no doubt regarding their existence. Moreover, because these realities are not completely disconnected from the material reality we see in front of our eyes, the conclusion is clear: some aspect of our material world mediates between realities. Thus, we could say that the soul is a medium that dissolves boundaries of consciousness.

## LOVE IS THE
## SOUL'S SISTER

We can appreciate the soul better when we get to know her sister. Just as the soul transcends the limits of time and space, so does her sister: love. Does love have time boundaries? Can we give love shape? Sometimes it may seem to have qualities when we put limits on it. In fact, in some situations, we are able to feel the symptoms of love. But this is transient, and love remains indeterminate, unbounded, timeless, and completely beyond our comprehension.

Love can be viewed as a unity, a ubiquitous oneness. Yet we experience love in its multiplicity: paternal love, maternal love, romantic love, passionate love, divine love, familial love, brotherly love, and so forth. Each of these expressions of love has a different quality. Each is its own reality.

Would you like to explain love to someone? How does it work? Why doesn't it always work that way? How do we measure it? You mean we can never determine what pulls people together or what drives them apart? Of course, love is a mystical experience. That is why it is called the soul's sister.

Does the fact that we cannot explain love mean that it does not exist? Of course not. We all experience love. Soul is exactly like this. It transcends all limits of consciousness.

At first, soul may seem more difficult to experience than love, but it really is not. We are experiencing soul all the time; we just do not name it. The sound of the sea, the flick of the fire, the wind at night, and the awesome spread of a starry sky all speak the language of the soul. The flight of a bird, shadow of a rock, purr of a kitten, and smile of a stranger pluck a mysterious inner chord.

Call it what you will. The mystic says this is the soul—enigmatic and paradoxical. When we say, "I love this person, I don't know why," we are dealing with enigma. When we say, "I love this person and I hate this person at the same time," we have a paradox. Many of us know both of these feelings. Enigma seems to be like a pixie; it plays with us. Paradox, on the other hand, is more tedious; it pulls and tugs at us, and can be quite tiresome.

In the same way, we can approach soul from a right-brained, intuitive perspective and enjoy an enigmatic dance, as if in a dream, never particularly wanting to awaken. Or we can dive into the paradox of the existence of a soul and wrestle with difficult questions, probing for a handhold, a way to grip the idea. Some say that the nature of paradox is so elusive that we will never succeed; others say that they have a way to turn paradox upon itself so that we can work with it.

## The Language of the Soul

Here are a few exercises that help us uncover the way the soul can be experienced. Each exercise can be done in less than five minutes. Pick any one of them.

1. Imagine yourself holding a newborn infant in your arms. Its eyes are open. You know that these eyes cannot focus, but they are looking straight into your own. Close your eyes and take two or three minutes to imagine this look and discover what it feels like.

2. Imagine you are holding an egg that has a live chick in it. Your hands are under a heat lamp, and you can feel the tap-tap of the chick trying to get out. Allow yourself to cradle this egg, feel the movement within, and imagine that as you hold the egg, the chick slowly breaks through the shell to freedom. Close your eyes and feel what this is like.

3. Try to remember the first time you felt that you were falling in love. Do you remember the physical experience? Did it affect your senses, the way you saw things, the way things tasted? What about falling in love was different from your normal, daily life? Let yourself dwell in this memory for a few minutes.

4. Imagine that you have finally met the wisest being that ever lived, whoever that may be. It may have been someone known, or someone completely hidden. In your imagination, notice what it would feel like to be with this person. What question would you like to ask this person? Imagine what answer the person might give to your question.

If you were able to take time to do any of these exercises, you discovered that the language of the soul is not cerebral, it does not speak in words. But it is quite clear nonetheless. The gaze of an infant's eyes touches a gentle tenderness within us. Unspeakable, it "hums," and our hearts are softened. The tap-tap of new life within an eggshell, about to be born, sends vibrations to the depths of our being. Life, quickening, bursts through to freedom.

Who can grasp falling in love? What is its language? Palpitation, heat, confusion, clarity, nausea, ecstasy, doubt, fear, an ocean storm, or a peaceful calm. Pick any or all of them, but none dwells in the realm of rationality.

The wise being within each of us may be silent, or it may speak recognizable words. If it speaks, often the message is so simple it is baffling: "Be yourself"; "You are doing just fine"; "I love you"; "Let go." And if she, he, or it does not speak, notice the experience of being in its presence. It may be calm, peaceful, comfortable, a feeling of coming home at last. Or, in fact, it may be questioning, curious, doubtful, wondering, or skeptical. This too is the language of the soul.

To attune ourselves, we need to broaden our range and let go of preconceived notions. We must learn to hear, see, feel every nuance of our moment-to-moment experience. The language of the soul lives at the edges of thought, or behind it. It is symbolic, metaphoric, poetic. There is always hidden meaning just a little out of reach. It does not matter that we are unable to grasp it with our minds because another part of us is touched, and this is sufficient.

Despite the limitations of our subjective truth, Kabbalists believe that via the soul, we get information from other realities. The way we attune to other realities is by using contemplative methods to pierce the veils that obscure our degree of awareness.

Commenting on Psalms 24:7, "Lift up your head, O you gates," the *Zohar* says: "The gates refer to supernal grades (higher levels of consciousness) through which alone it is possible for human beings to have a knowledge of the Almighty. Without this [awareness], human beings could not commune with God. . . . Some aspects of the soul can be known, some remain unknown. So it is with the Holy One. It is the Soul of souls, the Spirit of spirits, covered and veiled; yet through those gates [of awareness], which are the doors for the soul, the Holy One makes Itself known."[27]

## BRINGING A SOUL
## INTO THE WORLD

*C*ommonly held belief these days is that a soul chooses its parents. Often this idea is expressed in an ironic observation: "Well, you must have chosen a difficult father for a reason!" or, "I guess the fact that you don't get along with your mother was to teach you something about a past life."

An opposite notion is that randomness is the operative factor. Out of millions of spermatozoa, only one penetrates the wall of the ovum. It is happenstance which is closest, fastest, strongest, and this will determine the DNA of the fetus.

Jewish mysticism rests between these viewpoints. On the one hand, the existence of free will in the universe guarantees that a certain degree of randomness will always be present. On the other hand, because everything occurring in the lower worlds has its reflection in the upper worlds, there will be a relationship and mystical attraction between souls.

"When desire brings man and woman together, the child that issues from their union will be a combination of both of their forms because God produces the child in a mold that draws from both. Therefore the man and woman should sanctify themselves at such a time in order that the form be as perfect as possible."[28] This zoharic statement suggests that the outcome of conception is based not only on what is, but also on what could be.

On an individual basis, our "what is" part is related to our genetic makeup, the raw materials that we have to work with. Our "what could be" part is the result of choices we make in life, the way we condition ourselves. The interplay of these two factors determines who we are at any point in time.

The mystical level adds another dimension. The "what is" encompasses a history of soul connections, the complex assortment of assignments each soul has set before it, as well as the relationship of the soul to higher and lower realms. The "what could be" centers on simple acts of spiritual awareness expressed through free will, which becomes the fulcrum upon which the world turns.

Our lives, and the universe itself, are balanced on scales that measure deeds, words, and thoughts. Everything can turn on a word. A momentary thought can set a new spin to the universe. Each deed has the capacity to alter fate. Thus, the incredible drama that unfolds in each moment is awesome, for we never know what lies ahead. This mystical teaching is epitomized in conception, the archetype of newness.

## BODY AND SOUL

We know that alcohol, drugs, and cigarettes can be detrimental to a pregnancy. We intuit that undue stress during a pregnancy may be harmful, and that a well-balanced, relatively tranquil nine months may be beneficial; but there is no way to measure this. Moreover, wonderfully healthy babies often are born after traumatic pregnancies, and babies with colic or other complications sometimes are born after ideal pregnancies.

When we consider the soul, the teachings become even more ethereal. The Jewish mystic believes strongly that the level of our consciousness is a key factor in the attraction of souls. In other words, the state of mind of *both parents* at all times, including when they are engaged in the act that leads to conception, during the time of conception itself (even though it may be hours later), and throughout the entire pregnancy, affects the soul of the newborn infant.

A great deal of commentary in Jewish oral tradition discusses an array of ideas related to why someone becomes pregnant, and why not. Many of these concepts relate to merit, prayer, and past lives. In addition, on the mystical level, it is clear that souls have tasks to achieve while associated with physical form. Thus, it is assumed that there is a degree of selectivity, a choice process in the parents' physical situations, that will be relevant to the soul's task. Clearly, the parents' level of consciousness would be considered an important factor. Numerous hasidic stories describe the soul's selection of either saintly parents, on the one hand, or very average parents, on the other.

In addition, the sexual act has enormous mystical implications.[29] Mystics suggest that during lovemaking we should view each other as representations of the divine image. Moreover, we are advised that "it is important to avoid any extraneous thoughts during the sexual act. Partners should not think of any member of the opposite sex other than the sexual partner."[30]

Aryeh Kaplan, one of the more prolific modern writers of Jewish mysticism, suggests that deep meditation "can have an effect on the genetic structure of one's offspring, as well as the child's spiritual makeup."[31] He draws upon the description in the Torah in which Jacob controls the genetic reproduction of his sheep so that they will have body markings of spots, bands, and stripes. Jacob did this because he had to give the unmarked ones to Laban, who was corrupt. So Jacob peeled the bark off of rods and meditated on these rods to produce the desired effects in the propagating sheep.[32]

The operative mystical theory in this instance is that consciousness is connected with the soul realms. As such, our awareness will be a magnet to attract souls at similar levels. This is not something we can perceive logically. But if we are able to visualize all of creation as layers of awareness, each layer representing a different reality, we can begin to appreciate the dynamics of interaction with the soul realms.

We have a tendency to misunderstand the relationship between soul and body. If a body is lovely, emotions are balanced, and intellect is grand, we think that the soul of this person must be from a higher realm. If the body is impaired, the emotions are volatile, or the intellect is so-so, we assume that the soul must be from relatively lower realms. This is not at all the way it is presented in the teachings.

It is said in the *Zohar* that "when God delights in a soul, God inflicts suffering on the body so that the soul may gain full freedom."[33] And, in another place, "When suffering comes to a good person, it is because of God's love. The body is crushed to give more power to the soul, so that it will be drawn nearer to God in love."[34]

This teaching is difficult for us. It *should* be another way, we feel. Good things should happen to good people. But this clearly is not the mystical viewpoint. A soul has the task of mending itself and the world, to raise everything to a higher level of consciousness. There are an infinite number of ways to do so. Sometimes an impaired physical body is precisely what is needed to raise consciousness. Sickness, a difficult environment, a troubled relationship, poverty, suffering, untimely death of a loved one, any of a wide variety of demanding human experiences can lead to higher awareness. Because "gaining higher awareness" is another way to say "coming closer to God" or "fulfilling a primary purpose of creation," whatever we experience in these physical bodies that brings us to this goal is viewed as another opportunity to raise holy sparks.

Indeed, overcoming life's challenges does a great deal more to mold the character of a person than not being tested at all. Obviously there are many trials we would rather not have. Yet this may be what is on our plate. We do not necessarily get to choose. The way we learn to handle what we are given as our portion will affect the development of the soul.

I have worked with many families who suffer significant tragedies. Perhaps the most heartrending situation occurs when a parent has a child who has been diagnosed with a terminal disease—especially when the process lasts for years. God forbid this should happen to anyone you know, and yet the parents with whom I have worked in this plight are usually profound souls who have attained extraordinary levels of consciousness—not to speak of the amazing children I have encountered. We can never justify tragedy on this basis, but it helps us gain insight and compassion.

Situations need not be as dramatic as a terminal illness. A friend who had a difficult child once asked me, "How did this happen? We live well, we gave Tommy everything he needed. We loved him. We tried to give him the best education, which he resisted. We did not spoil him with too many material things, but gave him what counted. Yet, from the beginning, he was angry, miserable, combative, hateful, and destructive. He burned everything he could. He was a bully and stole from smaller children. We got all kinds of help for him: emotional, psychological. Nothing worked. What happened?"

I asked him, "Did you stop loving Tommy because he has a difficult life?"

"No, of course not," he answered. "It just causes me such pain to see him suffer so much."

Tommy's father did not love him any less because of Tommy's difficulties; perhaps this love was felt even more deeply because it was breaking his heart. We would not choose this scenario for ourselves. And Tommy's father did everything in his power to turn things around.

The question we must ask, however, is, What was happening with Tommy's soul? Or that of Tommy's father? Mother? Teacher? Psychotherapist? Brothers? Sisters? Friends? The entire world that he lived in was impacted by Tommy. He drew a great deal of attention to himself. And he touched many souls.

Who knows? Geniuses are born to poorly educated parents; mentally or emotionally challenged children often are born to the brightest, holiest, or most charitable people; seriously antisocial or amoral, incorrigible children are born to all kinds of families. We cannot draw soul comparisons to these events. We live in physical reality, but the soul dwells in many others.

# PERFECTING
## THE UNIVERSE

*T*he soul is the kabbalistic key to discovering the secrets of life and death. If we constantly remind ourselves that soul dimensions should never be construed as physical entities, but are "patterned forces" like bubbles passing through various realities, we can use the teachings about souls to gain an uncommon perspective on the spiritual nature of the universe.

In a remarkable zoharic passage, Rabbi Eleazar asks Rabbi Simeon a question: " 'Since God knows that people will die, why are souls sent down to the world?' "[35]

Rabbi Simeon answers, " 'This is a mystery that is explained in the verse "Drink water from your own cistern and running water from your own well."[36] The term "cistern" designates a place where water does not flow naturally. (This metaphorically represents a soul that is in this world, not its "natural" habitat.) When a soul is not defiled in this world, it returns to its designated (natural) place in a way that is perfect on all four sides, above and below. When the soul ascends in this way . . . the waters (radiations) of lower consciousness flow upward [to higher consciousness], as if a cistern were being transformed into a well with running water. This process of the returning soul brings a new dimension of union, foundation, desire, friendship and harmony to the universe. Thus, the return of the perfected soul completes a union that was initially aroused by supernal love and affection . . . [and by so doing, it adds to the overall perfection of the universe].' "[37]

This is an amazing idea, adding an entirely new dimension to the concept of soul. When the soul's host thinks, speaks, and acts in ways that benefit the world through lovingkindness, charity, bringing peace to neighbors, and other such deeds, then the higher dimensions of the soul are quickened, causing an activation in the realms of higher consciousness. Upon death, if a soul returns to its original source with its higher elements in a more perfected state, then *the entire universe benefits by gaining a new level of harmony!*

We are not dealing simply with "my" soul and "my" *karma*. We are not victims of circumstance, servants to the king, small cogs in overwhelming machinery that constantly turns, grinding us to powder. Rather, we are connected via our souls to the source of creation, and we can transform the flow of creation.

# FATE AND MIRACLES

Rabbi Zusha of Hanipoli (eighteenth century) was famous for his simple faith. Many stories are told about him, but perhaps the best known relates his response to students who asked why his teachings were different from those of his own teacher. Zusha's answer was: "When I come before the judges of the heavenly tribunal, they are not going to ask if I lived my life like Moses, or if I lived my life like Abraham. They are going to ask me if I lived my life to be the best Zusha I could be."

In his youth, Rabbi Zusha and his brother, Elimelech, traveled from town to town, learning with different rebbes. In those days, many Kabbalists were wandering ascetics, sleeping in the study halls and living on morsels of bread and scraps of food—except on Shabbat, when their stomachs usually would be filled. The Kabbalist learns much more from the experience of life than from books.

Zusha and Elimelech loved to attend joyous events: engagements, circumcisions, and especially weddings. Weddings have so much mystery, and yes, plenty of food, too.

In a traditional Jewish wedding, a number of rituals have kabbalistic importance. The *chuppah,* under which the bride and groom stand during the ceremony, represents a gateway to heaven. Before the wedding, in a separate ceremony called a *bedeken,* the bridegroom lowers a veil over the face of the bride. During her time under the veil, it is said that the bride is in direct communion with the souls of her mother, grandmothers, and great-grandmothers, all the way back to Sarah, the bride of Abraham. Moreover, during this time under the bridal veil, she connects with the souls of her children, her grandchildren, and her great-grandchildren, forward to the time when messianic consciousness will change our perspective of reality. Thinking about all of those connections was enough to make Zusha dizzy.

During the ceremony itself, when the bride first enters holding a candle, she circles the groom seven times. This symbolizes that she is bringing light to seven primordial levels of creation in which she and her groom are joining their souls. Seven blessings are said during the ceremony to commemorate the bond on each level. And breaking the glass at the end of the ceremony, although this act has many meanings on many levels, symbolizes for mystics the beginning of creation. That is to say, the light of each marriage is so bright it shatters all previous conceptions and opens the world to a whole new set of possibilities. For Zusha, weddings were not simply places to get good food, they were miraculous events. He believed that the world is balanced on each marriage.

This is a story of one wedding in particular that caught Zusha's attention. Many people think of hasidic stories as fables, folk tales, or anecdotes designed merely for entertainment or teaching. But great Kabbalists say that these stories are always real on some level.

This was a big wedding. People had come from all over the countryside to honor the bride and groom. The arrangements were lavish, food was abundant, music played constantly, and the dancing was ecstatic. Everything was designed to send wave after wave of joy to heaven so that a life of bliss and happiness would be assured for the couple during their time on this earth and in the world to come.

But Zusha was frightened. He had seen something happen in the wedding that worried him. It was a subtle thing, probably nobody else noticed, but it was the kind of incident Zusha spent his life noticing. You see, Zusha was one of the *lamed-vav tzaddikim,* one of the thirty-six hidden saints who quietly do their work in this world in a way that holds the entire universe together.[38] Without the work of a *lamed-vav*nik, the pain and suffering that would ensue would be unimaginable.

This incident had happened in the wedding ceremony itself. When the bride first came to join the groom under the canopy, she began to circle around him to enter the higher realms. For many people, these other worlds are a mystery, some would even say a fantasy. Many assume that these worlds are not important compared with tangible reality. But for Rabbi Zusha, these other worlds were as real as anything he could touch or see. Indeed, for him, these worlds were far more significant and more permanent than anything on earth.

At an early age, Zusha had discovered how to enter other realities. He had a mysterious inner vision. When a person acted in a certain way, it was a sure sign that something fortunate was going to happen to that person in the near future. Zusha learned to observe that when someone moved to the left or to the right, it was somehow an indication of their potential for success.

As a child, Zusha assumed that all people had this ability to observe and thereby anticipate things that would happen. Later, however, he discovered that although everyone did in fact have the capacity to foresee the future, most people did not allow themselves time to develop this unique and extraordinary gift. Indeed, he rarely met anyone who could see things in the same way as he. Thus, he was extremely disturbed when he saw that the bride circled the groom only five times rather than the required seven.

Too many people had crowded around the canopy. A number of rabbis and many family members had been crushed together at this critical moment. Everyone had been distracted at one point by a barking dog. The bride had done the best she could, but nobody was really counting. Nobody, that is, except Rabbi Zusha, who did this kind of thing automatically. In fact, for him the softest rush of wind was a message, the quietest birdcall, the color of a fly, or whether one was breathing in or breathing out when something was being said. Each and every detail in the universe unveiled something much, much bigger for this *lamed-vav tzaddik*.

The fact that the bride made only five circuits was a foreboding sign. A connection was not completed in two of the seven spheres, and thus the harmony of this couple's universe would be greatly impaired. It would falter, and the imbalance would bring about great tests and trials.

From his observations of the cycles of life, Rabbi Zusha knew that every married couple faces ongoing challenges, but that there are special difficulties in the seventh year of marriage. This is a time when all the worlds either settle into a new harmony for another seven years, or things get stuck in some kind of inflexibility. When this happens, they would fly apart. For our sweet couple, it was going to happen in five years. Moreover, it was going to be enormously difficult for them because their two worlds would be at odds. Rabbi Zusha was very much afraid for them.

But, thank God, fate is not as fixed as some people think. Everything we do affects how life will unfold for us. Of course, most of the time we do not realize the subtleties of the forces in life, so we miss many opportunities to direct our own fates. It is the job of a *lamed-vav tzaddik,* however, to constantly improve the destiny of those around him or her. Thus, Rabbi Zusha set out to do his work, to use his considerable influence in the cosmos to give the newly married couple a secret wedding gift. It was a gift that could never be discussed. Only Zusha himself five years from that day would be able to appreciate the fruits of his efforts.

In his prayers the morning after the wedding, Zusha deeply meditated on the problem and began to open vital channels. As a young man he had learned that just as he could observe the connections between the universe and individual acts, he could actually influence the universe by purposely doing something. For example, when he noticed that a person's particular action would invariably lead to a painful experience, he often distracted that person at a critical moment. If someone said something that surely would lead to trouble, Zusha would find a way to engage this person in a conversation and gently maneuver the subject to undo the damage. This was his responsibility as a *lamed-vav tzaddik.* He had no choice in the matter.

He even learned to observe when someone was in a dangerous state of mind, and he found ways to subtly tickle this person's psyche and break the mood. Sometimes, for no reason at all, we go from a bad mood to a good mood; it could be the result of a *lamed-vav*nik standing nearby. Indeed, sometimes we think we are having a casual conversation with a stranger, but in fact this other person is helping us avoid a serious tragedy. Moreover, many of us act as *lamed-vav tzaddikim* without even knowing it ourselves. But that is the subject of another story.

Zusha, in deep meditation, began to plead for this newly married couple in the heavenly court. If only people had the wisdom to see the importance of small actions. Of course, he understood that the bride had not caused the problem, as such. Rather, she was simply revealing something already in the hands of fate. Yet, the way things work in this world, had she been able to make the seven circuits, she might have influenced her fate and perhaps modified the decree through the power of her own free will.

Rabbi Zusha tried, in his way, to complete the two circuits. The argument in this heavenly court was quite complex. The lives of the bride and groom, and the lives of their parents and grandparents, were reviewed in depth. As with all human beings, mistakes had been made. Some had accumulated. The decree was not based on a single issue, which is often the case, but upon a series of events that led to an inevitable result.

Finally, Zusha made a plea bargain. The couple had a debt to pay. But if he could succeed in getting them to give more charity than usual and to perform many acts of lovingkindness during the subsequent three months, the decree would be canceled. It was agreed, signed, and sealed.

When Rabbi Zusha finished his meditation, he set out to find the couple, to persuade them somehow to fulfill an obligation that they did not know they had. He could not tell them, of course, and even if he had, they would not have believed him. No, he was obliged to do the work in his usual way, behind the scenes. If he were successful, they would not even know he had been around.

How does this story end? Did Zusha convince the young couple to give enough charity to save their marriage? We are not told, but we must assume that Zusha found a way. A *lamed-vav tzaddik* usually will be successful. The important points we learn here, however, are that our fate can be revealed in various ways, and that there are forces in the world that can modify fate.

$\mathcal{M}$ANY TIMES WE are drawn to acts of charity. Is it a *lamed-vav tzaddik* whispering in our ears? Are we under a decree that needs to be annulled? Even if we doubt this, what is there to lose when we feel an urge to perform an act of lovingkindness? Indeed, some say that all acts of lovingkindness give strength to the *lamed-vav tzaddikim,* and that these acts hold the world together. Who could argue with such a thought?

The sole purpose of the *lamed-vav tzaddik* is to raise holy sparks. In the process of doing so, he or she is constantly challenging fate. It is said that each of us has an aspect of the *lamed-vav tzaddik* within us. Does this mean that we can change our own fates and the fates of those around us? What is fate, how does it work, and how can we influence it?

# CHANGE YOUR NAME,
# CHANGE YOUR FATE

*M*oshe Steinberg was a professor of international relations at Hebrew University on Mt. Scopus in Jerusalem. His intellectual gifts were enormous, and his entire life was dedicated to academic excellence. Unfortunately, he did not tend to his own health. His long work hours, combined with neglect for rest and proper nutrition, led to a heart attack in his mid-fifties.

His son, Shlomo, was a friend of ours. He too was a brilliant scholar. Shlomo sent us frequent reports on his father's condition. Things seemed to get a little worse each day.

Initially Professor Steinberg had entered the hospital with severe chest pains. Within a few days it was determined that he needed immediate heart surgery. During the surgery, he went into cardiac arrest, and the doctors could not get the heart started for many minutes. At first the surgeons thought that the patient was lost. Although the medical team finally succeeded in their efforts to resuscitate Dr. Steinberg, considerable brain damage had occurred. After surgery, the professor seemed to be partially paralyzed. He could not speak and could barely lift his head or arm. The doctors were not sure if he would ever talk again.

One week later, the surgeons had to do another procedure to stop internal bleeding. This time the professor did not wake up after the surgery, and he lay in a coma for a few days.

Shlomo called us soon thereafter. There was a somber possibility that his father would never awaken. Even if he did, he would probably be an invalid the rest of his life.

Shlomo told us that a special prayer group was being organized at the Western Wall to recite psalms and to give his father a new name. The Talmud teaches that one of the ways to change someone's fate is by changing her or his name.[39] Shlomo and his family had done everything they could through prayer, charity, and commitments to come closer to God. Their last resort was to change Moshe's name.

The prayers lasted for a couple of hours. During that time, we gave the professor the new name his family had chosen for him: Raphael Brucha Steinberg, a name combining the healing power of God (*raphael*) with the spirit of blessings *(brucha)*. The next day, Raphael Brucha came out of his coma.

For a few days the doctors thought he would never walk again, and there was some question about his mind. However, less than a week after his renaming, the professor began to sit up and speak. He described to his family an out-of-body experience in which he dwelled on a plane where everything was made of light. He thought that he was dead, and the beings of light around him confirmed that this was so. He said that he had no regrets. But at some point he was informed that he was going to live as a completely different person than he had been. And then he woke up.

Professor Steinberg did in fact begin his life anew. After nine months of recuperation, he began to play music and fell in love with watercolor painting. Although he taught occasionally, his primary interest was to become an artist. Last I heard, eight years after his illness, he was spending his summers on the Italian Riviera, painting one or two canvases every day.

## FATE

*T*here is a saying: "The number of children one has, the length of one's life, and the degree of one's wealth do not depend upon a person's merits, but on *mazzal*."[40] In Jewish mysticism, fate is often referred to as *mazzal,* which is usually translated as luck, but which also means "the stars of the zodiac." The idea that we live under *mazzal* suggests that souls are fated from the beginning, dependent upon the flux and flow of the universe.

Kabbalists teach that the moon is the mystical vessel in which souls are gathered before they are released to the world. The moon in Kabbalah represents receptivity. When the moon is full, it is receiving the fullness of universal light and expansiveness. When the moon is new, it has no light and is in a more contracted state. Thus, the mystical implication is that souls are influenced by the phase of the moon when they become associated with bodies, each having different levels of expansiveness or contractedness. In modern terms, we would say that this describes why some of us are more extraverted while others are more introverted, which seems to be our fate.

Some people think of fate as a fixed scenerio, but mystics suggest that it is flexible. When we engage in activities that raise consciousness, fate adapts itself to support such things. For example, the Talmud says that the income one will receive each year is determined by fate, "except for the money spent on [celebrating] the Sabbath and other holy days. One who spends more is given more, and one who spends less is given less."[41] Thus fate is adjustable. In this instance, the celebration of Shabbat or another holy day is viewed as a consciousness-raising activity, and so we get *carte blanche* to invite as many guests as we wish to our Shabbat table. In essence, for these events, God (fate) says, "I'll pick up the tab."

Although our lives are influenced by fate, free will can dramatically alter our destiny. We are able to influence fate through skillful living. The more we realize the relationship between what we do and who we are, the more we regulate our own lives.

The Talmud says that we should be quick to offer bread to a poor person because "[mercy] is a wheel that turns in the world." Rabbi Gamaliel Beribbi said, "Whoever shows mercy to others is shown mercy by heaven; whoever is not merciful to others is not shown mercy by heaven."[42]

The High Holy Days of Rosh Hashana and Yom Kippur are built upon the idea that a person's fate is established for a year at a time. We say in the liturgy of Yom Kippur: "On Rosh Hashana it is inscribed and on Yom Kippur sealed [in the book of fate] how many will die and how many will be born, who will die at the preordained time, and who before this time [because of misdeeds] . . . who will rest, who will wander, who will be tranquil, who will suffer, who will be poor, who will be rich . . ."

Then the congregation says together, loudly, "But *teshuvah* (changing conduct), *tefillah* (prayer), and *tzeddakah* (charity) cancel the harshness of this decree."

Fate is a pattern sketched in a mystical book for the garment we call life. But the sketch of fate is only an outline. We can significantly affect the final design of our lives by the way we cut the cloth of our fate, how we sew it, how we trim it, and especially by the material of life we choose. Ultimately, although the design of our fate may follow an essential prototype, like a dress, a shirt, or pair of pants, we have a great deal of freedom to modify the finished product.

In addition to the fluidity of fate and the influence of free will as the modifying aspect, fate can be changed also by introducing a new factor into the universe, something unexpected. When the unexpected is also inexplicable, we call it a miracle. Miracles confront the laws of nature. Indeed, some say that fate is the natural order of things and that any change in the flow of fate is miraculous. Let us see what this means.

*S*criptural literature describes many miraculous events, such as staffs turning into snakes, water turning to blood, strange plagues, animals that speak, leprosy that comes instantly and departs just as quickly, the sun standing still, and a man being swallowed by a fish and regurgitated days later alive and whole.

The Talmud has its share of miracles as well: killing with a glance, resurrecting the dead, battling with demons, invoking divine spirits, teleporting from one city to another in a matter of minutes, visiting heavenly or demonic realms while still alive, incredible healing, assuring pregnancy in previously barren women, and casting spells with potions.

Miracles play a role also in the history of most holy days. The miracles of the splitting of the Red Sea and the ten plagues are associated with Passover. The appearance of God on Mt. Sinai is associated with Shavuot. The foiling of a plot for the massive genocide of the Jews is part of the Purim story.

Hanukkah is based upon a miracle that occurred twenty-two hundred years ago,[43] when the Maccabees defeated the Greeks. Upon reentering the Second Temple, the Jews found that the oil used for the menorah had been defiled and that there was a sufficient amount of pure oil to burn for only one day. The miracle was that this oil burned for eight days, just enough time to prepare and transport a new supply.

Often miracles are great, abrupt, and conspicuous. The most obvious biblical example is the parting of the sea at the time of the Exodus. A big miracle quite suddenly saved the Hebrews from annihilation. We often hear about these kinds of miracles: a terrible automobile accident with passengers unharmed; a parachute that fails to open but the skydiver somehow survives. Many miracles fall into this category. Some say, however, that for every big miracle, billions of little ones exist. Jewish mystics suggest that the mundane world is where the true miraculous nature of creation lies.

# MIRACLES PRECEDE
## CREATION

*T*he question of miracles was of considerable interest to the talmudic sages. Is the universe an orderly place? If it is orderly, as most believed, miracles had to be something other than out-of-the-blue events.

One of the ways ancient sages dealt with this question was to suggest that miracles had been preordained; they were in the mind of God, so to speak, at the time of creation. This is explicit in a Midrash in which Moses argues with God, saying, "If you split the sea, you will go against the natural order of things. Who could trust you? Indeed, you would be contradicting your own promise to keep the sea and the land separate."[44]

This is an important argument. If we cannot trust that there is an orderly universe, our faith will be challenged. God promises that things are going to go a certain way; water will not separate willy-nilly. If we discover that this promise does not hold 100 percent of the time, our sense of reality can be shattered. Thus, Moses is asking a critical question. God has put it in writing that water has certain properties but is about to break the rules at the Red Sea.[45]

The answer to this puzzle is found in a Midrash that states: "The Holy One stipulated [a precondition] for everything that was created in the six days of creation. [At the beginning of creation, the Holy One said,] I commanded the sea to divide . . . I commanded the sun and moon to stand still before Joshua; I commanded the raven to feed Elijah . . . I commanded the lions not to harm Daniel, the heavens to open for Ezekiel and the fish to regurgitate Jonah."[46] All this was done *before* the creation of Adam and Eve, and it implies that all miracles are a necessary part of the destiny of the universe.[47]

In essence, the sages used this approach to resolve a crucial question: Is there order to the universe, or not? They say yes. Even though a miracle seems to change the orderly flow of things, it is built into the mechanism of creation. The potential for miracles is a defined part of atomic structure. Although we have an orderly universe, the universe, paradoxically, has the potential to do extraordinary things that we would deem miraculous.

The well-known Kabbalist Nachmanides added a mystical dimension to this perspective. In response to Maimonides' viewpoint that miracles are used by God to reveal Itself to the masses, Nachmanides suggested that a level of reality supersedes nature, and in this higher reality, the miraculous is commonplace. Nachmanides said that a miracle is not a singular event in contrast to the flow of nature, but rather that miracles are an ongoing process.[48] The only reason we think that a miracle is opposed to the ordinary flow of nature is because we do not have a broad enough scope of these other dimensions of reality. If we did, we would see that everything is dependent upon miracles.

## AN UNREALIZED
## SEA OF MIRACLES

The Kabbalists teach that everything we do stirs up a corresponding energy in other realms of reality. Actions, words, or thoughts set up reverberations in the universe. The universe unfolds from moment to moment as a function of all the variables leading up to that moment. When we remain cognizant of this mystical system, we are careful about what we do, say, or even think, for we know that everything is interdependent; we know that a seemingly insignificant gesture could have weighty consequences.

For example, when we leave our home to go visit someone, we affect and are affected by our surroundings in thousands of ways from the time we step out of the door until we return. Where we place our feet, the people we see, the traffic we encounter, and the impressions we make all can be envisioned as intersecting lines in a great tapestry of life.

Now, what happens if the telephone rings just as we are about to leave? Our trip is delayed for a few minutes. This changes the design of the entire tapestry. Everything is different. The timing changes. The green light is now red; the person we smiled at is gone; the ant we never saw is now crushed.

In the new science of chaos theory, there is a well-known phenomenon called the "butterfly effect," in which the air moved in one part of the world by an insect can be the initiatory cause for a typhoon that occurs somewhere else in the world at a later time. The technical term is "sensitive dependence upon initial conditions."[49] This theory adds an incredible dimension to our lives. What does it mean that my automobile would push one air mass if I were not interrupted by a telephone call, and a completely different air mass if I were? What different reverberations are set up in the universe by those few minutes? Does one lead to a typhoon in my life, while the other does nothing?

Moreover, what if the phone ringing causes me to miss a terrible accident that otherwise would have maimed or killed me? A truck lost its brakes and came through a red light where I would have been had the phone not rung. Should I call this a miracle? Yet how would I even know that the accident would have occurred? Two minutes later, everything seems normal. Obviously, this would be an "unrealized" miracle.

In Jewish mysticism, the instant we open our eyes to the true dimensions of creation and causality, we find ourselves immersed in a sea of miracles. This realization is astonishing. At any instant, creation might unfold in a way that would be disastrous for us; therefore, each moment is bursting with the gift of life. Indeed, as a result of this awareness, the mystic loves life intensely and feels loved by it.

# ANGELS AND DEMONS

*G*ravity and magnetism have always mystified scientists. We can measure them, we can approximate what they look like, we know there is something happening that has strength and attraction, but they are invisible and not even discernible unless we have the right tools. You can place your hands next to a very strong magnet, and nothing happens. But if you have an iron bracelet strapped to your wrist, it could be pulled by the magnet so strongly that you would not be able to move your hand away.

In physical reality, every move we make is dependent upon electromagnetic energy. In the metaphysical realm, rather than call this energy electromagnetic, we could call it angelic-demonic. Every move we make is supported by an angel or demon. Moreover, everything we do creates new angels and demons. In this context, angels do not have personalities, nor are they entities. They represent lines of force, packets of energy like light photons, neither wave nor particle, and they cannot be distinguished except through results. The metaphysical magnets associated with the God realms are called angels, and those with the satanic realms are called demons.

When I bump my head, was I pushed? No. Nothing outside of myself pushed me. Yet I moved differently than I normally do, because I normally do not bump my head. Was this a malicious energy bundle? No. Was it a demon? Yes. How do demons work? A demon is a configuration of circumstances that ends up with me bumping my head. A set of combined variables is called a demon when an inevitable result occurs.

At any point along the way, however, one of these variables could change. I could turn right instead of left. So I would miss bumping my head. In that case, my turning was caused by an angel. I simply do not realize it because my head was never bumped. Therefore, each moment is packed with conditions that pull me closer to God and those that tug me farther away. Any of these, viewed individually or collectively, can be put on my good-and-evil scale. I am continuously surrounded by angels and demons.

## ANGELS

*T*he reference material regarding angels and demons in Jewish mysticism is extensive. Many details contradict each other. A large amount of information is based on medieval mythology, which was influenced by ideas from a variety of sources that extend far beyond traditional literature.

There are dozens of archangels, including four primary ones who are often identified in the oral tradition as Michael, Gabriel, Uriel, and Raphael. In addition to these are hundreds of angels mentioned by name in different mystical texts. Many names of angels begin with attributes that describe the qualities of the angel and end in *el* or *yah,* which are names of God. But the nature of individual angels is not always clear. *Gabriel* means "the strength of God," but Gabriel is also called the Angel of Fire and the Angel of War.[50] Raphael is usually known as the Angel of Healing, but it is also called the Prince of Hades.[51] Liliel is the Angel of the Night, but Lilith—whose name also means "night"—is considered to be the arch she-devil.[52] Michael is the Angel of Mercy and sometimes the Angel of Prayer, but Sandalphon also is known as the Angel of Prayer.

Jewish tradition describes an adversarial relationship between human beings and angels. Angels are jealous of humans because we humans have free will and they do not. The Midrash says that angels debated whether or not human beings should be part of creation. The Angel of Love felt that it would be a good idea to have humans in this creation because of our potential for expressing love; the Angel of Truth was opposed to human beings because we tend to tell many lies.[53] During this debate, God exhibited examples of humans for angels to see, but included only well-known characters from biblical lore. Of course, if at the start God had revealed the true nature of human beings to angels instead of showing them the greatest and most righteous people, there would have been an uproar in the heavens.[54]

Next, the Angel of Earth rebelled and would not give the archangel Gabriel any dust for God to create humankind. The Angel of Earth protested that the physical earth would be cursed and devastated because of human thoughtlessness; it insisted that God take personal responsibility rather than send an archangel as an intermediary.[55] This Midrash, thousands of years old, reveals parallels between the concerns of ancient sages and modern environmentalists. In the Midrash, God had to take the dust used to create humankind directly from the earth rather than send an angel to do it, suggesting an implicit covenant offered by God that the earth will not be destroyed by human ignorance.

The Angel of the Torah argued with God, saying that the days of human beings would be filled with suffering and that it would be far better if humans were never brought into existence in the first place.[56] Regarding this contention, God said (promised) that humans would endure despite the trials and tribulations of life.

God revealed the future to Adam and Eve in a book given to them in the Garden of Eden by the hand of the angel Raziel (secrets of God). This book contained sacred knowledge: 72 branches of wisdom that revealed the formation of 670 inscriptions of higher mysteries. In the middle of the book was a secret writing explaining 1,500 keys to the universe, which were not revealed even to the holy angels.

When Adam and Eve obtained this book, all the angels gathered around to hear it read. When the reading began, the angels exalted Adam and Eve as if they were God, whereupon the angel Hadraniel was secretly sent to them to say, "Adam and Eve, reveal not the glory of the Master, for to you alone and not to the angels is the privilege given to know these things."[57] Thereupon, Adam and Eve kept it secret and learned for themselves mysteries not known even to the celestial ministers.

When Adam and Eve transgressed the commandment of the Master regarding the Tree of Knowledge, the book flew away from them. Adam was so distressed, he entered the river Gihon (one of the rivers of the garden) up to his neck and stayed there so that his body became wrinkled and his face haggard. (We do not know what Eve was doing during this time.) God thereupon made a sign to the archangel Raphael to return the book, which Adam studied for the rest of his life. He left it to his son Seth, and it went through the generations to Abraham. It is still hidden today, somewhere in the world, for those who know how to read it.

Angels argued that humans would be a liability in the creation because they were always fouling things up. If the angels had their way, humans would be out of the picture, and the universe would run smoothly and predictably. This, of course, is precisely the point. What would be the purpose of a universe that was totally predictable?

The *Zohar* teaches that angels were created at the moment God said "Let there be light; and there was light."[58] In Hebrew it reads as a repetition: "Let there be light; and let there be light."[59] A mystical interpretation of this is "Let there be light (awareness) on the right side, the side of goodness; and let there be light (awareness) on the left side, the side of darkness." This interpretation is supported by the next line, which says, "And God saw the light [of the right side], that it was good, and God divided the light [of the right] from the darkness [of the left]."

The angels were created on this first day to have a permanent existence on the side of goodness. Rabbi Eleazar says that they will always continue to shine as brightly as they did on the first day.[60] There is a debate regarding the Angel of Death, however. The Midrash says that the Angel of Death (the dark side) was also created on the first day.[61] The *Zohar* says, however, that death was created on the second day because Genesis omits for this day the words "and God saw that it was good," though they are mentioned every other day of creation.

The giving of the Torah to human beings is described in the oral tradition as extremely threatening to the angels, because the Torah provides hidden information and secret names that give humans power over the angelic and demonic realms. The antagonism of the angels is revealed in the celestial conflict that Moses encountered when he went forth to receive the Torah from God.

Rabbi Eleazar said, "When Moses entered the cloud on Mt. Sinai,[62] he was met by a great angel, whose name was Kamuel, who was in charge of twelve thousand other angels. He (Kamuel) ran to attach himself to Moses [and thereby overpower him]. Moses opened his mouth, [and spoke the] twelve signs (names of God) that were taught and imprinted [in Moses] by the Holy One at the [burning] bush.[63] [As a result] the angel went away from him a distance of twelve thousand parasangs."[64]

Moses continued walking in the cloud, and his eyes glowed like embers of fire. Then another angel, more eminent than the first, whose name was Hadraniel (majesty of God), met him. This angel is set above all other angels and celestial beings by a distance of 1,060 myriads of parasangs (25 million miles).[65] Its voice penetrates 200,000 firmaments, which are surrounded by a white fire.

On seeing this angel, Moses was so awed, he could not speak any of the names of God, and he ran to throw himself from the cloud. But the Holy One said to him, "Moses, you talked about things with me at the [burning] bush where you gained knowledge of the secret holy names, and you were not afraid. Now are you afraid of something that I rule?" Moses was strengthened by the voice of the Holy One. He opened his mouth and spoke the seventy-two-letter supreme name of God.[66]

When Hadraniel heard the holy name spoken by Moses, he came close and said to him, "Praised be the distinguished Moses." It became apparent to Hadraniel what the other angels did not see. So he joined with Moses and they went together until they met an angel whose name is Sandalphon. Sandalphon is removed from all other angels by a distance of five hundred years. This angel stands behind the curtain of its master and weaves a crown from the requests of prayers. At a certain time, this crown rises of its own accord and goes past the Throne of Glory to settle in its place (on the head of God), at which time all of the heavenly hosts tremble and say, "Blessed is the glory of God in Its place."[67]

Hadraniel said to Moses, "Moses, I cannot go with you for fear that I may be burned in the harsh fire of Sandalphon." A great trembling came to Moses at this time. He ran past Sandalphon and across Rigyon, the stream of fire that burns (purifies) angels, who dip into it each morning and rise anew. The stream is beneath the Throne of Glory and is produced by the perspiration of the holy *hayyot* (higher angels), who fret out of fear of God. At this point Moses met the angel Gallizur, who is called Raziel. This angel also dwells behind the curtain, and sees and hears everything.[68]

Now Moses came to the angels of terror, who surround the Throne and are the mightiest of angels. But God told Moses to hold on tightly to the Throne so that no harm would come to him. Thus, the Holy One brought Moses close and taught him Torah for forty days.[69]

This description of the journey of Moses to the highest realms gives us a sense that there are levels upon levels of angelic forces, each increasingly fantastic in its dimension.[70] It also suggests that Moses had the capability to transcend even the most imposing angel, Sandalphon, to sit and be instructed directly by God. Sandalphon is considered the "brother" of Metatron, who is the chief of all angels. Metatron is associated with Enoch, and Sandalphon with Elijah. Both Enoch and Elijah are included among the few mortals who never died.[71]

## DEMONS

*D*emons are ubiquitous but are not cited in the literature as often as angels. The head of the demons is Satan, who is also named Samael and Beelzebub,[72] while the king of demons is called Asmodeus.[73] Asmodeus married Agrath, and they are attended by tens of thousands of other demons.

Just as there are many types of angels, there are various types of demons, which include *shedim* (devils), *se'irim* (hairy demons, satyrs), *mavet* (death), *dever* (pestilence), and *azazel* (the demon to whom the scapegoat is sent on Yom Kippur).[74]

Demons are viewed as between angels and humans. They have "wings" like angels and can move quickly, assume any form, and have the ability to read the future. But they eat, drink, propagate, and die.[75] They can have sexual relations with humans, and this is a source of new demons. But demons do not have real bodies that cast shadows, so propagation with humans occurs in dreams or other nonphysical contact. Humans give birth to demons through the imagination.

Demons can be overpowered by humans. The queen of demons, Agrath, once met Rabbi Hanina ben Dosa. She revealed to him that the only reason she did not cause him harm was because heaven had given him immunity for his extensive learning. This was a mistake on her part. Once Hanina ben Dosa knew that Agrath could not harm him, he put a hex on her. He said, "If heaven takes an accounting of me, I order you never to pass through populated areas."[76] This, in essence, put her out of business. She immediately began to plead with him, so he relented and gave her freedom to do her demon work on two nights of the week: Wednesday and Saturday.

The Talmud reports a similar incident between Agrath and the sage Abaye. (Apparently she did not learn from her other experience.) This time Abaye did not yield, but we find that demons still frequent narrow places where few people go, like dark alleyways.[77]

In addition, if one knows how to capture a demon's power, the demon can be put into service. The archangel Michael provided King Solomon with a magic ring which gave him power over all the demons. King Solomon discovered the names of angels that influenced the demons he wanted to control. Through the use of his magic ring, King Solomon captured Asmodeus.[78] Asmodeus taught Solomon the secret of the *shamir.* Some say that this was a worm that could split rock. The building of the Temple of Solomon depended upon the ability to split rocks without iron tools, for the use of metal had been forbidden by God.[79]

Once King Solomon had the *shamir* under his control, he could build the altar to God. This information gave him sufficient mastery over the demons so that he used them in the building of the First Temple.[80] Thus, the First Temple, the holiest site in Jewish history, had a team of demonic builders—suggesting that demons are not necessarily evil. The point of this story is that when we have power over demonic forces, they can be put to good use. On the other hand, when demonic forces have power over us, our lives can be miserable. We see this theme emphasized in the continuation of the story.

At one point, Asmodeus tricked the king. When Solomon chided Asmodeus, saying he was not much of a demon if he could be captured by a mortal and put into chains, Asmodeus replied that he would be happy to demonstrate his greatness if the king would loan him the magic ring. Solomon was foolish enough to do so (giving away his power), and Asmodeus instantly threw him a thousand miles away from Jerusalem. Then Asmodeus cast the magic ring into the middle of the ocean so that it could never again be used against him, and he assumed Solomon's appearance, pretending that he was the king.[81]

Solomon wandered as a beggar for three years and took a job as a cook in the royal household of Ammon. He was a great cook, and soon he became the chief of cooks. This is how the king's daughter, Naamah, came to notice him. She fell in love and would not be swayed by the king to give up Solomon. So the Ammonite king sent the lovers to a barren desert, where it was presumed that they would die by starvation.

The lovers wandered to a city by the shore of a sea. They begged for enough money to purchase a fish to eat. Naamah found a ring in the belly of the fish. Sure enough, it was Solomon's magic ring, and the couple was instantly transported to Jerusalem, where they dethroned Asmodeus, who had been posing as King Solomon for three years.[82]

This tale contains the secret of the use of power and is a teaching story about raising sparks to attain messianic consciousness. One of the hidden features of the story is that the mother of Asmodeus, in essence the mother of demons, was also named Naamah. Thus the story relates a circle of events, in which Naamah, the wife of Solomon, makes a *tikkun,* a fixing, to raise the sparks of Naamah, mother of the demons. In this process, Naamah, the wife of Solomon, becomes a matriarch in the lineage of the messiah that comes from King David, the father of Solomon.

Just as demons are not always used to produce disagreeable results, angels are not always pleasant to be around. It is true that many are desirable, such as angels of grace, healing, justice, love, mercy, moon, mountains, paradise, peace, praise, stars, trees, truth, and water. But there are also angels of confusion, destruction, fear, fire, hail, insomnia, reptiles, storms, terror, and thunder.[83] These are considered angels rather than demons only when their purpose is to draw us closer to God.

Actually there are angels for every atom in the universe. Each snowflake has a multitude of angels around it; each blade of grass has an angel over it, saying, "Grow, grow."[84] Every characteristic, emotion, thought, or phenomenon has angels identified with it.

All the descriptions of angels and demons are meant to help us approximate qualities we find within ourselves. When we are feeling caressed, loved, comforted, or pampered, our angels are described as soft, gentle, refined, careful, and considerate. When we are anxious, frustrated, worried, or nervous, our angels are pushy, critical, demanding, accusing, and relentless. When we are having serious troubles and our lives seem to be falling apart, we have demons who are cruel, malevolent, hateful, odious, and fiendish.

This should not be interpreted to mean that the mystics believe that angels and demons are imaginary. Just the opposite. They are quite real, and they manifest in an infinite number of ways. If the results of something are viewed as good, we generally call it an angelic influence. However, if something draws someone away from God, even though the initial motivation may have been well intended, we say that there was a demonic influence.

It is important for us to understand that an intention behind an act does not ensure its results. Intention must be balanced by awareness. The greater the awareness, the greater the probability that something good will come out. The denser the awareness, even though one's intentions may be good, the greater the risk that things will not turn out so well. We could do something kind-hearted for someone without realizing that this could bring enormous grief into his or her life.

We may ask, "If our intentions do not assure that things will turn out for the good, what do we do?" The answer is that we must attune ourselves to the constant ebb and flow of ongoing creation through our contemplative practices and through spiritual work that builds awareness, as described in various sections of this book. And we must make every effort to attain the highest level of consciousness so that our actions may be inspired by the ingredients of judgment and wisdom, spiced with a large dose of faith.

# THE EBB AND FLOW
## OF MYSTICAL FORCES

$\mathcal{M}$ystics say that energy flows in cycles. Daytime cycles are related to the rotation of the earth; monthly cycles to the moon; and annual cycles to the relative position of the sun and stars. Light and dark are connected to expansion and contraction, lovingkindness and restraint. Kabbalists apply this mystical cosmic framework to everything, including angelic and demonic energies.

According to mainstream Judaism, days begin and end at sundown. Kabbalists naturally follow this calculation from the point of view of Jewish law, but from an energetic perspective, the daily kabbalistic cycle flows between the zenith of high noon and the nadir of midnight.

From noon until midnight, the sun appears to be declining, which means that the power of lovingkindness is waning. When the sun reaches its lowest ebb, the time in which the energy of darkness is strongest, accusing angels have their greatest power. The Kabbalist says that this point is the darkest of the night, the moment when restriction and judgment are at their full power. If we were abandoned in the mystical midnight of creation, we would disappear. We could not survive the judgment. Thus, in the poetic language of Kabbalah, at precisely this instant, God "enters" the celestial Garden of Eden.[85] That is to say, at the moment when the physical universe is in greatest jeopardy, the darkest moment of the day, the force of expansion materializes and revitalizes the center of creation.

Of course, Jewish mystics understand that midnight in one part of the world is different than in other parts. They know that God is, so to speak, continuously entering the garden. It may be difficult to envision midnight as a moving line, but from the viewpoint of God-ing as a process, this imagery is perfect. From where we stand, the lovingkindness of the Divine brings Its light to our midnight, exactly when we need it for survival. When we become objective, however, we realize that it is always midnight somewhere. Thus, God is perpetually entering the garden, forever bringing Its light to everybody's midnight at all times, a continuous process.

Angels are also constantly "angel-ing." The *Zohar* says that accusing angels move about the world during the dark hours before midnight. Clearly this time is relative to the observer. Objectively, however, it could be midnight a thousand miles to the east (one hour's difference), in which case God has already entered the garden (there), which by definition sends the accusing angels into hiding.

This is another interactive relationship. Angelic and demonic energies are not independent and self-sufficient, but are parts of the system of the universal ebb and flow. The more we can begin to understand this cosmic fluctuation, the more our horizons widen and we are able to appreciate the intricacy of the interrelational process between Creator and creation.

Another example is the zoharic statement that all celestial beings chant praises to the Holy One. As soon as night falls, three hosts of angels arrange themselves in three parts of the universe. Over these three hosts of angels stands a chieftain called a *hayyah,* an angelic force which is said to be the support for the divine Throne. The nighttime chanting continues until daybreak. Then humans take up the praises three times a day in prayer. Accordingly, praise is offered six times in twenty-fours, three by human beings during the day, and three by angels at night.[86]

Kabbalists are well traveled, so it does not take much to figure out that when I am offering praise in my morning prayers, the angelic hosts not far from me are still engaged in their nighttime praises. Thus, the idea of praise being offered six times a day applies only to where one is standing. From an objective viewpoint, however, praise and prayer are continuous day and night, unfolding as the earth revolves. This movement resembles a kaleidoscope ceaselessly opening, or a flower constantly blooming, and is a wonderful image to contemplate.

## INVOKING ANGELS
## FOR HEALING

Not long ago I heard from a dear friend whose son had been the victim of a freak accident. He had been hit in the back of the head by a golf ball. His recovery was not going well, and a blood clot in his brain was causing pressure that potentially could paralyze him for life, or kill him. The boy had been in intensive care in a semicomatose state for ten days when his mother and I first spoke. For some reason, he did not improve and his prognosis was not good. High-risk surgery with possible brain damage was a fast-approaching option that everyone wanted to avoid.

In the course of our conversation, the boy's mother asked for a meditative/prayer practice, and I suggested an archangel meditation. In it, we surround ourselves or someone dear to us with angelic energy for the purpose of protection and healing. Soon after our talk, her son had to be put into a medically induced coma so that he could be kept quiet and out of pain in the hope that the swelling would be reduced.

My friend began frequent guided meditation and prayer with her son, despite the fact that he was in a coma. The subconscious mind can absorb meditative guidance; moreover, the soul never sleeps. She continued consistently for many days. Indeed, when he was brought out of the coma, he was repeating the words of the meditation.

From that time on, each step along the way, just before a major invasive decision had to be made, he would improve. Hours before they had to put in a permanent shunt to draw off the cerebral fluids, the pressure stabilized. Thanks to modern medicine, the boy is alive and well. The doctors and nurses deservedly get credit for the miracle. His mother, father, and I firmly believe that angels had a great deal to do with it as well.

## Archangel Meditation

Each evening, traditional Jewish bedtime prayers include the following invocation: "May Michael be at my right, Gabriel at my left, Uriel in front of me, Raphael behind me, and above my head, the *Shekhina*—the Divine Presence." This is one of my congregation's favorite meditations; it works well for adults and children. As a meditation, it can be used to develop a sense of protection, comfort, healing, and security. It is one of the few meditative exercises recommended at bedtime.

When we call upon angels to be with us, we tap into an infinite resource of good will. It is as if we plug into the magnetic core of the earth to keep ourselves centered. Archangels represent the God-center of the universe; they draw nourishment from Its infinite supply. The only impediments to connecting with this energy are doubt and cynicism. If we can recognize these as they arise in our minds and find appropriate cubby holes in which to keep them in reserve for the times when they are useful, we can instantly benefit from the feeling of angelic presence.

1. Try to find a quiet place where you will not be disturbed for twenty to thirty minutes, such as in bed at night, when falling asleep. Close your eyes, relax your body, and breathe normally. Allow your attention to focus on the experience of your body and the movements of your chest and stomach around your breath.

2. Let yourself imagine that you can feel a presence along the right side of your body and the right side of your face. It can feel like a subtle pressure, a tingling, a vibration, heat, coolness, or some other sensation. If you cannot feel anything, simply think that something is next to you, almost touching you on the right side.

3. Give this experience on the right side the name of Michael. The archangel Michael is often viewed as the messenger of God. Whatever this may mean to you, pretend that the messenger of God is totally present on your right side. Be with this experience for a while.

4. When you are ready, let yourself imagine another presence on your left side. Feel the pressure, just like on your right. This is the archangel Gabriel, which is known to represent the strength of God. You can experience both sides simultaneously. The messenger of God on your right, the strength of God on your left. Stay with this experience for a while.

5. Allow yourself to sense something behind you, anywhere along the back side, particularly supporting you as you are sitting or lying down. Imagine this is part of what is holding you up. This is the archangel Raphael, generally known as the healing power of God. Now you can do all three simultaneously: Michael, the messenger, on the right; Gabriel, the strength, on the left side; Raphael, the healer, supporting you from behind.

6. Next, with your eyes still closed, imagine a light is shining ahead of you, in front of your face. Allow it to be as bright as you can. This is the archangel Uriel, the light of God. Now you are surrounded on four sides: a messenger, strength, healing, and light.

7. Finally, imagine a huge, benevolent cloud of light hovering above your body. The is the *Shekhina,* the feminine presence of God. Allow the light of the *Shekhina* to slowly descend, surrounding you with love, enveloping you with tender protection, cradling you in the softest, most peaceful state of mind you have ever experienced. Surrounded by angels, you are also in the arms of infinite kindness, absolute security, and safety.

8. If you are in bed, this is a wonderful way to drift off to sleep. If you are sitting, stay as long as you wish in this state of mind. When you

are ready to end the meditation, however, do not get up too abruptly. It is much better if you are able to reverse the process, slowly allowing the *Shekhina* to rise up again to hover over your head. Then let go of the angels one by one, making sure they do not go too far away but give you freedom of movement. Even though you let go of the meditative state, you will probably feel a residual of this experience once you begin moving around.

You can practice this meditation as often as you wish. We cannot overload on angelic energy; it is always beneficial. This is a great meditation to share with children. Most people who are ill gain enormous benefits from this guided meditation; you can do it in their homes or in the hospital. I have done this even over the telephone. But be sure that the person meditating will not be disturbed for at least twenty minutes, and most important, you should be well practiced in it yourself before offering it to others.

## ANGELS, AND JACOB'S LADDER

A number of sections of Torah refer to angels, one of the more famous being the portion dealing with Jacob. At one point, Jacob dreams of a ladder that reaches from earth to heaven.[87] Angels go up and down the ladder, and God stands above it, talking to Jacob, promising to give him the land that surrounds him. Later, Jacob wrestles with and defeats an angel. Afterward, he is renamed Israel.

All biblical commentary attempts to resolve difficulties in the text. In this instance, the problem that is of concern is why the Torah says that the angels first ascend the ladder and then descend. Logically, assuming angels start off somewhere other than earth, the text should say that the angels descended first and then ascended. So, naturally, this turn of words invites comment.

Some obvious questions arise: Since angels do not walk—they move in some other way—why do they need ladders? Moreover, why do we envision them with wings? It is written in the Midrash that some angels have six wings, and some have twelve.[88] It is said that demons have six wings.[89] And the *Shekhina,* the divine feminine presence, is also said to have wings. Why is this? None of these beings needs wings to get from one place to another. What do the wings represent?

Although in the Torah wings are used literally for flying, the code for the word "wing" means "a covering; under the influence of something." As it says in Psalms 36:8, "How excellent is your love, God; for people find shelter under the shadow of your wings." When we are under the wings of the *Shekhina,* we are surrounded by light and lovingkindness. When we are under the wings of a demon, we are surrounded by darkness. The wings of angels surround us with angelic wisdom.

It is said that an angel is given a job to do, just one job at a time, usually to deliver a message. For example, we learn that every living thing has a momentary guardian angel that gives a vital message: Live! The next moment, another angel appears with the identical message. What happens to the first angelic energy once it has delivered its message? It has nothing else to do. Its whole purpose was to do this one act. You see, once the message is given, the angel no longer has wings, so to speak. It disappears.

Angels and demons are like orbs of spiritual energy in an effervescent liquid that is constantly bubbling. When a bubble rises to the top, it disappears. The bubble is defined by the liquid and not by itself. We must be careful when we speak about orbs of energy because we tend to think of them in terms of boundaries, but angels do not have physical boundaries. So we must try to imagine angels as ephemeral bubbles that exist everywhere, often overlapping with one another, not surrounded by liquid, not even having dimension.

The Talmud gives us a way to exercise our imagination regarding angelic energy. It says that the width of Jacob's ladder had to be eight thousand parasangs, which equals about twenty thousand miles.[90] Why? Because the wording of the passage that describes angels ascending and descending suggests that two were going up and two were coming down at the same time. Using talmudic logic, the ladder had to be wide enough for four angels abreast!

The Talmud goes on to quote Daniel 10:6, which says that the angel Daniel saw had a body like Tarshish. Whereas some translate Tarshish as a precious stone, the secret meaning is that it is the name of a sea that is two thousand parasangs wide. Thus, the Talmud concludes that if each angel is two thousand parasangs wide, four abreast means that Jacob's ladder was eight thousand parasangs in width.[91] This, of course, is wider than the earth.

A similar teaching can be found in the *Midrash Rabbah,* which explicitly says that the size of an angel is one third of the world.[92] In this teaching, four angels abreast would have the "dimension" of 1 ⅓ worlds. In either measurement, Jacob's ladder is substantially larger than the world. If this is so, what does the ladder rest on?

Obviously it is not any kind of ladder that fits into our imagination, nor is it a ladder that is logical. Indeed, it is not a ladder at all, but a sign of higher consciousness. The *Zohar* is quite clear on this, saying, "The ladder of Jacob symbolically allowed him to see all levels of consciousness as one, all awareness knit into one whole. Each side of the ladder represents a dimension: Abraham on the right (*chesed*/expansion) and Isaac on the left (*gevorah*/contraction). Jacob in the middle (*tiferet*/beauty) is the culmination of the balance and harmony required to be able to stand on the highest rung, above either side. This (Jacob) is viewed as a completion, a wholeness, the potential for the totality of consciousness in its sum rather than in discrete parts. The whole of the ladder forms one sacred chariot (the vehicle leading to total awareness)."[93]

Each rung on the ladder represents a level of consciousness. Jacob is viewed in Kabbalah as the peak of human perfection, more than any of the other biblical characters. He stands on the top rung, the highest potential achievement, held up on either side by the pillars of lovingkindness and justice. Justice, it should be noted, in kabbalistic terminology, is comparable to what other traditions call *karma*. That is to say, cosmic justice is the spiritual law that every action, word, or thought reverberates throughout the universe.

We see here that angels are concentrations of cosmic influence. They do not have dimension, per se, but represent forces that raise consciousness. The ladder symbolizes the journey of higher consciousness, which is implied by the angels' ascending the ladder before descending it.

Jacob "wrestles" with an angel all night, and after this transformation of consciousness is renamed Israel. The word "Israel" is composed of two words in Hebrew: *yashar* and *El. Yashar* means "to go straight"; the word *El* is one of the primary names of God. Thus, Israel can be interpreted to mean "that which yearns to go directly to God." It is implicit in creation that every particle of matter and every being has within it an aspect of Israel, a yearning to return to its source. This idea is reinforced by the teaching that the name Israel does not apply to angels because they are already eternally connected to God.

The Midrash teaches that when the angels realized that they were praising the God of Israel, they began to wonder about who represents Israel. When Adam was born, they asked, " 'Is this the one for whom you are proclaimed God?' God responded, 'No, he is a thief, he stole the forbidden fruit.' Noah? 'No, he drinks too much.' (Noah got drunk after the flood.) Abraham? 'No, his father was an idol worshiper.' Isaac? 'No, he loves his undeserving son Esau.' Jacob? 'Yes, he is the one.' "[94]

So Jacob is the ideal, the force within each of us that constantly pulls us to God. In this we are different from the celestial beings. Angels have no need for this pull because there is nothing pulling them in any other direction. Angels are fully immersed in God, they have no free will. This is true as well for demons.

Jacob represents the highest part of humankind. Our other components are pushed and pulled by angelic and demonic forces. Jacob wrestles and wins. This is one of the most important spiritual teachings of the Torah. In essence, it says that once we clearly recognize the part within us that is connected with God, we can never be defeated.

## Guardian-Angel Practice

1. Find a quiet place where you will not be interrupted for at least thirty minutes. Sit comfortably and focus your mind on the experience of this moment, simply being present. It will be useful for you to have a watch or alarm with a beeper that you can set for thirty minutes. At the end of this meditation, you may need to reorient yourself.

2. Imagine that somewhere quite close is your guardian angel. It can take any form you wish. Let your imagination be free. Your guardian angel can be in a body or not; it can take form or be a thought; it can speak, report through telepathy, or use other nonintellectual means of communication that you will understand. When you are able to sense something close to you, notice how it feels, and describe to yourself what it looks like.

3. Try to communicate with this guardian angel. If you have difficulty with this exercise, let yourself pretend, and examine whatever thoughts come into your mind. Pretending does not matter in this practice; we can learn something from the hidden sparks in every thought. Therefore, however the guardian angel chooses to communicate, find out the following:

   a. When did it come into your life?
   b. What does it do for you at this time?
   c. How often is it with you?
   d. How was it born?
   e. How is it nourished?
   f. How does it make decisions?
   g. What can it do for you in the future?

4. Now, say to it:

  a. What can you tell me about death?
  b. Describe hell to me.
  c. Describe heaven.
  d. Will you be with me after I die?
  e. Will I see relatives or friends who have already died?

5. Finally, say: "Please, give me an experience right now for a few minutes of the heavenly realm after life. Just for a short time, let me experience heaven, deceased loved ones, angelic forces, or the Throne of God. Show me what this is like."

   Allow yourself to completely relax and be carried to the heights of the upper realms. (You will be able to relax more if you remembered to set a timer for thirty minutes.)

6. When you return from your soul voyage, be sure to reconnect with your guardian angel and affirm that you will want to have future conversations. See if it is willing to do so. Then come back to the experience of your body, and after a few deep breaths, open your eyes.

When we are able to establish a relationship with a personal angelic force, we gain access to angelic realms, which are realities that transcend our own. Once we know how to enter this frame of mind, we slowly alter our sense of individual identity and time. For example, our experience exploring heavenly realms—especially in contact with deceased loved ones—quickly opens new possibilities for the meaning of eternal life.

Using techniques such as these visualizations, our ordinary perspectives of reality can be dramatically altered. We can become more attuned to subtle aspects of creation. Some people experience this through conjuring invisible creatures like fairies, gnomes, or elves. Others become sensitive to the delicate messages given by nature that alert us to more than meets the eye. Yet others become attuned to nuances in everyday life that reveal hidden meanings of otherwise mundane events. These are mystical phenomena. Our awareness of them can be nurtured by any spiritual practice that opens us to the possibilities of experiences that transcend the mind.

# GOOD AND EVIL

*R*ebbe Zalman Schachter-Shalomi calls himself "the Last of the Mohicans." With Shlomo gone, Zalman is the final bridge between the old country of tradition and modern post-Holocaust Judaism that chooses to look to the future as much as to the past. Reb Zalman is sometimes referred to as the cybernetic rebbe. His computer skills are well advanced, and his future planning often includes technology yet to be developed.

Still he is an old-time rebbe, filled with hasidic tales and anecdotes that embrace the heart. He teaches in many languages, and even his English is multidimensional. His sharp and unusual insights are invariably provocative and inspiring for audiences.

I remember one particularly powerful tale that opened for me a new understanding of the difficult and complex questions regarding the issue of good and evil.

"My dear friends," he said, "I was recently asked about the question of evil. Is there evil in the world? If so, how can it exist if God is all-powerful and all-good? As many of you know, this is a question that has been problematic for thousands of years. So let me tell you a little story."

Zalman closed his eyes and began to rock back and forth. In his eldering years, he has taken on the role of a spiritual *zayde,* a grandfather, for dozens of rabbis and thousands of students. Stroking his beard, he told this story.

"When the Baal Shem Tov was only five years old, his father, Eliezer, became fatally ill. On the last day of his life, young Israel's father called to the boy and said, 'My son, remember that the Enemy will always be with you, but no matter what happens, the soul within you is pure and whole. The Enemy can neither enter it nor blemish it; your soul belongs to God. Fear no man, and do not fear the Enemy, for God is always with you.' Then Eliezer, the father of the Baal Shem Tov, died.

"Israel's mother had died soon after his birth, when he was circumcised. So now that Israel was orphaned, the people of his village raised him. He was not much of a student, and he constantly gazed out of the classroom window. Actually, he hardly spent any time in the classroom, for he was always wandering in the woods, eating roots and berries and singing with the birds.

"His life outdoors was his primary education. He followed ants, slept in the moss, talked with animals, and most of all, he quietly listened. He listened to the wind, the creak of branches, the flutter of leaves. In his silence he could hear things others could only imagine: spiders weaving, beetles breathing, plants growing. This is how he learned the language of nature.

"At the age of ten, Israel became the helper of the schoolmaster in the village of Horodenka. His job was to guide younger children to the schoolhouse each morning, and back to their homes in the afternoons. He was wonderful with the younger children, and soon they became radiant. Often the children were late arriving at school or going home, but the parents did not mind because the children seemed to be so cheerful; their cheeks were rosy with laughter, for they were constantly singing. The adults were pleased that their children were so happy.

"Only the children knew that Israel took them to and from school by a roundabout way. Rather than walking down the road, the way most people would have, they cut across the fields and through the forest. They called to the chipmunks and whistled with the birds. Most of all, they sang songs to God that Israel taught them.

"The children walked through the woods with young Israel the son of Eliezer, chanting wonderful tunes. And just like us, the children were carried to the heights of joy!

"The heights of joy, indeed. Their songs were so filled with innocent love that they broke through the barriers that guard the heavenly realms. Soon these songs were filling the palaces of the Divine, and a rumor began that the messianic time had come. When Satan, the Enemy, heard this rumor, he instantly appeared in the heavenly courts, and with a fury that caused a great peal of thunder, he cried out, 'Someone in the world is meddling and must be stopped.'

"The prophet Elijah, who has the job of announcing the arrival of the messianic era, came forward and said, 'They are only children.' But in truth, Elijah himself was uncertain. This was the closest the world had ever come. Perhaps the innocent joy of the children actually heralded the arrival of the messianic era.

"Satan scowled at Elijah and demanded of God in a booming voice (Zalman roared), 'Let me challenge these children!'

"God acquiesced (Zalman spoke sweetly), 'Go, challenge.'

"Thus, Satan came to earth and began his search for something or someone that could do his work. As everybody knows, the Enemy can instigate things, but actual deeds must be performed only by living creatures.

"Satan checked the entire insect world, looking for one that would carry his poison into the bloodstream of the boy called Israel. None of the insects would agree. He checked all the animals to find one who would attack Israel. But the boy knew the language of nature, and all the animals refused. There was not a single living thing that would cooperate with the Enemy to harm the boy.

"Finally, Satan found an old man who lived as a charcoal burner. He was one of an extremely rare breed, for he had been born without a soul. His body functioned as a normal body. But there were no feelings whatsoever. He did not know right from wrong. He could not be with human beings. Indeed, when he had been born, his mother had abandoned him in the woods, for she instinctively knew he was more animal than human. He was nursed by a she-bear and learned to survive by eating ants and grubs.

"But he had higher intelligence and would spy on people who camped in the woods. This is how he learned about fire, and from that he learned to make charcoal. He had been spotted on numerous occasions, but was so weird-looking, making such strange sounds, people avoided contact. Yet they pitied him. People who wanted charcoal would take what they needed and in return would leave behind food and drink. He always hid when people came around to take his blackened wood. In this way, the charcoal burner never had to encounter a single human being his entire life.

"This was the perfect creature for the Enemy's purpose, one that could not say no to his evil designs. Even before this time, Satan had sent a demonic power to exercise itself through the charcoal burner's body. On nights that were lit by a full moon, the pathetic brute would grow fur. Then, standing on all fours, he would howl at the moon. People talked about a strange werewolf living in the woods, but they never had the courage to search out the truth.

"Satan, however, had a much more insidious scheme this time than simply turning loose a werewolf. When he found the charcoal burner sleeping, he reached into his body and removed his heart. Then Satan took a piece of his own heart, the heart of evil, the nucleus of the darkest void, and placed this black heart within the empty chest of his creature.

"The next morning, Israel led the singing children across the fields toward the line of trees that marked the forest. As they approached the trees, suddenly a huge, shadowy creature stepped out of the dark forest, snarling, growling, spitting. Its eyes gleamed red; its nostrils sent plumes of orange fog spiraling in the early-morning air. Standing on its hind feet, it was as big as a tree, twenty feet tall. When it spread its hairy arms, it could grasp a team of horses. But most frightening was its wail as it howled and yelped and shrieked.

"The children either fainted dead away or ran for their lives. They scattered in all directions, except for those lying in a heap behind young Israel. Israel was the only one to stand his ground, facing this monster, never moving. After a while, the immense werewolf returned to the woods, and all was quiet once again.

"Each time Israel revived one of his fallen charges, the child screamed upon awakening and ran directly back home. Soon, Israel was standing all alone by the edge of the forest.

"The parents of the village were angry with Israel for having taken the children through the forest. Everyone knew a werewolf lived there, even though they thought that the children were exaggerating its size. Still, it had been foolish to take them into the wooded area. Little did they know that the children were not exaggerating at all.

"Israel told the adults that there was nothing to worry about. In truth, nobody had been hurt. The children had been frightened, that is all. He assured them that the next day they would get over their fear, and this would be a good thing. After a while the parents agreed with Israel and said that he could guide the children the next day.

"The following morning, the children huddled together as they approached the trees that marked the beginning of the woods. Sure enough, at the same place as on the previous day, the hideous creature once again appeared, bellowing and howling at the edge of the tree line. Israel cautioned the children to stand still, or to lie down and cover their faces if they must. He would deal with the creature."

Reb Zalman now got quite still. His eyes were closed, and his rocking was more subtle than before. It seemed as though he were standing before this creature himself. We were the children; he was the warrior facing the unknown. We waited. Nobody moved. Slowly, he began again.

"Israel walked forward alone, placing himself directly between the were-wolf and the children. As he got closer to the beast, it loomed larger and larger, until it was like a black cloud that enveloped him. He was frightened, to be sure, but his dying father's words kept repeating themselves in his mind: 'Do not fear the Enemy, for God is always with you.'

"He kept walking. The werewolf did not move. Closer and closer. He walked up to it. And then the dark cloud descended, and Israel found himself inside the demon. In the murky shadows, he saw its smooth, black heart—the heart of darkness. He reached out, took it in his hands, and stepped backward. Once again, he was outside of the creature's body.

"The heart writhed and pulsated in his hands. It was slippery and repulsive, but Israel kept his grip tight. In this moment, young Israel had in his power the opportunity to destroy the heart of evil. If he did so, the world would never be the same.

"But he noticed a drop of blood trickling down one side of the heart, and his soul was touched to its depths. He could see that this heart was in torment; it was in agony. It too suffered the enormous pain of separation just like everyone else in the world. For even the heart of evil has within it a spark of the Divine, and it too yearns to be returned to its source.

"Thus, the compassion of young Israel opened wide and his only choice was to release the heart. He placed it on the earth. At that moment, the earth split open and swallowed the heart into its depths.

"The next day, the villagers found the body of the charcoal burner. It is said that he had a peaceful look on his tormented face. It is also said that the children never were as happy again, for the heart of darkness continued to do its work. The fear that it left behind was now inside the children, influencing their actions, feelings, and thoughts. Indeed, they were now more like their parents than the innocent children they used to be."

*W*E SAT SILENTLY for many minutes, pondering what we would do if we had the chance to destroy the heart of evil. What kind of world would it be? Reb Zalman rocked from side to side. Then he said, "You see, my friends, while at first this story seems sad—perhaps it would have been better if Israel had destroyed the heart—it is still a story of great optimism. For it teaches us a big lesson. The lesson is that even the heart of Satan has a divine spark; even the heart of evil yearns to be redeemed.

"This is important, because we learn that our job is not to set up a battleground to eradicate evil, but to search out its spark of holiness. Our task is not to destroy but to build; not to hate but to find a place of yielding; not to polarize but to discover the points of commonality so that we can work together. Learn this lesson, dear friends, it will serve you well."

### The Mystical Perspective of Good and Evil

*T*he universe can be viewed as a metaphysical magnet, with one pole called good and the other called evil. Good is represented by God, and evil by Satan. The more we engage in certain activities, the closer we are drawn to God. Of course the opposite is also true.

It is important to keep in mind that we are discussing God and not *Ein Sof. Ein Sof* is beyond good and evil; we must not attribute "goodness" to It. To do so would exclude evil, and this would leave It deficient—which It is not. Of course, it would be just as foolish to call It evil as to call It good. Simply said, *Ein Sof* embraces everything, including the totality of good and evil.

In our reality, in the simplest terms, we say that good is whatever brings us closer to God, and evil whatever draws us away. When an iron filing falls to the surface of a paper that has a magnet beneath it, a number of variables determine whether it will be drawn to the positive side of the magnet or to the negative side. How close does it fall to either side? How strong is the magnet? How much friction (resistance) does the surface of the paper have? What is the shape and smoothness of the filing itself?

We could ask similar questions about ourselves. How close do we feel to God? How strong is the influence of God consciousness in our lives? How easy is it to access awareness of God's presence? How much time do we give ourselves to explore the deeper meanings of life? How much are we conditioned by habitual behavior that makes our lives routine and unconscious?

When we answer these questions, we get a sense of how connected we will be to the magnet of goodness.

Notice that the iron filing itself is neither positive nor negative before it becomes magnetized. We are neither good nor evil in our nature. We are simply the product of the accumulated influences in our lives, plus the most important variable: our free will. We can place ourselves closer or farther away from things, as we choose. These choices, of course, will influence where we end up.

Nothing is ever stationary, because the forces of the universe are constantly tugging and pushing. Higher consciousness, the light of the Divine, is a powerful source of attraction. Yet it is balanced by an influential opposing force. Some name this opposing force the "evil inclination" *(yetzer hara)*.

In human beings, the evil inclination has a wide arsenal at its disposal, including but not limited to lust, greed, status, fame, fortune, popularity, acquisition, cleverness, talent, and power. None of these characteristics is inherently evil, but each has the potential of seduction to draw us deeper into our ego-structures and farther from our connectedness with the Divine.

The constant tension of opposing forces is a universal law. In magnetism it is called positive and negative; in space, up and down, right and left, forward and behind. In the East the principle is described as *yin* and *yang*. In Kabbalah it is called *gevurot* (restrictive powers) and *chasidim* (expansive powers).

The dynamic tension between *gevurot* and *chasidim* appears continually in major biblical motifs: Adam and Eve, Cain and Abel, Abraham and his nephew Lot, Sarah and Hagar, Ishmael and Isaac, Lot and his daughters, Esau and Jacob, Joseph and his brothers, and on it goes. In each instance, the Kabbalist perceives a universal relationship of one representing more the side of restriction, and the other the side of expansion. This cosmic push and pull is the nature of creation and the principle upon which good and evil are based.

## PURIM: NO DIFFERENCE
## BETWEEN GOOD AND EVIL

*P*urim is a holy day derived from the Book of Esther that celebrates the miracle of Jewish survival when the evil Haman tried to commit genocide. In religious circles, Haman is often equated with

Hitler, and some mystical teachers suggest that parallels to the Third Reich can be found in the Book of Esther.

Purim is viewed by Kabbalists as a highly significant holy day, yet it is the most hidden day of celebration; hidden because God's nearness is not as obvious on this day. On Passover, for example, God is quite present, causing miracles to get the Israelites to a new land. On Rosh Hashana and Yom Kippur, the idea of being judged for the coming year makes the presence of the Divine almost palpable. So too Shavuot, with God on Mt. Sinai, giving the Torah; and Sukkot, in which God's protection is a primary theme. But it is well known that God is never mentioned in the Book of Esther.

The celebration of Purim is festive and colorful. Many people dress in costumes; absurdity is the theme of the day. The more ridiculous a statement, the more it is in the spirit of Purim. Major newspapers across Israel print headlines on this day like "Knesset Goes Out of Business," or "Taxes Abolished," or "Leviathan Spotted in Dead Sea." In synagogues everywhere, prayers are sung in strange melodies and the Book of Esther is read with inflections and innuendos that are often riotous.

In Jerusalem during Purim, I usually shopped around from one congregation to another to enjoy the flavor of different people reading the text. Some of the more sedate rabbis go from Jekyll to Hyde on this day. In one of my favorite *shuls*, a large chandelier was ripped out of the ceiling by a highly respected Kabbalah teacher who decided to swing during the middle of the *megillah* reading.

Purim and Simchat Torah, the celebration just after Sukkot, when the cycle of Torah readings begins anew, are among rare occasions when inebriated people are seen on the streets of Jerusalem. Purim's festivities arise from the traditional teaching that we should reach a state of mind in which we cannot tell the difference between the hero of the story, Mordecai, and the arch-villain, Haman.

The source of the idea of becoming intoxicated on Purim comes from a talmudic statement made by Rava that says it is our "obligation" to fill ourselves with the spice of Purim (Rava never mentions wine or alcohol) until we cannot tell the difference between the words "cursed be Haman" from the statement "blessed be Mordecai."[95] Kabbalists point out that the Hebrew words for "blessed be Mordecai *(baruch Mordecai)*" have the value in gematria of 502, which equals the value of the Hebrew words for "cursed be Haman *(arrur Haman).*"[96]

Thus, for Jewish mystics, the words themselves indicate that the archetype of good, represented by Mordecai, and that of evil, represented by Haman, suggest an implicit relationship because they have the same numeric value. This mystical concept is echoed by the fact that the word for serpent *(nahash),* which represents evil incarnate in the Garden of Eden, and the word for messiah *(meshiach)* also have identical gematria.[97]

Rava's teaching is that we must immerse ourselves in the sweet spices of deep wisdom until we have attained an intimate understanding of the nature of good and evil. When we reach a transcendental point in which good and evil overlap to the extent that we can perceive how either can transform into the opposite, the intensity of the experience can be so great that we lose our sense of personal identity. If we do so, we can enter into a world that is called *devekut,* constant awareness of God. But the process of understanding the relationship of good and evil is paradoxical and not as easily accomplished as it sounds.

The essential message that Rava communicates is that good and evil is not a dichotomy at all, is not a split between opposites, but an enclosed universe of curved time and space. A mobius strip gives us a graphic example.[98] If we take a strip of paper and, before attaching the two ends, we twist one of the ends to its opposite side, we have a mobius strip. Now, if we pick up this strip and start drawing a line, we will end up with a line on both sides without ever removing the pencil from the paper. The two sides geometrically are actually one.

This is not to say that good is really evil and that evil is good. Not at all. Rather, that each has the spark of the other, and if pushed too far, this spark can be ignited.

The complexities of the question of evil push us to the limits of reason. At these limits, we must extend beyond the mind and draw upon resources that surpass the intellect. We do this through contemplative exercises, meditation, visualizations, study, and intense devotion. In this process, we move to a new mind-state. Only with a revitalized perspective can we gain insight

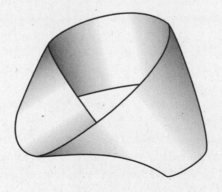

into the issue of good and evil. It is therefore said that when enough people accomplish this understanding of the nature of evil, we will enter a new era of awareness. Indeed, the mystics say that Yom Kippur, the holiest day of the year, is really like Purim, and that Purim itself represents what things will be like in the era of messianic consciousness.[99]

## IS EVIL NECESSARY?

In the traditional paradigm, "good" is doing things the way God wants us to do them, and "evil" is doing things another way. From this perspective, evil is considered to be poison. It is something that should be obliterated. Our task is to avoid it at all costs, but should we encounter it, we must exterminate it.

The mystical teaching of the Baal Shem Tov, however, presents us with a new paradigm. It says that evil has divine nature within it. As the *Zohar* describes, "There is no sphere of the Other Side (evil) that entirely lacks some streak of light from the side of holiness."[100] Rather than destroy it, our task is to uplift it. This adds considerable complexity to the law, for whereas tradition would have it black and white, the mystics say that there are an infinite variety of shadings, each of which can be raised to new heights.

Kabbalah teaches that in reality, evil as we know it can never be eradicated, even if we wanted, for it fulfills a primary function in creation.[101] Without something pulling us away from the Divine, we would be overwhelmed by God, we would lose our free will, and creation could not exist as it does now.

The old paradigm views good and evil as a simple dichotomy: God is in one direction, and Satan is in the other. The new paradigm suggests that God is in every direction, represented by light, and Satan is also everywhere, represented by veils. From this viewpoint, evil is defined as a force that dims the light.

The old way of looking at things is that something is inherently evil. For example, money is the root of all evil; there can be a bad seed that produces an evil outcome; a person can be evil to his or her core; a serpent is evil. The new way says that evil is not a *thing;* rather, it is related to awareness. Money can be good *or* evil, depending upon what we do with it. A bad seed can produce an infected fruit, or it can be converted into something useful. Mold can be discarded as harmful, but certain kinds become penicillin. A person can be evil and even a potential murderer, but there may be a way to bring out a different quality that could benefit humankind. A poisonous serpent may strike at us, or we may milk its venom to use for medicine.

Our tendency is to hold on to old ways of seeing things. It seems easier to clearly define good and evil and to know exactly how to deal with it. Yet difficult questions do not yield easy solutions. And the question of good and evil is one of the most difficult of all.

# Part Three

## HIGHER AWARENESS

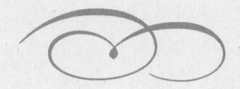

### MA'ASEY MERKEVAH

(The Work of the Chariot)

# THE MYSTICAL
# CHARIOT

Rebbe Nachman of Breslov told the story of a king who discovered that his entire supply of grain had been contaminated by a strange fungus. The grain looked the same and tasted the same as normal grain. There was no way of knowing anything was different, except for one little problem. Anyone who ate this grain lost all contact with true reality. In simple terms, when a person ate this grain, he or she became deranged.

The king and his advisor were the only ones who knew about this problem. They discussed their options. They were rapidly running out of uncontaminated grain, and there were no alternatives for feeding the nation. In two more days they would have to open the contaminated storehouse, or all the people of the kingdom would starve. A new grain supply would not be ready for almost a year, and there was no assurance that even that would be uncontaminated.

At first they thought that they would give the grain to the people but would not eat it themselves, so that at least two people in the kingdom would maintain their sanity. Then the king realized that he would not be able to govern the masses if he did not understand what people were thinking. So he suggested that he should eat the grain but that his advisor should stay sane.

Then the advisor realized that it would be impossible to give advice to the king if he was seeing true reality but the king was not. They understood that in order to rule a kingdom of people with a different reality, they both had to eat the contaminated grain so that they could see things like everyone else. The only hope for the future of the people was the possibility that someone would be able to realize that the world they were experiencing was not the true reality.

So the king and his advisor put out an edict to the people that everyone was required by law to put a mark on their foreheads, and every morning when they saw that mark in the mirror, they were to ask themselves, "What does this mark mean?" Their hope was that people would wonder why everyone was obliged to ask themselves this question, and eventually, at some point in the future, this mark would lead the nation to the realization that their reality was illusory.

This is where the story ends. We never find out what happened because in fact we are still living the story. We have a mysterious mark within us that continually has us asking the questions "Is this real? Is this the way life is supposed to be?"

Rebbe Nachman's story is a wonderful spiritual metaphor. On the fast track of modern life, our natural priorities to attain wisdom and connect with the truth of this existence have been eroded by the demands of the outer world. The nervousness and breathlessness that accompany our constant need for more time have fed an illness of epidemic proportion during the last half of the twentieth century. Not many people yet realize the severity of this affliction. I used to refer to it as the "time demon," but now the world has become infected with what I call TDS, pronounced "tedious," which stands for Time Deficiency Syndrome.

A major symptom of this disease is a distorted sense of priority. Whenever work encroaches upon personal relationships and the relationships take a backseat, this is TDS. Tens of millions of marriages and family relations suffer because so many people have their priorities confused.

Another symptom is the dependency on the "quick fix." Pharmaceutical companies have become rich because we seek instant relief for aching bodies and depressed minds. It is far simpler to take a painkiller than to work with the stress causing the disease.

Perhaps the most prevalent symptom of TDS is a sense of angst and purposelessness. One woman told me that she felt as if she were drowning in a sea of commitments and responsibilities. There was so much to do, and so little time to do it. She could feel herself strangulating, blacking out, going numb, and she was terrified. As a mother, she was a chauffeur, cook, cleaning woman, accountant, washerwoman, and slave; she rarely had time to look inside, to feel her self, and life had lost most of its meaning.

Even though she had a beautiful home, three children, and a husband who was a good provider, she had no sense of joy. From the outside, her life looked wonderful. Inside, it was worse than a nightmare. She could not point to anything specific; it was not like the daily soap operas. She trusted her husband and loved him. It was simply the fact that she had no time to nurture herself, to feed her soul, and she was dying of spiritual malnutrition.

The disease of insufficient time is a malady that eventually leads to self-destruction. When the soul is starved, the body begins to exhibit many unhealthy signs. We are more easily irritated, and we tend to engage in mind-numbing activities. We drink more caffeine to stay awake, and ingest more soporifics to get to sleep. We constantly think about utilizing our time well, and we often try to do three or four things at once. This attempt at "efficiency" comes at a price: we sometimes have to become ill just to get time off to be with ourselves.

Although our life expectancy is increasing, the real question is whether or not the quality of our lives is improving. Does our affluence assure us of deeper connections with the meaning of life? Do we have a higher caliber of relationship with our families? Are we more integrated with nature? Are we genuinely happy?

Some would say that the contaminated grain that we have been ingesting for a long time is called desire. We are acquisitive; we want more of everything: status, fame, fortune, and possessions. We are never satisfied with what we have. Others would say that the grain is power. We want to control things, to be in a position of superiority, to lord over others.

Whatever name we give it, most would agree that this grain is food for the ego rather than the soul; it is food that nurtures our sense of separateness. The more separate we feel, the more we are driven by desire, power, and other motivations that distinguish us from the rest of humanity. In this continuous search for distinction, our priorities shift to meet the requirements of a reality dominated by a materialistic world. Thus we surrender time—the time to sit quietly by a pond and reflect, or the time to absorb ourselves in deeply meaningful activities. We get nervous when there is nothing to do, and we try to fill up every spare moment with activity. Our desires push us onward, while our famished and neglected souls plead with us to stop, reflect, and bring quality into our lives.

We are human vessels that hold the light of awareness to the extent that we are able to contain it. Every move we make that is harmful to ourselves or others creates new leaks in our vessel. Most people have vessels that are so leaky that they can contain only a small fraction of their potential light of awareness.

Yet even though it is a fraction of our potential, the light that each of us has within is the source of our yearning to be connected with the Divine. This light does not have a name. A scientist cannot locate where it dwells. But the quest for truth is an essential part of our makeup. In Rebbe Nachman's story, this yearning is the sign on our foreheads, the sign of sanity.

One of the more important secrets of mystical teaching is hidden in our desire to connect with the Divine. While the intrinsic nature of yearning is to acquire something, get somewhere, or accomplish a goal, we ultimately discover that there is nothing to get and nowhere to go. The yearning itself holds a secret; its own existence is an answer rather than a question. Our delusion is the belief that this yearning is mine or yours; the teaching, however, is that it is an important way we experience the presence of God. In effect, it would be more accurate to say that this is God-ing yearning through each soul for the truth of creation-ing to be realized. In the modern idiom we would say that the medium is the message. Our sanity, our connection with true reality, is in the yearning itself.

But the urge to be with the Divine is not sufficient. Jewish mystics learned long ago that we must involve ourselves in activities that heal our leaky vessels, sealing the cracks one at a time so that our inner lights will become brighter and brighter. By minimizing our harmful acts and directing ourselves to actions, words, and thoughts that raise holy sparks, we gain enormous insight into the nature of our relationship with God.

We can read about possibilities for the future, we can talk about great teachers, we can think about wonderful wisdom-teachings. If, however, we do not begin to accept the responsibility of bringing a new consciousness to humankind, it will continue to elude us. It is up to us to work toward higher awareness right now in whatever way we can.

The process of putting a high priority on raising our own consciousness and that of the world is called the "work of the chariot." The mystical chariot in Judaism is a vehicle to higher awareness.

The third section of this book is designed to be a modern chariot for the coming millennium. It is composed of stories and spiritual exercises that can transform us. Many of the spiritual practices described here are elementary to Judaism. They are the vehicle through which we can fully recognize the limitations of our current level of awareness and find ways to regain a clearer view of reality. The mystical chariot is the key to the attainment of a world-consciousness that is far beyond the level at which we live in these days.

## VEHICLE TO
## HIGHER AWARENESS

In ancient times, before the word "Kabbalah" was used, Jewish mystical practitioners were called *yoredei merkevah,* those who descend in the chariot.[1] They had many other names as well: masters of the mystery, children of the king's palace, those who know wisdom, the understanding ones, those who entered and left in peace, those who reap the field, and so forth.

These mystics were immersed in teachings that collectively were called *ma'asey merkevah,* the work of the chariot. The teachings were closely guarded secrets, and an aura of great reverence was built around *merkevah* mysticism. As an added preventative to keep the secrets hidden, the mystics let it be generally known that dabbling in these secrets would result in serious illness and possible death. Thus, a spell was cast around Jewish mysticism, supported by statements such as the talmudic dictum "The work of the chariot may not be taught to anyone, unless this person is a sage."[2]

The Talmud contains a famous story of four scholars who "entered the *Pardes*" (garden/orchard). The *Pardes* in this context was not an ordinary garden, but a realm of expanded consciousness, some say Paradise. The experience these four sages had was so overwhelming, one died, one became demented, one gave up his faith, and only one, Rabbi Akiva, survived unharmed. This story, which has been part of Jewish folklore for the last fifteen hundred years, is typical of the general attitude in Judaism toward the pursuit of dangerous mystical wisdom.[3] Only in the last half of the twentieth century has the enormous wealth of Jewish mysticism been made more available to the general public.

Essentially, the teachings of the chariot have to do with specific meditative methods that were used for ascending to the highest spiritual realms.[4] Many of these methods were never written down. Some, however, are described in the texts of the *Hekhalot* (palace chambers). These texts refer to practices that, apparently, were performed more than two thousand years ago. The texts describe in detail the architecture of other realities. They give the names of the angelic guardians of the many gates that had to be passed, and they provide actual formulas of magical incantations, primarily variations on names of God, used to alter consciousness.[5]

The father of Ecstatic Kabbalah, Abraham Abulafia (thirteenth century), is known for his contemplative methods for reaching transcendent states of awareness in order to gain God consciousness.[6] Abulafia's technique was to sit in a quiet, darkened room, gazing at letters of the Hebrew alphabet, mentally permutating them into various words and phrases. The intense concentration required to master this technique leads to high states of ecstasy.

Techniques like these that alter states of consciousness fit under the general heading "works of the chariot," the chariot being the medium by which layers of awareness are traversed. Modern mainstream Judaism has all but forgotten these methods. Indeed, many Jewish teachers today believe that contemplative practices are not acceptable in the Jewish world. The emphasis of twentieth-century Judaism has been on the study of Torah, meeting the requirements of Jewish law, and celebrating the holy days. Yet a clear strand in the weave of Jewish fabric has always emphasized contemplative practices and the goal of attaining states of mind categorized as prophesy. It goes all the way back to writings that are included in the Bible.

Ezekiel is viewed in Kabbalah as the prototype of prophetic vision. Although the word "chariot" does not appear in Ezekiel's prophecy, he describes "living creatures" *(hayyot),* about whom he says, "Their appearance and their work was like a wheel within a wheel. Wherever the spirit *(ruach)* went, they (the *hayyot*) moved, and the wheels were lifted up along with them; for the spirit of the living creature was in the wheels."[7]

Later, Ezekiel says that the living creatures he saw were cherubs *(keruvim),* and he uses the same descriptive language as earlier: "When the cherubs moved, the wheels moved with them."[8] The root letters of the Hebrew word for cherub *(krv)* are identical with that of chariot *(rkv).*[9]

In the Holy of Holies of the Temple, the ark was covered in gold. Sculpted over the ark were two golden cherubs with wings outstretched, facing each other. The wings symbolized a boundary within which the Divine Presence would reside when communing with mortals. In the Torah, God says, "And I will meet with you there and will speak with you from above the covering [of the ark], from between the two cherubs which are upon the Ark of the Testimony."[10]

The mystical cherubs atop the ark are viewed by Kabbalists as the source of all prophecy. They represent the archetype of the chariot, and within their wings they enclose the secrets of every experience that removes the veils cloaking our awareness. The mystics teach that once we fully realize the true dimension of the inherent light of consciousness dwelling within each of us, we will attain messianic consciousness, a new way of experiencing reality entirely different from reality as we now know it.[11]

Messianic consciousness is the next plateau of human development. Just as we know that there was some kind of paradigm shift from animal consciousness to prehistoric human consciousness, and that human consciousness has gone through stages measured in various ways, such as social awareness, technological development, or basic intelligence, Jewish mystics say that there is yet to come a major paradigm shift toward an entirely new level of awareness. In this advanced state, pain and suffering as we know it will vanish, war will end, our relationships with one another will dramatically be altered, the lion will lie with the lamb, so to speak, and life will be completely different from anything we might imagine. This is what messianic consciousness is all about.

Today, many of the tools early mystics used in the work of the chariot are forgotten. Many practices as well were relevant only to those times. Methods such as living in great austerity, being hermits, chanting secret names of God, and being meticulous in certain behavior may not work for people in our day, even if we knew the specifics. But many wisdom-teachings have been transmitted in considerable detail through talmudic and midrashic literature. All of them are designed to give us access to our inner light. These are the chariots for our day, and, perhaps more important, the mystics promise they will lead us to a new world.

## METHODS FOR ATTAINING HIGHER AWARENESS

*T*here are three traditional methods for attaining expanded consciousness. Many of them are easy to describe but difficult to master. The first approach is to immerse oneself in activities and studies that have provocative content and meaning. In a Jewish context this means scrutinizing one's own behavior, developing a regular rhythm of study of inspirational works, paying more attention to one's spiritual life, devoting one day a week to spiritual practice, and so forth. This approach, common in many spiritual traditions, is based upon the principle of adaptation. We adapt to our surroundings, the food we eat, the words we read, and the exercises we undertake.[12]

The second approach for raising awareness includes the first, but the direction is much more internal. The main objective of this strategy is for one to gain insight through seclusion, contemplation, and soul-searching. Although we do not see much in modern Judaism that supports withdrawal from the busy world into an environment of personal retreat, the practice of seclusion and deep meditation was commonplace among Jewish mystics.

The third approach is what I call *kavvanah* practice. Normally, the translation of *kavvanah* is "intention." It is discussed in the context of prayer or observance of Jewish law. The sages asked if there is more merit in performing a religious duty when one's intentions were clear, or if the doing of the act itself is more important than what is going on in the person's mind. Obviously the ideal situation is when one's mind and heart are connected with what one is doing. But what if they are not? The sages ultimately divided on the issue, and as with many other aspects of talmudic scholarship, we can make a strong case for either side.

But this idea can be taken one step farther. *Kavvanah* can be applied to everything in our lives. *Kavvanah* comes from the root word *"kavvan,"* which means "to direct, aim, or attune." As we have noted, Jewish mysticism is built upon the idea that every aspect of creation interrelates with every other, resulting in the precept that every thought, word, or action reverberates throughout the entire creation. Moreover, whether a religious obligation or not, every event that arises has the potential for raising holy sparks.

In this context, *kavvanah* suggests a continuous awareness of the implications of everything we do. Therefore, *kavvanah* is of crucial importance to Jewish mystics. Indeed, Kabbalists were often referred to as *mekavvanim*, meaning "those who are always intentional" or, better, "those who are constantly attuning." The Kabbalist wants to have focused awareness in every moment. We can utilize a special practice for developing this awareness, just as we did on page 40.

### THE PATH
#### OF AWARENESS

*H*ere is a simple exercise: Stop reading for five minutes and do nothing but notice when you inhale and exhale. That is all. *Do not think about anything.* Don't count on your fingers, don't use a pad of paper. Simply close your eyes and be aware of your breathing. How long can you maintain this awareness without thinking?

"Thinking" means shifting attention to anything that arises that is not simply the experience of the here and now. A sound is simply a vibration; if we identify it in any way, knowing it is a "bird," "airplane," or whatever, that is a thought. If we ruminate about something that happened, or plan for something about to happen, that is a thought. If we find ourselves wanting more of something, or wishing something would go away, that is a thought. Are you able to notice your breaths for five minutes without having a single thought?

*M*OST PEOPLE DISCOVER that they cannot stop thinking for even one minute at a time. We are not the rulers of our own minds! This is a depressing experience for some people. Thoughts come and go on their own, and there seems to be *nothing* we can do about it.

This being the case, the mind takes us to places throughout the day which may not be related in any way to where we are standing or what we are doing. The mind takes us so fast and so far, we enter our own universes and play out our own dramas time and time again throughout the day. We lose all sense of time and place; we lose all awareness of what is happening around us.

This experience is not an aberration that occurs a couple of times a week or at odd moments of the day. It is happening constantly, hundreds or thousands of times *each hour!* It is like a mind blink. Do you realize how many times you blink your eyes each minute? We don't think about blinking because it is automatic. We don't realize the number of excursions our minds take because we have become accustomed to them. Indeed, we believe that this is the normal condition of the mind. Unfortunately, this belief is profoundly mistaken.

In spiritual traditions around the world, the most elementary contemplative practices are designed to help the student realize the degree to which the mind is out of control. Sitting meditation, mantras, mudras, walking meditation, moving practices such as *t'ai chi chuan*, controlled breathing, silence, prayer, and so forth all quickly reveal the chaotic mind. Every meditator discovers this in the first session. Everyone who has attempted to pray soon comes to the realization that the mind simply will not stay concentrated for long.

Whenever I offer a new class for people who want to learn about meditation, a frequent question that arises in the first or second session is, "My mind is so busy; how do I stop it?" This question is the result of a widespread misunderstanding about meditation and what it is supposed to do. Inexperienced people think that with practice we can stop our busy minds. Unfortunately, this erroneous belief is exacerbated by some meditation teachers and schools who promise that their method will lead to bliss and total control of one's thoughts. This is nonsense.

The students of the Baal Shem Tov heard that there was a great teacher coming to town, and they asked their master permission to learn with this person. The master gave his consent. Then they asked him, "How will we know if he is truly a great teacher?" The Baal Shem Tov replied, "Ask him to advise you on what to do to keep unholy thoughts from disturbing your prayers and your studies." Then the master continued: "If this teacher gives you advice, you will know that he is not worthy. For it is the service of every person to struggle every hour until their death with extraneous thoughts, and time after time to uplift these thoughts and bring them into harmony with the nature of creation."[13]

We use contemplative practices in Judaism to raise the sparks of whatever we engage. The goal is not to attain a state in which no thoughts arise, but to deal quickly and appropriately with whatever comes up, whether they are situations with other people, or thoughts in our minds. As we practice this, we do indeed become much more refined, calmer, and more in control. But we will never eliminate disturbing thoughts entirely until we pass out of these bodies.

The process of learning to deal appropriately with our thoughts and anything we encounter is elementary in all contemplative work. It is the practice of building awareness. In Judaism, it is related to the way we live our lives in general.

There are many ways to bring a heightened degree of *kavvanah* into our lives. One of the more interesting is to spend one day a week trying to do everything opposite from our normal routines. If you usually get up at 7 A.M., try getting up at 6:00 or 6:30 A.M.; do something unusual during the extra time. If you do everything right-handed, try it with your left: combing your hair, brushing your teeth. If you dress yourself right to left, try it left to right. See how many things you can reverse throughout the day without jeopardizing your safety, your job, or causing harm to others.

Much of our loss of awareness is the result of our routinized lives. By forcing ourselves to change our habits once a week, we become aware of little things that we had not noticed before. This new noticing is the key for developing skills on the path of awareness. The more we notice trivial detail, the more we gain in awareness.

Normally we spend only a small fraction of time during the day really being aware, perhaps less than one percent. By doing the simple practice outlined above, and those that follow, we can improve our awareness quotient two or three times, or maybe more. That is still only a tiny percentage of the day. But the rewards are enormous. Life becomes more vivid, colors seem sharper, events are more interesting, situations more provocative, and our own sense of purpose becomes heightened. Moreover, if we are diligent in becoming sensitive on a moment-to-moment basis, a high degree of *mochin de gadlut,* expanded consciousness, can be attained, and we thereby achieve a new plateau in the process of enlightening.

The goal of the following exercises is for us to learn to bring awareness of the Divine to everything we encounter, and thus expand our consciousness. It may be relatively easy for us to do so when wonderful things happen to us; however, we must do likewise in every facet of life. When we are able to experience the presence of God-ing during difficult events, and even in our own disturbing thoughts, we begin to grasp the sparks of holiness within those events or thoughts and raise these sparks back to their source.

Here are two specific practices for raising awareness. Either can be done daily for only twenty minutes, and within a matter of weeks the practitioner will notice changes in his or her awareness. The first one is based on traditional Jewish morning blessings.

## Practicing Kavvanah: *Part 1*

1. Sit very quietly and notice the experience of the body, the feeling of the chest rising and falling. Whenever you notice you are thinking about other things, stop what you are doing, take a couple of deep breaths, and come back to the experience of the body. When you know you are centered, continue with the exercise.

2. Allow yourself to appreciate being here right now, saying to yourself something like: *I am aware. I am free to make choices in life. I am a whole person, and I am thankful for being alive.* Notice your awareness, your sense of wholeness, and how your feeling of thankfulness expresses itself.

3. Now, let yourself focus on your mind, what it does for you, how it works, and its potential. Whisper to yourself something like: *I am grateful to have the ability to see things, to understand, to notice light from dark,*

*truth from falsehood. My mind works, and I am grateful for having insight.* Notice this mind and be grateful for its capacity.

4. Now, let yourself focus on your body. Many of us have poor body images. This is not the time to be body-critical, but rather to be body-positive. Think of the body in its wholeness; be aware of its strengths. Examine the parts that are in good working order. There are thousands of parts that are functioning well, and perhaps a few that are not. Offer thankfulness for the parts that are working.

5. Stand up and walk across the room. Notice as many movements as you can in the process of walking. How does it feel to lift and move your body? Try to notice the ankles, knees, hips, thighs, the feel of clothing on your skin. Notice how the shoulders, arms, back, neck, and head move while walking. Go as slowly as you wish. During this time, give thanks for the ability to move and to feel the movement. Give thanks for each part of the body that does its job while you move.

6. Return to your seat and sit down again. Keep your eyes open and look straight ahead without moving your eyes or your head. How much can you be aware of seeing without moving? Notice that you try to identify and put names to the things that you see. Try simply to notice shapes, colors, shadows, and movement without naming. Notice any sounds that are occurring. Try not to dwell in a sound, but to be aware of each new sound in every moment. Give thanks for the ability to notice so many things and that life can be so full.

7. Now, simply sit quietly and notice everything that happens in each moment, to the best of your ability. You will discover that when the mind is active, you will not be able to remain as aware. Whenever you realize that the mind is thinking, pulling you out of your physical awareness, gently come back to the experience of the body. In time you will be able to observe your thoughts without being overwhelmed by them. Once again, give thanks for the wonderful gift of awareness and the richness of life in each moment.

8. If you do not already have one, get an inexpensive watch that has a timer. Set the timer for approximately, but not exactly, one hour. Throughout the day, whenever the timer beeps, stop what you are

doing as soon as possible and take ten to twenty seconds to conduct a body scan; be aware of what is happening in your own body and around you. You can do this even while you are engaged in another activity. Simply notice where you are, how you are feeling, what is happening in different parts of the body, what sounds are occurring, and your general visual experience. Each time you do this, give thanks for the fullness of the moment, your awareness, and the abundance of life around you.

9. Every few days, change the time by a few minutes so that this meditation never becomes a routine. Soon you will become aware of things spontaneously, without the timer, and your perspective will begin to change. In a matter of a few weeks, you will begin to notice the difference and will be much more present in your body. Being present adds an entirely new dimension to life.

## *Practicing* Kavvanah: *Part 2*

1. Sitting quietly with your eyes open, trying to be very still, allow yourself to *think* about a simple physical movement, like turning the page of a book, reaching to pick something up, scratching an itch, *but don't move.* Simply notice what you want to do, but don't do it.

2. Be aware of the tension of wanting but resisting. At some point you will do something, but do not do it just yet. Your mental task is to observe exactly what must happen in order for your desire to overcome your resistance not to move. Sooner or later you will allow yourself to reach for the book or turn the page. While you are waiting, what thoughts go through your mind; what does it take to get the body moving?

3. At the precise moment you begin to move your hand, are you able to observe your own will that draws you to a particular movement?

4. Now, imagine that every aspect of existence is connected to a power source. If any particular connection were to be cut, that piece of existence would instantly cease. Nothing can exist without being connected to its source. Now, imagining the presence of the source of life, that which empowers all movement, repeat steps 1 to 3 above.

5. When you are ready, reflect on everything around you from the per-spective that the source of creation is constantly present. This source vitalizes every movement and attends every action, word, and thought. Experience this as the presence of the Divine.

6. Set the timer on your watch to go off every two hours or so. Each time it sounds, reflect on the presence of the Divine for as long as you are able to do so. This will become automatic. A major aspect of the enlightening process is bringing the presence of the Divine into as many moments of your life as possible. As in the previous exer-cise, in a few weeks you will begin to experience the change.

The first exercise, being aware of every physical stimulus arising in each moment, is easy to describe but difficult to master. In its early stages we make quick progress. But usually we find the required concentration too much to sustain, and we slip into our old patterns. Actually, as simple as it sounds, this is an advanced method which has parallels in a number of traditions. In Zen Buddhism it is called *shikan-taza,* the state of mind of a highly skilled samu-rai whose life depends upon acute awareness. In Tibetan Buddhism it is called *Dzogchen* or *Mahamudra,*[14] considered to be the most lucid discipline of awareness practice.

The second exercise, sustaining a sense of the continuous spiritual pres-ence of the Divine, is also difficult to maintain. This, however, heightens the sense of the immediacy of the source of life in everything that unfolds, and then slowly melts barriers of self-identity which keep us believing we are separate. Once we fully realize the degree to which we are integrated into the spectrum of awareness—that is, that we are part of it—our perspective of life changes dramatically.

## MENDING THE SOUL, MENDING THE WORLD

*T*he body is composed of different organs and millions of cells. Each cell is a shell containing a soul spark. Therefore, the body is a physi-cal shell for millions of soul sparks.

Who "owns" the physical shell? Is this *my* body? Is that *your* body? And if it is mine, where am I? Where does the "I" live that owns it?

When we follow an inquiry of where, who, what, why, and how in reference to our "selves," we encounter a hall of mirrors that regresses into infinity. We are not our names. We are not our addresses or our telephone numbers. We are not our identities. We are something other than the person we watch as we brush our teeth. We are something more than the accumulation of experiences since birth. Indeed, as we pursue this inquiry, we ultimately come to realize that this body is a caretaker for the source that gives it its light. Our body is not our essence; it is simply physical matter.

We call the accumulated sparks that give life to this physical matter the soul. However, the body does not "own" the soul; the soul does not belong to it, for the soul is simply a vital force that gives existence to physical matter. Just as each soul spark of every living cell in our bodies makes up that which we call our soul, so too do all living souls in the world cumulatively make up part of a universal soul. Indeed, Jewish mysticism teaches that the soul giving us vitality is connected to, and draws sustenance from, a universal soul.

One of the more important concepts in Kabbalah teaches that whatever happens anywhere in the universe reverberates throughout the totality of creation. Thus our lives are affected by what is happening everywhere; moreover, whatever we do in our lives affects everything in the universe.

Perhaps this sounds a bit pretentious. We often view ourselves as inconsequential specks of dust in a universe in which distances are measured in light-years and the number of known stars exceeds the limits of our imagination. This sense of individual limitation is a natural outcome of our linear thought process. As we saw earlier, however, the kabbalistic approach is that awareness is a holistic continuum. Once we enter a holistic frame of reference in which all parts are complete and are replicas of the whole, then everything in the universe, by definition, is integrally connected.[15]

Whereas lower forms of consciousness have limited choice in the way their lives will unfold, human consciousness enters an entirely new level: It can commune with its source, and it has the quality of free will. We can analyze and contemplate the implications of life and can freely move in a chosen direction. Thus we can engage in activities which we calculate will raise our consciousness and the consciousness of those around us.

Each time we do something that raises consciousness, we lift sparks of holiness to new levels. This is called *tikkun ha-nefesh,* mending the soul, and *tikkun ha-olam,* mending the world, bringing it closer to its source. Although initially the ideas of mending the soul and mending the world seem different, in reality they cannot be separated; we cannot raise sparks in ourselves without raising those in the world, and vice versa. Even more important, according to Kabbalah, the process of expanding awareness in ourselves and the world is the fundamental reason for our existence. In fact, when we make no effort to raise our own consciousness and that of the world, we abdicate our humanness.

We can help ourselves and others in many ways. The Talmud says, "These are the precepts whose fruits a person enjoys in this world but whose principle remains intact for him or her in the world to come. They are honoring mother and father, acts of lovingkindness, early attendance at the house of study, hospitality to guests, visiting the sick, providing for a bride, escorting the dead, absorption in prayer, bringing peace to fellow human beings . . ."[16]

Additionally, Jewish mystical teachings describe hundreds of other spiritual practices to mend souls and raise holy sparks. In modern life, we often learn to cultivate negativity. Most radio talk shows epitomize this process. But the sages taught us that negativity separates us from humanity and God by psychologically covering our hearts with a thick membrane. We are strongly advised to avoid thinking negative thoughts or saying negative things about others. Rather, the idea is to cultivate positive states of mind, which we can accomplish in many ways: by spending quality time daily in contemplation, meditation, and prayer; by living skillfully so as to avoid causing harm directly or indirectly to any form of life; by being modest in our own needs, respectful of the needs of others, and satisfied with our station in life; and by letting go of pride and envy.

Of course, these ideas have been around for a long time. As thoughts, they are noble. As actions, they are transformative. When we act on these ideas, we not only make our lives more harmonious, but we bring the world ever closer to messianic consciousness as well.

The mystical side of Judaism has always been focused on the development of spiritual practices that carry us to ever expanded states of awareness. Greater awareness includes more caring about everything that exists: people, animals, plants, and all of nature. Along with greater awareness comes a new love and compassion for all beings. By definition, greater awareness means less self-identity, for the sense of self continuously dissolves as we merge into a vast interconnectedness with all of creation.

In biblical times, the goal of this kind of awareness practice was prophesy. In talmudic times, the goal was to gain access to the mystical chariot so that one could dwell in higher realms of consciousness. In hasidic times, the goal was to annihilate one's sense of self in order to merge with God.

In our times, the goal of raising holy sparks is nothing less than the attainment of messianic consciousness for all of humankind. In this context, the individual cannot be separated from the integrated whole; the collective enlightenment of humanity is clearly as relevant as any focus on individual attainment. Thus, the practices we will discuss not only enhance personal development, they move the totality of creation ever closer to the goal of higher awareness.

## THE MESSIANIC IDEAL

*A*lthough the messianic ideal was never mentioned in the Torah, the sages of the Talmud discussed it in considerable length. They said that seven things were created before the world: the Torah, repentance, the Garden of Eden, *Gehinnom* (hell), the Throne of Glory, the Temple, and the name of the messiah,[17] suggesting that these seven features are pillars upon which the creation of the world depends. Implicit in the discussion is the idea that because the seven things mentioned were created before creation itself, they are realities not limited by time and space.

Talmudic sages believed that the messiah symbolizes the end of evil. Discussions in the Talmud often center upon how things will be in messianic times.[18] However, one sage, Rabbi Zera, pleaded with everyone who calculated the coming of messianic consciousness, saying, "I beg you not to postpone it [by wasting your time and getting confused with conjecture], for it has been taught that three things come when you least expect them: messiah, finding a lost article, and a scorpion."

According to Rabbi Zera, as long as we are anticipating the messiah, our hopes and expectations might have the opposite effect.[19] Rabbi Zera's subtle point was that we must be present in the here and now to reach a level of awareness necessary to attain messianic consciousness. Anticipation, by its nature, pulls us out of the moment.

Actually there are two messiahs in Kabbalah, one from the lineage of Joseph, and the other from the lineage of David. As with all mystical concepts, there are widely divergent predictions regarding how these messiahs manifest, how long they live, and what life will be like when they exist.

Abraham Abulafia felt that the messiah represents the human intellect developed to its highest capacity.[20] Rabbi Levi ben Abraham, who lived during Abulafia's time, compared the messiah of Joseph's lineage with the practical intellect, and the messiah of David's lineage with the speculative intellect.[21]

The Lurianic approach is that the messiah comes through the continuous preparation of humans who constantly raise holy sparks until the world ultimately attains a higher consciousness. At that time the appearance of a being who embodies all of the characteristics of a messiah will be the *result* of this new awareness rather than its herald.[22] Luria's depiction is the context in which messianic consciousness has been presented in this book.

The old model of the messiah suggests that a savior will come in one of two ways: the world will be primed, or the world will be so debased that it will be on the edge of total collapse. In either instance, the messiah is the hope for the future.

These teachings suggest that the messiah is a savior. This savior has a presence that emanates peace, which affects everyone and everything. A simple meditation gives us insight into what this experience might be like.

You may want to try this. Give yourself a few minutes, and imagine what would happen if the messiah were to come into the room. Reflect on an event of the past day or two, and imagine how this event might have unfolded had the messiah been present. How would you have acted? How would others have acted? How would you have felt? Close your eyes for a few minutes, and think about this.

WHEN WE IMAGINE the presence of the messiah, typically we think about things like more lovingkindness, great gentleness, pure calmness, extraordinary peacefulness, deep understanding, infinite caring, enormous sympathy, and so forth. The presence of the messiah is a dream hidden in all of our hearts.

The question we must ask ourselves, however, is this: "What are we waiting for?"

The new paradigm suggests that while waiting for something to happen, we are unbalanced, constantly "leaning into the future." Whenever we dwell on the future, we miss what is happening right now. As Rabbi Zera indicated, whenever we conjecture about the coming of the messiah, we are drawn away from the essential element required for messianic consciousness, which is to be fully present in the here and now.

It is not difficult to stumble into the pitfall of missing what is happening as we plan for the future. In their eldering years, my dear parents, God rest their souls, took a number of vacations to foreign countries and sites they had dreamed about all of their lives. While traveling, anxious to be on time for connections, worried about hotel reservations and where they were going to eat their next meal, they were constantly preparing for what was going to happen. They would be ready hours before a scheduled departure, and often would not sleep the previous night for fear of missing the alarm. They prided themselves for never missing a train or airplane, but, of course, they often did not appreciate where they were. Only photographs after the fact brought them back to an experience, and even then they frequently disagreed about where the photos had been taken.

We all do this in one way or another. We say to ourselves, "When I retire, I am going to have more quality in my life"; "When the kids leave home, we will have time to really enjoy things"; "When I finish this task, I will feel much better." We are leaning into the future, filling ourselves with hope.

These expectations for the future desensitize us to what is happening right now. We shut off, attempting to avoid the discomforts of our present experience by contemplating what we hope or expect to be a better future. But the truth is that although each nuisance in our lives eventually ends, a new one is certain to arise. As a result of ignoring this fact, many of us spend our lives in numbness and denial, waiting for the problems and difficulties of life to end.

Waiting is self-defeating. We have whatever we need. This realization often is hidden behind veils, but as we peel these veils away through our awareness practices and our actions to improve ourselves and the world, we discover that everything we ever wanted is right here.

Messianic consciousness is not something that comes in the future; it is our intrinsic nature. It is our birthright, available to all of us here and now. Although obscured over the millennia by clouds of ignorance, its light continues to shine in the divine sparks at the core of our being. Despite the fact that this ideal seems to be unreachable, the Kabbalah teaches that all we need do is make a place in ourselves for higher consciousness, and immediately we will be filled with new luminescence. As the Holy One says, "Offer me an opening no bigger than the eye of a needle, and I will widen it into openings through which wagons and carriages can pass."[23]

# THE PATH OF
# THE *TZADDIK*

## (Jewish Enlightenment)

*I*n guiding students on the ultimate path of awareness, the Talmud says in the name of Rabbi Phinehas ben Jair, "Study leads to precision, precision leads to watchfulness, watchfulness leads to cleanliness, cleanliness leads to restraint, restraint leads to purity, purity leads to saintliness, saintliness leads to humility, humility leads to fear of sin, fear of sin leads to holiness, holiness leads to the holy spirit (prophecy), and the holy spirit leads to life eternal."[24]

Each of these twelve steps represents an inclusive spiritual process that contains many elements of practice. A well-known eighteenth-century Kabbalist, Moshe Chayim Luzzatto, wrote an entire book on this subject alone.[25] In essence, it describes in detail what might be called the Jewish path of enlightenment.

In our modern vernacular, adding contemplative tools to traditional Jewish teaching, a similar enlightenment model could be stated: Learning leads to respect, respect leads to generosity, generosity leads to acts of lovingkindness, acts of lovingkindness lead to moderation in living, moderation in living leads to purity of thought, purity of thought leads to joy, joy leads to selflessness, selflessness leads to awe, awe leads to equanimity, equanimity leads to extraordinary mind-states, and extraordinary mind-states lead to life eternal (God consciousness).

Following this model, I have combined twelve Jewish paths of heightened awareness with spiritual exercises, meditations, and hasidic tales. In this way, one not only sees what the ladder looks like, but also learns how to ascend it. Anyone wishing to explore the Jewish enlightenment path will be able to develop a personal program of specific practices.

# 1. The Path of Learning

Study *(Talmud Torah)* is the first rung on the ladder—the base from which everything ascends. The essential idea of this foundational practice is to reframe our priorities. In this context, study means that we dedicate a certain amount of time in our lives to the pursuit of spiritual wisdom. The act of bringing our consciousness out of mundane arenas into the study of spiritual texts directly affects the way we see things in the world. Even if we give only thirty to forty-five minutes a day to this effort, we quickly see results.

When used more extensively, the path of learning can be a meditative process. Just as musicians, athletes, and others who practice specialized skills for many hours a day experience altered states of awareness, so too does one experience a new way of looking at things after spending hours in spiritual study.

When we focus on a task day after day, it affects our view of the world. If what we are doing is on a spiritually evolved level, it helps us; if it is not, we get a distorted perspective of things. Thus, in the broadest terms, the path of learning is the process of refining our awareness by dedicating time each day to the study of uplifting material.

When we read inspirational books, our hearts soften. This path of practice, however, requires more than an occasional book. Rather, it requires that we assume the habit of daily study and thereby continuously add spiritual and mystical sweetener to our lives. From this base, we can move to far more comprehensive practices.

## 2. THE PATH OF
## RESPECT

*T*he next level is to develop the quality of precision *(zhiruth)*, which comes from realizing that there are no casual actions, words, or thoughts. Therefore, we pay close attention to everything we do. The implication of being precise is that we have an underlying basis to differentiate beneficial acts from those that are harmful. This ability to distinguish is based upon study and careful observation. It is said that three things detract from our ability to develop precision in our lives: too much worldly involvement, too much frivolity, and too much association with people in realms of lower consciousness.[26]

One of the best spiritual practices for cultivating precision is to develop great care in the use of speech. Before we go into detail, let us enjoy a wonderful hasidic tale that emphasizes this point.

## *Yosele the Holy Miser*

Once a beggar named Koppel came to a strange city and went straight to the best section in town, looking for money. He saw a big, beautiful house, and rang the bell. The owner of the house, Yosele, invited him in. They sat for a while, having tea and cake, discussing many things. Finally, Yosele asked Koppel, the beggar, what he wanted. It should be no mystery; Koppel said that he needed some money to get a place to stay and food.

Well, the change in Yosele was from day to night. His face turned dark with anger. He yelled a few obscenities at Koppel and then threw him out into the street, telling him never to return.

Koppel brushed himself off and went to the town's spiritual leader, Rabbi Kalman. The good rabbi gave Koppel advice on where to go and where not to go. One thing for sure, he said, never try to get anything out of the town miser who lived in a big house in the wealthy section and whose name was Yosele.

"I've met him already," said Koppel.

"So, *nu?*" asked the rabbi.

"You are correct. He was pleasant at first. But when I asked for money, I was out on my head."

"That is the way it is with him," Kalman said. "He seems nice, but, *oy vey,* what a temper!"

So, Koppel, the beggar, followed the rabbi's advice and found a place to live. He must have done something right because the next Friday morning when he awoke, he discovered an envelope under the door with the exact amount of money needed to buy food for Shabbat and to carry him through the week.

The following Friday morning, the same thing happened again. So it went for many months. Every Friday morning an anonymous friend slipped money under his door. In this way, all went well for Koppel, the beggar.

One day Rabbi Kalman heard that Yosele the miser was quite ill and there was a good chance that he would die. The kindly rabbi went to visit Yosele. He talked with the dying man and said, "Yosele, your life may be ending soon, yet there is still time for you to make amends. The people in this town are angry with you, and you do not have a single friend. You don't even have someone to bury you. Why don't you do something about it?"

Yosele turned his head and looked directly into the rabbi's eyes. "What do you think I should do?" he asked.

Rabbi Kalman hemmed and hawed for a while and then stuttered with great anxiety, "Maybe, maybe you should think about . . . uh, giving some *tzeddakah* (charity)." The rabbi hurriedly blurted out, "As you know and everybody knows, *tzeddakah* opens the gates of heaven. Really . . ." but he could go on no longer because Yosele had closed his eyes and turned his head away.

As Rabbi Kalman departed, he thought to himself sadly, *Once a miser, always a miser.*

Yosele died. Because he had no friends, and no money could be found in his entire house, he received a pauper's burial. Just a hole in the ground without a marker.

The next Friday morning, Koppel, the beggar, was astonished to discover no envelope under his door. Nothing. He felt his stomach get a little queasy. Shabbat was coming, and he had no money. He had grown comfortable over the months and had almost forgotten the art of begging. What was he to do?

Koppel ran over to Rabbi Kalman's house. When he arrived, what a hub-bub! The living room was filled with all of the beggars in town. Every one of them had the same story as Koppel. Their Friday-morning anonymous donation was missing. After a while of scratching their heads, they came to the conclusion that only one person in town could have been the anonymous donor: Yosele, the miser.

They decided to pool their meager resources and give Yosele a proper burial, which they did the following Sunday. Rabbi Kalman officiated. At the end of the ceremony, he felt faint and lay down in the grass. He went into a deep sleep, and dreamed. In his dream he saw Yosele. Rabbi Kalman apologized profusely for allowing him to be buried as a pauper, and even more for having had derogatory thoughts.

"Don't worry about me," said Yosele, "I was well attended at my burial. You see, Abraham came, and Moses came as well. So did David, and Isaac, and Jacob. Everybody came. It was a fine funeral."

"So, what can we do for you, Yosele?" asked the rabbi. "We all are so embarrassed."

Yosele answered, "Truly, there is nothing. Heaven has everything." He continued, somewhat poignantly, "I must say, however, that there is something I miss. Here I cannot help anyone; after all, it is heaven. But I don't get the feeling I used to have before sunrise on Friday mornings when I delivered those envelopes. That time is over for me now. I just want you to know that there are some things even more important than heaven!"

Not long after he was buried, the townspeople set up a marker for the grave, which read: "Here lies Yosele, the Holy Miser."


*T*HE PATH OF respect teaches us that we are never in a position to judge another person. Yosele had his way of doing things. He needed to be anonymous, and the only way he knew to do so was to feign anger when people asked for money. So the entire town turned against him. Even the rabbi had doubting thoughts. They spoke harshly about him behind his back, and left him isolated. If only they had known.

Many hasidic tales have a similar theme, in which someone who is an outcast is really a saint in disguise. The people around this person usually say or do disrespectful things. They discover only after the fact that they missed the opportunity to learn the secrets of the universe.

But more important than what was missed is the weight of darkness that rests on people when they have negative thoughts about others. When we gossip about somebody, we may think we are having fun at the other person's expense, but usually we have a peculiar discomfort and we hope that nobody is around the corner, listening. In fact, when a friend occasionally finds out that we gossiped about her or him, our embarrassment is enormous.

Gossip is subtle and dangerous. A word misused can destroy a person's reputation in seconds; it can ruin a life. A word planted in someone's mind can poison a relationship forever.

Most gossip is idle. We pass the time talking about others, not intending to be malicious. It is the way we convey information. But the teaching of *lashon hara*, "evil tongue" (derogatory or damaging speech), suggests that almost anything said about a third party has the capability of injuring that person on a subtle level, as well as oneself.

Virtually every business office, every organized group, and every spiritual community is riddled with little wormholes of gossip. We spend an enormous amount of time talking about one another. Dozens of times people have come to me in tears, saying, "She said that he said that she said . . . such and such about me." Of course, when we trace back to the original source, invariably the accused will say, "I never said such a thing!"

Derogatory speech is so common, we usually do not realize what we are doing even after the fact. We are so accustomed to idle gossip in ordinary conversation, we fail to appreciate what it does to us and what it can do to others.

In the spiritual practice of paying attention to the use of language, we watch what we talk about and especially what we say about people. The ideal is to minimize, if not eliminate, all negative conversations about people, whether we know these people or not.

Any attempt to censor our own speech is an interesting process. One teacher said that when he tried to exclude references to other people in his normal conversation, he discovered that *90 percent* of his everyday speech was in one way or another connected with gossip. That is to say, he noted that the subject of conversation led to gossip about somebody nine out of ten times. Even if the ratio for you is only five out of ten, it means that half of the things you talk about will soon lead to the subject of other people.

Unskillful speech about others reverses the process of raising sparks: we don't raise them, we lower them; we encapsulate holy sparks in shells of misinformation, distortion, fabrication, and simple misunderstanding. Everyone I know, including myself, is guilty of this. We all talk about others, and we all are subjects of damaging speech at one time or another, when others talk about us.

The following is a spiritual exercise for mending our own souls and mending the world at the same time. Those who are able to work with this practice will be startled to discover how much it applies to our daily lives.

## Practicing Respect

1. Starting now, each time you finish talking with someone, try to take a minute or two to reflect on the topic of the conversation. Try to remember any individuals mentioned during the conversation. What was said about them? How do you feel about each person? Did you bring this person up in the conversation, or did someone else bring her or him in? Simply notice this, and if you have time, take a few notes so that you can remember.

2. After doing the reflections in step 1 for a while, you will become more sensitized to the subject. Notice how the presence of an individual gets drawn into the conversation. Does it simply happen? Is there usually an association that draws the person in? How does the energy of the conversation alter when the name is brought up? Notice if you are feeling completely at ease, or if there is tension when discussing others. Take more notes when you have time.

3. In a few weeks, you will be ready to do some self-censoring. During a conversation, when you feel the urge to bring up somebody's name, try to hold back. This will feel uncomfortable at first. Experiment with this. Occasionally you will bring up the name anyway. Notice what happens to the conversation on the subtlest level you can observe. Try to censor yourself as often as you can.

4. In a few more weeks, you will gain some success in self-censoring. Now the process becomes more difficult. You will notice others introducing names into your conversations. Try to gently guide the conversation in a new direction without offending other participants. If you are able to do so, move quickly off the subject or try to ignore the introduction of a third party. This is not easy, and it takes practice. If the subtle method does not work, a more direct approach can be tried gently: "I'd rather not talk about this person right now, if you don't mind. Let's move on."

The habit of moderate gossip is ingrained in all of us. Once we are able to minimize or eliminate gossip, we discover a fresh breeze in our communications. We talk less and cover more. However, when we roast someone with gossip, we cannot help but get smudged. Everyone becomes contaminated by the ashes of gossip—the people about whom we are speaking, everyone who is listening, and the person gossiping. It affects the way we will think about the person and how we will relate to this person from that time on.

Although we might feel titillated in the moment, we usually end up feeling some tightness in our hearts, for we know that a soul is being harmed by this kind of talk. Thus, gaining skills in this arena can be of enormous benefit to the world. It is said that learning to master skillful speech is one of the more fulfilling paths of spiritual development available to us.

## 3. The Path
### of Generosity

fter developing skills in the level of precision, we turn to the quality that the ancients called watchfulness *(zrizuth)*. This is sometimes translated as zeal, but is primarily focused on the characteristics of bright awareness and active interest. For example, we can perform a service for someone halfheartedly, or we can do it full of eagerness and good will.

When we contemplate the effects of our good deeds on the continuous unfolding of creation, realizing how we are copartners in this process, we develop the aspect of active interest. On the other hand, when we have aversions to any task and prefer our personal comfort, we lose this sense of interest.[27]

One of the clearer expressions of active interest is generosity. Implicit in generosity is caring. Each time we surrender possessions, we release ourselves a bit more from the clutter of self-identity, which makes us feel separated from the world and ultimately alienated.

The giving of *tzeddakah* (charity) is viewed by the Talmud as one of the more important acts in the human repertoire for raising sparks. It makes this quite clear: "Ten strong things have been created in the world. Rock is hard, but iron smashes it. Iron is hard, but fire softens it. Fire is hard, but water extinguishes it. Water is strong, but clouds carry it. Clouds are strong, but wind scatters them. Wind is strong, but the body breathes it. The body is strong, but fear defeats it. Fear is strong, but wine expels it. Wine is strong, but sleep dissipates it. Death is stronger than all, and *tzeddakah* saves us from death, as it is written, '*Tzeddakah* delivers from death' (Proverbs 10:2)."[28]

The idea that *tzeddakah* saves us from death is treated literally and figuratively. Literally, when anyone is seriously ill, their families reach to the bottoms of their pocketbooks and give to anyone in need to the maximum of their capacity. This is based on the idea we learned earlier that four things can change fate: charity, prayer, changing our ways, and changing our names.

Figuratively, the power of *tzeddakah* to overwhelm death is derived from the mystical view that a time will come when we relate to death in an entirely different way. *Tzeddakah,* understood as righteousness through which the Divine Will is expressed, in the truest sense requires selflessness. And selflessness implies less concern about death because of the realization that something beyond this body is interconnected with all of creation. Thus, selfless giving, *tzeddakah,* by definition, overwhelms death.

## Tzeddakah *and the* Shnorrer

While living in Jerusalem, I often went to the Western Wall for morning prayers. I carried with me ritual prayer articles, *tallit* and *tefillin*, and I always filled my pockets with coins. The Western Wall is a magnet that draws a wide variety of *shnorrers*,[29] people who solicit all passersby for charity.

Tourists are often irritated by *shnorrers* because there seems to be no sense of propriety where *shnorr*ing is involved. One might be standing before the Wall with closed eyes, in the middle of a prayer, when an insistent tug at the elbow signals the arrival of a another *shnorrer.* Sometimes the *shnorrer* will glance at the open page of your prayer book to ascertain whether or not you are in the section called the Amida, a central prayer which requires quiet concentration. But this is not always the case, for I was interrupted countless times during silent prayers.

My method at the time was to quickly withdraw a coin from my pocket and hand it over, often without even turning to see the face of the person receiving this *tzeddakah*. In this way I was fulfilling my obligation while being minimally distracted. Many old-timers do the same.

I have had quite a few experiences involving remarkable *shnorrers*. Just after I ran out of coins one day before the end of my prayers, a *shnorrer* who was at the Wall every morning came to me and put out his hand. I asked if he had change for a fifty-sheckel note, worth about forty dollars at the time. He proceeded to reach into his pocket and pull out a wad of bills that clearly was worth hundreds of sheckels.

I laughed, knowing that a tourist would have thought that this *shnorrer* was a fake. What gall! What *chutzpah!* The tourist would think that this guy lived in a mansion and probably had millions in his mattress. But the truth was that this one *shnorrer* raised funds for more than two dozen families. I knew for a fact that he lived in a one-room hovel and that most of those who were close to him, particularly the families he supported, believed him to be the saintliest person in their lives.

One tourist commented to me that he was upset because he felt that too many *shnorrers* were arrogant and seemed to be self-righteous. Some *shnorrers* even gave him the feeling that they were doing him a favor! This tourist represented many people who assume that a person begging for money should be appropriately submissive and demonstratively appreciative. But the Talmud teaches: "He who causes others to do good things is greater than the doer,"[30] and there is no reason for someone begging to feel any less a person than his benefactor.

The *Zohar* makes an even stronger case. It says, "When the Holy One loves someone, It sends this person a gift in the shape of a poor person, so that the loved one should perform a good deed through giving charity. Through this merit, the giver of charity will draw to himself or herself a 'cord of grace,' from the universal source of lovingkindness, which will wind around his or her head and imprint a mark on the forehead so that when punishment falls on the world, the destroying angel will notice the mark and leave him or her alone."[31] From this perspective, if we are in a position to be donors, we should be grateful whenever we have an opportunity to give charity.

As with the beggar mentioned above, *shnorrers* themselves are regular givers. I remember a time when two *shnorrers* walked into a study hall of a *yeshiva* during the afternoon prayer session just before the High Holy Days. This is a time when giving increases, when people build up spiritual merit in preparation for the upcoming heavenly judgment day. I recognized one of the beggars. He always seemed a little loony to me, especially because his right eye wandered in one direction while the left eye stared directly ahead. This walleyed look was winsome, and I noticed that people were always gentle with him. Almost everyone gave him money. His approach was childlike, shy, and because of his strange gaze, he seemed to be looking at your face and the back of your head simultaneously.

The other beggar was grim, shaggy, and depressed. He shuffled around the room, barely pausing, his half-opened hand trembling a little out of reach. He was not as successful as his colleague in raising money. Indeed, when both had circled the study hall, the loony one had a fistful of coins, while the grim one had a meager sum clasped tightly in his palm.

At that point, the loony *shnorrer* walked over to his buddy, glanced at the paltry sum he had received, and tithed out of his own collections a wad of money for his friend. Actually, they may not have been friends. I had seen each of them alone, but this was the only time I ever saw them together. Nonetheless, this was one of the most poignant acts of pure charity I had ever seen.

After some time, I began to look forward to giving *tzeddakah* whenever possible, and especially during prayers. I realized that the process of giving was often a more profound spiritual experience than prayer itself. I began to notice what was in my mind when the interruption occurred, as if God were calling to me through the medium of this *shnorrer.*

I noticed as well how the intrusion set an entirely new spin to my thought process. Initially, I was irritated when interrupted, which, I later realized, was a reflection of my sense of separateness and an illusion of control. That is to say, when I was irritated, I had the feeling that some "otherness" had stepped into my world and had disturbed "my" consciousness. I experienced this feeling as tightness in my heart and mind. After a while, deciding to follow the practice of indiscriminate giving, trying never to pass a beggar without handing him or her a coin, I found that my mind became less contracted and my heart was far more open. This experience transformed the way I view myself as an individual, how I relate to my own possessions, and how I experience my own role as a vehicle through which divine providence acts.

## Selfless Giving

The Jewish philosopher Maimonides described a number of ways to give charity, teaching that it is preferable to be anonymous. One of the higher forms of charity, he noted, is to help a person stand on his or her own rather than become dependent upon the good will of others.

Rebbe Nachman of Breslov said, "Charity has the power to widen the entrance to holiness. When a person wants to embark upon a certain path of devotion, he or she first needs to make an opening in order to enter this new path. This is why all beginnings are difficult. But giving charity makes the entrance wider."[32]

Choygam Trungpa Rinpoche, a Tibetan master who, before he died in 1987, influenced thousands of followers in North America, once was asked to describe the most important quality needed for enlightenment. He responded with one word: generosity. In the Buddhist world, this is called *dana,* selfless giving. In Judaism, it is called *tzeddakah.*

The giving of *tzeddakah* is important on many levels. On the physical plane, it balances the world's resources; on the emotional level, it is one of the better methods for opening the heart; in the intellectual world, it breaks down ideological constructs as the lines between differences begin to blur. But the most profound consequence of constantly giving *tzeddakah* is the subtle disintegration of the boundaries that define the self as separate from others.

At first, giving charity is distinctly experienced as a subject-object phenomenon. *I* am giving to *you*. After a while, however, the benefit of giving equals the benefit of receiving, and all is connected in a closed loop. Some are nourished though the opportunity of giving; others through that of receiving.

The idea of *tzeddakah* adds an important dimension to our normal approach to charity. *Tzeddakah,* as righteousness, suggests that there is more involved than one person simply helping another.

The sages asked whether it is better to give from the heart or out of obligation. Imagine a scenario in which a person who has just closed a business deal is walking down the street. This person has made a profit of a hundred dollars and is obligated to tithe 10 percent for *tzeddakah*. The person encounters a filthy, obnoxious, thankless beggar and gives him ten dollars. The beggar sneers at the money, spits, and turns away.

Another person, who has already met her *tzeddakah* obligations for the week, walks down the street. She sees a woman beggar holding a child. Her heart is touched. She pulls a few dollars out of her purse and gives it to the woman begging. The beggar is enormously grateful and smiles deeply as she pockets the money.

Which of the two is the highest form of *tzeddakah*?

Although we might think that giving from the heart is a deeper expression of authentic giving, the sages taught that the one who gave out of obligation was actually performing the higher level of *tzeddakah*. Why? Because he was not personally involved. He was simply acting as a conduit for the *tzeddakah*. He understood that possession and ownership are transient in this ephemeral state we call life. Receiving and giving follow laws of nature and destiny. Giving a part of our wealth when we are able to do so is a natural law of maintaining a balance in the universe.[33]

The woman, on the other hand, felt that she, herself, was doing something. She was personally satisfied about helping a beggar in need. She had already fulfilled her obligations; this was something extra. And so there was just the slightest tarnish to her act: a touch of personal ego along with the will of God. Obviously, there is nothing wrong with what she did. Indeed, it was a wonderful, meritorious act. Give it a 9.9 on a 10-point scale. Everyone is encouraged to give from her or his heart.

This illustration simply points out that the idea of *tzeddakah,* righteousness, includes in it the sense that we are vehicles through which the Divine Will can be expressed. When the will of God is invoked, rather than when our personal wills are the motivating force, the righteousness is purer.

The Talmud advises, "If a person is anxious to give charity, the Holy One will furnish the money to do so."[34] This idea completely reverses our normal survival mechanism that says, "Take care of me first." It suggests that if one is really concerned more about helping others than oneself, the means will be found.[35]

## Practicing Generosity

1. Take one dollar and fold it a few times. Put a paper clip on it and keep it handy in your pocket or purse. The next time you see a stranger who is asking for charity, no matter what he or she looks like, give away this dollar. Try to have a dollar in your pocket each day to give away.

2. Write a check for five or ten dollars, leaving the name blank. Put it on your fridge with a magnet so that you will be constantly reminded of it. The next letter or advertisement you see asking for charity, fill in the name and send this check. Try to do this at least once a month.

3. Calculate your net income. Determine a percentage that you intend to give away. Make the percentage low enough that you can actually fulfill your commitment. (Some traditions, including Judaism, suggest 10 percent, but for many people these days, this is too much of a burden. Even 1 percent is sufficient for this practice. The important thing is to decide, and then to do it!)

4. Whenever you gamble, buy a lottery ticket, or receive any kind of financial windfall, commit to giving to charity at least 10 percent of the found money. If you win, send the charity off within one or two days. Don't delay.

5. When you know someone who seriously needs money but is too proud to ask for it, find a way to send a significant donation anonymously. You can have a messenger deliver an envelope of cash, or you can have a cashier's check drawn and request not to have your name

on the check, and then send it without a return address. Once sent, forget about it. Never tell the person, or anyone else, about what you have done. Never.

6. Each time you receive your paycheck or any other money, always reflect upon the conditions that allowed that money to come in: your mental and physical health, your family support, your background and training, your business relationships, the economy, the weather, and most important, the presence or absence of God-given events. This reflection and contemplation are vital parts of coming to terms with what ownership and property are all about, and how tenuous is our personal wealth.

## 4. THE PATH
## OF LOVINGKINDNESS

*T*he path of generosity was enormously respected by the sages. The Talmud says, however, that "Our rabbis taught that lovingkindness (*gemulit chesed*) is superior to charity in three ways. 1) Charity can be done only with one's possessions, while lovingkindness can be done with one's person and one's possessions. 2) Charity can be given only to the poor, while lovingkindness can be given to both rich and poor. 3) Charity can be given to the living only, while lovingkindness can be done both for the living and the dead."[36]

Acts of lovingkindness are far more subtle than charity; they require a letting-go of more than property. This letting-go might come easily and naturally. A person may trip and fall in the street, particularly a child or an older person, and we automatically hurry to their aid without a moment's hesitation. But letting go might also come with considerable resistance. Our elderly parent may call on the telephone for the umpteenth time to ask a favor. We are busy. We have our own lives to lead. We resent being a primary caretaker. Still, Mom needs help, she sacrificed many times, and who else is there for her? So we let go and fit the errand into our lives.

In many ways, charity is simpler, cleaner, and easier than lovingkindness. Once we hand it over, we are done with it. However, there is never an end to acts of lovingkindness. Given the extent to which we inflict pain on one another, the world has an almost insatiable need for lovingkindness.

One's social status does not matter. Rich and poor alike yearn for a loving touch. Who does not respond to a genuine, heartfelt smile? Whose soul does not warm when given a simple little gift, even if it costs only a dime?

Acts of lovingkindness are not just for humans, by the way. Our kind treatment of animals comes under the category "pain of living animals" *(tza'ar ba'alei chayyim)*. It is a talmudic edict that we pay special attention to domestic animals so that they are not caused undue suffering. We must feed our animals before ourselves,[37] and we must relieve an animal's pain even if it means breaking the Shabbat laws.[38] One is not permitted to purchase an animal unless he or she has the means to take care of it.[39] Causing an animal to suffer, or imposing a blemish, is also forbidden.[40] Hunting in general is frowned upon, since the kosher laws do not allow the consumption of meat from a *treif* (torn) animal, which usually results when an animal is killed by a hunter.[41]

What does it mean that acts of kindness can be done for the dead? The talmudic commentary says that offering tributes at a funeral, accompanying a person to the grave, and saying blessings over the dead are acts that lift the sparks of the soul of the deceased in other realms. Moreover, as we will see in the chapters on death, we can help the soul of someone deceased with kabbalistic meditation techniques.

Acts of lovingkindness do not have to be overt. A person may not even realize that he or she has done something. We can help someone indirectly by acting as an intermediary; we can casually hint to another at something we know will help a person. We can pray for the person in the quiet of our own hearts. "When we concentrate mind and heart on the Source of Sources, blessings can be drawn from the depths of the 'cistern,' the Source of Life, the stream from Eden. Prayer draws this blessing from above to below."[42]

The mystical approach to each act of lovingkindness is that it is the binding force that holds the world together. It is said: "Sometimes it happens that the world is exactly balanced between people whose good deeds bring life and those whose evil deeds bring death. Then, one righteous person can turn the scale and the world is saved. But should it ever occur that one wicked person is left, then the world would be destroyed."[43] The *Zohar* goes one step further and asserts that "a person should always imagine that the fate of the whole world depends upon his or her actions."[44]

In the talmudic process we always question ourselves, testing the deeper meanings of things. What does it mean that our actions are so important? Isn't it said in Ecclesiastes, "All is futility! What profit does a person have of all their labors under the sun?[45] . . . The work that was done under the sun was grievous to me; all is futility and striving after wind"[46]? If this is so, what do our little acts of lovingkindness accomplish after all?

In response, the *Zohar* says that "futility, in this case, refers to acts of humans that are done 'under the sun.' However, righteousness and lovingkindness are acts done 'above the sun.' "[47] These acts work in this world and transcend it at the same time. From the perspective of this world, history seems to repeat itself. But the transcendent perspective is that we are propelled inexorably toward higher levels of awareness: "Man's purpose is to move in the direction of higher consciousness and not toward lower consciousness. Therefore it is meritorious for human beings to love each other and to expel animosity toward each other, so as not to weaken higher consciousness."[48]

Our acts of lovingkindness not only matter, they are the medium through which we can bring the world together in a new era of human relationship. Many practices in Judaism are described with fixed times and amounts. However, lovingkindness is one for which there is no fixed measure.[49] We can perform these acts from morning to night throughout the week. We can set lovingkindness in our souls as a lifelong practice that will always call to us.

The path of lovingkindness leads directly to the highest realms. This path is illuminated by untold billions of sparks that are continuously being released from their husks, while all along, each day of the process, we constantly widen the expanse of our hearts and of those around us.

## Practicing Lovingkindness

1. Buy a blank journal, a large one, that will be your lovingkindness record book.

2. Spend thirty minutes writing down every act of lovingkindness you can ever remember doing. Leave one or two inches of space under each entry. Each of these will become a category.

3. Two or three times a week, or more often if you wish, check off specific acts of lovingkindness that you have done in their respective categories. If you have done new things not on your list, record them as new categories.

4. After a while, you will have a long list of acts of lovingkindness, some of which have only a couple of check marks, some of which have many checks associated with them.

5. Start a new section near the back of the book under the title "Opportunities Missed" for doing an act of lovingkindness. Make a note of these. The point of this exercise is not to feel guilty about missed opportunities, but to be alert to possibilities that have come and gone. This awareness itself can be a loving act if converted into a prayer. It is better to notice something missed than to be oblivious altogether.

6. Do not discuss this journal or what is listed in it with anyone, except perhaps a spiritual guide. The journal is for your personal use; the work you do in this area is between you and God.

The purpose of this exercise is to heighten awareness. We should neither be prideful of areas with many checks, nor regretful of those lonely deeds that went unattended. Rather, we want to be attuned to the needs of the world around us and to the possibilities for offering a piece of ourselves. There are no measures in this for success or failure. We are simply working on heightening our own consciousness and raising one spark at a time.

## Other Practices of Lovingkindness

1. When you read in the newspaper or hear on television about someone who touches your heart, write a brief note to that person and send it to her or him via the newspaper or television station. Letters from strangers are wonderful to receive.

2. If you think of someone you may have wronged in the past, write her or him a letter from the depths of your heart. You do not have to send the letter if you don't want to, but writing it is important. Of course, you can also send it.

3. Think of someone you know who is physically or mentally ill. Concentrate your thoughts and prayers on this person, holding him or her in your imagination as completely healthy. Think positively; send the person healing angels. The person does not need to know you

are doing this for it to be successful. Do this practice each day for as many people as you wish.

4. Search out a soup kitchen, charity, or other local service organization and contribute food, clothing, anything you can. Volunteer at the local thrift shop, home for the elderly, hospital, Meals on Wheels, Salvation Army, etc. Even a couple of hours a month is great.

5. Try to find a way to invite needy guests into your home once a month for a meal. You may have to provide transportation as well. This is work, but enormously heartwarming.

You get the idea. The opportunities are limitless.

## 5. THE PATH
### OF MODERATION

The key to the higher levels of spiritual development is said to be restraint *(haprishut)*. Mastery in general is the ability to hold back, to focus on the task at hand without being distracted, to have a clear sense of priority in the midst of temptation. The master in a particular field is usually someone who has devoted a great deal of time to developing particular skills. Occasionally mastery comes through talent alone, but normally it is the result of sincere effort.

Rabbi Bachya ibn Paquda, eleventh-century author of the classical text on Jewish spirituality *Duties of the Heart,* said that many interpretations of the practices of restraint and moderation suggest extreme abstinence and renunciation. In his opinion, however, a better definition suggests that we simply meet our essential needs without requiring anything in excess.[50]

Judaism has never encouraged asceticism. In the eleventh century, it was common for spiritual aspirants to renounce worldly life. They lived as hermits in rocks and caves, dressed in rags, and completely withdrew from all social contact. Rabbi Paquda frowned upon extreme expressions of piety like this.[51] The general view is that excessive asceticism is ironically an act of self-indulgence with considerable ego-attachment. Moreover, the gifts of this world all have divine sparks and should not be scorned.

Rather, the goal is to willingly undertake some abstinence, to constrain oneself mindfully. Moderation gives one an opportunity to experience every part of this creation, in modest amounts. Paquda said that *haprishut* includes the qualities of fairness, simplicity, humility, forbearance, resoluteness, consideration, temperance, patience, and resignation, among others.

The path of moderation can be applied to everything we do: the quality and quantity of food we eat; the choice of media we take in; the amount of time we work, party, socialize, or entertain ourselves; and the amount of money we spend on clothes, furniture, toys, and automobiles. Indeed, moderation should apply as well to our spiritual aspirations. Excessive attachment to any aspect of our lives will often produce unfavorable results like pride, arrogance, conceit, or other egotistical behavior.

Moreover, if we do not develop the skills of moderation, we remain trapped in our desires, always wanting what we do not have, never content, never in harmony. Desire has an infinite appetite: the more we have, the more we want.

There are natural boundaries that keep us somewhat in check. The day has only twenty-four hours, our credit cards have limits, our stomachs can fill only so far, and our bodies need to rest. Relying strictly on these natural regulators, we survive.

The teaching of moderation suggests, however, that if we want to achieve peace of mind in our lives, we must learn to hold back from the flood of abundance, lest we be swept away. This does not mean that we must avoid the sweets of life (heaven forbid). Rather, we need to learn how to be content while consuming fewer of them.

Moderation is the key to mastery. One approaches it slowly. It is not difficult if we are gentle. We cannot force ourselves into a moderate lifestyle, because force and moderation are contradictory terms. Rather, we can embrace moderation in increments, and the excess baggage of our lives will slowly melt away.

## Practicing Moderation

1. Assess the following aspects of your life on a subjective scale: too much, too little, just about right.

   *a.* I work . . .
   *b.* I eat . . .
   *c.* I watch TV . . .
   *d.* I read magazines . . .
   *e.* I entertain myself . . .

    *f.* I spend time with the family . . .

    *g.* I work on my inner life . . .

    *h.* I work on spiritual practices . . .

    *i.* I read inspiring books . . .

2. Add anything to the list that comes to mind as a quality you feel is represented too much or too little in your life.

3. Look over your list to determine those things that you feel are excessive. For each, calculate the amount that you consume each day (such as four hours of TV, or three full meals a day plus snacks and extra dessert after dinner).

4. Now, assuming you had to diminish the quantity of only one of the things on your list by 25 percent, which would it be?

5. Imagine how you would go about cutting back 25 percent of this thing (such as, "I'd watch television an hour less each day"; "I'd cut out a percentage of my snacks and dessert"; . . .).

6. See if you can actually do this for a week. If so, do it for a month. If you succeed, you can reward yourself by adding to your life something on the list that says "too little." Otherwise, keep trying, or choose another thing on the list.

7. Each time you have success, give yourself a reward by increasing the time given to "too little" items. Work on your list until there is nothing left that says "too much."

## Other Practices of Moderation

1. Pick something that you want to master that can be started right away without a great deal of preparation or costing too much money. Suggestions: becoming skilled in learning to play a musical instrument, writing prose or poetry, learning a foreign language, painting with watercolors, sculpting in clay, reading through an entire encyclopedia (for people who are interested in Judaism, the *Encyclopedia Judaica* is highly recommended), cooking special pastries for others, and so forth.

2. Choose the best time of day when you can devote thirty to firty-five minutes to developing this practice. It should be a time that can be totally dedicated, without interruption, at least five days a week.

3. Make this time each day sacred. Let the family know that you are not to be interrupted (except in emergencies). Do not answer the telephone (get an answering machine). If you like music, put on a headset to cut out all distracting noise. Give yourself permission to be completely devoted to your practice this time each day.

4. Stay with it. Gentle self-discipline is the key. You will love this time with yourself, and after a while you will become skilled in whatever you are doing. But the skill is not the goal. Much more important is giving yourself the time. This is where you will gain self-confidence, and with self-confidence comes more peace of mind. This practice teaches us how to develop mastery one step at a time.

The path of moderation is one of the primary elements in a more extensive practice that leads to the ultimate level of enlightenment in Judaism. The more we practice moderation, the more we are able to reprioritize our lives for the things that will deepen our spiritual practice.

Moderation gives us a clearer perspective of who we are and what we need to survive. When we practice it, modifying the degree to which we are driven by incessant desire, we soon realize that we are surrounded by thousands of chariots to higher realms—thousands of new opportunities to connect with God. Every interaction in life is a new opportunity to take the reins of these chariots. We have more choice over our destiny than most people realize. It is a matter of setting our priorities, slowing down, reflecting, simplifying, and paying attention.

## 6. The Path of Purity

*T*he goal of purity in the context of spiritual exercise is to minimize or eliminate thoughts that cause inner conflict. We attempt to clarify the difference between our own will to do something, and God's will. Purity is a level of attachment to God in which thoughts have more of a selfless quality. By attaching ourselves more to the presence of the Divine, by placing God before us, always, we are able more to "do deeds for the sake of their creator and speak about them for their own sake."[52]

Mastery in purity comes through contemplation. We closely observe how the world operates and thereby gain wisdom. We experience the transient nature of things, that fortunes rise and fall, that good times come and go, and that life is ephemeral. In this, we gain greater awareness of our own limitations, and greater appreciation for the way things unfold.

It is said that we can be distracted from developing purity by pursuing pleasure, fame, honor, or status.[53] Each of these is temporarily ego-gratifying but is ultimately an insatiable and disheartening quest.

Earlier in this book we explored the concept that the higher level of soul is always pure. We can use this idea in a meditative practice to deepen the realization of the part within us that is always connected to God. Once we fully appreciate the implication of this teaching, it changes the way we relate to others forever.

## Practicing Purity: Tehora He (The Soul Is Pure)

1. Sitting with your eyes closed, imagine that you have X-ray vision and can penetrate yourself as if you were composed of translucent material. You can notice many small parts interconnected in your body.

2. Looking very closely, imagine that a subtle being is illuminated within. The light that allows you to see comes from somewhere deep inside and fills the body with a glow.

3. Imagine your body many years younger than you are now. Notice that although the image of the body may change, the light that illuminates it remains the same. It is simply light; it does not change.

4. Try to imagine yourself many years from now. The body will again change, but the light will stay the same.

5. Now imagine a beloved. Notice how his or her body is completely different from yours, but the light illuminating it is of the same quality as yours. Light is light.

6. Do this exercise with people you know and love, and with people you may not get along with so well. Again, the light will be the same

as yours. You may discover that the reality of sharing the same light affects the way you feel about these people.

7. Do this exercise a number of times until you have the image clearly within. Then, when you are on a public street, allow yourself to imagine that each person is illuminated from within by this light. As we described earlier, you can say to yourself quietly, *"Tehora he"* (She—the soul within—is pure). You will find yourself feeling an affinity for strangers. This is the purpose of the practice, to remember that we all are connected to the same source and therefore to one another.

## 7. THE PATH OF JOY

Rebbe Nachman of Breslov, the great grandson of the Baal Shem Tov, was famous for his teachings on joy. Joy is a major theme in his stories. He said that the roots of depression are "husks *(kelippot)* which are at war with all that is holy." Whenever depression takes hold, the Divine Presence *(Shekhina)* goes into exile. Therefore, "the strength of the forces of holiness and the destruction of the shells that imprison holy sparks depends upon joy."[54]

According to Rebbe Nachman, the value of joy is its ability to combat the destructive power of our imagination. "The human's image-making faculty is the source of all temptation. If it becomes dominant, it results in depression . . . forgetfulness takes hold and one forgets one's purpose in life. We have to fight back and aim to be continually happy so as to break the power of our imagination."[55]

Kabbalists use the imagination to attain higher realms. But if it is not harnessed, according to Rebbe Nachman, imagination can be the source of our sense of alienation and separation from God.

Rebbe Nachman said, "You may fall to the lowest depths, heaven forbid, but no matter how low you have fallen, it is still inappropriate to give up hope. The ability to return to God *(teshuvah)* surpasses everything, and so there is no room for despair. Even sins can be transformed into virtue; even your failings and shortcomings can be brought back to God.[56] The most important thing is never to give up, but to continue to cry out and pray to God."[57] To make his point, Rebbe Nachman told a story.

One upon a time there was a farmer named Moshe who lived in the Ukraine in the nineteenth century. Moshe was known as "Moshe Simcha" (joyous Moshe) because he was rarely seen without a big smile. He had a happy soul and seemed content with the world. Moshe's life as a farmer had not been easy, but his high spirits stayed with him nonetheless. He figured he had the choice to smile and laugh, or to frown and moan. He knew that no matter what he chose to do, the world would not change that much. So he decided that he might as well enjoy his lot in life.

One day Moshe was plowing his land when a huge, strange stone turned up in the soil. He picked it up and knew at once that it was valuable. It had a dazzling, almost blinding light shining in its center, as if it contained its own sun.

Moshe carried the stone to the city, where he showed it to his brother-in-law, Shabbtai, a jeweler. When Shabbtai saw the stone, big as a fist, he almost choked on his herring. "Where did you get such a stone?" he asked in awe. Moshe shook his head and pointed his thumb upward, silently indicating "Only God knows."

Moshe asked quietly, "How much do you think it is worth?"

Shabbtai smiled and raised his thumb, returning the gesture he had just received. Then he said, "You will have to take this stone to the market in Amsterdam, for that is the only place they will be able to pay for such a large gem."

Amsterdam! How would Moshe get to Amsterdam? He had no money. It would be too dangerous to go overland. The best way would be to go by boat, from Odessa through the Black Sea to the Mediterranean, past Gibraltar, and then up to Holland. But he could not possibly pay for such a passage.

Shabbtai agreed to help. He contacted a captain, a shady character, who was in the business of smuggling. The captain agreed to take Moshe, with promise of payment at the other end. Payment, of course, at ten times the going rate. But who cared? Moshe would get his ride.

The deal was cut, and Moshe went onboard. He had his own cabin and was served daily by the steward. The captain was a gruff, dark-bearded man with a patch over one eye, who looked very much like the pirate he was rumored to be. He spent every day with Moshe, joking about the people he had thrown overboard, which he claimed he did whenever he was in the mood. He related every gruesome detail, trying to intimidate Moshe, but Moshe had a joyous soul. He pretended the captain was joking, and laughed himself silly.

They got along wonderfully this way. As long as the captain laughed with him, Moshe felt safe. Relatively.

Each day at lunchtime, Moshe took out the stone to admire its inner glow. He sat there, mesmerized by it. He did not think so much about the money this stone would fetch; he was much more interested in its intrinsic beauty. It was a magnificent stone, and he grew to love it.

When they were two weeks away from landing in Holland, an awful thing happened. Moshe fell asleep at lunch. He was still asleep when the steward cleared the table. And he was still asleep as the steward did his daily cleanup by throwing overboard everything that was left on the table but the cup, the dish, and the silverware. All the scraps of food, crumbs of bread, and on this day, the piece of dirty, old glass that must have been rolling around in the bilge—all of it was thrown overboard in one heave-ho.

When Moshe awoke, his stomach immediately knotted. The gemstone was gone. He knew it would be gone forever. And if the captain found out that Moshe could not pay his passage, he knew that he too would be gone forever.

Yet when the captain came that afternoon, Moshe was as jovial as ever. They joked and laughed just like every other day. Of course, Moshe had not told the captain about the stone in the first place, for fear that he would steal it. Now that it was gone, Moshe had even more reason not to tell him.

Day after day for the next couple of weeks, the two of them were together, joking like old friends. The day before arriving in port, the captain came to Moshe and asked him to do a favor. He told him that his reputation was not the best in these parts. Then the captain asked Moshe if he would be willing to have the entire shipment put under his name. This would minimize the suspicions of the customs officers. If Moshe was willing to do this, the captain would pay him a fine fee.

Of course, Moshe agreed. What did he have to lose? Even if he got caught smuggling, it was better than being thrown overboard. So the contracts were pre-dated and signed. On paper, Moshe owned the entire cargo, worth a huge sum.

That night there was a strange wind. It shook the rigging and howled in a way that pierced to the marrow of one's bones. Sailors know this wind as a cry that comes from a world far beyond our own. The next morning, the captain did not appear on deck. Indeed, when they went in search of him, sailors found that the captain had died during the night.

When the ship docked that day, Moshe was instantly a wealthy man. He paid all the sailors triple wages and still was exceedingly rich. Everyone was happy.

When Moshe returned home, his neighbors saw that he was as joyful as ever. Moreover, he gave away so much money, his joy became infectious. Indeed, from that time forward, everyone who ever knew Moshe always smiled whenever his name was mentioned. Even today, when people hear the story of Moshe Simcha, they often seem to smile for no apparent reason, just as you may be doing right now.

REBBE NACHMAN TAUGHT that Moshe's joy and laughter changed the world around him. In fact, Moshe's survival depended upon his joyous countenance. Indeed, he was a messenger of joy. The s tone he had found was merely a means to get him aboard the boat. We never know how things will turn out. All we can do is maintain our joy no matter what happens.

The hasidic movement was built upon the idea of "serving the Lord with joy." In fact, the early *hasidim* became so ecstatic in their prayers that they were ridiculed by opponents for their wild dancing and acrobatic tumbling. But their joyous relationship with God could not be suppressed, and Hasidism spread across Europe.

Enthusiasm and joy are infectious. We feel good, our hard edges are softened, our critical minds are pacified, and we gain a new sense of equilibrium. Most of us experience joy spontaneously and assume that it comes on its own. But joy can be invited as a guest, and it can be cultivated to remain for extended periods of time.

## Practicing Joy

Rebbe Nachman said that the pathway to our true destiny is joy. Indeed, joy and enthusiasm are important aspects of the spiritual path in many ways. The wonderful part of this practice is that it nurtures us while we are doing it, and usually helps us see things from a different perspective.

Here are ten practices to warm the heart and fill the soul with joy. Any one of them can change your day.

1. *Music:* If you don't already own one, get a miniature audiotape player and comfortable earphones. Find pieces of music that move your soul. Play them repeatedly when you are engaged in mundane activities. Play them so much that they are in your mind even when the player is not on. Also, sing! In the shower, in the car, spontaneously, whenever you wish.

2. *Dance:* Find a room in the house where you will not be interrupted and nobody can see you through the windows. Move the furniture so that

you have a clear space to dance. Play some music you love, and move your body any way you wish for twenty minutes. This is a dance for you alone. If it does not make you feel wonderful, choose another piece of music next time.

3. *Nature:* Make it a point at least once a week to spend two hours in a raw, natural setting with as few people around as possible. Go to the beach, mountains, forest, desert, someplace filled with the beauty of nature. During this time, *try not to think about yourself.* Rather, act as a nature-loving tour guide for yourself who is constantly saying things like: "Look at that ant"; "Listen to that wind"; "Smell that flower"; "Touch the bark on that tree"; "See how the sun glistens off the water"; "Be very still and listen." Try to spend the entire two hours without thinking about your own life. You may wish to carry a notepad so that if distractions arise, you can make a brief note to attend to these concerns after the two hours are up.

4. *Selectivity:* We choose fairly carefully the food we eat. We know what does not agree with us, and we usually try to avoid it. The same should hold true for what we choose to feed our minds. For one month, try to be selective of the type of programs you watch, the quality of radio you listen to, the magazines you read, the movies you go to see. You may choose to minimize experiences that titillate and excite, which often include scenes of violence, anger, and general mayhem. This kind of material may entertain us, but it does not give us joy. Indeed, it does the reverse. Try one month of selectivity, and substitute one of the following choices:

5. *Books:* Take an hour and browse your local bookstore or library without any goal. Let yourself be guided by whim. Find a seat and read parts of a book or magazine that catch your fancy. The idea is to discover new areas of interest or simply to be lightly entertained, with no objective in mind.

6. *Playground:* Take an hour and walk in a local park or playground. Ride a swing. Sit on a jungle gym. Lie in the grass. Hug a tree. Talk with a child you don't know. Try to be with your own inner child, not thinking about adult things. As in step 3, *see if you can spend an hour not thinking about yourself.*

7. *Museum:* Spend a morning or afternoon exploring a local museum, just hanging out. Ponder the works of the artists. Let your fantasy flow. Again, try not to think about your own past and future during this time.

8. *Fantasy:* Pick up travel brochures, get videos from the library on nature or distant lands, and let yourself fantasize about traveling around the
world. Pick a place you would really like to go. Get books from the library
and study everything you can find about this place. Plan your trip, even if it
is years away.

9. *Soak:* Fill a tub with warm water. Use bubble bath if you like. Soak
your whole body for at least a half hour, trying to keep your mind free. If
you begin thinking about yourself, make up a fantasy and float away.

10. *Thanks:* Speak words of thankfulness to God. Reflect on your
physical gifts: eyesight; hearing; and the abilities to speak, stand, walk, touch,
smell, taste, and so forth. For each thing, give thanks. Reflect on your shelter, food, safety, kitchen, bathroom, and give thanks. Whatever comes to mind,
find something in it for which you can be thankful. Try to get into the habit
of thankfulness (rather than the normal habit of complaint). Each night as
you go to sleep, see how many things you can think of to give thanks for
that day. You may discover that the list is so long, you will fall asleep before
finishing it.

Notice that all of the above suggestions require taking time for yourself. Of course, there are many joyful practices that involve being with others. Take advantage of these as well. But be assured, our joy is ultimately not
dependent upon other people, but on our individual relationship with life.

Obviously, there are hundreds of activities that lighten the heart and
nourish the soul. As noted above, you do not have to wait for joy to arrive
on its own; you can invite it in through the front door this very moment.

## 8. THE PATH
### OF SELFLESSNESS

Humility *(anavah)* in Jewish mystical teachings means selflessness. The idea of selflessness is to let go of all of the trap-
pings of self-identity, which include our notions and beliefs about who we
are, our preferences, our desires, and our expectations or aspirations. The practices that are described in kabbalistic literature for attaining this state are
*bittul ha-yesh* (nullification of the "there is") and *meserit nefesh* (surrender of
the vital soul).

Humility does not mean meekness. Moses is viewed in the Torah as the humblest of people, yet he could be quite fierce with the Israelites, and even more, he argued with God on a number of occasions. Humility means to be clear, confident, and accepting without pride, self-interest, or ambition.

We strengthen our sense of humility by habituating ourselves by consistently choosing the most diminished position among a group of people. We select the hardest seat at the end of the table; we walk in the back of a crowd; we wear the most modest clothes; we pick the smallest portion of food.[58] The idea is to diminish our sense of self-importance, but it is crucial to keep in mind that even here, the rule of moderation applies. Thus, one does not *always* seek the most subordinate position.

In our culture, outward expressions of self-diminishment generally run counter to essential beliefs of rugged individualism. Self-assertion has strong currency these days; it is important to be heard. On the other side, some people are extremists in denying themselves any minor indulgence, which can border on asceticism, or, equally unhealthy, they may be self-righteous in their martyrdom. Rare indeed are the people who are balanced between these poles, who do not struggle to achieve something, who are not self-aggrandizing, who do not care about status on the one side, or, on the other, who are not full of themselves in glorification of abstinence, purity, and false modesty.

Therefore, the position in which we find ourselves is not as important as how we feel about it. Although we may attempt to break down our sense of self-importance, it is far more relevant for us to assess the degree to which we are concerned with our rank. This concern is a reflection of the degree to which we are self-oriented, and is inversely related to our measure of humility.

It is taught that if one is in a position of authority, wealth, success, or fame that invites flattery and admiration, it is important to seek out friends and teachers who are willing to give advice and even admonishment, if necessary, so that one will remain grounded and centered on the path.[59]

## Binah *Consciousness: Being Here and Now*

One of the best ways to develop on the path of selflessness is through a meditative practice that leads to what is called in Kabbalah *binah* consciousness. When one masters this practice, it evolves into the next level, *chochma* consciousness, which is the highest meditative state attainable.

*Chochma* and *binah* are at the top levels of the Tree of Life, except for *keter* at the crown. But because *keter* is ephemeral, for nothing can be said about it, *chochma* and *binah* represent the aspects of creation closest to the Divine Source that we can experience. *Chochma* represents the element in which the first spark of a thought is initiated. *Binah* represents the element in which the thought is actually formed. *Chochma* is "higher" than *binah,* and more nebulous.

*Binah* consciousness can be distinguished from ordinary consciousness in a simple way. It does not have a personal identity; there is no sense of I/me. Thinking without a sense of ego-awareness is difficult, but with practice we can experience the quality of uncontaminated *binah* consciousness. One of the means for determining the presence of ego is by examining our relationship to time. Invariably, if one's thoughts are dwelling in the past or preparing for the future, we can be assured that ego is somewhere nearby.

The experience of being in *binah* consciousness is completely sensual. One does not dwell in reviewing past events or in planning for the future. There is only the experience of each moment as it arises. In this state of mind, each sound is exquisite, each visual impression unique, each odor is captivating. Once we are free of our sense of our own selves, we enter a state that is often defined as rapturous. Quite simply, it is delicious to be alive without having to remember who we are.

The best way to notice our own mental processes is through traditional contemplative practice. A basic technique is to focus on one's breath. Sit comfortably but fairly straight so that you can be still for thirty to forty minutes. Pay attention to the experience of the body, the rising and falling of the chest as the breath comes and goes, or any other body experience that arises, whether an itch, an ache, or other physical phenomenon. Try not to *think* about any of these things, but simply notice them as they are happening.

Many people have the misunderstanding that simple meditation practices like this belong to Eastern traditions. However, sitting quietly and observing our physical experience is a generic meditation practice that has been described by mystics in a wide variety of traditions, including Judaism. It is so natural, children sometimes do it without realizing that they are meditating. Invariably, the objective is to let go of our mental process and be present with what is happening in the moment.

Though it sounds simple, this is not easy to do. The mind is quite active. Each time we notice that we are thinking, we gently try to bring our awareness back to the body. It is self-defeating to become frustrated and angry with our own minds, because the fact is that mind activity rarely ceases. Anger is just the opposite of what we are trying to accomplish. Our goal is to *notice* thoughts rather than be caught by them. We simply draw our attention back to the body each time we are aware that thoughts have carried us away, and we focus on the breath or whatever physical sensation is happening in that moment. Indeed, the very noticing of the thought is a moment of awareness, which, if anything, should have us satisfied with our success rather than frustrated.

The mind is remarkably active. More than 99 percent of our thinking process fits into the ordinary mode, perhaps as much as 99.9 percent. Yet we can enhance our *binah* consciousness more than we think. If we are able to observe our own minds closely enough, we can recognize the presence of the Now underlying every thought. It is the seed around which thought rapidly gathers. The mind, however, works so fast that *binah* consciousness is blanketed and quickly converts to ordinary thinking.

When we are able to be still and notice the inner workings of our minds, we begin to experience the difference between the sensation of *binah* consciousness and all the other feelings that arise in ordinary thinking. Ordinary mind-states have a wide range of emotions but usually a clear sense of personal involvement with the world. This identification has an insidious quality of separation built into it: me and you, me and the world, me and everything that is not me. This sense of separation clouds our relationship with the world. In *binah* consciousness, on the other hand, we feel alert, mindful, bright, luminous, expansive, inclusive, soft, and lucid. We integrate with everything happening around us, feeling connected, whole, and relaxed.

The more we recognize *binah* consciousness for what it is, the greater our capability to stay with it before ego overwhelms it. The experience of extended *binah* consciousness feels so different from ordinary consciousness, it is viewed as a higher stage of enlightenment. This is the first objective of a strong meditative practice.

When we become more skilled in our meditative practice of *binah* consciousness, we gain more mastery over our emotional reactions, bringing a new sense of calmness and a greater sense of equanimity to our lives. We are able to see things more clearly, have more refined judgment and a more balanced appraisal of how things will unfold. *Binah* consciousness gives us an experience of ongoing lucidity that dramatically affects our lives.

## Chochma *Consciousness: The Experience of Nothingness*

The next level of consciousness is *chochma* consciousness, which is far more subtle than *binah*. We need to spend considerable time working with *binah* consciousness to get to the *chochma* level. It is what the ancient Kabbalists called *ayin,* Nothingness. Actually, as discussed earlier, Nothingness is "something" we can actually experience.

Many people confuse the mental experience of numbness, blank thoughts, or sleep with Nothingness. For example, when meditating, people occasionally feel they are doing well when nothing is happening. They feel nothing; they know nothing. In this instance, they are most likely asleep sitting up. *Chochma* consciousness is completely different. It is the experience of pure awareness. No thoughts, per se, belong to the person. But everything that is going on in that moment is "noticed," not with the cognitive mind, but as sensory input. There is "nobody" here to notice, no identification with self-ness, no one to react; it is simply noticing.

*Chochma* consciousness is not yours or mine to have; it belongs to the universe of awareness. When we enter this universe, we become invisible. The body does not stop functioning—it continues to breathe; it even continues to think. But none of that is relevant when we enter *chochma* consciousness.

Whereas we can conscientiously use meditation techniques to experience *binah* consciousness, *chochma* consciousness comes only through grace. We cannot force it, but we can invite it in. We do this by being vigilant in our *binah*-consciousness practice. The more we master the experience of being constantly in the moment, the better our chances of experiencing *chochma* consciousness.

This state of mind is the Jewish way of expressing a degree of enlightenment. Many believe this is the prerequisite for attaining *devekut,* constant awareness of the Divine, which is the goal of almost all contemplative practice in Judaism. When we work with this practice it invariably brings us closer to sensing the immediacy of God.

## 9. THE PATH OF AWE

The sense of awe arises out of the true understanding of the relationship between the process of God-ing and that of creation-ing. The role that each of us plays in this process is dynamic. The sense of responsibility for each of our actions, words, and thoughts can be heightened to such an extent, we tremble when we consider the potential.

The Psalms say that "the beginning of wisdom is the awe of God."[60] The sages said, "Happy is the person who fears always," which is interpreted to mean one who is always in awe of the Divine.[61] True wisdom comes from understanding that the universe is balanced on our actions, each and every one of us. Our understanding of the significance of this mystical fact leads us to an awesome conclusion: Each one of us is responsible for how the universe will unfold.

Kabbalah says that once we appreciate that the Divine Presence is everywhere, we come to realize that nothing is too small to be excluded from It.[62] No gesture is inconsequential; everything has meaning—a falling leaf, a birdcall, the shape of a cloud. If this is true, we can barely imagine the implications of the things we do. This is how we cultivate awe.

## Alone with God

Modern Judaism places great emphasis upon participation in the community. Indeed, many Jewish scholars and rabbis believe that individual spiritual practice is antithetical to the tradition. We need ten people to form a *minyan* for prayer, holy days are celebrated collectively, the community is an important network of support for maintaining many laws regarding Shabbat and being kosher. It is almost impossible to sustain an observant Jewish practice without a community.

Nevertheless, Jewish mystics have always been drawn to practices of introspection, contemplation, and seclusion *(hitbodedut)*. They point to the fact that the revelation of the Torah occurred when Moses was alone on the mountain for forty days. Moreover, many prophets practiced seclusion, including Elijah and Elisha.

The Talmud quotes Shimon the son of Rabban Gamliel as saying, "All my days I grew up among the sages and I have not found anything better for oneself than silence."[63] In the *Zohar,* Rabbi Eleazar says, "My keeping silence was the means of building the sanctuary above and the sanctuary below."[64] The sanctuaries above and below are the places where one has intimate communion with God.

Abraham Abulafia (thirteenth century) said, "Choose a lonely house where none shall hear thy voice. Sit there in thy closet and do not reveal thy secret to any living person."[65] There are dozens of examples of well-known Jewish teachers who took extended solitary retreats, including Isaac Luria, the Baal Shem Tov, Chaim Vital, the Kotzker Rebbe, Joseph Karo, and Rebbe Nachman of Breslov.[66]

For the Kabbalist, one of the hidden directives regarding silence comes from Ezekiel's prophetic vision, which says, "A storm wind came out of the North . . . and from its midst [came] the appearance of an electrum *(chash-*

*mal)* in the middle of the fire."[67] The Talmud says that we should divide the word *"chashmal"* into two parts: *chash,* which means "silent," and *mal,* which means "to speak."[68] This is the "speaking silence" which holds the mysteries of creation.

We see it again in another famous prophetic passage from when Elijah the prophet retreated in solitude for forty days and nights and then was guided to stand on a mountain. Here a strong wind appeared, but the answer was not in the wind. Then an earthquake occurred, but the answer was not there either. Then a fire, but not there. Finally "a still small voice" emerged that revealed to Elijah the hidden truth.[69]

Silence, for the contemplative practitioner, means inner silence. One could be standing on Fifth Avenue during the lunch-hour rush, in the middle of cacophony, and be immersed in a total state of inner silence. On the other hand, one could be isolated in a cabin in the middle of the woods and have no inner silence whatsoever. Inner silence means having the ability to perceive the feather's weight of the subtlest thoughts that can arise in the mind.

Normally we are aware of our gross thinking process. Thoughts are like loud diesel trucks pounding in our consciousness. They capture us and overwhelm us with their urgency. Sometimes we are able to quiet ourselves so that our thoughts become softer. We lie on the beach and ruminate through the sands of time. Thoughts flicker, images flash by, and we feel comforted by the scope of our life experience. But these are still solo instruments in a quieted orchestra hall, still clear, distinct, and overpowering. We may not yet be fully concentrated, because we do not notice the squeak of a mouse under the seats of the third balcony row.

That subtle movement of a hidden mouse, small and elusive, is what we want to observe. How quiet must the inner chambers of our minds be, how still! This is the inner silence sought by the contemplative mystic. Here a new reality takes shape, one much more connected with the realms of higher awareness than is available to us in our normally noisy mental playing field. Here, the still small voice of God can be heard.

*Hitbodedut* is the reflexive form of the verb *"boded,"* which means "isolated" or "secluded." Thus, *hitbodedut* means "to isolate or seclude oneself intentionally." One can isolate oneself physically, by going out of the everyday world to a location that assures being alone, or by withdrawing into the center of one's being while in the midst of a crowded room. In our busy world, it is not easy to do.

The Breslov *hasids* (students), followers of Rebbe Nachman, actively engage in *hitbodedut* as a major aspect of their spiritual practice. They usually go into the woods in the middle of the night and separate until each person is alone in the darkness. Then they speak to God directly, in their own language. They say whatever is on their minds, anything.

I went with a small group once. As soon as we divided and I was alone, I was frightened half to death. The woods at night are a scary place for me. I am always conjuring up bears. Every shadow is a creature with sharp teeth and claws, every sound is a slithering snake. I stood quietly, trembling, terrified.

Then I heard in the distance one of my compatriots calling out in a sobbing voice, "God, where are you? What are you? What is taking you so long? Why can't I feel you? I don't even know what I'm talking to. Why do you make it so damn hard?" And then he burst into louder sobbing.

Somehow I was reassured by this plaintive call. It made me want to cry. I did cry. More than a little. And then I began my own call. Not as loud as my friend's, for I was embarrassed. Besides, God—if there was such a thing— could hear my whisper, or even my mind, for that matter. But the instructions were that we had to articulate words. We could not simply think the thought. Speaking was an important part of the experience. Saying the words out loud, even in a whisper, adds an emotional quality and coherence that thoughts never attain.

I said, "I need help with this. I don't know what I'm doing here. I'm scared. I need help." I repeated "I need help" as a mantra for many minutes. I became quiet. I began saying again, "I need help, I need help," over and over. I repeated this for a half hour, maybe longer.

Finally I burst into tears and found myself saying, "Thank you, thank you," to nobody and for no apparent reason. With whom was I speaking? What was happening? I had no idea, but for some reason I felt better. My fear dropped away. The woods became friendly. It was no longer dangerous because, for some reason, I no longer felt alone.

## Yearning to Merge with God

A number of years ago, I led a workshop at Lama Foundation, in the mountains of the high desert near Taos, New Mexico. It was an eclectic retreat with four teachers: a Buddhist, a Sufi, a Christian, and a Jew. I was amused at the time because three out of the four teachers were Jewish by birth. Almost half of the participants were Jewish as well. This is not unusual, even today, at spiritual conferences.

During the mornings I led contemplative Jewish practices, which always included chanting the main prayer: *Shema Yisrael, Adonoy Elohaynu, Adonoy*

*Ehad* (Hear, O Israel, the Lord is Our God, the Lord is One). The way I explain the meaning of this prayer is as follows: Listen closely *(Shema),* that part within each of us that yearns to go directly to God *(Israel—Yashar El),*[70] the transcendent, unknowable source of sources *(Adonoy)* and the God that we are able to relate to in Its immanence in everything we experience around us *(Elohaynu),* both the transcendent *(Adonoy)* and the immanent, are actually, paradoxically, one and the same *(Ehad).*

Near the end of the monthlong retreat, the entire group decided to walk up Lama Mountain to a higher plateau. The trail is long, winding, and steep. At night it is difficult to follow, even with a good light.

One of the women who had been in my morning prayer group, a Christian who was interested in Jewish mysticism, tried to come down from the plateau on her own around midnight, without a flashlight. Soon she was lost. But there was another problem—quite a serious problem. She had a body chemistry that exploded whenever she became nervous. She would flush, and patches of skin all over her body would turn deep scarlet. If she became really frightened, she would break out in hives externally and internally. Her esophagus could clamp down and suffocate her.

Lost on Lama Mountain, this woman went into a severe panic attack. She gasped for air as her entire system froze. She could not go up or down, and she could not stay where she was. Death was in the neighborhood.

Then, for no apparent reason, she began to chant the Shema. She told me later that it surged within her and she knew it was her only chance for survival. She chanted the words of the Shema over and over again, and her breathing passages began to clear. As the panic lifted, she realized that she could see the trail almost as if it were phosphorescent. She simply walked down the mountain at that point, calmly and happily, chanting the Shema all the way.

The words of the Shema are wonderful, especially when understood in their mystical context. They connect us, Jew and non-Jew alike, with a common inner essence that longs to be at one with the source of creation. In her chant, she merged with the part of herself that yearned to be with God. When she was able to speak directly to the Unknown, her reality changed.

Mystics would say that it was God calling to Itself through her.

## *Practicing Awe: Part 1*

1. Find someplace in your home where you can be alone and undisturbed for half an hour.

---

2. Take an inspirational book with you, something that can be opened to any page and will give a meaningful phrase in a few lines. Many books are good for this purpose: the Bible, Psalms, poetry, spiritual autobiographies, meditation guides, books about saintly people, prayer books, and so forth.

3. Spend the first ten minutes "warming" your heart by sitting quietly, eyes closed, perhaps humming a quiet melody to yourself.

4. For the second ten minutes, imagine that you are able to communicate with God, whatever that means to you. Speak out whatever is on your mind. The subject does not matter. Just continue speaking nonstop for ten minutes. If you are embarrassed to do this, speak about the embarrassment. If confused, speak about that. Speak about anything: anger, frustration, love, whatever.

5. During the last ten minutes, open the book you are holding to a page at random. Read a few lines, no more than a paragraph, and then close the book. Continue to sit quietly.

6. Do this practice once a week for at least ten weeks. After each half-hour session, immediately write your experiences in a journal. At the end of the ten sessions, read over the entire journal. If you have never once felt a special connection, this practice is not for you at this time. If you have, one or more times, then continue with the practice until you feel you have gained intimacy with your inner voice. From this point on, you can continue the practice at random, for you will now have ready access to your inner voice.

## Practicing Awe: Part 2

1. Schedule a minimum of three days for a personal retreat. It can be longer, but three days is enough to begin this practice. (If there are children at home, you will have to make arrangements for their care or find a separate room for yourself in the house.)

2. Whether you live alone or with a partner, designate a sacred space where you will not be disturbed during the entire retreat.

3. Sleep and eat in your sacred space. Turn off the telephone; do not answer the door; do not listen to the answering machine. In other words, really honor the time you are giving yourself—your soul— during this retreat.

4. During the retreat, minimize your "doing" part and maximize your "being" part. Recommended activities include noticing your breath, gazing, chanting, hatha yoga, praying, noticing your thoughts, staring at candles, eating simply, doing absolutely nothing, and any other endeavor (or nonendeavor) that will enhance mindful presence. Activities not recommended include casual reading, writing at length, watching television, listening to radio, listening to music, studying, using the computer, eating complex foods, practicing golf putts, and any other activity that allows us to be mindless.

5. The idea is not simply to pass the time, but to notice what happens in our minds when we have nothing to distract ourselves. After the initial boredom, anxiety, discomfort, and frustration, we engage ourselves on a new level. This is a challenging practice.

6. Keep a simple journal, limiting yourself to a short, fixed time period for writing.

For more guidance on setting up personal retreats, see my books *Silence, Simplicity, and Solitude* (Bell Tower, 1992), and *Renewing Your Soul* (Harper-SanFrancisco, 1995).

## Practicing Awe: Part 3

1. Whenever you are feeling good or thankful about something, at the first opportunity, whisper a personal statement of thankfulness to the universe.

2. Whenever you are feeling estranged, negative, angry, sad, bitter, frustrated, disillusioned, or in any way out of sorts, always ask for assistance. At the first opportunity, whisper to the universe something like: "I'm feeling very sad and I could use some help to feel better. Please, help me."

3. Whenever you feel deficient in something—you need more time, more money, more clothes, more support—at the first opportunity, whisper something like: "I feel the need for more money, so I am asking for help in this—either to have more or to find peace of mind with what I do have." When you do this, the goal is not necessarily to fill the deficiency, but to find a place of comfort with what is.

4. Whenever you feel like speaking spontaneously to the universe for any reason whatsoever, at the first moment, find an opportunity to do so. The idea, obviously, is to develop a relationship. Occasionally we all feel somewhat alone. The purpose of this practice is to fill that sense of aloneness with companionship for the soul. It can provide us with enormous strength in dealing with life's ongoing trials.

## 10. THE PATH
### OF EQUANIMITY

*a* Jewish wisdom-story tells about an advanced student in Jewish mysticism who traveled to a secret institution which housed the most enlightened beings of the time. This student wanted desperately to gain admittance so that he could grow in his wisdom. But he had to pass a test to be accepted among these learned people, who were called the Masters of Concentration.

One of the elders said to the young man, "My son, you are on the right path and your goal is admirable. But to join our community you must have reached a level of equanimity *(hishtavut)*. Can you say to us that you have achieved equanimity?"

The young man had not expected such a question. He asked the elder, "Master, please, explain what you mean by equanimity."

The old man said, "My son, if you know one person who honors and praises you, and another person who despises and insults you, are both of these people the same to you?"

The young man sat quietly for a while, carefully investigating his own feelings. Then he replied, "Master, clearly I derive pleasure and satisfaction from the person who honors me, and pain from the one who insults me.

But I can say in all honesty that I do not feel any sense of wanting revenge, nor do I bear a grudge. So I believe that I have attained equanimity."

The elder shook his head. "No, my son, you have not acquired equanimity by our measure. The fact that your soul experiences the pain of an insult means that you will not be able to attach your thoughts entirely to God. Our level of concentration requires that you cannot waver, even for a moment. Therefore, go in peace until you become truly equanimous so that you will be able to concentrate."[71]

The entrance requirements for this mystical academy seem quite rigorous. Is it not enough that we are able to overcome our disturbing thoughts? Can we actually reach a state of mind in which such thoughts never arise in the first place? The Jewish sages said yes, as do major teachers in most spiritual traditions.

The state of mind that we need to attain is called *ayin,* Nothingness. We have to be nothing in our own eyes, and therefore nonreactive. As we have just seen, we can achieve the level of *ayin* through the contemplative practice of *bittul ha-yesh,* the path of selflessness.[72] Thus, selflessness is a precondition for equanimity.

In the state of *ayin,* we discover an entirely different relationship with questions such as: Who am I? What am I? Where am I? Am I a name? Am I a relationship to my family? Am I something distinguished by an address, driver's license, social-security card, library card, or telephone number? From the perspective of selflessness, we realize that although we may be identified by and associated with objective symbols, our essential souls are something else, something that transcends names, numbers, measurements, or other common forms of identification.

Who am I? I am nobody. There is no I. There is only that which enables the question to be asked in the first place. Who is asking? God-ing is asking through this body, this mind. Who is thinking? Who is reading these words?

Like a child who endlessly asks why, we use this practice to put our "who" questions against every proposed response. And just like we ultimately reach an enigmatic conclusion with the child, "Only God knows why!" so too will we be stumped by our "who" questions, for they are never finally resolvable. They do lead to insight, however, and this insight is the key to the advanced state of mind that leads to selflessness. This is not self-annihilation—we don't cease to exist in this practice. Rather, it is the realization of the ever-present nature of divine consciousness. When a Jewish practitioner reaches a level of awareness in which he or she enters the realm of selflessness, it leads to a realization that God's presence is everywhere, including one's own consciousness.

In the eighteenth century, the Maggid of Koznitz, Rabbi Israel Haupstein, said, "There are two kinds of spiritual leaders. One is the great leader who constantly does God's will, but who realizes that he or she is doing it. Such an individual does not have the power to bring everything back to its root (i.e., redeem all the holy sparks) or make one realize that all is derived from God's will. The reason for this is because this spiritual leader does not [fully understand] that even his or her own worship *ultimately comes from God* [because they have too much of a sense of themselves].

"There are other spiritual leaders who are nothing in their own eyes (selfless). They realize that God's power is everything and that without it there is absolutely nothing. These leaders can bring all attributes and thoughts to their root. Such a spiritual leader may be like nothing inside (selfless), but light and all holy influence radiates to the world."[73]

Herein is the mystical secret that holy sparks are raised when we fully realize that we are nothing but vehicles for the expression of Divine Will. Paradoxically the vehicle itself has its own free will. When the conductors (you and I) of this free will believe that we are separate identities, we limit and detach ourselves from the source of life, and the sparks thereby cannot be returned to their root. When we appreciate that we are empowered by a central force, then our free will is used for the benefit of this central force, and the holy sparks are returned to their root.

As Rabbi Levi Yitzhak of Berdichev said, "At every instant, all universes receive existence and sustenance from God. It is human beings, however, who motivate this sustenance and transmit it to all worlds. When a person nullifies the sense of self completely and thereby attaches Thought to Nothingness, then a new sustenance flows to all the universes. This is a spiritual sustenance that did not previously exist. A person must be so in awe of God that the ego is totally nullified. Only then will this sustenance flow to all universes, filled with everything good."[74]

The merging of our free will with the Will of the Divine causes a new "sustenance" to flow in the universe. That is, this combination raises sparks and brings about a new level of consciousness in all of the universes of this creation. This is the product of attaching Thought, the mind, to Nothingness, the center of creation.

Thus, we practice the path of equanimity, which involves attaining the mind-state of selflessness, for much more than personal enlightenment. It is viewed as the path of true wisdom, and it is the process by which new consciousness is raised throughout the universes.

## Practicing Equanimity: Part 1

1. Sitting quietly, allowing the mind to reflect, try to recall as many times as you can during the past year when you were angry, and what caused it.

2. Try now to remember as many times as you can in your entire life when you were angry. How many details can you remember?

3. You will notice that no matter how much you try, you will be able to remember only a relative handful of times; even for these, many of the details will have disappeared. Notice that more than 90 percent (and it may be as high as 99 percent) of the angry experiences you have had are completely forgotten. Reflect upon this for a few minutes.

4. Now, try to remember all of the experiences of great joy that you have had in your life. Try to remember all of the details as best you can.

5. Of course, you will have noticed that more than 90 percent of the joyous experiences also are completely forgotten. It is true that at various times something will happen in our lives to cause us to remember an angry, sad, or joyous moment, but the point of this exercise is to realize that experiences of great emotional power do not last for long and most of the time are forgotten. Again, reflect upon this for a few minutes.

6. This is all there is to the practice. The more we reflect upon the ephemeral nature of our emotions, the more we realize that the next time we are caught in an emotional response, it will surely pass and be forgotten, even though we may not feel this way in the moment of our passion.

## Practicing Equanimity: Part 2

1. Sitting quietly, allowing the mind to reflect, try to think of a recent event in which you were personally involved that was highly emotional for you.

2. Imagine observing this event from the level of the soul. Assume that you can see clearly the cosmic implications of the event and can appreciate what happened from a universal point of view. Notice that the soul has a highly objective viewpoint.

3. Select another evocative event and reflect upon it from the perspective of the soul, contemplating all the variables that had to come together for this event to occur. Think of how it will affect the near and distant future.

4. Do step 3 repeatedly for as many emotional events as you can recall, whether negative and angry or positive and joyous. Each time you will notice that a broad overview affects the intensity of the emotions.

5. As you strengthen your inner observer, work with this process on all of the events in your life. Do this practice on a regular basis, perhaps once a week, reflecting on your relationships from a soul perspective. Over time this builds a reservoir of understanding which helps modify the ripples in your life. A disturbance in a shallow pool causes major turbulence; the same disturbance in a deep reservoir causes only modest ripples.

# 11. THE PATH
## OF EXTRAORDINARY
## MIND-STATES

*J*ewish mystics often engage in soul-travel to other realms. In a way, this is a practice of dying. The more we experience these excursions, the more comfortable we become with the prospect of what happens after death. In many traditions it is taught that we must die out of our own self-consciousness to enter states of higher awareness.

In Jewish mysticism, higher awareness has always been connected with the prophetic state of mind. This is called *ruach ha-kodesh,* the holy spirit, the fountain of prophecy that is the source of divine inspiration. Whereas little is known about the spiritual practices of ancient prophets, there are many descriptions in mystical Judaism of various techniques to develop *ruach ha-kodesh.* These include extensive prayer, solitary retreat, continuous acts of lovingkindness, absorption in contemplation of the Divine, repetition of holy names of God, and so forth. Once we attain this higher state of awareness, we are ready for the ultimate goal of *devekut,* merging with the Divine. Obviously, this advanced state of contemplative practice requires considerable discipline in daily life.

For more than a thousand years, Kabbalists have used visualization in order to dwell in higher planes. The mystical theory "As above, so below" is based on a holistic viewpoint that everything is connected. Whereas many traditions await visions of other realities, Kabbalists actively use imagination to enter these realms. In principle, if we can imagine it, it is as if we are doing it.

The following visualization may be difficult for some readers. It can be done in stages or all at once. In either case it should be repeated at least a half-dozen times, or until the images are clearly implanted. This meditation can be done on one's own but is best accomplished when one person reads to another. If working alone, the meditator may wish to record the visualization and then play it back, turning the machine on and off to allow for flexibility. The meditator must always set the pace, even when being guided.

*Whenever ending this visualization, quickly reverse the order of the steps to the beginning of stage one. This visualization must always begin and end with the initial instructions of noticing one's breath and body movement. This is important.*

While doing this visualization, be sure you will not be disturbed. Put a note on the door. Disconnect the telephone. Never leave a person alone in the middle of a visualization, and never push anyone farther than she or he is willing to go.

If guiding another person who is inexperienced in visualization work, the guide should read the following.

When doing visualizations, we should not have expectations of how they work. Some people see images as if a video screen were working in their minds—others have strong sound impressions. Some people have vague images, shadows, or other blurry sensations, and many people "visualize" by merely thinking. There is no right way to do this, as long as you are able to stay with the process.

# Throne-of-God Meditation

## Stage One: The Cave of Machpelah

1a. "Close your eyes and breathe deeply. Let yourself relax, and notice your chest rising and falling with the breath." *(Reader: Wait one minute.)*

"Now, imagine you are standing in a field that has a large group of rocks to one side; you can see that there is an opening that leads to a cave. A guard stands at the entrance to the cave. You will approach the guard, and the guard will ask you a question, a password, or something else that you must do to gain entry. Tell me if you are able to enter the cave." *(Wait silently. Do not make any sign of impatience. Getting into the cave can take less than a minute, or significantly longer. If the person is not able to get into the cave, or they drift away for some other reason, STOP AT THIS POINT and try the exercise again some other day.)*

1b. *(If the person indicates they are inside the cave, ask:)* "Please describe for me in as much detail as you can what you see, feel, or experience in this cave."

*(After hearing a detailed description of what is in the cave, ask:)* "Would you like to continue on now, or is this enough for today?"

*(If the person wants to move forward, go to step 2a. If it is enough for today, say:)* "Please go back out of the entrance that you came through, past the guard, into the field where we first began. Notice your chest rising and falling with the breath." *(Wait 30 seconds.)*

"Now, take a couple of deep breaths and open your eyes."

## Stage Two: The Garden of Eden

2a. *(Begin with stage 1, then continue:)* "Now that you are inside the cave, look around until you notice a special place where you can sit. When you find it, please describe it to me." *(Wait silently until the person describes the seat. Never give approval or disapproval of anything the person says. If the person has difficulty finding a place to sit, encourage her or him to continue looking. If the person continues to have trouble, stop at this point, reverse to the beginning, and end the visualization.)*

*(Once a seat is found:)* "Sit in this place. It has magic. Imagine you are closing your eyes as you sit here in the cave. You will be transported to a new place. You are outside a large garden surrounded by

a big fence with a gate. Two angels are guarding the gate. Describe to me what you see and how it feels to be here." *(Listen to the full description.)*

"Now you will be tested by the angels with a question, a password, or something else that is required for you to gain entrance. See what happens, and let me know if you are able to enter through the gate." *(Wait silently. If the person is not able to get into the garden, or he or she drifts away for some other reason, stop at this point. Be sure to reverse the visualizations, return to the cave, and come out of the cave into the field.)*

2b. *(If the person indicates being inside the gate, say:)* "You have entered the Garden of Eden. Please move around as much as you wish, and describe for me in detail what you see, feel, or experience in this garden."

*(After hearing a detailed description of the garden, ask:)* "Would you like to continue, or is this enough for today?" *(If the person wishes to continue, go to step 3. If not, return to the cave and then out into the field.)*

## Stage Three: Angels Deliver a Bodily Garment

3. *(Do everything up to step 2b, then continue:)* "Now that you are standing in the Garden of Eden, four angels will approach you. They will bring you a garment that will give you a new body. Describe to me what these angels look like. Describe what you look like when you put on this garment that gives you a new body." *(Wait until the person is finished.)*

*(After hearing a description of the new body, ask:)* "Would you like to continue, or is this enough for today?" *(If the person wishes to continue, go to step 4. If not, go back to the cave and then out into the field.)*

## Stage Four: The Gates of Righteousness

4. *(Do everything up to step 3, then continue:)* "Notice that to one side is a pillar of light made up of three colors. A guard stands in front of it. You will be tested with a question, a password, or something you must do to gain entrance into the pillar of light. See what happens. Let me know if you are given permission to enter the pillar of light, but do not enter it yet." *(Wait.)*

*(If the person does not get permission, return to the field via the cave. If the person does get permission:)* "When you enter this pillar of

light, it is going to carry you to a place called the Gates of Righteousness. Let me know what it looks and feels like when you arrive." *(Wait.)*

## Stage Five: The Being of God

5. *(Do everything up to step 4, then continue:)* "Look around and you will see that there is a special place with gates being guarded. These are the Gates of Righteousness. You will have to answer a difficult question, a puzzle, or you must undertake a hard task to get past the guard. This will be a challenge. See what happens and let me know if the guard is willing to let you pass." *(Wait.)*

   *(If the person cannot get past, return to the field via the garden and the cave. If the person gets permission to pass:)* "When you pass this guard, you will be transported to a new heavenly realm where many angels live. This is called the Being of God. When you arrive, describe to me your experience, how it feels, and what you see." *(Wait.)*

   "Would you like to continue?" *(If YES, go on to the next stage, step 6. If NO, reverse direction back to the cave and into the field where you began, ending the meditation.)*

## Stage Six: The Inner Sanctum of God

6. *(Do everything up to step 5, then continue:)* "There is only one more level that we will do. A special angel will approach you. This angel has a difficult question for you, a riddle, a test, or some task it wants you to do. This will not be easy. See what happens, and let me know if the angel is willing to take you up to the next realm." *(Wait.)*

   *(If the person cannot pass the test, return to the field via the Gates of Righteousness, the garden, and the cave. Remember, never ask about a test or riddle unless the person expresses a willingness to share it. If the person passes the test:)* "This angel is now going to transport you to the highest plateau, where you will be totally in the presence of the Divine. This stage is called the Inner Sanctum of God. When you arrive, describe to me your experience, how it feels, and what you see." *(Wait as long as you can. When the person is finished, remember to return to the field, quickly and gently going through all the stages in reverse.)*

This is a wonderful, peaceful, meditative place. It is sometimes difficult to return. Stay as long as you can, but at some point, as gently as possible, come back. Otherwise, the shock of returning too abruptly could be quite traumatic.

This guided meditation is based upon the journey of a higher soul level *(neshama)* after death that is described in considerable detail in the *Zohar.* According to the Jewish mystics, if a soul is worthy—well advanced in the process of redeeming sparks—it can become attached to God. Obviously, this imagery goes well beyond the boundaries of the intellect, but experientially it has profound importance—for the goal is *devekut,* merging with the Divine. Indeed, in this description, the soul can ascend to the level in which it beholds the Inner Sanctum of God—an exalted state of uniting with the Divine. After the soul enjoys the supernal delight of this lofty heavenly realm, it can continue its ascent, according to the *Zohar.*[75] However, the description ends at this point, suggesting that higher ascent is entirely enigmatic.

This visualization is extraordinarily powerful. It changes our relationship with death and helps us look forward to new opportunities beyond this life. When dwelling in higher awareness, we become more intimate with the extraordinary mind-state of *ruach ha-kodesh.* The word *"kodesh"* (holy) is a synonym for God, as in the phrase *"Ha-kodesh Baruch Hu,"* which is translated: "The Holy One, Blessed be It." Some translate the holy spirit as the "breath of God."[76] In a famous phrase in the Torah, God says, "I will fill him with the breath of God *(ruach Elohim),* with wisdom *(chochma),* understanding *(binah),* and knowledge *(daat)."*[77]

This level and the next represent the culmination of spiritual practice in the Jewish model of enlightening. Up to this point, aspirants must consciously make efforts to direct their own spiritual growth, but *ruach ha-kodesh* and *techiat ha-maytim* (life eternal) come only through grace.

# 12. THE PATH
## OF LIFE ETERNAL
## (GOD CONSCIOUSNESS)

*T*he final stage of the Jewish enlightening process could be translated literally as "enlivening the dead." Judaism believes that death is an illusion and that life eternal is everyone's destiny in the world to come. The essential Jewish belief of resurrection submits that all but the worst elements of human existence will be revitalized in an entirely new paradigm when our level of awareness attains new heights.

The teaching of this conclusive stage is that one need not wait for the future to achieve the awareness of eternal life. It is available to every one of us, here and now.

We will see later that death can be cheated; at least eleven people entered the heavenly realms without dying. Indeed, stories of transitions of great sages in many traditions suggest that some people do not die, but consciously move to another level of awareness.[78]

We must emphasize the word "consciously." In death, we all pass over to another level of awareness. But almost all of us do this unconsciously. As a result, the lower soul must go through purification, and most of us are reincarnated for the purpose of raising more sparks. Still, there are some who consciously go through their transition and attain a level of reality that in Kabbalah is called *tzaddik*. They have achieved life eternal. We can accomplish this over many lifetimes, or, with committed spiritual practice, we can do it in this one.

The level of awareness called *tzaddik* in Jewish mysticism is a timeless, spaceless realm that transcends duality. There are no clear boundaries of self and other in this realm, for all of creation is interconnected and interdependent. There is no subject or object, for each arises simultaneously with the other and cannot exist on its own. With no past or future, there is no birth or death; there is simply a continuous unfolding of the present moment. Herein lies the ultimate truth of existence, God-ing and creation-ing as one process everlasting.

Each of us has an aspect of the eternal *tzaddik* dwelling within us. This is the piece that holds together our world and the world around us. The more we deepen our practice, the closer we come to becoming the highest *tzaddik,* one who fully transcends this world. Even those at this level are called upon to keep the universe balanced in times of great need.

Although the *tzaddik* resides in an exalted state of mind, we can appreciate this awareness through an excellent exercise called "Through God's Eyes." It allows us to envision reality from the perspective of God, so to speak. At this stage in spiritual development, having not the slightest self-illusion, we see things in an entirely new way, observing veils within veils, realities within realities.

## Through God's Eyes

The essential understanding of messianic consciousness lies in appreciating the nature of process as an ongoing phenomenon. God is God-ing, creation is creation-ing, you and I are verb-ing, continuously unfolding in a dance with the Divine.

This awareness alone is sufficient to raise our consciousness to its highest potential. It is not something that awaits us in the future. It is simply a matter of realizing the consciousness within us in this moment.

In this final exercise, we learn to experience the process as it continues. This practice will alter consciousness and in a short time will change one's perspective on life.

1. Try to find a place where you will not be disturbed for twenty to thirty minutes. Sit quietly, comfortably, breathing normally.

2. Imagine that you are on an empty, protected beach on a warm, sunny day. You are sitting or lying on sand, fully relaxed. You can let go of all of your cares and worries while on this beach. You are alone here and completely safe. Look around you and describe to yourself what you see. Notice how you feel.

3. At one end of the beach is an empty house with at least three rooms. Let yourself walk toward this house, but do not enter it yet. Describe to yourself what the empty house looks like.

4. Walk through the front door of this house. The first room you enter will have a full-length mirror. Stand before this mirror and look at yourself. You can see yourself in great detail. Try to notice as much as you can about how you look in this mirror. How are you feeling while you do this?

5. After a few minutes of looking at yourself, you will enter the next room. Here too is a mirror. But this is a magic mirror that allows you to have a vision of what God looks like. Let your imagination flow and pretend that this is a window into heaven. Through it, you can see God. Allow yourself to spend a few minutes immersed in this experience of envisioning God.

6. Now you will enter the third room. There is yet another full-length mirror in this room. When you stand before it, you will experience a combination of the first two rooms. Look at yourself in the mirror and experience the presence of the Divine at the same time. That is to say, in this mirror you will see yourself as God sees you. Look

at yourself through the eyes of God, so to speak, and notice what you look like from the perspective of the Divine.

7. When you see yourself through God's eyes, notice how you feel. Observe how different you may feel from your experience with the first mirror.

8. When you are ready, leave this house by the same way you entered. Return to the place on the beach where you began this exercise, and sit or lie in the sand, allowing yourself to feel free, relaxed, totally at peace. Remain here for a few minutes. When you are ready, take a few deep breaths and open your eyes.

When we are able to let go of our inner critic for a while, we instantly realize a new relationship with life. In the eyes of God, we are perfect.

Each moment, as God-ing unfolds, we begin anew. Each moment is an opportunity to be fully who we are, or even who we think we want to be. It is always available to us.

God-ing is here. We are here. This is it.

# Part Four

## BEYOND THIS LIFE

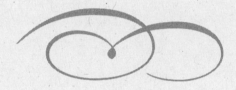

### OLAM HA-BAH
(The World to Come)

# REWARD,
# PUNISHMENT,
# AND DIVINE
# PROVIDENCE

One Tuesday morning, the Baal Shem Tov called together a number of his students, harnessed up the horses, and took off for parts unknown. The students always looked forward to these mysterious trips and the adventures that came with them. Usually the master would use his magical powers to travel great distances in a matter of hours. This time, however, the journey seemed to drag on endlessly; they rode in the carriage day after day and wondered if it would ever end. A number of students began to feel that this was not interesting at all; indeed it was downright wearisome.

On Friday afternoon, about an hour before sundown, they found themselves in a dense forest. Had it been any other sundown they would have been irritated; but this sundown led into Shabbos, the holy day of rest. What kind of Shabbos would it be in the middle of the woods? No wine, no *challah,* nothing to eat? It was a disaster.

Suddenly they saw a clearing with a cabin and a small barn. When the carriage pulled up to the cabin, the students jumped out and knocked on the door. After a while, it was answered by a large, unshaven, nasty-looking fellow in his undershirt. He snarled at them through broken, yellowed teeth, "What do you want?"

"Dear sir," they replied, "we are traveling with our master, and in a short time it will be Shabbos. We have nowhere to stay. Would you mind if we joined you and your family for Shabbos?"

"Mind?" he spat out. "Of course I would mind! I know your type. You want to sing and dance and tell stories during all of Shabbos. Not in my house!" He slammed the door in their faces.

What were they to do? There was no place else to go. So they knocked once again on the door and cowered together when the angry brute answered. This time his face was crimson, his eyes flared, and his lips dripped spittle. They said, "Dear sir, please, we have nowhere to go. We will sleep in the barn. We will not eat much. But please, let us stay."

"On one condition," he responded, "that you do it my way. No singing, no dancing, no storytelling. My way, or no way."

They agreed, wondering what their master had gotten them into. The room inside the house was dingy. Dead insects were scattered across the floor, and every corner had cobwebs.

They sat at the table. The Baal Shem Tov seemed to be in deep contemplation, constantly grooming his ample beard with his fingers. The students, however, were visibly upset. What could be worse than having a Shabbos in a dismal place like this? Moreover, what could be worse than a Shabbos that could not be celebrated with song and dance?

Well, actually, it did get worse. The host, if we could call him that, brought out just a touch of wine for the *kiddish* blessing, and then slobbered down most of it before passing the cup. The bread was stale, and each person at the table received only a crumb. Still more, believe it or not, he sneezed in the soup tureen before serving meager amounts to everyone at the table. The meal was ghastly in every respect.

That night they slept in the barn. The next morning they sat down to the second Shabbos meal, and it was worse than the first. He served cold leftovers, more stale bread, another smidgeon of wine, and some greasy lukewarm water with a limp piece of celery floating in it. This was called soup.

The third meal, just before sundown, was no better. The students could hardly wait for nightfall so that they could get back into the carriage and go home. By all measures, this was everyone's worst Shabbos; indeed, it was the most unpleasant experience they ever had with their teacher. Some even dared to whisper that he had lost his power and they were going to look for another rebbe.

All along, the Baal Shem Tov stroked his beard and quietly contemplated the events as they unfolded. He seemed completely unperturbed. Clearly he was not his joyous self like he usually was on Shabbos when he would tell marvelous stories, sing incredible *niggunim,* and dance around the table. But he did not argue with the gruff old man, nor did he use his magic to win the man over. He just sat and waited.

Night finally arrived. The young men hurried to get their belongings. But the surly old man said, "And where do you think you are going?"

One of the students responded, "Sir, we thank you for your kind hospitality, and we will now be going on our way."

The big man glared at the students. "Thanks ain't enough. I expect payment for the meals and lodging. I know you don't have money, and I don't want money anyway. There's plenty of work to do around here."

The students were flabbergasted. Payment for a Shabbos meal? In the past, they had eaten the best food in the best company and nobody ever suggested payment. Yet when they inquired of the master if the host could demand payment, the Baal Shem Tov rolled his eyes and shrugged his shoulders, indicating that the man had the right to ask for compensation.

Could it get worse? The next day they were cleaning the barn, moving the hay, spreading manure, building a new shed, and repairing a roof. Indeed, that Shabbos meal had been quite expensive. The miserly wages compounded the insult, for at the end of each day the old scrooge would tell them that they had to work the next. By the middle of the week, they wondered if they ever would be able to leave.

All along, the Baal Shem Tov worked shoulder-to-shoulder with his students, hardly speaking but never complaining. He had a distant gaze in his eyes, like a mariner searching through a thick fog for a beacon that would lead him home. As the week wore on, he became increasingly contemplative and often closed his eyes to explore inner realms.

By Thursday, the students had the sinking feeling they would be spending another Shabbos in this awful place. Indeed, Thursday night the ogre said that one more day would be required to fulfill their obligation.

All day Friday they were heartbroken, resigned to their fate. They agonized over the possibility that they would have to pay for the coming Shabbos by working all next week. An endless cycle would imprison them. There would be no escape.

## A New Shabbos

Late in the afternoon they finished their labors and prepared for Shabbos as best they could. The old man described to them a stream not far away where they could bathe. It was the first gesture of kindness he had made all week. They hurried to the stream, and behold! It was truly beautiful. A hot spring bubbled nearby so that they could soak their aching bones. The stream itself was deep enough for each to submerge in the living waters for purification. This was more like it. Too bad they had to go back to that awful house for another miserable Shabbos dinner.

As dusk was falling, they reluctantly returned to the cabin. When they entered, they could not believe their eyes. It had been transformed. It was filled with light, the walls gleamed, and the floor was highly polished. The table was set with a pure-white cloth, beautiful dishes, golden cutlery, and lovely wineglasses. The man's wife, whom they had never seen—perhaps she had been away—was dressed in a gorgeous white outfit. She lit candles all over the room to welcome the Shabbos; and what a Shabbos it was! Freshly baked *challah*; wine that flowed endlessly; perfect gefilte fish; piles of sweet, roasted chicken; on and on it went.

But the most amazing thing of all was the old man. He was transformed. He wore a beautiful robe and an embroidered skullcap. His face radiated a rosy glow of satisfaction and happiness. Even more astonishing, he sang and told amazing tales. He had an enormous amount of information at his fingertips.

At one point, the man's wife went up to the Baal Shem Tov and said to him, "Master, do you recognize me?"

He looked at her very closely, and then said, "My goodness, you are Rivka. My dear, it has been over thirty years since I saw you last. You must have been twenty years old when you left our home."

"Eighteen," she said. "Do you remember the last Shabbos I spent with the family?"

The fog began to clear a little. Rivka had been a maid in the Baal Shem Tov's home. There had been some problems, he remembered. His wife was not happy with her work. But he could not recall the details.

Rivka continued: "That last Shabbos, I remember so well. You had many guests. I had prepared a large amount of soup and put it in your biggest urn. It was very heavy as I brought it from the kitchen. I have always been a little clumsy; things seem to slip through my fingers. I tried to be so careful. But . . ."

Now it came back to the Baal Shem Tov. He could see Rivka carrying the urn from the kitchen. Suddenly, for no apparent reason, the whole container went crashing to the floor. Soup splattered everywhere. His wife was very angry with Rivka and criticized her until the young maid had been reduced to tears. It was a disaster. He remembered it well.

Rivka said, "Master, I was mortified. I realized it was my mistake. I decided to seek different work so that this would never happen again. Six months later, I left your house and found another job.

"After I left, I had a dream. In my dream, you were on trial. Angels accused you of a terrible misdeed. Do you know what it was?"

The fog cleared even more, and the Baal Shem Tov could see the flicker of the beacon that would illuminate his soul. He waited.

Rivka continued: "The angels accused you of allowing me to be embarrassed in public. You never did anything to bring comfort to the situation. And for this, the angels felt that you deserved to die!

"There was a lengthy debate in heaven. I saw it all in my dream. You had many defenders. Every prayer you have spoken and every person you have helped was represented by a defending angel. The heavenly argument continued for a while, and finally it was decided that you should be able to live. But you had to pay a grave penalty; they specified that you would have one Shabbos completely ruined."

The beacon now flashed brightly. Finally, after a week of reflection, he understood. He knew that the gruff man was acting a role, but he could not put the puzzle together until now. This man, the husband of Rivka, was a *lamed-vav tzaddik.* His whole task in life was to make sure the world would keep turning smoothly. He carried out the orders of heaven, even if it meant putting someone through a hellish experience.

The Baal Shem Tov looked across the table at the *tzaddik,* and the *tzaddik* looked back. Each of these wise sages had a grin stretching from ear to ear. The students looked from one to the other, not completely understanding what was happening, but overjoyed as light filled the room.

This was a Shabbos beyond any they had ever experienced. They were carried to indescribable realms, moving from one heavenly plateau to another, until they reached the highest moment—a taste, just a taste, of the seventh heaven. This one instant was more than payment for the week they had spent. Indeed, it was priceless.

They never uttered another word of complaint from that time forward. When they returned home the next week and shared this experience with others, they were proud to have been among those who spent the ruined Shabbos with the Baal Shem Tov, a holy day that had been traded for his life.

## The Value of Shabbos

Many wisdom-teachings are illustrated in the story of the *lamed-vav tzaddik*. Although we enter the world with fate as a steady companion, we can generate new fate while we are here. A simple act can have dire consequences, especially if one is at a high station of awareness and knows better. Everything we do creates an accusing or defending angel, which means that our actions, speech, and thoughts create ripples that ultimately work in our favor or as stumbling blocks.

When adversity strikes, it does not do much good to complain. The master remained calm but pensive, searching for the answer. The students, on the other hand, needed to learn more about faith. In the end, however, they were rewarded for their labors.

A *lamed-vav tzaddik* may hide in many disguises. The person giving us the hardest time actually may be saving our lives. We can never tell from one moment to the next if an event is for our well-being, so it is wise to give everything and everyone the benefit of the doubt.

In this story, one ruined Sabbath was traded for dozens of years of the Baal Shem Tov's life. The meaning of the Sabbath is to "rest" from our mundane consciousness and allow ourselves time each week for spiritual reflection. This reflection helps us stay finely tuned, alert to adjust our daily decisions, whenever necessary, so that our quality of life is enhanced. Without regularly taking this time, life can spiral into one dreary task after another, like the week that followed the ruined Shabbos in this story, until we no longer feel the spirit that resides within. In this sense, life can feel meaningless. Thus we have the teaching that Sabbath is almost as important as life itself.

One of the more interesting aspects of this story is the fact that a misdeed had a negotiable "punishment," and that it took many years for this punishment to be given. In this is a kabbalistic teaching about the nature of creation that is revealed in a story about the training of angels.

# THE MOST EXCELLENT
## HUMAN QUALITY

*I*t is taught that during Rosh Hashana and Yom Kippur there are accusing angels and defending angels. If the defending angels do not do their job well, the world cannot continue. So God prepares all defending angels by sending them to do a task that deepens their understanding. In one situation, God said to an angel, "Go find the most excellent quality of human experience, and return to tell me what it is."

The angel searched around the world. It saw many things. But what most impressed it was an event in which a confused man was standing in the middle of a busy road. To one side another man saw that a large truck was coming down the road too fast and would not be able to stop before hitting this dazed man. So the man on the side rushed out from the curb and reached the other just in time to push him out of the way. Unfortunately, he could not save himself and he was killed by the truck. The angel gathered up a drop of his blood and took it to God, saying, "This, I believe, may be the most excellent thing in human experience, the willingness to sacrifice one's life for another."

God replied to the angel, "You have found an excellent experience, but it is not the most excellent. Go back and find it."

The angel returned to earth and searched once again. It scanned the world, and this time the angel was attracted by the experience of a woman giving birth. The woman moaned and writhed for a long time until at last the infant was born. When she saw its little body, her pain dropped away and a warm ecstasy filled her with love. The angel reached over, took a drop of sweat from the woman's body, and returned to God, saying, "This, I believe, may be the most excellent thing in human experience, bringing life into the world."

Once again, God said to the angel, "Indeed, this is an excellent human experience, but it is not the most excellent. Try one more time."

So the angel returned again to find the most excellent human experience. It searched very carefully, and being an angel, it could view thousands of events at the same time. Suddenly something caught its attention. A man was running through a wooded area, and he was clearly in a violent mood. The angel quickly reviewed this man's life and found that he had just been released from jail, having served many years for another man's crime. Now, furious, he was out for revenge.

The angel followed him through the woods and saw him approach a cabin. The guilty one lived inside. He was the one who should have served the prison term. When the running man came close to the house, he saw a light through the window.

Standing at the window, still bent on revenge, he looked inside and saw his intended victim. The man and his bride of one year had just returned from the hospital with their new daughter. They were as happy as people can be. The angry man looking through the window watched carefully, and slowly his heart broke into pieces. He began to weep and then turned away into the woods, never to return.

The angel gathered up one of his tears and returned to God, saying, "This, I believe, is the most excellent thing in human experience—forgiveness: the ability to transcend anger, hatred, and the desire for revenge."

God congratulated the angel, saying, "Indeed, the ability to forgive is the most excellent gift in human experience. Many other things are important, but this is one of the few traits that distinguishes human potential. As a defending angel, it is imperative that you understand forgiveness; it is the only reason my creation continues. Without forgiveness, all would disappear in an instantaneous flash."

The Jewish mystical point of view is that creation is based upon compassion and lovingkindness. For the Kabbalist, forgiveness does not mean we need to embrace someone who has done a despicable act against humanity. Rather, it is focused on the degree to which we hold on to our anger or our negative feelings.

If the creation were based upon a pure system of reward and punishment, in which punishment would be the instant result of one's actions, we could not survive for long. We do things, say things, and think things that would surely overwhelm us if we had to make instant payment for unskillful behavior. The very idea that there is a time period between one's actions and the resulting "punishment" suggests that the universe is willing to wait, so to speak, for something to mediate the potential punishment.

## REWARD AND PUNISHMENT

The traditional approach to the concept of reward and punishment is that the hand of providence is in everything as a payment for past deeds. Good actions receive good payments; actions that are not good can cost a heavy price. Traditionally, we learn through revelation or prophecy about what we are supposed to do, and then must live our lives accordingly.

In theory, this idea may seem logical. In reality, we see that it does not work this way. We discover through experience that people who live good, clean lives often suffer greatly, while others who are not so careful often seem to have everything they need. This raises the issue of why bad things happen to good people. The ancient rabbis were greatly troubled by this question.

The Talmud tells of a father who sent his son to the roof to bring down some young birds. The son went as instructed and fulfilled the requirement of the law by sending away the mother from the nest before collecting the chicks. On his way down, the son fell off the ladder and was killed.

Two specific Jewish laws in the Torah say that people performing particular commandments will live extended lives. The first of these laws is that of obeying one's parents; the other is that of sending away the mother bird from her chicks.[1] In this instance, the boy had fulfilled both laws, yet was the victim of an early death.[2]

The rabbis wondered if there had been extenuating factors. Perhaps the son or even the father was thinking something "sinful" as the boy was descending from the roof. But it was decided that the commission of good deeds should protect someone from thoughts such as these. Moreover, when one is engaged in the performance of a good deed, it is said that this person cannot come to any harm.

This situation distressed the rabbis. They simply did not know how to deal with it. Indeed, it was said that one of the greatest sages, Elisha ben Abuyah, turned away from his religious beliefs and stopped practicing his faith because of a similar incident in which he witnessed someone being killed in the performance of a good deed.[3]

Some of the rabbis tried to solve the problem by saying that there is life in this world, and life in the world to come. They suggested that when the law described the prolongation of life by doing good deeds, it was referring to life in the world to come, but the length of one's life in this world was never assured.

However, this idea contradicts other rabbinic dictums based on the principle that everything is repaid in the world measure for measure *(middah keneged middah)*."[4] There are many examples along this line of thinking. The Talmud says that famine comes from not giving tithes, pestilence comes from performing mortal sins, war comes from perversion of judgments, harm from wild beasts comes from swearing, exile comes from idolatry or incest, and bloodshed comes from not allowing the land to lie fallow in the seventh year.[5]

Throughout the Talmud, punishments—in this world—are described as retribution for misdeeds. But this still is not satisfactory. All we need do is look around us to see the heartache and misery of wonderful people, or the comfortable lives of tyrants and thieves.

There is yet another talmudic approach to the question of reward and punishment. In this, good deeds are their own reward, and misdeeds are their own punishment. Each good deed leads to another; this makes for a pleasant life. Conversely, each misdeed also leads to another, and this results in a confused and difficult life. The advice given here is: "Do not be like servants who serve their master with the expectation of receiving a reward, but serve without expectations."[6]

According to this viewpoint, reward and punishment should not be part of our calculation, either in this world or in the world to come. Simply being present in the moment is all we really can do. This talmudic idea is a rejection of the belief of measure for measure; it says that God is forgiving and filled with lovingkindness. Even if 999 accusing angels declare a person's guilt and only one says the person is innocent or deserves forgiveness, mercy will prevail.[7]

Along these lines, the *Zohar* asks, "How is it that so many sinners and transgressors are alive and active?"[8] If punishment were swift, as some say, these people could not live long. However, it says that if there is a possibility that a sinful person may become virtuous, the person is judged favorably. In addition, if the person is destined to bear a virtuous child, the judgment is always lenient.[9]

Thus we see that the idea of reward and punishment runs the full gamut from guaranteed reward or retribution, either in this world or the next, to living each moment in its fullness, trusting in the merciful and forgiving nature of the universe. None of these ideas, however, is fully satisfactory. On the one hand, all of them leave us with the feeling that we are constantly being judged, and on the other, there seems to be no correlation between one's actions and the rewards of a good life.

## DIVINE PROVIDENCE

The mystical approach to the difficult issue of divine providence brings us a wholly different perspective on the question of reward and punishment. The original sin recorded in the Torah is eating the fruit of the Tree of Knowledge, as if God did not want it to happen. We could ask, Did the eating happen by accident? Were Adam and Eve programmed to eat the forbidden fruit? Was it preordained that they should eat? And if it were any of these, where does the punishment fit in? It seems that they did what had to be done; it was divine providence. If so, how does divine providence work?

This question has plagued mystics and metaphysical thinkers for two thousand years. It is extremely difficult to address as long as we remain fixed on the old paradigm of God as a noun. However, once we move to the concept that God is a verb, and that the process of creation is relational, we gain new insight, for creation-ing cannot unfold without God-ing, and vice versa. It is like two gears turning against each other—if one gear is withdrawn, the other immediately stops.

Thus God-ing and creation-ing have a symbiotic relationship that reveals itself as each moment unfolds. Divine providence is the role that God-ing plays in the relationship. God-ing brings all of the variables of the universe to bear upon each moment. This means that as long as I am in process, or you, or anyone, or anything, the universe in turn is in relationship with this process. This relationship is what we call divine providence. Some examples will help clarify what God-ing means in this context.

A person learning how to draw discovers that there is a relationship between the object being drawn and the space just around that object, called negative space. Rather than draw the outline of a flower, for example, one can be trained to draw the shape of the space around the flower. When drawing this way, we still get the flower, but we do it by focusing on the space that is "not flower." So by drawing everything around an object, we end up drawing the object.

We also could look at the flower from the perspective of everything that allows it to be what it is: earth, water, nutrients, seed, warmth, light, and air. Thus, we can relate to a flower from the viewpoint of what allows it to exist in this moment. If it were surrounded by a vacuum instead of its current air pressure, it would immediately wilt and die. If it were moved to a different location, it could be severely traumatized. From a mystical perspective, if its angelic energy were withdrawn, it could not survive.

The space around something defines the thing. I am David-ing, but everything around me defines what I am. Some would say that we are what we eat. But that is too narrow a viewpoint. Rather, we are what we see, hear, touch, and taste; we are the accumulation of our experiences, and we are in process with a continuous flow of experiential input. Change the experience, and we change. Every moment we exist, we are in relationship with that which defines who we are.

What David-ing brings to each moment is the compilation of my life—a collection of events—plus a monkey wrench called free will. Most of the time, the gears of the ongoing relationship between God-ing and David-ing turn in a fairly predictable way. But the monkey wrench can be inserted into the gears, affecting my direction and ultimately the direction of the universe.

What divine providence brings to each moment is the accrual of everything that has occurred in the universe up to that moment. In the Garden of Eden, the system is completely pristine, for there is no prior history. It is the beginning of a new consciousness. In this context, divine providence was single-pointed. God-ing says that Adam and Eve should not eat from the tree because it will cause death. This is precisely what the Tree of Knowledge did. Clearly, the garden could have been structured to keep Adam and Eve from tasting the Tree of Knowledge. Death is not a punishment, but the reality of a creation that has duality. Duality requires separation. Yet the ultimate truth of the Divine is Oneness. Part of the process of separation merging back into Oneness is what we call death.

So reward and punishment in our reality is a continuous process of the unfolding relationship between God-ing and creation-ing. God-ing endlessly gives us clues: "Watch out, if you eat too much chocolate, you are going to regret it"; "If you split the atom, it will come at a great cost"; "If technology becomes too advanced, the nature of the human mind will change forever"; "If life becomes too busy, you will lose contact with your soul." God-ing consistently informs us that our lives are balanced upon the decisions we make.

Our day-to-day actions, words, and thoughts continuously affect our sense of harmony with the universe. The more harmony we have, the more we could say we are being rewarded. But our harmony is not simply a function of our individual deeds, for just as human beings bring free will into each moment, God-ing brings divine providence. Because divine providence includes every ripple that has been sent into the universe by every person who has ever lived and every event that has ever taken place, we can never second-guess it. From this perspective, reward and punishment is not related only to individual decisions; it is the product of the collective history of creation. It affects not only individuals, but the process of creation-ing as a whole.

This is a central Jewish teaching. Our conscious actions and good deeds are not simply for the individual, but for the entire world. Our goal is to bring all of creation into greater harmony. It is for this reason that all of the prayers of the High Holy Days are structured in the plural. Our efforts are for the community of all beings.

The Talmud teaches that when a wild she-goat is laboring to give birth, she may be standing at the top of a mountain. In this situation, the newborn kid will be maimed or killed when it drops. God-ing prepares an eagle to catch the kid in its wings as it is born, and thus save it. God-ing notes: "If the eagle were one second too soon or one second too late, the kid would be killed."[10]

This is a marvelous example of the "spontaneity" of divine providence.[11] But we must ask, What brought divine providence to the place in which the newborn kid could be saved? And the answer is that this can happen only when there is a particular harmony in the universe. Too often we are aware of situations where divine providence does not intervene to save life. Whales beach themselves, birds fly into windows, horses break legs, "accidents" happen naturally everywhere.

We know today that nature often provides millions of offspring in the process of reproduction to assure that a few will live. The scientist tends to focus on the millions that do not survive as a proof of randomness; the mystic focuses on the few that do survive as a proof of divine providence.

The goal is not to avoid every accidental injury or death, but to work toward a higher consciousness that sustains a harmonious balance in the universe. We do not know which newborn kids need to be saved. Nor can we clearly understand death on any level. But we have a deeper wisdom that guides and informs us. It is upon this inner knowing that we must rely.

At each moment, creation-ing continuously evolves along with God-ing; humans add the ingredient of free will, and God-ing provides a mixing bowl called divine providence. This system is fundamentally causal, and yet is spontaneous and unpredictable because an unknown variable always can be inserted between the cause and the effect, through either free will or divine providence.

The teaching that God is a verb and that creation is an ongoing process brings a new vitality to each moment and opens up for us an infinity of possibilities. By understanding the way the process works, with God-ing and creation-ing unfolding simultaneously, we gain enormous insight into the mystical architecture of the universe.

The approach of Jewish mysticism regarding divine providence and fate is twofold. First, we do everything in our power to live, to fix ourselves, to change the world for the better. Every breath is a new opportunity for confronting fate and bringing us closer to a new reality. Second, we realize that life, as we know it, is ultimately fated to end in death. For this we practice equanimity. We learn how to balance the highs and lows, and we develop a center of inner peace that will sustain us through difficult times.

---

Life is not an *either-or* proposition; it always includes the spirit of *and*. There are times for one approach *and* there are times for its opposite. Sometimes we fight to make change; sometimes we gracefully accept fate. In any case, we must be very careful of anyone who suggests that she or he has answers to questions that have been with us for thousands of years. A great teacher once said, "In reality as we know it, many questions are meant only to be asked—never answered."

# DYING AND FEAR

*S*ome people say that waiting for dying to begin is far worse than dying itself. Nursing homes are filled with people who anxiously await death's visit. This can last for years. Fear pervades day after day during this time. The fear becomes accentuated when empty chairs are inevitably noticed in the dining room. Every few weeks, another person disappears, evoking terror in one's heart.

When is it going to be my chair? What is going to happen? Will it hurt? Where am I going? Will I know who I am? Will I ever return?

## DAD

*A*s I was writing this book, my father, Sampson D. Cooper, aged ninety-two, made his final passage. He had been living in a nursing home and for many years had been confined to a wheelchair. He felt trapped in a body that simply would not function in the way that he wanted. His intellectual capacity diminished dramatically near the end of his life, and he increasingly became disheartened when words and entire sentences disappeared into a black hole that slowly consumed his mind.

For a couple of years, I received weekly telephone messages that Dad had been found on the ground near his wheelchair. He would slip while moving from his bed or the toilet. Sometimes, I think, he would just lie down on the floor to sleep because the extra few feet to get to the bed demanded too much effort. An independent person, he would not tolerate being strapped into the chair. Fortunately, he was never hurt in these incidents, except for occasional bruises.

One evening, however, we got the message that Dad had been found unconscious. We went straight to the nursing home. When we arrived, his eyes were open but he was unable to speak. It did not look good.

We stayed with him until late that evening, and I returned early the next morning. Since he was not able to eat or drink, the doctor knew that he could not last for more than a day or two. So I sat with him, speaking, singing, being quiet. Shoshana arrived around noon. We spent the afternoon swabbing his lips and mouth with water, trying to help soothe any discomfort. Most of the time we meditated.

My mother had died nine years earlier on the holiday called Tu b'Shevat, the Festival of Trees, while we were living in Jerusalem. On the long flight from Israel to California, where she had lived and would be buried, I remember looking across an expanse of clouds, feeling Mom's presence everywhere. Her spirit permeated everything. It was a wonderful feeling. I remember wondering if death were really so expansive.

Late in the afternoon with Dad, I noticed a change in his breathing. Throughout the day, he had pushed our hands away, not wanting to be touched. We respected his needs and left him alone. But now something had changed. He reached out and wanted to hold my hand. His eyes were wide open, but he was still unable to speak.

As I moved in close enough to whisper to him, he began to emanate a light of life-force that bathed the room. I felt myself carried into a completely different realm, fully conscious, and I sensed more strongly than ever the presence of my mother. My head was two inches from Dad's. I knew that he could feel her as well. He was quite still, looking straight ahead, holding my hand tightly.

I found myself saying, "It's okay, it's okay."

Dad was not religious. He had been angry with just about everything for the last fifteen or twenty years. Mom had given up along the way. But she had asked me to promise to see him through his final years. This was not easy to do. He could be quite nasty. Still, when we returned from Israel, he moved from California to Colorado so that we could spend extended time together.

Now, however, there was not the slightest hint of the anger I knew so well. The last half hour of his life was calm, connected, and extraordinarily powerful. His breath got fainter, I continued to whisper, and Mom's presence got stronger. At one point I sensed a deep gratitude from her, and from a part of him, for seeing him through, and especially for what was happening right now.

Then I felt the presence of my mom indicating that she would take over, for he was about to go somewhere that was beyond my limits.

He never closed his eyes until the final shudder when his breath stopped. In that last moment, I began to say *kaddish*. Wherever he was, he heard me. A tear formed up in the corner of one of his eyes. I was stunned. And then he was gone.

All the years of our estranged relationship were wiped away in that final half hour. Words did not need to be spoken. The life-force that spread through that room and beyond was all that needed to be communicated. Indeed, it is here with me now as I write these words.

## WORKING WITH THOSE
## WHO ARE DYING

Working with dying people means dealing with fear: our own, that of those around us, and that of the person dying. Although most fear of death is diverse and extensive, it essentially falls into three main categories: fear of personal failure in this life, fear of pain in the dying process, and fear of the unknown after death.

When we make peace with our own concerns about death, we are more able to work with others. Many practices in Judaism help us develop skills for this kind of work. Following are exercises that open our awareness and slowly help to alleviate our fears.

We all are familiar with the feeling that we have not done things well; we feel that we have botched jobs or relationships, and we sense that we have left tracks behind that we wish would disappear. We hope that time will heal these wounds, but when we are approaching death, old pains often loom quite large in our universe of regrets. If only we could do it over again; if only we had more time to fix things.

People in the process of dying worry about promises unkept, responsibilities avoided, and life goals unfulfilled. They worry as well about liabilities that are being left behind for others. They are distressed about abandoning people who relied upon them, whom they nurtured, loved, or sustained. And they are troubled about people who may have served and loved them but were never properly acknowledged.

As long as people focus on the empty part of the cup, the list of concerns grows longer and longer. Many times dying people have their heads and hearts so filled with a sense of personal failure and missed opportunities that they are immersed in a sea of remorse that keeps them, and everyone else, from attending some important issues: forgiveness, openheartedness, acknowledgement and the expression of unconditional love.

It has been pointed out by health professionals who work with dying patients that the most important quality we need to have when attending someone in the dying process is the ability to be present: to be able to listen, support, and be noninvasive. In doing so, however, we sometimes do not have an opportunity to "get real" with a dying person. I was not able to do so with my father; he was somewhere else that last day. And my mother left suddenly, so I never had the chance. Nonetheless, I have been in many situations in which people are able to let go of old patterns and make new connections that bring about a healing for everyone involved.

Whether or not this will occur depends upon a wide set of variables. It should *not* be a goal. Many people simply are not prepared to be more vulnerable or to take risks in the highly stressed environment that often accompanies the dying process. If, however, there seems to be willingness on everyone's part to explore deeper questions, here are some practices for working with others in the dying process.

## Fear of Failure

### 1. Offering Confession and Asking Forgiveness

In Judaism, this practice is often associated with the High Holy Days: Rosh Hashana and Yom Kippur. At that time, we communicate with the Divine, confessing things we regret having done, said, or even thought.

At any time in the year, however, we can take on the spiritual practice of confessing our regrets to another person, or listening to someone else's confessions, particularly someone who is in the process of dying. Obviously, this is not easy to do and must be accomplished with considerable skill and sensitivity. People are reticent to reveal things about which they feel guilty. Many would prefer to take these secrets to the grave, and they should be entitled to do so.

The success of this practice is not measured by the amount or intensity of information divulged. Rather, success is measured by the degree to which a safe haven is provided in which a person can choose to discuss his or her regrets. Clearly, it must also be safe to *not* discuss sensitive issues—pressure must never be brought to this situation.

This practice requires only two people. We begin by sitting quietly, remembering as many events as we can in which we may have done, said, or thought some things we now regret. Sometimes simply sitting quietly like this is sufficient, for in mystical terms, the souls are communicating on different planes of reality which do not require verbal expression. It goes beyond a glance or gesture. Indeed, even if a person is in a coma, the soul can connect in unknown ways.

Most of the time, however, in this process it is quite useful to speak aloud what is in our hearts. The purpose of this exercise is to be willing to admit mistakes and to ask for forgiveness. When we are able to do so, the process can be profoundly moving. It often opens a potential for new understanding between people, and is highly recommended for healing old wounds. Either or both people can speak.

## 2. Annulment of Vows

This is another spiritual exercise that is normally done during the High Holy Days but can be addressed at any time during the year. As noted, people in the dying process often feel that they have unfinished business. Releasing them from these concerns can be a true source of liberation.

First, at an appropriate time, we ask a person, "Do you feel that you have made promises or commitments that are still unresolved?" If the person says yes, we attempt to find a way to release these commitments that is satisfactory for the person. If it is a promise the person made to you, you can say something like: "I wholeheartedly release you from this promise and any other commitments you may have made."

If it is a commitment to someone else, try to find a way to free the person. You might bring in others who are involved. You might use reason. You might take on some things yourself, though you should never assume an obligation of another out of a sense of guilt. You might invite angels to help, use prayers, call on God.

The very fact that these issues are being discussed is liberating; it usually leads to much more peace of mind and clarity. In one's final days or hours, a great deal can be accomplished along these lines to help her or him through the transition process.

## 3. Tashlich

Annulment of vows is one of a number of purification practices. Another is *tashlich* (sending away), which is done annually on the afternoon of the first day of Rosh Hashana. Usually we say prayers at a body of water into which we cast bread crumbs, which represent residual aspects of traits, habits, or memories we would like to discard. The following is a variation on this.

If people in the dying process can write for themselves, have them do so. If they need help with the writing and are willing to let you help, you may write for them. On scraps of paper, write responses to the following:

   *a.* Things I have done in my life that I regret
   *b.* Anything I may have said to harm someone
   *c.* Events I would replay, if I could
   *d.* Things I wish I had said to someone
   *e.* Promises I made that were never kept
   *f.* Hopes and dreams that never worked out

Anything can be added to this list. Each scrap of paper should be crumpled up and burned over a small fire, slowly, contemplatively, until all are gone. In a hospital, or anywhere that fire is not permitted or not practical, each scrap of paper can be cut into tiny pieces and destroyed in some way.

## 4. *Family History*

If the dying person is a parent, grandparent, or elder relative, an excellent practice is to record as much family history as he or she is willing to offer. Who did what when? What are some of the rarely told family secrets? Try to gather as much detail as you can. Exploring the past in great depth is a wonderful form of healing.[12] It allows people to reflect on the meaning of their lives, the impacts they have had, the continuity they have engendered. Although these reflections can open old wounds, for the most part they are usually provocative and soul-satisfying. This process is highly recommended.

## 5. Meditation Exercises

Many of the meditation exercises suggested in this book are recommended for working with the fear of failure, particularly: Awe (p. 219), Equanimity (p. 225), The Soul Is Pure (p. 205), Joy (p. 209), Archangel Meditation (p. 144), Guardian-Angel Practice (p. 149), and Through God's Eyes (p. 232).

## FEAR OF PAIN

*M*ost physicians these days will prescribe sufficient medication to deal with any pain involved in the dying process. Everyone has different pain tolerances, and ultimately only the patient can determine her or his own comfort level. Once appropriate medication has been arranged, there are a number of complementary ways to work with pain. One of them is meditation.

Guided meditation is often invaluable for people who have not had meditation experience. The secret of being a competent guide is to learn how to participate in the meditation while directing. Never simply read the words. This will not work. You must enter into the spirit of the meditation. Your own state of mind will influence your timing, voice modulation, sensitivity to the needs of the other, and management of the content of the imagery. The following are examples of guided meditations that can be of particular help to someone in the dying process.

## 1. Inspiration

One of the basic Jewish meditative techniques is to read inspirational scripture out loud. Psalms, the Song of Songs, the Shema, other prayers, and any other parts of scripture can have insightful meaning when read slowly and used as contemplative material.

Many people have strong negative feelings about biblical literature. This is often related to the language rather than the subject. Try to work with material that is as close to everyday language as possible. If a meaningful scriptural reading cannot be found, use poetry or something beautiful from another culture that touches your soul.

If using inspirational readings, be sure to review the selection before beginning, to make certain it is appropriate. Do not read for content, but for inspiration. One line followed by a full minute or two of silence is fitting. The idea is not to "get somewhere," but to in-spire the silence. This process has great value.

### 2a. Speaking to God

For ten or fifteen minutes, speak to God in your own words. Every-one participating should try to find a space alone in order to speak in a whisper and have a certain degree of privacy. Try any of the fol-lowing subjects (or any others that seem appropriate).

> *a.* What I did right in my life
> *b.* What I might have done better
> *c.* What I need right now
> *d.* My prayer for others
> *e.* How to deal with my pain and anxiety
> *f.* How to open my heart and accept things

### 2b. Reflection of God

Repeat this process of speaking to God, but this time speak to each other as if your partner were the vehicle through which God is lis-tening. One speaks, one listens. After five or ten minutes, partners should switch. Pray to each other, and let your heart connect inti-mately with your partner's.

### 3. Singing Together

Sing or chant together some holy songs, names of God, lines from liturgy, wordless melodies, or anything else that helps you raise your voices in song. Singing together has great healing power.

### 4. Nature

If you can go for a walk; be in nature; or sit by the ocean, on a moun-tain, in the desert, by a stream, or anywhere different and alive, try to do so. Just sit quietly and listen. (If the dying person is unable to do this, it is still highly recommended for the caretaker.)

### 5. Other Meditations

Other meditations in this book that are useful in working with the fear of pain are: Equanimity (p. 225), Archangel Meditation (p. 144), and Guardian-Angel Practice (p. 149).

# FEAR OF
## THE UNKNOWN

*H*asidic and kabbalistic literature, the Talmud, and the *Zohar* all have descriptions of realms of reality that transcend the mind. Because these other realms are not rational and are difficult to describe, one of the best ways to enter the experience of dwelling in these realms is through guided visualization that allows the meditator total latitude in forming his or her own internal images. When we utilize our imagination in the context of guided meditation to explore other realms, the effect can be to gently alleviate fears of the unknown. Indeed, when we enter heavenly realms in our imagination, we often feel comforted within. It is as if our souls have memories far beyond the limits of our minds. Guided meditations, such as Guardian-Angel Practice (p. 149), Archangel Meditation (p. 144), and Throne-of-God Meditation (p. 228) are very useful in this process.

When working with people who express great fear of dying, I often lead them through a series of guided meditations like these. We travel together on a creative inner journey to realities that we imagine could be like after death. The imaginative mind has marvelous access to other realms of reality. The point is not whether or not we are making things up, but instead that, as discussed earlier, if we can imagine it, some aspect of it exists—"As above, so below." Thus, we can explore the other side of death.

Guided visualizations are not supposed to suggest concrete forms. Rather, the idea is to set intentions and to encourage the person experiencing the visualizations to explore with great freedom the images of his or her own mind. The guide is merely a facilitator when the person needs help to break through her or his own self-imposed limitations. Once this is accomplished, a whole new inner world opens up for the person who is visualizing. This can be accomplished in one extended session lasting a couple of hours, or in a number of sessions over the period of a week. It is usually a rich experience and often leads to a different perspective of life after death.

Yet with all these practices available to us, fear of dying still is a major obstacle for many people. As we will see, the greatest sages in Judaism often reached out for help to deal with the fear of death. They generally agreed that dying itself was a far easier experience than dealing with the process of dying, in which fear plays a dominant role. There are no simple answers to this challenge.

# THE SOUL'S
# TRANSITION
# AFTER DEATH

*a* traditional Jewish ritual during a person's last hours of life is for someone to light a candle in the room of the dying person, which symbolizes the flickering of a human soul. We give deference to her or his final wishes. A person is gently encouraged to confess and ask for atonement. This confession can be as simple as "May my death be an atonement." A person often recites the Shema when preparing for death.[13] It is said in the Talmud that being with someone when she or he dies is a great deed of lovingkindness, for a soul in transition is comforted by a soul in a peaceful state.

In Jewish tradition, we say that someone has died when breathing has stopped and there is no pulse. Traditionally a feather is put across the lips and watched for any sign of movement for eight minutes. The eyes are gently closed, and the arms and hands are extended alongside the body. Water standing in the vicinity is poured out. The body is never left alone, for its vital soul is temporarily disoriented. During the period between death and burial, traditionally about twenty-four hours or less, psalms are read continuously to help ease the passage.[14]

In religious communities, the body is prepared for burial by a *chevra kaddisha* (holy community). In this process, called *tahorah* (purification), the body is cleansed with lukewarm water while attendants recite biblical verses and psalms. The idea is to honor the one who has passed over, and also to heal the soul in transition. *Tahorah* is an enormously powerful experience for those who perform this ritual, and deeply meaningful for the survivors. When the preparations of the body have been completed, a large amount of water— at least four and a half gallons—is poured over the body while it is held in an upright position. This represents a final purification in preparation for burial. Afterward, the body is dried and placed in shrouds.[15]

Many traditional rituals have been put aside by non-Orthodox Jews. This, I believe, is a mistake. I was once called by a man who was facing serious surgery. He was worried about dying. He wanted Tibetan Buddhist rites of passage first, and then a Jewish burial. I asked him why, and he responded that his body would be constantly attended and that prayers would be said to assist his transition. I told him that Judaism has a similar ritual using different prayers but the same process. He was surprised to hear this; most Jews are completely unaware of the depths of the tradition.

It would be helpful for non-Orthodox Jews to revisit this particular aspect of the tradition and to seriously consider paying more attention to honoring the mystery of death. As we learn more about the Jewish mystical approach to dying, soul journeys, raising sparks, and bringing the consciousness of the world to a higher level, we need to pay closer attention to the value of some of our ancient rituals.

Jewish practices after burial are generally well known. For the first seven days, immediate family members sit *shiva* (*shiva* means seven), which traditionally includes sitting low to the ground, burning a candle for the entire week, not wearing leather footwear, covering mirrors or turning them around, and having a prayer *minyan* (ten adults) in the house for three daily prayers (morning, afternoon, and evening after dark) so that *kaddish* (prayers for the dead) can be said. This process with the accompanying ritual can be highly therapeutic for the family. It brings the community together, strengthens bonds of relationship, and gives a framework of support in the face of a difficult experience. It also gives one a sense of connectedness with the tradition, knowing these observances have been done for thousands of years. Many who do not ordinarily observe traditional Jewish practices have found great merit and deep meaning in sitting *shiva*.

Mourning continues for thirty days *(sheloshim),* during which time mourners are not supposed to cut their hair, wear "pressed" clothes, get married, attend festive events, or embark on business journeys. *Kaddish* is said every day at prayers (traditionally three times a day) for eleven months for a parent, child, or spouse.

Most of the mourning rituals are designed to help people through the grieving process. On the mystical level, they also help the soul during its transition. This is particularly true of the prayers that are sent to support the soul needing redemption. We will see that the power of prayer for those who have died is an important part of the redemption process.

Whether or not we are attracted to traditional mourning practices, we cannot help but think about the loss of a loved one. We can be a major resource for the departed soul by simply sending our love and support. When we are able to feel that we are doing something, it helps us in our grieving process, and, mystics say, it truly helps the soul.

s discussed earlier, there are five levels of the soul. The higher levels, *neshama, chayah,* and *yehidah,* function in a way that they cannot be directly affected by what a person does to his or her consciousness. However, they are indirectly affected by the states of the *nefesh* and *ruach.* After death, the higher levels of the soul will return to their home "regions," but they must await the redemption of the *nefesh* before finally resting in their natural states.

If the *nefesh* does not get redeemed, the *ruach* cannot be "crowned" in the lower Garden of Eden. If it cannot be crowned, the higher soul levels cannot reach the center of awareness. In this sense, all of the levels are "punished" by having to await the redemption of the lowest level of soul, the *nefesh.*

It is said that the *nefesh* wanders between the grave and the dwelling place of the deceased for the first seven days after death, looking for its living body. After, the *nefesh* is purified in *Gehinnom,* and then it wanders the world until it has a garment (signifying an awareness level).[16] This process of purification takes twelve months. Once it has its garment, it gains access to the lower Garden of Eden, where it joins the *ruach.* The *ruach* then gets crowned, the *neshama* unites with the Throne, and all is well.

In a remarkable section, the *Zohar* outlines the process of the purification of the *nefesh* during the twelve months after death, suggesting a completely different scenario from what most of us have been taught. The Jewish mystical system is designed to continue the process of *tikkun olam* (mending the universe) even after death. The reader must keep in mind that the language of Kabbalah is poetic, the images are metaphors, and the intention is to arouse the soul rather than the mind. From this perspective, let yourself enter these mystical teachings as a garden of delights.

Once a *nefesh* no longer has a body, it loses its free will, which is associated only with living people.[17] Therefore, it no longer can redeem itself, but needs the guidance and help of a living being with free will. In this context, there are a number of ways in which a *nefesh* can be redeemed.

## Assistance from a Living Tzaddik

First, there are *tzaddikim* (saints) who dwell in other realms. These saints are born into this world when the scales of good and evil in the world tilt dangerously to the side of evil. In this situation, the *tzaddik* has the job of maintaining the world so that it does not go out of kilter.[18]

When there is a living *tzaddik* in the world, unredeemed souls—wandering souls—primarily those in the first twelve months after death—are used by this saint as "workers" to keep the world running well. They act in the same way as angels, for they can perform tasks in realities other than the one we normally experience. As they serve the saint, the souls raise sparks and are redeemed by the merit of the work they do in service of the *tzaddik*.

## Prayer

If no *tzaddik* is alive in the world, the Torah scroll defends these souls. That is to say, all the prayers of the world are drawn upon to keep unredeemed souls illuminated. Thus, family and friends who pray for someone recently deceased can be of critical importance for the redemption of that soul. Once again, we who have free will can accomplish things that are beyond the capacity of a soul in the death realms.

## Merit of Ancestors

Next, the *ruach* level of the soul is drawn from the Garden of Eden to help illuminate, and thus uplift, the *nefesh* level of the soul. In this process, three times a day, a *ruach* goes into the Cave of Machpelah, that is, to the graves of Abraham, Sarah, Isaac, Rebecca, Jacob, and Leah. Its presence stimulates their bones, like the presence of a great-great grandchild warming the spirit of the great-great grandparent. This "warming" attracts supernal dew, the essence through which life becomes manifest. Once the dew is stimulated, it descends from heaven, level upon level, until it reaches the lower Garden of Eden. Here, the supernal dew bathes and perfumes itself in spices. The aromatic dew now enters the Cave of Machpelah, and the fragrance of the Garden of Eden raises the spirits of the patriarchs and matriarchs. In their merit, the world is healed and the souls in the death realms redeemed.[19]

---

If none of the above processes takes place, and the world is endangered because the matriarchs and patriarchs are asleep (not protecting the world), then the *nefesh* informs the *ruach,* the *ruach* informs the *neshama,* the *neshama* informs the Holy One, and the Holy One sits on the Throne of Mercy. This arouses an emanation of a stream of dew from the Ancient Holy One *(Ein Sof).* The stream flows to the "Head of the King" (the upper limbs of the Tree of Life: *chochma, binah,* and *daat),* which causes the lower limbs, the spirits of the patriarchs and matriarchs *(chesed, gevorah,* and *tiferet),* to be blessed. As a result, everything in the world is blessed, which helps all unredeemed souls.[20]

*T*HE DIFFERENCE BETWEEN the kabbalistic approach to redemption of the soul and some of the descriptions we find in other Jewish literature is so pronounced, we must pause to reflect. Here we see the treatment of the soul in a completely different light: its redemption is virtually assured. Whether through service to the *tzaddik,* the merit of prayer, the merit of the patriarchs and matriarchs, or, as a last resort, the outflow from the source Itself, the after-death scenario is filled with merciful lovingkindness.

Compared with concepts of reward and punishment in other Jewish literature, the idea of mercy in this instance is not personal, per se, as much as it is the quintessence of the universal design. Although a *nefesh* may carry the burden of life, the thrust of the universe is to raise all levels of consciousness. The *nefesh* will be lifted by this urge to a level in which it will be able to garment itself in higher consciousness, and thus it will join with its sister, *ruach,* in the Garden of Eden. When this is done, the sister-soul of the *neshama* comes to its highest potential.

As noted earlier, the levels of soul are connected, as on a violin string. This string will not resonate well if anything impedes it. Thus, this process of redeeming the lower levels of the soul releases the upper levels, and the string of our violin is completely liberated to join the cosmic symphony in perfect pitch.

# REINCARNATION

*T*he death of children is perplexing, cruel, and seems so senseless. How do we deal with it? Visions of other worlds do not alleviate the pain of heartbroken parents who lose a child, especially a young child who never had a chance to experience life.

Our friends Yakov and Miriam asked us to be the godparents of their firstborn son, Hanoch. At his circumcision, something caught my attention. Normally, the quick surgery results in a fair amount of blood. The infant cries for a few seconds, until a cotton ball dipped in wine is placed between his lips. But Hanoch bled only a slight amount and hardly cried at all. It was as if he knew something the rest of us had missed.

This same day his mother, Miriam, was quite ill. We thought it was post-partum weakness, but a year later we found out that Miriam had AIDS. This happened before the general public knew much about the disease. She had been a medical professional and somehow had come in contact with infected blood, probably via a needle stick before the inception of the meticulous procedures common today. Miriam died six months after that. Hanoch tested HIV positive. He may have been the first child in Israel with this disease. He died when he was eight years old.

Everyone who has been involved with the serious illness or death of a child experiences a test of faith in the core of her or his being. If life has purpose at all, what is the meaning of a child's death? Moreover, once we personally experience the grief of a loss so terrible, we cannot help but wonder about the suffering in the world. Why is there so much starvation, so many senseless deaths, so much cruelty? Why have there been wars throughout history, plagues, disease, tyranny, poverty, torture, and murder? What kind of a God oversees this?

Clearly, nobody has adequately answered questions such as these. Spiritual traditions, however, do attempt to offer cosmologies that raise insight regarding things like fate, *karma,* reincarnation, and soul journeys. The teachings of Jewish mysticism begin with the premise that life and death as we know them are reflections of other realities. What we see as beginnings and endings are merely segments of something without boundaries.

The teachings of reincarnation are of value when we have nowhere else to turn in the tragedy of a death. Whether it is the death of a young child or of a young adult in his or her prime, sometimes we can find solace in understanding that the task they came to do was completed and they had to move on. Indeed, there is a teaching that says, "The good die early so that they do not risk being corrupted, and the wicked live longer so that they have more chance to repent."[21]


## OLD DEBTS


*O*nce a man named Baruch went to the Baal Shem Tov with a long list of complaints. Life really had not treated him well. He never got a good education because from a very young age he had to support his family. He had difficulties with women. He could not keep jobs for long. People treated him poorly, and his reputation was always on the rocks. What happened? What did he do to deserve this fate? And what could he do to change it?

The Baal Shem Tov listened carefully, stroked his beard, and then said, "Baruch, I want you to go to the city that I will write on this piece of paper. In that city, you must find Yishai ben Shabbtai. Keep looking until you do, for when you find him, you will understand everything."

Baruch went immediately to the town. He went to every *shul,* looking for Yishai ben Shabbtai. He asked the butchers, the merchants, the town tax collector. Nobody had ever heard of this person. Baruch searched for weeks. He could not believe that the holy Baal Shem had sent him on a wild-goose chase.

Finally he was exhausted. He ended up in the local graveyard, talking with an old, wrinkled gravedigger. He told the old man his story. The gravedigger looked at him from behind shaggy eyebrows and asked, "Did you say Yishai ben Shabbtai?" Baruch nodded, and the old man began to chuckle.

"Amazing," he said. "He was buried in the first grave I ever dug, fifty years ago, and since that time not a single person has inquired about him. You see, he was the stingiest, meanest, cruelest man that ever lived."

The old gravedigger guided Baruch to the other side of the cemetery, where a small stone marked the grave of Yishai ben Shabbtai. The gravedigger said, "Here he is, but I must tell you that he would never have helped you; he would have spit in your face like he did to everyone else."

Baruch was confused. He returned to the Baal Shem Tov and told him the story of his search. "Why did you send me to find someone who died before I was born?" he asked. The Baal Shem Tov looked deeply into his eyes and said, "Baruch, look inside yourself, for you have the reborn sparks of the soul of Yishai ben Shabbtai, and this is the answer to your question. Every problem you face raises another spark that he caused to fall."


## GILGUL:
## REINCARNATION

*A*s with all the mysteries surrounding death, the question of reincarnation has been highly controversial in mainstream Judaism. Even today, when I tell hasidic tales that include the idea of transmigration of souls, people often approach me from the audience, saying, "I did not know that Judaism believes in the doctrine of reincarnation."

Actually many Jewish texts discuss the issue. Moreover, "in contrast with the conspicuous opposition of Jewish philosophy, metempsychosis (reincarnation) is taken for granted in the Kabbalah."[22] *The Bahir* (twelfth century), one of the earliest books in Kabbalah, refers to reincarnation, and in the sixteenth century, Chaim Vital wrote a number of books on the subject. The most comprehensive work available today is the excellent book *Jewish Views of the Afterlife,* by Simcha Paull Raphael (Aronson, 1994).

Early writers on the subject typically viewed reincarnation as a punishment. Later, the Jewish approach to reincarnation was influenced by Lurianic Kabbalah, which suggests that sparks from root souls can be collected into individual souls. As has been discussed, one of Luria's primary doctrines suggests that the task of humanity is to redeem the fallen sparks of primordial humankind. Each root soul must therefore raise up the 613 limbs that represent Adam and Eve. This is called the *Shi'ur Komah,* meaning the "measurement of the body."

The *Shi'ur Komah* is a metaphysical measurement, despite the misunderstanding that it was a literal attempt to measure the body of God. Indeed, this doctrine was one of the most secret parts of the early kabbalistic teachings, for it used metaphors that were likely to be misunderstood by uninitiated readers. For example, physical dimensions of God are estimated at 236,000 parasangs—about 600,000 miles. This naturally caused outrage among rational readers, but was actually a reference to a typical kabbalistic interpretation of a verse in Psalms.[23]

The true teaching of *Shi'ur Komah* is actually quite profound. Following the idea described in the opening of this book that creation resulted from the Shattering of the Vessels, we can see that all of the fallen sparks collectively represent the body of God, so to speak. If these sparks were gathered together, they would merge into the light of the Divine. Thus, all of creation is the metaphorical body of God, and every person in the creation embodies the potential to return divine sparks to their point of origin.

Jewish mystics say, "The shape of humans corresponds to the mystical shape of the Godhead . . . Everything in the human body, each of the 248 limbs and 365 sinews, corresponds to a supernal light as they are arranged in the primal shape of the highest manifestation of God. The human task is to bring our true shape to its spiritual perfection, to develop the divine image within ourselves. This is done by observing the 248 positive and 365 negative commandments of the Torah, *each one of which is linked to one of the organs of the human body,* and hence one of those supernal lights."[24]

There are actually thousands of laws within the scope of Jewish observance. Attempts have been made to isolate 613 from the Torah (248 plus 365), but there are many variations in these listings, which often include a significant percentage of laws that apply only to priestly activities in the Temple. From the mystical perspective, the number 613 represents archetypal categories into which the laws could be organized. This is a metaphor for the design of the universe, and is equated hypothetically with the "body of God," so to speak. The language of the *Zohar* says that they are the 613 organs that give us insight into our souls.

In simple terms, the meaning of this teaching is that everything we do in life is a key that enables us to peek at a part of the soul, and some things allow us to look more deeply than others. The only way we connect with the soul, however, is through insight. Our gentleness as well as our anger, our compassion as well as our fear, are wonderful teachers if we can see the sparks hidden within them.

The trick is to learn to observe closely how and when key personal traits reveal themselves in our lives. When we are able to note how they affect us and those around us, we gain insight. Through insight we open new gateways. We discover that all of our personality quirks, habits, behaviors, conditioning, and individual characteristics form a template, like a pattern on a curtain. When we shine a light through this pattern as an observer, we can perceive aspects of our own soul. Under close scrutiny, the pattern reveals to us what the soul is and what it needs to do. Through this process, according to Kabbalah, the source of life makes Itself known.

From this perspective, reincarnation has vast potential. It is not a punishment for sin as much as an opportunity to raise any of the sparks that have not yet been redeemed in a root soul. As the *Tikkunei Zohar* says, "If there is even one organ in which the Holy Blessed One does not dwell, then the person will be brought back into the world through reincarnation because of this organ, until the person becomes perfected in all of her or his parts, that all of them may be perfect in the image of the Holy Blessed One."[25]

## Healing-the-Dead Meditation

For thousands of years, people have used dreams to communicate with the dead. By actively engaging an altered state of consciousness that simulates the experience of dreaming, Kabbalists are able to enter unknown realms. This process is based on the kabbalistic principle that our imaginations are connected with higher realities. Today we call this method "waking dreams."

We can utilize the same process that the sages used for connecting with our own loved ones who have died. We can visit with anyone—it need not be a parent or even a relative. It should, however, be someone we knew well when she or he was alive. This practice is especially recommended on Yom Kippur, during the Yizkor (remembrance) service, when we bring to mind the memories of our parents.

Initially, some people are skeptical about the exercise that follows, inhibited by an inner censor who says we are making up this contact with our imaginations. After all, we have strongly conditioned beliefs concerning death. If this voice is loud within you, let it have its way. Nonetheless, let yourself "pretend" as if it were really happening.

Do not begin this practice with someone who brought great violence or severe abuse into your life. After a while you may choose to work with such a person, but begin with someone toward whom you have kindly or neutral feelings.

1. Find a protected, quiet place where you will not be disturbed for about thirty minutes. Sit in a comfortable position, close your eyes, and let your attention rest on bodily sensations.

2. After a few minutes of relaxation, allow the images of dear ones who have died come into your mind. Notice how you feel as these images arise.

3. Pick only one to work with. Let this image rest in your mind. Try to communicate with it telepathically, or even by using an imaginary voice inside your mind. Ask the image anything you wish. Some possible questions are:

   a. What is it like where you are?
   b. What was it like when you first died?
   c. Who else is there with you?
   d. Have you visited any living person in their dreams?

4. Now, say to the image: "Tell me the things that you feel you did well while you were alive. What are the things that you are proud of having done?" (Let it speak to you.)

5. And: "What are the things that you feel you did not do so well in your lifetime? What are the things you regret the most?" (Let it speak. You may find yourself getting sad at this point. Try to stay connected as best you can.)

6. Then: "If you could choose one thing that you regret the most, what would it be? If you could live your life over, what would be the most important thing you would change?"

7. Now, allow the image to fade into the background. Try to remember a situation that actually occurred with this person when he or she was alive. You want to bring this event into your imagination *as if your deceased partner were living her or his life over again. Your task is to remember this event as if it occurred the way they would have wanted so that the person would not have regrets.* See the event anew, in its more per-

fect form. Let yourself replay it in this new way over and over again for a few minutes.

8. Let go of the event and invite the image back into your mind. Notice how you are feeling. Ask it, "Is this the way you would like to be remembered?" If it says yes, agree to try to build up these memories. If it says no, find out what it would like, and try to do it that way the next time.

9. Promise to return, and ask if it will come back again. Hopefully, the image will agree to do so. Bid farewell for now, and give it a hug if you can. Take a couple of deep breaths, and open your eyes.

Once you have identified a particular attribute to work on for someone who has died, allow yourself to meditate regularly on the person, always imagining situations in ways that idealize how this person would have acted if given the chance to do it over again. Soon your feelings toward this person will begin to change and soften, and that heals and helps redeem the dead.

The key to this practice is obviously the reframing of our memories. If we want to hold on to old and painful memories because "that is the way it was," we remain stuck, as does the one with whom we are working. If we can use our imaginations to re-create our memories, we begin to free ourselves and thereby release sparks for the souls of the dead.

This practice is not one of denial. It is a practice of forgiveness and regeneration. Everyone enters this life with a pure soul. We are stuck with our fate, the work we have to do, and our intrinsic strengths and weaknesses. We often make a mess on one level or another. Just as we hope we will be forgiven, we need to find a way to forgive others. Each time we are able to do so, the universe is raised one more notch in its consciousness.

# DYING AND DEATH

*R*eb Shlomo Carlebach told wonderful hasidic tales. He would usually begin with something like: "Holy brothers, holy sisters, listen closely, as I tell you the holiest of the holy... the deepest, deepest, *mamash* (really!) deepest of the deep." His eyes would roll back in his head, and his eyelids would flutter as he entered heavenly realms.

One winter Shabbat weekend during the late 1980s, Shoshana and I visited Moshav Modi'in, between Jerusalem and Tel Aviv, where many students of Reb Shlomo's lived. We knew that the rebbe would be here this weekend, and we wanted to experience an entire Shabbat with him.

At the end of the Friday-night service, which consisted of close to ninety minutes of shouting, hand-clapping, and floor-thumping, all participants moved into the dining area, where a traditional Shabbat meal was served. Almost two hundred guests sat at long tables, and every so often someone in the room spontaneously began to chant a new *niggun*. Soon, people pounded on the tables so that silverware and dishes clattered in rhythm to the beat. The *niggun* would end. We would have a few minutes to eat a bit more chicken and kugel, and then another *niggun* would start up. When the dessert was served, Reb Shlomo told one of his stories.

This particular evening, he offered a teaching about the mourner's *kaddish* prayer. *Kaddish* is one of the most famous parts of Jewish liturgy. Its opening words are well known by Jews and non-Jews alike. They are intoned at funerals, remembrances of the Holocaust, *yartzeits* (anniversaries of deaths), memorials for national losses, and other somber occasions: *"Yitkadahl v'yitkaddash sh'may rabbah . . ."* (May Its great name be exalted and be sanctified . . .).

When someone in our immediate family dies, we say the mourner's *kaddish* daily for eleven months, based on the belief that the soul takes twelve months to pass from one level to another. *Kaddish* is viewed as a means to help a loved one through the transition to higher realms. The twelfth month is omitted because of the assumption that the deceased person has enough merit by this time to make it on his or her own. Saying the *kaddish* the last month would imply that the person did not have sufficient virtue, and this would be inappropriate.

Reb Shlomo began: "Dearest friends, did you know that in the old days, if someone owed rent, the landlord could take the law into his own hands? He could empty the house of its furniture and sell it; he could put the people in jail; he could even, God forbid, take the people off and sell them into slavery.

"It happened a hundred and fifty years ago in the house of one poor *shlepper* and his wife, Feigelah, that they were many months behind in the rent. One day, after Feigelah went off to the market, the landlord showed up with the local police and carried away the husband and the eight children. When Feigeleh returned from the market, the neighbors told her what had happened.

"So this holy wife went to the landlord to find her husband and her children. The landlord told her that he intended to sell them into slavery for the back rent. She pleaded with him. She begged him. The landlord thought about it, and realized that perhaps he could get twice as much as they would fetch on the slavery market. It would be an outrageous sum, but he had nothing to lose. So, finally, he agreed to ransom them back. He asked for one hundred rubles for the overdue rent, and nine thousand nine hundred rubles for his trouble. He told the wife that the extra money would go to bribe the police and other officials to release her husband and the eight children.

"The woman stared at him with unbelieving eyes. Ten thousand rubles! It would have been hard enough to come up with one hundred. But ten thousand was a fortune beyond all possibility.

"She left the landlord's house and slowly walked along the dirt road that led back to her own home. What could she do? She reached into her pockets and counted three rubles. This was everything she had to her name. Three rubles. There was nothing to sell. Everything had been stripped from the house just to feed the children. It seemed to her that all was lost."

At this point in the story, Shlomo closed his eyes and rocked back and forth. "And now, sweetest, dearest friends, listen closely," he said in a singsong voice. "I'm going to tell you what happened to this holy woman. Listen carefully, but don't listen with your ears. Listen with your heart—deep, deep in the center of your heart. In the deepest depths, listen, listen . . .

"This woman was walking, when suddenly a thought arose. This thought said to her, 'Feigelah, when your husband dies, who will say *kaddish* for him? Who will know when he dies?'

"This thought terrified Feigelah. So she found a poor Jew on the road, and she gave him one ruble and said to him, 'Please, say the mourner's *kaddish* for my husband.' She told this beggar her husband's name and walked away.

"As she was walking. . ." Shlomo began his singsong once again. Whenever he did this, something extraordinary, something profoundly mystical was about to happen in his story. So we leaned forward to listen a little more closely. "As she was walking," he repeated, "another thought arose in her mind, and it said, 'Feigelah, what about all the people who die and nobody says *kaddish* for them?' "

Now Shlomo began to sing a little *niggun,* repeating this question until all of the souls in this crowded room were humming it together: "What about people who die and nobody says *kaddish*?"

Soon we were completely hypnotized by the power of this mantra. As Shlomo sang, I could sense a meltdown; all of us were thinking about our own parents and grandparents or other relatives who had passed over to the other realms without having had *kaddish* said for them. Moreover, how many strangers had died without any family to send them prayers? I thought about people lost in the Holocaust, whole families with nobody left behind to say *kaddish*. Reb Shlomo could have stopped his story at this point, for the tears had already begun to flow. But he continued.

"So this holy Feigelah ran back to the beggar who she had asked to say *kaddish* for her husband, and she gave him yet another ruble and said to him, 'Dear sir, please, say *kaddish* for all the souls for whom nothing has ever been said. Please, say *kaddish* to help them in their passage through the heavenly realms.'

"Feigelah turned from the beggar, deeply touched. But as she began to walk away, yet another thought arose in her mind. She turned back to the poor *yiddin* sitting there with two rubles in his hand, and she gave him a third, the last ruble she owned, the end of everything she had, and she said to him, 'Dear sir, when you say *kaddish* for all these lost souls, really, really, really put your heart into your prayers; don't hold back in any way.'

"For the next few hours, Feigelah sat in the fields not far from this beggar. As the sun went down that evening, she heard him pray. *Oy,* did he pray. He prayed with a broken heart, calling out with all his might and all his pain. She felt her face drenched in tears as she was carried to the heavenly realms in a chariot of flames. His prayers shattered the celestial gates and released a flood of souls who had waited so long to be rescued. Then he was finished.

"Friends, what a vision she had! She began to walk home, and somehow her step was lighter. As she was walking, a shining carriage with four horses appeared on the road. It was unusual; she had never seen a carriage like this before. It stopped next to her, and the well-dressed man inside asked directions. Then the stranger did something most unusual: he offered her a ride.

"She did not know what to do. She had never been in a carriage like this. At first she declined, but he insisted. When she was certain that he was sincere, she accepted. After all, it had been a long day. Soon they were deeply engaged in a conversation.

"The stranger asked her many questions. Slowly he was able to get the entire story about her husband, her children, the landlord, and the ten thousand rubles. As he was letting Feigelah out of the carriage, he did an amazing thing. He reached into his pocket and wrote out a check for the full ten thousand rubles.

"She was astonished. Ten thousand rubles. The next day she ran to the bank. When she handed the check to the clerk, he looked at her strangely and told her to wait a few moments. She began to panic. Was it real? Perhaps the man in the carriage had played a cruel joke and there was no money in the bank. She waited, getting more nervous as the moments passed.

"The clerk brought his supervisor, who looked her up and down. Then the supervisor took her by the arm and directed her to the office of the president of the bank. This was a big office, and the man behind the desk looked at her with a scowl on his face.

"'Where did you get this check?' he asked her. She told him the story of meeting a stranger in a carriage; and she told the story of her husband and children. The man behind the desk then pointed to the dozens of pictures hanging on the walls of the room, and asked, 'Do you recognize anyone in any of these pictures?'

"Feigelah looked and instantly identified the large portrait behind the desk as the man who had been in the carriage. When she said this, the bank president turned pale. You see, the check he held in his hands was signed by his father. And the portrait behind him was a picture of his father. His father had died five years earlier, and the bank president, an only child, had never said *kaddish* for his father."

*S*IGNALING THE END of the story, Shlomo began to sing a series of *niggunim*. I glanced around the room and saw a deluge of tears. How many unspoken *kaddish*es were represented in that room?

## THE TEACHINGS
## OF DEATH

*D*eath fascinates the living. We want to know as much about it as we can. We do not want to believe that death is the end, so we explore wisdom-teachings that are thousands of years old to find a clue. Almost all traditions suggest that death is not an end but a transition. It is intriguing that the world's wisdom-teachings agree on this point. Despite a wide variety of interpretations of what happens, how it happens, or where it happens, the end result is that death is a gateway to other realities.

We do not know what part of us death takes, or even if we should identify with what is taken. We cannot say that there is something to "look forward to." Yet mystical traditions throughout the history of humankind have said that reality as we experience it is nothing but a drop in a vast sea of possibilities.

In the Talmud, Rabbi Jacob says, "This world is like an antechamber before the world to come. Prepare yourself in this antechamber so that you may enter the banquet hall."[26] The question that arises is, How did Rabbi Jacob know about the world to come? Where do the Buddhists get their information about the *bardo*s, or the Hindus about the astral worlds? How do Native Americans know about the power of medicine, or Aboriginal tribes about spirit-gods? Why did the ancient Egyptians dedicate so much of their lives to death?

Is this a cross-cultural, international conspiracy that has been perpetrated on the consciousness of humankind to deceive us into thinking that we are not living useless lives? Is it that we *want* so much to believe in such ideas that we will grab at any straw placed before us? Perhaps.

Or perhaps there is a universal message built into our genetic code that initiates a particular tape loop when human consciousness enters certain levels. People who have experienced this level say that there is an ocean of mystical fragrance. It has a scent to it, a special aroma that alerts the soul.

The whisper of a mystical experience is quickly recognized. The language is soft, yielding, inclusive, and saturated with love. This is what mystics say:

"At once my physical body lost its grossness and became metamorphosed into astral texture. I felt a floating sensation . . . I gazed at my arms and moved them back and forth, yet could not feel their weight. Ecstatic joy overwhelmed me . . . My realization deepened that the essence of all objects is light."[27]

"I was . . . indissolubly one with all nature. Deep in the soul, below pain, below all distraction in life, in a silence vast and grand, an infinite ocean of calm which nothing can disturb."[28]

"I stood enraptured in ecstasy, beside myself, and my every sense was endowed with understanding."[29]

"What talk is this? How could the lover ever die? That would be truly absurd—to die in the water of life!"[30]

"Strong trembling seized me and I could not summon strength; my hair stood on end . . . and behold, something resembling speech emerged from my heart and came to my lips . . . I said: 'This is indeed the spirit of wisdom.' "[31]

As a well-known teacher was about to die, he sat in a lotus position and called out to those around him: "Don't be misled! Look directly [at what is about to happen]. What is this?" He repeated this so that they would pay close attention, and then he calmly died.[32]

Do we need to say whether these ecstatic quotes come from Muslims, Christians, Hindus, or Jews? In fact, mystics in all of these traditions are represented above, but what difference does it make? The commonality of the experience is the point; deathless reality is a vital experience in all traditions.

# NEAR-DEATH
# EXPERIENCES

*T*he *Zohar* tells of Rabbi Jesse going to visit a poor neighbor who was ill. While the rabbi was sitting by the man's bedside, he heard a [heavenly] voice, which said: "Wheel, wheel [of destiny], a soul is come to me before its ordained time. Woe to those neighbors in his town who have not done anything to help him."[33] Rabbi Jesse realized that this voice from heaven was warning that the town would pay a great price if his neighbor died without anyone caring. He quickly got a special herb, a mystical potion, for he knew that he had to intercede in the man's fate. The herb made the man sweat so much he miraculously recovered from his illness.[34]

Later the recuperated man said to his rescuer, "Rabbi! My soul had actually left my body and I was brought before the throne of the King. I would have remained there forever, but God wanted you to have the merit of restoring me."[35]

Today, modern medicine has its own magic potions, bringing people back from the gates of death more than ever before in history. Thousands have returned from the twilight zone of other realities to report their visions. They speak in the language of mystics, with awe, transformation, and filled with love.

For many years, researchers studying death have recorded out-of-body and near-death experiences. Many are unique, but the parallels are quite remarkable. Bright lights are frequently seen, a feeling of comfort and surrender is often noticed, dead relatives appear to the person undergoing the experience, and often there is a feeling of enormous relief that the burdens of life finally have been lifted.

It is important to clarify, however, that experiences of dying are not always wonderful. Indeed, many are exceedingly difficult. Some people die with considerable physical pain and suffering, as well as an extraordinary amount of emotional distress and anguish. Despite mystical reports of the wondrous things to come when we reach the other side, we still have to get through the process of dying.

The Talmud says that there are 903 types of death, from the easiest, described as a kiss, to the most difficult, which resembles pulling a thorn backward out of wool.[36] As may well be imagined, the Jewish sages had many discussions of death. The words "dead," "death," and "dying" are mentioned more than five thousand times in the Talmud.

*T*he Angel of Death is a messenger of God. It has been associated with the dark angel Samael, who represents Satan, but acts only under the direction or approval of God.

Many stories describe the battle between the Angel of Death and humans. This angel sometimes must resort to deception, for it is not all-powerful. Indeed, occasionally Death is defeated.

King David once asked God when he would die. God responded that no person would ever know in advance the time of her or his death.[37] But because of David's merit, he learned that he would die on a Shabbat when he was seventy years old.

So David spent every Shabbat exclusively in the study of Torah, for it is said that the Angel of Death has no power over anyone fulfilling one of the commandments. One Shabbat, which was also the holy day of Shavuot, David heard a strange, wondrous sound in his garden. He went to see what was making the noise, and the steps leading to the garden collapsed, killing him. The Angel of Death had caused such an alluring noise, David forgot that Death was near.[38] The Angel of Death has many tricks up its sleeve.

On the other hand, when the sage Rabbi Joshua ben Levi was about to die, the Angel of Death was directed to carry out one of his wishes. The scholar asked Death to show him what it looked like where he was going, which the angel agreed to do. But before departing, Rabbi Joshua said, "Give me your knife [which you use to kill people], lest I be frightened along the way." This is how Rabbi Joshua got the Angel of Death to hand over to him the instrument of death.[39]

When they arrived at Paradise, Rabbi Joshua jumped over the wall, thereby entering without first dying! The Angel of Death grabbed the corner of his garment, but Rabbi Joshua swore that he would not return to his earthly life (only to await death).

The Holy One had to intervene, saying that Rabbi Joshua's oath not to return to life would be valid only if in his entire life he never made an oath that had to be annulled. This, of course, is almost impossible, for we are always making casual oaths, like promising ourselves that we are going to do something that we never do, or, conversely, swearing that we will never do a thing again, and then do it anyway. It is the reason Jews say the Kol Nidre prayer at the time of Yom Kippur, so that unintentional vows and unfulfilled oaths are not held against someone. But in the life of Rabbi Joshua, he had never said or thought anything that he did not fulfill. So his vow not to return back to life was honored.

The Angel of Death pleaded with him, "You must return my knife!" for without this knife, nobody would ever die again. Rabbi Joshua refused to return the instrument of death. It was a standoff, and the entire universe held its breath.

Finally, a *bat kol* (a heavenly voice) boomed out: "Return it to him, for mortal creatures require it!" Thus Death was reestablished. What would the universe look like if "mortals" ceased to die? Afterward, the Angel of Death was never again misled into giving away its knife, even though another sage tried the same maneuver.[40]

So Rabbi Joshua tricked Death and entered Paradise without dying. Ten others are said to have entered Paradise "alive," the best known of whom being Elijah the prophet; Hanoch, the father of Methuselah; Serah, the daughter of Asher; and Bithiah, the daughter of Pharaoh (who was given this reward for having saved Moses).[41]

Kabbalah adds another dimension to death, suggesting that it is not monolithic but has a number of levels. It says that the Angel of Death is protected and "ridden" by the Shadow of Death. Although they have different energies, they are inseparable partners. Moreover, they have different gateways into the realm of death, for there are "gates of death" and "gates of the shadow of death." Indeed, it is said that there are innumerable, mysterious passageways to death "hidden away from humankind, who know them not."[42]

Death, therefore, is far more complex than simply a realm of nonliving. The actual dying process, the transition, the time immediately after death, and the entire first year following one's death all have unique qualities. All along the way, those who are living can serve, support, and be advocates for those who are dying or who have entered the death realms. Many people feel helpless in the face of death, but the truth is that by understanding the many facets of death and dying we come to realize that there is a great deal we can do.

## THE DEATHS OF SAGES

*T*he Talmud records a number of deaths in which sages return in dreams to describe the dying experience. In one story, Rava was attending his dying friend Rabbi Nachman. Nachman asked Rava to intervene with the Angel of Death, to use his influence so that Death would not torment Nachman. Rava was surprised and asked Nachman why he did not make the request himself of the Angel of Death, for Nachman was highly reputed and had great merit. Nachman replied that when the Angel of Death has been instructed to end somebody's life, that person no longer has any influence.

The story continues. Rava asked Nachman to return in a dream after his death to describe what dying was like. Indeed, Nachman did return in a dream. "Did you suffer pain?" Rava asked. Nachman responded, "[Death was like] the taking of a hair from milk." He added, however, "If the Holy One told me to go back into the world, I would rather not, for the fear of death is too great."[43] Despite his advanced awareness, Nachman was still deeply afraid of the possibility of a painful death.

This story teaches many things. People with merit can influence the Angel of Death, except when they themselves are about to die. This influence can be used to ease suffering for those in the dying process, and normally is accomplished through prayer, which is the primary tool used to reach angels and Death.

Additionally, the story informs us clearly that Jewish sages communicated with other realms. Nachman told Rava from the other side that his experience of death was quite easy. Nonetheless, the fear of death far exceeds the experience, so much so that Nachman did not want to return to go through it again, even though the actual experience for him was as simple as taking a strand of hair out of milk.

In another talmudic story, when Rava himself was dying, he was attended by his brother, Rabbi Se'orim. As in the previous story, Rava asked his brother to tell the Angel of Death not to torment him. His brother asked him, "Are you not his intimate friend?" Rava's response was, "Since my *mazzal* (fate) has been delivered to him, he does not pay attention to me."

In this story as well, Rabbi Se'orim asked his brother to return in a dream after his death to describe what dying was like. Rava did so. When asked if he suffered, he replied, "As from the prick of a cupping instrument."[44]

Cupping is an ancient technique in which glass spheres are heated and then placed on a person's skin. As the cup cools, a vacuum forms inside and the skin is drawn up by suction. Ostensibly the process draws toxins from the body, through the skin. The Chinese use this method today, and I have experienced it. The sensation is unusual, but not uncomfortable. In fact, the pulling of a bandage off skin is far more irritating.

So the sages are clearly informing us that the dying experience is altogether tolerable, but that the potential for being tormented in the dying process is unbounded. No matter what our station in life, how many good deeds we have done, how pious a life we have lived, the Angel of Death does as it wishes when taking someone to the other side. Yet if someone has an advocate who speaks on her or his behalf, the dying process can go much easier. This information is important for anyone who is in a position to help a person going through this transition.

Also, the sages apparently asked others to return after death, to describe not only death itself, but what it is like in the death realms. As noted earlier, dreams are usually the vehicle for this transmission between different realities.

Almost everyone dreams of close relatives who have died. These dreams are often quite vivid. Sometimes they occur soon after death, and often they reoccur for months or years.

The sages trained themselves to work with dreams. We can do the same. When we are skilled in this process, we can communicate in exactly the same way these stories describe. We can ask dream images questions like: "How was death for you?" or, "What is it like where you are?"

## SLEEP IS
## ONE-SIXTIETH
## OF DEATH

While we are awake, the soul hovers above us. When we sleep, however, an aspect of the soul travels to the higher realms. Sometimes an angel reveals future events to this traveling soul,[45] but sometimes it does not deserve this revelation and the soul "falls into the hands of the Other Side (evil), who lies to her about the future." The unworthy person is thus shown a happy but false dream to draw him or her farther from the path of truth.[46]

The Talmud teaches that sleep is one-sixtieth of death. Each night our souls enter a magical theater of high drama. They move through other realms of reality, constantly challenged by a variety of spiritual entities. If a soul is burdened by any clutter carried by its earthly body, it will be weighted down and vulnerable to the seductions of corrupting forces. The degree to which it gains a true or false image of other realities is dependent upon the baggage it carries. As the Zohar says, "A person's soul testifies at night about whatever he or she does in the day."[47]

Despite the testimony of our soul, however, the judgment is always lenient. Otherwise, except for the most virtuous people, we would never get anything but false dreams. "If the soul is found deserving to continue in her present state, she is allowed to return to this world. In this judgment, good and evil actions are not weighed in the same way. No account is taken of harmful acts which a person is likely to perpetrate in the future. But with regard to good actions, not only those already performed in the past, but also those which will be performed in the future are taken into consideration."[48]

The scales that balance our actions are therefore loaded in our favor. Everything "good" from the past, present, and future is placed on one side; everything "not-good," but only from the past and present, is placed on the other side. As our capacity for doing good deeds in the future is enormous, the scales will normally weigh in our favor.

The Kabbalah suggests that dreams are not simply messages to the psyche, but are essentially prophetic. If we know how to interpret dreams, they inform us what is going to happen. Therefore, "a person should not tell his or her dream [indiscriminately] to a friend lest the listener cause a delay in its fulfillment."[49] This means that we should be careful to share our dreams only with people who are objective and open. A dream is like a fragile embryo that must be handled tenderly. If we understand its potential and nurture it carefully, it can attain its fullness. The capacities for prophecy and for seeing into other realms of reality lies latent within all of us.

"When a person goes to sleep, the soul rises according to its level. The Holy One teaches the *neshama* with signs of future things to come in the world. . . . There are different grades of dreams which teach secrets. The lowest is the dream itself, next is the grade of visions, and highest is the grade of prophesy."[50]

Rabbi Hiyah asked, "It is said that a dream uninterpreted is like a message undeciphered. Does this mean that the dream comes true without the dreamer being aware of it, or that the dream remains unfulfilled?" Rabbi Simeon answered, "The dream comes true, but without the dreamer being aware of it. For nothing happens in the world without advance notice of it being announced in heaven from where it is broadcast to the world. When there were prophets in the world it was announced through them; when there were no more prophets the sages took over. After the sages, things were revealed in dreams, and if there were no dreams, the birds in heaven would announce it."[51]

Whether we appreciate it or not, we experience things that have already been anticipated in our dreams. This may explain some of our experiences of déjà vu, our unpredictable anxieties when we feel something is about to happen, our "knowing" who is at the other end of the line when the telephone rings, our sense of destiny when we know a stranger is important in our lives, or our eerie sense of comfort in some situations and discomfort in others. We have an untold number of dreams whispering in our conscious and subconscious minds, messages from the Unknown, secrets shared by angels.[52] When we understand the language of dreams, we gain admission to an inner world that holds the mysteries of the universe.

## SOUL JOURNEYS
## IN THE NIGHT

The Baal Shem Tov was seated at a large table, surrounded by his disciples. One of these students was Nachman of Horodenka, who was the grandfather of Rebbe Nachman of Breslov.

The Baal Shem Tov talked about a great many subjects, and the evening wore on. He stopped at one point late in the evening, reflected for a while, and then said suddenly, "The time has come for me to reveal to you, my faithful students, the deep secrets of the bath of immersion: the *mikveh*."

He began to tell them about the meaning of being purified in living waters, and spoke of the four mystical rivers that emanate from the Garden of Eden. He discoursed on the roots of souls connected to universal oceans. As he talked, his face became illuminated, until the room was filled with light. Then, in a moment of ecstasy, the master threw back his head and went into a reverie, a silence that shimmered.

The disciples sat transfixed, trembling in joy and awe. They stared at their motionless master. They had seen him in altered states, but never like this. The students waited, but nothing happened, except that the Baal Shem Tov continued to glow, his face turned upward, his head slowly moving from side to side. Ten minutes passed, twenty. Some of the students closed their eyes. The evening was late. Nachman of Horodenka was so tired he put his head down on the table and fell asleep.

Nachman had a dream:

He was in a city. Everyone walked in one direction. They were going toward a huge building. Nachman followed. Inside the building were throngs of people in an enormous room. All were hushed, listening to an eminent teacher speaking at the other end of the room.

The teacher was talking about the *mikveh*. He went on for a long time, and after a while, Nachman realized that these teachings were different from those of the holy Ari, Rabbi Isaac Luria, upon which so much mystical teaching is based. Indeed, at one point, the teacher himself said openly that he was in opposition to the Ari's teachings on this issue.

Suddenly, someone came through the door. A flutter rippled through the mass of people. A figure of exceptional magnetism passed through the crowd. The Ari himself, the distinguished Isaac Luria, had entered the room. He walked slowly to the pulpit, and the crush of people following him carried Nachman to the front of the room.

At the pulpit, Nachman was overwhelmed. There he saw his teacher, the holy Baal Shem Tov, who had been the one speaking all along. Now his teacher was face-to-face with Isaac Luria, who had died almost two hundred years earlier. An unprecedented debate began. Each of the masters quoted the *Zohar*. Each gave his own interpretation. Words flew like fire. They quoted Torah, Talmud, Midrash, each developing a stronger and stronger case. Finally they reached the end of their argument and the heavens were asked to decide.

The room was frozen. Nobody moved. Then the heavens quaked, and the Ari raised his hands and bowed his head. He said quietly that the decision had been made in favor of the Baal Shem Tov.

At that moment, Nachman awoke from his dream. He realized that he was sitting at a table with fellow students. The other students also were awakening, and the master was coming back out of his trance. Nobody said anything as they all became alert. Then the master, the holy Baal Shem Tov, looked directly at Nachman. The first words he said were: "And it was you I chose to accompany me as my witness."

## SUSTAINING LIFE

*D*reams connect us with other realms, but we can have dreamlike visions while fully awake. Shoshana worked part-time as a nursing instructor at Hadassah Hospital in Jerusalem. She has worked a great deal with dying patients in geriatrics and oncology. One of her patients at Hadassah was a very old man, Rabbi Avi, who was clearly in a terminal stage of his disease. His body was covered with pressure sores; his bandages needed to be re-dressed every few hours. He was in a room with three other very sick patients, who often cried out in pain.

Except when he was visited by students, which was quite often, this old teacher constantly read or prayed. He had a stack of books by his bedside. His students treated him like a saint, and Shoshana knew he was an important teacher.

Rabbi Avi did not flinch as his dressings were changed. In fact, he kept reading. Whenever other patients clamored for help and a half-dozen nurses and doctors filled the room, he continued to read. Even in a code-blue emergency, when someone died, he remained focused on his books.

Shoshana came home after work one day and related a strange incident. Rabbi Avi's health was declining, his sores were getting worse. Shoshana said to me, "He seems to be holding on beyond all normal limits. While I was working around his bed, wondering what this was all about, I silently sent him a thought-message. I said to him, 'You do not have to hold on. You can let go whenever you want.'

"I have done this before with people, but this is the first time someone yelled back at me, telepathically. I was shocked. My mind filled with a strong voice that said, 'Stand back! You have no idea of what is happening here!' Just at that moment, I glanced at Rabbi Avi, and he glared at me from behind his book. He rarely looks at people, so I must admit that it sent shivers down my spine." This experience deeply touched Shoshana and has affected the way she has worked with dying patients ever since.

Judaism honors life above all things sacred. Every law in the books can be broken if a life is endangered. In Judaism, we try to squeeze the last ounce out of a life, because each breath is viewed as an opportunity to raise another spark. It is never too late to redeem oneself while still alive.

Death is viewed as both friend and enemy. It is our friend in the sense that once we are on the other side, like the sage Nachman, we have no interest in returning to this life. Life is difficult. In fact, the Talmud describes a famous debate between the house of Hillel, who defended the position that it is better to have been born than not to have lived at all, and the house of Shammai, who said it would have been better not to have been born in the first place. This debate went on for two and half years. The final vote was that it would have been better not to have been created, but now that we are here, we need to make the most of it.[53] In this sense, death is our friend.

For the living, however, death represents the enemy in that it steals our free will. After death we no longer have the potential to be copartners in the creation. Only the living can raise sparks, only the living can process with God-ing. In the death realms, we rely on the merit we acquired through life or the support of living beings who hold us in their memories and prayers, for we can no longer act on our own.

So the traditional Jewish approach is not to "go gently into that dark night." We don't give up so easily. We do everything we can to sustain life. Obviously, when life loses quality to the extent that we can no longer raise our own sparks, things are different. Then death becomes our friend once again, for life has little value without free will.

The mystical viewpoint is that thirty days before one's death, a proclamation is made in heaven, and even heavenly birds announce the person's doom. During these last thirty days, his or her *neshama* departs each night and ascends to the other world to see its place there. This is different from normal soul journeys, which are often reported back in dreams. In this instance, because the soul is now under the wings of the Angel of Death, the person does not have the same consciousness or control of the soul as previously.[54]

In addition, it is said that one's shadow becomes more faint during the last thirty days.[55] The mystic understands this as a metaphor. The light that fades is not that of the sun; the sun's shadow does not disappear. Rather, the vital light that is connected with the life-source begins to diminish. In the contemporary idiom, the shadow of our vital light is called an aura, and this aura begins to subside thirty days before death. Some people can see these things.

The *Zohar* describes the story of Rabbi Isaac, who realized that he was about to die. He went sadly to his dearest friend, Rabbi Judah, and told him that he perceived his soul was leaving each night without enlightening his dreams. He could see also that his shadow (aura) had faded. In a touching scene, Judah said that he would fulfill any request of Isaac's after his death. In return, Judah asked Isaac to reserve a place by his side in the world to come so that they would again be together. In tears, Isaac begged Judah to stay with him until death took him away.

The drama now became profound. They went together to visit Rabbi Simeon bar Yochai. As they entered the room, Rabbi Simeon noticed the Angel of Death dancing in front of Rabbi Isaac. Rabbi Simeon, the greatest of mystics, stood by the door and forced the Angel of Death to leave the room. Looking at Isaac, Rabbi Simeon saw that there were only a few hours left.

Rabbi Simeon asked the doomed man, "Have you seen the image of your father today?" It is known that our relatives come to us at the time of departure from this world and they accompany the soul to the other realms.[56] Rabbi Isaac answered that he had not yet seen his relatives.

So Rabbi Simeon prayed aloud that the Holy One should give Rabbi Isaac a reprieve. Then Rabbi Simeon called in his own son to hold on to

Rabbi Isaac, for he saw that Isaac was in great fear. The story now moves into another realm of reality.

Rabbi Isaac fell into a deep sleep in which he saw his father. He asked his father what it was like where he would be going, and his father described the chamber that had been prepared for him. Then the father said to his son, "We were on the point of departing [to bring you here] when a voice went out [in heaven], saying, 'Be proud of Rabbi Simeon, for he has made a request [that Rabbi Isaac should live] and it has been granted him.' "[57]

Although the death edict had been set for Rabbi Isaac, it was changed. Even if a person knows of his or her impending death, it is never too late for someone to intervene.

## L'CHAIM: TO LIFE

Ⓐ wonderful tale was told by Reb Zalman about a student named Yehuda who traveled a great distance to visit the famous Seer of Lublin for a Shabbat weekend. Yehuda arrived on Friday morning and immediately went to see the rebbe. As everyone knows, the Seer could look into the future. Almost as soon as Yehuda walked into the room, the rebbe asked him not to stay for Shabbat.

Yehuda was shocked. "But rebbe, I have come so far. Is there any way I can spend Shabbat with you?"

The rebbe looked at him with sad eyes. "The truth is, my young friend, I see death surrounding you, and it seems that you are destined to die this Shabbat. It would be better for you to go to a small village and die there."

Reb Zalman said, "Can you imagine how Yehuda felt? The Seer of Lublin told him that he had one more day to live. His heart was broken. He slowly took up his small bag and dragged himself out of town."

On the road, Yehuda encountered a wagon loaded with students. They were singing loudly and having a wonderful time. The wagon stopped when they saw him going away from the city.

"Friend," they yelled out, "you are walking the wrong way. The Seer of Lublin is this way. Come with us."

Yehuda turned slowly, and sadly said, "I cannot go. The Seer has sent me away."

"But why?" The students surrounded him. This was astonishing. The Seer never sent anyone away.

Yehuda told them that the rebbe had said he was going to die and that he should find a small village.

The students at once said, "Nonsense. You do not have to leave. Why should you die all by yourself, where you don't know anybody? Maybe the rebbe was worried that it would ruin our Shabbat. But it won't. Come. If you have to die, do it at the rebbe's table. This way, if you get sick and need help, we will be there to hold you up. Come, friend, do not worry about a thing."

So Yehuda joined this singing group and climbed into the wagon. They started toward Lublin, and one of the students said to Yehuda, "Friend, as long as you are going to die, if you have any money, we could use a keg of schnapps to keep us all warm." Indeed, he did have money.

They stopped at the first tavern and bought a great deal of schnapps. Each time someone lifted his cup, he turned to the benefactor, Yehuda, and cried out, "*L'chaim, l'chaim,* may you live a healthy, long life." One after another of these blessings rang out.

Yehuda began to get rosy in the cheeks. He forgot what the Seer of Lublin had said to him. Actually, everyone was having too much fun to be thinking about tomorrow. And so, round after round, the blessings poured in for him.

They arrived at the Seer's home in a very happy state. When Yehuda once again went to greet the rebbe, the great Seer of Lublin looked at him with amazement. The rebbe's large eyebrows arched, and he said, "It is wonderful, my young friend. The Angel of Death is gone. What a rebbe cannot do for his students, his students can do for one another with their blessings of *l'chaim.*"

"You see," said Reb Zalman, "a rebbe may have enormous merit, and many wondrous things can be done in a rebbe's name. But when a group of people gather together as a collective to send blessings to someone, the potency of this is even greater than that of a rebbe.

"May we all be blessed to have good friends and beloved ones who defend us and praise us in the heavenly realms."

# HEAVEN, HELL, AND RESURRECTION

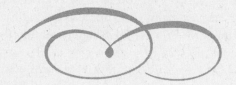

ANY STORIES DESCRIBE the difference between heaven and hell. In one, a person who dies is met by the heavenly gatekeeper. "What does hell look like?" wonders the newly deceased. She is taken to a room with a large table surrounded by people. The table is set with delectable things to eat and drink. But the people are continuously angry and miserable, starving because their arms are encased in locked, metal sleeves and they cannot bend their arms to bring their hands to their mouths no matter how hard they try.

Heaven is the room next door. It also has a table filled with food, and the people in this room also wear sleeves over their arms. But the people in this room are happy and calm, for they have learned to feed one another.

In another tale, a person dies and awakens in a beautiful garden. The keeper of the garden is quite solicitous and gives the person whatever he asks for. He wants a beautiful house, and the house of his dreams instantly appears. He wants a perfect spouse, and the ideal spouse materializes. Each day he requests something new, and each day his wish is fulfilled. This goes on for many months. His wishes become more extravagant. He gets everything he wants. Nothing is lacking. He runs out of things to request. Days go by without a wish, then months.

He becomes bored. There is nothing to look forward to, nothing to challenge him. The taste of everything goes flat. Finally one day he says to the keeper of the garden, "I've been thinking that maybe I would like to see what things are like on the other side."

The garden keeper says, "The other side, what do you mean?"

"I mean that I wish I could see what it would be like to be in hell."

"Oh," says the garden keeper, " but, my friend, where do you think you have been all this time?"

*H*EAVEN AND HELL are not necessarily what we think they are. The same experience can be heaven or hell, depending upon our point of view. So too the idea of resurrection, life after death. If we view it as something out of reach in the distant future, we are wearing mental mind-sleeves, so to speak. We are separated from it and cannot bend our thoughts to nourish our souls. But if we see the ongoing relationship between God-ing and creation-ing, we fully connect with the understanding that resurrection is a continuous process, happening right now.

## GEHINNOM

*R*ebbe Nachman of Breslov said, "Everyone says that there is a dimension of reality called 'This World'(*Olam ha-zeh*), and another called the 'World to Come' (*Olam ha-bah*). Maybe there is [actually] a reality called 'This World' somewhere [else], but given the constant suffering we see around us, it appears that we currently live in *Gehinnom* (hell)."[58]

In Judaism the netherworld is usually referred to as *Gehinnom*, which comes from the name of a valley south of Jerusalem, the Valley of Ben-Hinnom (Gei Hinnom), where idolatrous tribes sacrificed children by fire to the god Moloch.[59] It was known as a place of torture. The prophet Jeremiah said it would be designated forever as the Valley of Slaughter.[60] From these references it became known as a place of retribution, where punishment was doled out.

The netherworld is also known by a variety of other names: *Sheol*,[61] the grave, the dust, *Abaddon*, silence, the depths of the pit, and the land of darkness. There are widely differing views about what happens in the netherworld, but they are universally gruesome: eternal suffering from fire, freezing, hanging, suffocation, disemboweling, and any other awful crippling or maiming that could be conjured by a fertile imagination.[62]

Each Rosh Hashana, which is a Day of Judgment, souls are divided into three groups: the thoroughly righteous, the thoroughly wicked, and the intermediate.[63] The house of Shammai said that the righteous will go straight to Paradise, the wicked will be doomed to *Gehinnom* forever, and the intermediate will be punished and then released.

The house of Hillel disagreed. They said that God is always merciful, and therefore the wicked are not punished forever. According to this view, most souls spend a maximum of twelve months for purification and then are released. Only a handful of crimes, such as not believing in the eternal nature of the soul,[64] scoffing the Torah, or informing on an innocent person, result in extended residence in the netherworld beyond twelve months; but even then, hell does not last for eternity. The house of Hillel said, "*Gehinnom* will be consumed [in the messianic era], but [those condemned for extended time in hell] will not be consumed."[65] In other words, they will outlast *Gehinnom*. Indeed, the Talmud says outright, "There is no *Gehinnom* in the world to come."[66]

The ancient sages suggested that the proportions of *Gehinnom* are enormous compared with the world. They said, "Egypt is one-sixtieth of Ethiopia; Ethiopia is one-sixtieth of the [known] world; the world is one-sixtieth of the Garden [of Eden]; the garden is one-sixtieth of Eden; Eden is one-sixtieth of *Gehinnom*. Therefore the entire world is like a [tiny] pot lid compared with *Gehinnom*."[67]

Hell is 3,600 times larger than the Garden of Eden, and 196,000 times larger than earth. No wonder our lives seem to be in *Gehinnom* so much. From this, we gain perspective into the rabbinic view of the world to come. If the huge dimension of *Gehinnom* were eliminated, a world without suffering would ensue, which would seem like Paradise.

Although there are differences of opinion regarding what the world to come represents, it is generally viewed as a time of messianic consciousness.[68] Following the idea that there would be no *Gehinnom* at that time, the concept of divine retribution would take a different form. Then, it is said, the Holy One will take the sun "from its sheath and the righteous will be healed and the wicked judged."[69] The idea of the sun being drawn from its sheath means that a light far brighter than the sun will be applied. This would be the *Ohr Ein Sof,* the infinite light of awareness which illuminates every corner of the universe and all the wisdom of creation.

## PARADISE

*P*aradise is generally associated with the Garden of Eden, which is represented on two levels in Jewish mysticism. The lower garden is paradise on earth, while the upper garden is related to heaven. Descriptions rarely differentiate between the terrestrial and celestial gardens. Because the mystical approach to all of creation is that everything below has its reflection above, there may be no clear difference between the two.

The garden is described in luscious terms, filled with spices, trees, angels, perfumes, precious metals, and jewels. Of course, all righteous beings dwell here: great sages, the matriarchs and patriarchs, the well-known biblical figures, scholars from all ages, and the messiah. In the midst of this, God sits and explains the Torah.[70]

Paradise is viewed as being on the right side of God (lovingkindness), while *Gehinnom* is on the left (justice). The Midrash asks what the distance is between the two. Rabbi Yohanan said the breadth of a wall; Rabbi Hanina said the breadth of a hand; but most of the rabbis generally agreed that Paradise and *Gehinnom* are side by side, having a common boundary.[71]

Where is this boundary? It is precisely where we stand each moment. Paradise and *Gehinnom* meet in the center of our being. We can reflect upon the past from either perspective, and our future depends upon the side toward which we turn for the choices we make. We are never more than a hair's breadth away from either heaven or hell.

Regarding the world to come, the mystics go one step further. They say that the Torah, which represents the mind of God, so to speak, was revealed as a handshake—black fire on white fire.[72] When two hands clasp each other, the boundaries of each become blurred, and we must look closely to determine which is which.

In the world as we know it, we seem to be able to differentiate between the opposites of left and right, good and evil. The boundary between opposites is defined by both sides simultaneously. In the world to come, however, our perception will shift dramatically, and the handshake will become fully integrated.

Thus, just as the Garden of Eden is the starting point of human consciousness, is it also our destiny. Life eternal is a fundamental tenet of Jewish faith. It is life in the garden, but not life as we know it, because opposites will blend into each other, evil will no longer exist, and suffering will disappear.


## RESURRECTION

Resurrection is one of the thirteen principles of faith proposed by Maimonides,[73] and is the second benediction of the Amida in the daily prayers.[74] It is said that if a person does not believe in the idea of resurrection, he or she will not have a portion in the world to come.[75]

Resurrection is a different idea from reincarnation. Reincarnation is continual rebirth to redeem fallen sparks in the process of perfecting the creation. Resurrection is the heralding of a new era, a transformation into a consciousness previously unknown in which reality undergoes a profound change.

Although resurrection is a principle of faith in Judaism, we find a wide variety of conflicting viewpoints on what it means. There is general agreement on only one issue: the source of life cannot be thwarted by death. However, when resurrection occurs, how it happens, and to whom all are points of contention. As a result, it is not surprising that Reform and Reconstructionist Judaism resolve the problem by discarding the notion of *Gehinnom* and of resurrection altogether.

Kabbalah, however, follows a different track of thought. If the root of all souls is *Adam ha-Rishon* (earliest human awareness), resurrection represents the culmination of the rectification of holy sparks that have fallen and have been returned to their original source.[76]

The *Zohar* reports, "Rabbi Abba said, 'All people will rise from the dead. God is the fountain of mercy. Since people in this world suffered, they will not suffer in the world to come.' "[77] The *Zohar* also says, "After the resurrection of the dead, the world will be perfectly renewed and will not have death."[78]

Life after the resurrection will not be like anything we can conceive. Yet the description in the *Zohar* is interesting. In our current reality, the body is a garment or a shell *(kelippah)* for the soul, which is viewed as a spark. In the world to come, the body will no longer be a shell for a spark, but will become the flame of that spark, enhancing it rather than confining it. The body will look like the one we see currently in our mirrors, yet it will be fully il-luminated, like the glow of Moses as he came down from Mt. Sinai, when he was incandescent to the extent that he had to cover his face with a veil.[79]

Thus the *Zohar* says, "It is apparent that there will be a new creation from the one bone that remains intact (the *luz* bone), which never decays, and from which will expand the whole body.[80] . . . Then God will cause the iden-tical body and the identical soul to return to the world . . . and will cause the dew to descend upon them . . . the dew of lights; supernal light through which the Almighty will pour forth life upon the world."[81]

The *luz* bone is sometimes referred to as the nut of the spinal column, a mysterious bone that rests at the base of the spine. The Midrash says that it cannot be dissolved in water, burnt in fire, ground in a mill, or split with a hammer.[82] Indeed, when someone attempted to smash a *luz* bone, the bone remained whole, while the hammer and anvil split.[83]

Obviously there is no physical entity in the body that is indestructible. Rather, the mystics suggest that there is a sustaining quality for each being that contains all of its codes. This mystical essence can be cloned any time in the future. We could describe it as an angel, an eternal bubble of energy, that retains the prototype of a particular being. It is from this energy bubble that the new body is ultimately resurrected.

As an aside, one of the primary reasons the rabbinic tradition does not allow for cremation is the concern that the *luz* bone will be lost in the process. However, as we see from the Midrash, the *luz* bone cannot be burnt in fire. This is an issue of great concern for modern Jews whose parents or relatives choose to be cremated, as mine did. Reb Zalman points out that millions of people were involuntarily cremated in the Holocaust, but we dare not say that they will be denied resurrection. In view of this reality, the Jew-ish laws regarding the issue of cremation need to be articulated with greater sensitivity.

## DEATH HAS
## NEVER EXISTED

*A* modern Kabbalist said about resurrection, "This is the only level of consciousness which is completely beyond human experience: that of continually dying in the 'kiss' [of God] and being resurrected. In this final stage of creation, all reality will be reunited with God, not only the sparks but also the shells (bodies) of physical reality. Having died—the unrectified, natural ego being finally 'dead'—the soul will experience life as an eternal pulsation or oscillation of living/dying into God."[84]

This viewpoint provides a perfect summary of the evolution of the kabbalistic perspective. Resurrection represents a new level of consciousness well outside the boundaries of human experience. In it, humans will not sense an ego barrier of separation, but will be united in the totality of the universe. In this realm, we do not live and die as disconnected entities, but expand and contract as an extension of God, each of us representing an eternal pulse-beat of the Divine.

The *Zohar* asks, "Is not a sinner dead even though alive?"[85] In this context, "sinner" means one who has distanced her- or himself from God, which of course includes everyone but a handful of righteous beings. Thus we could read this question, "Are we not all dead even though we think we are alive?" What does it mean to be alive in this context? It means to be fully aware of the presence of God-ing and to appreciate our role in the continuous unfolding of creation.

Solomon ibn Gabirol, an eleventh-century Jewish poet and philosopher, developed a contemplative system that leads to freedom from death.[86] This approach was developed in his main philosophical work: *Mekor Hayyim* (Fountain of Life). The first step is to contemplate God and to live an ethical life so that the soul can attach itself to its source. From here the soul will rise in contemplation until it reaches the level of "first universal matter," the level of archetypes. Next, our contemplation leads to appreciation of the Will of God, which leads to the source: the Fountain of Life. When we fully connect with the Divine through contemplation, our communion with God releases us from death.[87]

Because resurrection is in a timeless domain, it penetrates any reality limited by time and space. In other words, resurrection is not something for which we must wait. It is always here. Our challenge is to move from ego consciousness to God consciousness. Creation-ing is the pulse of God-ing. No matter how far we have expanded outward from the Divine, we are still part of It.

This is the secret of resurrection and the reason the sages were so concerned about communicating it to us. Despite the limitations of language and concepts, the underlying principle that we constantly live in the presence of the Divine assures the certainty of resurrection. Each moment we are sustained in life as we know it, it is as if we are being raised from the dead. Our entire life is a perpetual experience of resurrection, if only we were able to perceive it in this way.

Abraham Isaac Kook, one of the foremost Kabbalists of this century, believed that death is imaginary. Our view of death is distorted by our confused perception of reality. In time we will come to realize the full connotation of the Hebrew words *"Lo hayah mavet me-olam,"* which mean, "Death has never existed."[88]

# EPILOGUE

## THE DIRTY PENNY

In the city of St. Petersburg two hundred years ago, a desperate situation arose in which a ransom of ten thousand rubles was demanded for a young bridegroom. This experience was not uncommon in those days, when unscrupulous police, military, or other people in power would arrest or kidnap Jews and demand ransom, for they knew that Jewish law required the Jewish community to do anything—including selling a pr ___ us Torah scroll—to save a Jewish life.

Three talmudic students in the area realized that the only place to get such a sum was from a wealthy man named Ze'ev. Now *ze'ev* is the Hebrew word for wolf, and this man was aptly named. He was ravenous for wealth and would do anything to acquire it. He could also be vicious when turning people away who requested donations. He never contributed to anything.

These three rabbinic students were to become famous rebbes. The youngest of the three was later known as the Alter Rebbe, Shneur Zalman of Lyady. He was the leader of the three because he was certain that they would be successful with Ze'ev. The other two were Reb Levi Yitzhak of Berdichev and Reb Mendel of Vitebsk. They were far more skeptical about getting money out of Ze'ev, and were concerned about wasting precious time. But they wanted to accompany Shneur Zalman to provide protection. He agreed on condition that they would not say anything during the fund-raising, no matter what happened.

Ze'ev was stunned, and somewhat honored, to see a delegation of three rabbis at his door. He also was suspect, but he invited them in nonetheless. They had tea and talked about the weather for a while. Finally Shneur Zalman got around to telling the story. He told of an orphan boy who had no family and whose wedding was only a week away. The boy had been arrested on a trumped-up charge, and now he could not be released without the paying of a ten-thousand-ruble ransom.

As Shneur Zalman spoke, Levi Yitzhak and Mendel could see tears welling in Ze'ev's eyes. At the end, Ze'ev said, "Such a sad story. You have touched my heart. So I would like to help." Levi Yitzhak and Mendel were startled. How had Shneur Zalman done it? Then quite suddenly their delight turned sour, for Ze'ev reached into his pocket and pulled out one rusty, dirty kopek—worth a penny—which may have been in his pocket for ten years. He handed this paltry sum to Shneur Zalman as if it were a major contribution.

The two older students were shocked by such miserliness, but they had agreed before coming not to say a word. This was Shneur Zalman's project.

What did Shneur Zalman do? He began to praise in the most lavish language imaginable this wonderful contribution: "Oh, sir, you do not know what this means to us. We are so grateful for your generosity. I want to bless you and your wife and your children that you should be successful in your business, you should be the beneficiary of good health, you should be graced with love . . ." On and on he went, giving blessings in abundance.

Finally, when Shneur Zalman had finished, the three rabbis gathered to leave. Ze'ev stood at the door. As they were departing, Ze'ev said, "You have touched me so much with this story, I feel that I must give you more." He reached into his pocket and pulled out another dirty kopek.

Reb Levi Yitzhak and Reb Mendel were infuriated, but they said nothing, as they had promised. Reb Shneur Zalman, on the other hand, began a new round of praises and blessings that lasted another ten minutes.

Finally they were out on the street, walking away from the house. Levi Yitzhak said to his friend, "Are you crazy? We just spent an hour for two lousy kopeks!"

"Hush," whispered Shneur Zalman.

Sure enough, when they were about a hundred feet from the house, the front door opened and Ze'ev called out, "Teachers, come back."

They returned to the front door. With a great deal of fuss, Ze'ev proudly handed them a one-ruble coin. "I want to make a serious donation." Of course, Shneur Zalman spent yet another five minutes with new praises and blessings.

They began walking away. Mendel said, "The way I calculate it, we just spent over an hour to get one ruble. At this rate, it will take us ten thousand hours. We ought to have the boy out of jail in four or five years."

"Hush," whispered the future Alter Rebbe.

Again the front door opened and Ze'ev called out. They returned, but this time he gave them ten rubles. A few minutes later it was one hundred rubles. Then five hundred; then one thousand. Finally, after a dozen returns, he wrote out a check for the balance so that they had the full amount of ten thousand rubles.

The two skeptics were numb with amazement. It had taken a few hours, but they had the entire sum. As they walked away, they asked excitedly, "How do you do it? How did you know he would give so much?"

Reb Shneur Zalman said, "When our hearts are covered with a thick shield, the barrier not only keeps things from coming in, it also keeps them from going out. There is no way to remove this shield over the heart all at once. So what we must do is find a way to make the tiniest crack. Then each little opening of generosity leads to another.

"This idea of slowly breaking down our barriers is the secret of all success: it works for charity, it works for learning, it works for love. Every time we do a good deed, it builds the capacity to do more. No matter what you want to accomplish, you can begin with something that may seem trivial, even a dirty penny. Let yourself slowly evolve, widening the crack. Ultimately you will be able to pass through easily."

THE STORY OF the dirty penny is a metaphor for attaining messianic consciousness. We have many wisdom-teachings about the potential for human awareness, but unless we begin to actualize these teachings, they remain in the realm of ideas, conjecture, and abstraction. To bring about the new reality of messianic consciousness, we must find a way to make a crack in our own barriers so that the light of awareness will shine through.

This story suggests that we can reveal the light of higher awareness by opening ourselves to it one step at a time. Once we make a crack, the barrier can be split open quickly. Higher awareness is a huge reservoir. All we need do is remove our fingers from the dam of self-identity. If we have the courage to do so, we will be flooded in light.

May each and every one of us be blessed to realize the messianic consciousness within us; may we gain strength and insight to open our eyes; may our lives be filled with the ongoing truth in which we are saturated with love, caring, and kindness. And may we serve the world from this level of awareness.

And let us say: "Amen."

# ENDNOTES

INTRODUCTION

1. Aryeh Kaplan, *Chassidic Masters* (New York and Jerusalem: Moznaim Publishing, 1984), p. 115.
2. Because we have dual citizenship in Israel and the USA, Shoshana and I choose to observe one-day holy days as Israelis.
3. The fifty-sixth year represents *chesed* of *gevorah*. For a discussion of kabbalistic cycles, see "Template of Creation."
4. Moshe Idel, *Studies in Ecstatic Kabbalah* (New York: State University of New York Press, 1988), p. 132.
5. Ibid.
6. See David A. Cooper, *Silence, Simplicity, and Solitude* (New York: Bell Tower, 1992), pp. 59–73.
7. *Encyclopedia Judaica,* vol. 7, pp. 1391, 1403–20.
8. See Larry Dossey, *Healing Words* (San Francisco: HarperSanFrancisco, 1993).
9. *Zohar* I:4a.
10. See Idel, *Studies in Ecstatic Kabbalah.*
11. Moshe Idel, one of today's foremost scholars of Kabbalah, points out that "certain Kabbalists saw divine inspiration as the *sine qua non* (essential condition) for fathoming the sublime secrets . . . [and they also believed] that altered states of consciousness were a prerequisite for a more profound understanding of the sacred text. . . . One must return, or at least attempt to return, to the level of consciousness that characterized the person who [originally] received the inspiration or revelation." Moshe Idel,

*Kabbalah: New Perspectives* (New Haven and London: Yale University Press, 1988), p. 234.

12. Zalman Schachter-Shalomi, *Paradigm Shift* (Northvale, NJ: Jason Aronson, 1993), p. 258.

13. Ibid., p. 267.

14. Ibid., p. 268.

15. Ibid., pp. 266–68.

16. Ibid., p. 280.

17. Ibid., p. 257.

18. *Avoth d'Rabbi Nathan* 15:3.

19. The dates of the Jerusalem Talmud are not clear. See Maimonides' introduction to the Mishnah Torah.

20. Rabbi Adin Steinsaltz points out that Hillel suggests 7 principles, Rabbi Yishmael suggests 13, Rabbi Eliezer ben Jose Ha-Gelili suggests 32, and the Malbim (R. Meir Loeb ben Yehiel Michal) compiled a list of 613 principles, which was not exhaustive. See Adin Steinsaltz, *Steinsaltz English Edition of the Talmud: A Reference Guide* (New York: Random House, 1989), pp. 147–54; and *Encyclopedia Judaica* 8:366–71.


PART ONE: THE PAST

1. *Mamash* was one of Shlomo's favorite words, used to emphasize things. The closest idea in English would be "really," as in, "He was *mamash* a big person."

2. A *mikveh* is a gathering of "living water"—connected to a natural source—used for spiritual purification by completely immersing the body. Religious men use the *mikveh* before Shabbat or holy days. Religious women use the *mikveh* after menses in preparation for intercourse.

3. Gershom Scholem, *Major Trends in Jewish Mysticism* (New York: Schocken Books, 1941), p. 280.

4. Genesis 1:2.

5. See Rashi on Genesis 1:2.

6. Aryeh Kaplan, *Inner Space* (New York: Moznaim Publishing, 1990), p. 80; see also *The Bahir* (New York: Samuel Weiser, 1979), section 2.

7. The Hebrew letters for the word "deep" *(tohum: tav-hey-vav-mem)*, can be rearranged to mean "death" *(ha-mavet: hey-mem-vav-tav)*.

8. The word "bohu" can be divided into two words: *bo* and *hu*, which means "It is in it." See *The Bahir*, section 2.

9. Kaplan, *Inner Space*, p. 82.

10. The Ari teaches additionally that there are 288 fallen sparks. This is derived from the next line in Genesis (1:2), "and a wind of God moved over (*merachephet*) the face of the waters." *Merachephet* is spelled *mem-resh-peh-het-tav*. The first and last letters— *mem, tav*—spell *met* (death); the remaining letters—*resh, peh*, and *het*—add up to 288. This is also the value of the word "*ibbur*," which means gestation. So, death and re-

birth both are represented in the opening to Genesis. It is significant that 288 is four times seventy-two, representing the number of letters in the most hidden name of God (72), repeated once each in the four worlds. See Kaplan, *Inner Space,* pp. 78–83, for more information on the Shattering of the Vessels.

11. *Zohar* I:156a–b.
12. Song of Songs 7:11.
13. *Zohar* I:88a.
14. Ibid., I:129a.
15. Ibid., I:53a.
16. Ibid., I:60a.
17. Ibid., I:156b.
18. *Encyclopedia Judaica,* vol. 10, p. 494.
19. Ibid., 9:35.
20. *Zohar* I:19b–20a.
21. Genesis 1:26.
22. Gerald Friedlander, trans., *Pirkei De Rabbi Eliezer* (New York: Sepher-Hermon Press, 1916), chapter 13.
23. *Zohar* I:35b. Samael (Satan) rode the serpent, but the serpent itself is also considered to be Satan.
24. The Hebrew letter *gimel,* when spelled out, uses the letters *gimel, mem,* and *lamed.* The word *golem* uses the same letters. It is the word for the Frankenstein-like creatures that ancient Kabbalists are said to have created by using magical formulas of various names of God. The numeric value of *golem* or *gimel* is the same as *chochma,* which is usually defined as wisdom. The letter *gimel* equals 3, *mem* equals 40, *lamed* equals 30. Total: 73. *Chochma* is made up of the letters *het* (8), *kaf* (20), *mem* (40), and *hey* (5). Total: 73. Kabbalists call *chochma* the kind of pristine wisdom that lies in the realm of formless matter. *Chochma* can be divided into two words: *koach* amd *ma.* This means "the power of 'what,'" in which "what" is a code word for formless matter, which is the essential meaning of *golem,* thus closing the circle. See Yitzchak Ginsburgh, *The Hebrew Letters* (Jerusalem: Gal Einai Publications, 1990), p. 58.

The Talmud, in a section that deals with many issues of demonology, says that Rabbi Hanina and Rabbi Oshaia were able to create a small calf (a *golem*) through studying mysteries revealed in the kabbalistic text the *Sefer Yetzirah* (*Sanhedrin* 65b). It says that these rabbinic sages ate this calf.

The Talmud also says that Rabbah (fourth century) created a "man." Rabbah sent this creature to his study partner, Zera, who upon speaking to it realized that it was not human, and with a word returned it to dust. Zera was one of the great talmudic contemplatives in Jewish history. It is said that he "fasted" hundreds of times, which I understand to mean that he withdrew into silence and solitude on a regular basis. He would test himself by placing his feet in a hot, burning oven to see if his concentrative powers were strong. But the rabbis around him were jealous, and one day they did something to distract him. As a result, his legs got a little burned. As he was short in stature, he got the nickname "Short man with singed legs." (*Baba Metzia* 85a.)

Within all of these strange teachings is a key to deep understanding. The Hebrew that forms the sentence "Rabbah created a man" is *"Rabbah bara gabra."* The wording is similar to the well-known incantation *abra-kadabra,* which means "I will create as I speak" [Aryeh Kapan, *Sefer Yetzirah* (York Beach, ME: Samuel Weiser, 1990), p. xxi]. Kaplan points out an interesting side note that the word *abra-kadabra* contains the word *bara,* to create, and the remaining letters add up to 26, which is the value of the tetragrammaton (Y-H-V-H). This is all magic.

Kabbalists traditionally obfuscated secret teachings to be certain that people would not misuse them. In the sentence *"Rabbah bara gabra,"* each word has the same three letters: *bet, resh,* and *aleph,* which in that order mean "to create." But the last word of the sentence *(gabra)* adds one additional letter, *gimel.* We could read this sentence, "Rabbah created a *gimel*-creation," the meaning of which is, "Rabbah discovered the creative power of the principle of fragmentation, the essential ingredient of physicality, the satanic force."

25. During the holy days of Sukkot, one of the primary rituals is to hold an unopened palm branch, a citron, and myrtle and willow branches, and shake them in the six directions. This is viewed by Kabbalists as a way to bring a *tikkun,* a mending, to the separation caused by the physical universe. The palm branch represents a *vav,* the number six, and the citron (a lemonlike fruit) represents the Tree of Knowledge in its most "beautiful" state of unity and undifferentiation—when it is united with the Tree of Life. During the ritual shaking, the six directions are mystically drawn into the citron, representing the person's heart. The intention of the ritual is to break through the illusion of separation and to return to the unity of the symbolic garden.

26. "The level of the material [world], beneath the level of form is called Satan. Matter denotes that which undergoes generation and corruption and is constantly changing; whereas the forms of the species do not deteriorate" [Moshe Idel, *Studies in Ecstatic Kabbalah* (New York: State University of New York Press, 1988), p. 35].

27. Genesis 2:8–17.

28. Ibid., 3.

29. *Encyclopedia Judaica* 7:326.

30. Ibid., 13:78.

31. Ibid.

32. *Eruvin* 19a.

33. *Tamid* 32b.

34. Ibid.

35. Ibid.

36. Louis Ginzberg, *The Legends of the Jews,* 7 vols. (Philadelphia: The Jewish Publication Society of America, 1937),vol. 1, p. 55.

37. Ibid.

38. Friedlander, *Rabbi Eliezer,* chapter 12.

39. Ibid.

40. Deuteronomy 20:19. This Torah section stipulates that when a city is besieged, it is forbidden to destroy the trees around it. In that context it asks a rhetorical question: "Is man a tree of the field that you should besiege it?" The structure of the Hebrew allows this to be a question or a statement. As a statement, it completely reverses its meaning to "Man is a tree of the field . . ." which is the way Rabbi Eliezer chooses to read it.

41. Song of Songs 4:12.

42. Friedlander, *Rabbi Eliezer,* chapter 21.

43. *Midrash Rabbah, Bereshit* 15. In other sources it is called a nut, palm, or carob tree. The belief that it was an apple tree may have come from references to the citron as the "apple of paradise." See Ginzberg, *Legends,* 5:97–98.

44. Friedlander, *Rabbi Eliezer,* chapter 12.

45. Ibid., 1:70, and notes on 1:17.

46. *Zohar* I:7a.

47. Ibid., I:26b.

48. Ibid., II:133b.

49. Aryeh Kaplan, *Meditation and Kabbalah* (York Beach, ME: Samuel Weiser, 1982), p. 225. An example of the *atbash* method is described by Levi Yitzhak of Berdichev. He points out that there is an aspect of God that is hidden, and an aspect that is revealed. Both aspects can be discovered in the word *"mitzvah" (mem-tzadi-vav-hey).* A *mitzvah* is the performance of a religious duty; it is also considered to be a meritorious deed. Levi Yitzhak says that when we do a *mitzvah,* we connect with the hidden God and the revealed God. The first two letters of *mitzvah (mem, tzadi)* represent the hidden God. Hidden in the sense that using the *atbash* code, *mem* equals *yod,* and *tzadi* equals *hey.* These are the first two letters of the tetragrammaton *yod-hey-vav-hey.* As we can see, the last two letters of the tetragrammaton are also the last two letters of the word *"mitzvah,"* indicating the revealed aspect of God. See *Kidushit Levi, Bereshit.*

50. *Hagigah* 12a.

51. The *Ohr Ein Sof* is described as the vehicle of inner illumination that gave prophetic insight to King David and especially to Moses. This was the reason why Moses was glowing so much when he came down from Mt. Sinai that he had to cover his face with a veil (*Zohar* I:31b).

52. *Zohar* I:34b.

53. Ibid.

54. *Midrash Rabbah, Bereshit* 8:1, *Adam ha-Rishon* was androgynous, being both male and female, rather than hermaphroditic (bisexual, or suggesting one who has male and female genitals). This statement was challenged in the same midrash: "But is it not written, God took one of Adam's ribs *(tzela)*?" And the response was, "The word *'tzela'* here means side, as it is used in Exodus 26:20, 'For the second side *(tzela)* of the tabernacle.' "

55. Genesis 1:27 and 5:2.

56. *Adam ha-Rishon* was considered so "beautiful," nothing could look at it. After the "sin," the beauty was diminished and its height was reduced to (only) 100 cubits (150 feet tall). The beauty of *Adam ha-Rishon* is related to profound faith, meaning total clarity. Jacob, who represents the essence of beauty, is compared with *Adam ha-Rishon* in this regard. See *Zohar* I:142b.

57. "The Tree stood to a height of 500 parasangs and its circumference was 60,000 parasangs" (*Zohar* II:2a). One parasang measures approximately 2½ miles.

58. Ginzberg, *Legends,* 1:70. If a person walked only 6 miles a day, 40 miles would be covered in a week, 2,000 in a year, a million in 500 years.

59. Leon Hurvitz, trans., *Scripture of the Lotus Blossom of the Fine Dharma (The Lotus Sutra)* (New York: Columbia University Press, 1976), pp. 158–59. "Thousands of myriads of millions . . ." One thousand of one myriad of one million equals ten trillion. This reference is far more than that.

60. Swami Pradhupada, *Krishna: The Supreme Personality of Godhead* (New York and Bombay: The Bhaktivedanta Book Trust, 1970), II:165.

61. Genesis 3:21.

62. Ibid., 3:5.

63. Ibid., 3:22.

64. Ibid., 1:28.

65. The *Zohar* clearly differentiates between the creation in "potential" and that of "essence." "All things were 'created' in potential through the use of the name *Elohim* [in the first section of Genesis], but that which was created in potential was not actually made in form until the full name, Y-H-V-H/*Elohim,* is used. Creation came out of potential and received its essential substance at this time [in the second chapter of Genesis]" (*Zohar* II:113b).

66. Genesis 3:12. "She gave to me from the tree, and I ate."

67. Ibid., 3:13.

68. The verb is translated as *nisha (nun-shin-aleph).* We can change the letter *shin* into the Hebrew letter *sin,* now reading it *nisah,* which dramatically changes the meaning. As the Torah is written strictly in consonants, without vowels or diacritical marks, this method of rereading a word is commonly used by religious Talmudic scholars. One might disagree with this reading, but not the method used to derive it.

69. Genesis 3:14.

70. Rashi on Genesis 3:14; see also *Bechorot* 8a.

71. *Zohar* I:124a.

72. Serpent is the word *"nahash"*: nun (50)-*het* (8)-*shin* (300). Total: 358. The word "messiah" is *meshiach: mem* (40)-*shin* (300)-*yod* (10)-*het* (8). Total: 358.

73. Traditionally, Rosh Hashana marks one of four different "New Year" days in the Hebrew calendar: the first of the month of Nisan (in the spring), the first of Elul (one month before Rosh Hashana), the fifteenth day of Shevat (in January or February), and the first day of Tishri (Rosh Hashana). Each of these days represents a point of

reckoning to determine the beginning of a year for purposes of tithing, ascertaining the length of contractual obligations, when it was permissible to eat certain fruits, and so forth.

74. Other judgment days in the Hebrew calendar are: 1) Passover, determining the grain crop for the coming year; 2) Shavuot, for the fruit harvest; and 3) Sukkot, for the annual rainfall—thus including all vegetables and domestic animal life.

75. The judgment is first pronounced on Rosh Hashana but is not sealed until Yom Kippur. Mystics say that everyone has one last chance to change this judgment on Shemini Atzeret, at the end of Sukkot.

76. Aryeh Kaplan, *Sefer Yetzirah,* p. 186.

77. The Talmud has many references to "pre-creation" times. In one section, for example, describing Moses' ascent to the heavens to receive the Torah, Moses was opposed by angels, who said, "Sovereign of the universe! How could you give to flesh and blood the secret treasure (the Torah) which has been hidden for 974 generations *before* the world was created?" (*Shabbat* 89a).

78. Kaplan, *Sefer Yetzirah,* pp. 167–90. The seven letters are *bet, gimel, dalet, kaf, peh, resh,* and *tav.*

79. Kaplan, *Sefer Yetzirah,* p. 185. This is a highly esoteric doctrine that describes worlds within worlds within worlds. For example, in the universe of Beriyah, there are seven chambers, themselves worlds, given the names Holy of Holies, Desire, Love, Merit, Luster, Essence of Heaven, and Brickwork of Sapphire. Many qualities that we experience such as fear, anger, hatred, jealousy, and so forth are considered worlds in themselves, separate realities. From this the Baal Shem Tov teaches that no matter what we are experiencing, it is a world containing a divine spark that can be liberated through higher consciousness.

80. The Buddhist perspective is that each moment has tens of thousands of beginnings. Modern science suggests that each subjective moment of our reality is composed of millions of synaptic firings in the mind. Mystical Judaism says that the continuity of time is a function of an unbroken flow of creative force, without past, future, beginning, or end as we know it.

81. Steven Hawking, the noted scientist, has said, "The uncertainty principle had profound implications for the way in which we view the world. Even after more than fifty years they have not been fully appreciated by many philosophers. . . . The uncertainty principle signaled an end to . . . a model of the universe that would be completely deterministic; one certainly cannot predict future events exactly if one cannot measure the present state of the universe precisely." Stephen W. Hawking, *A Brief History of Time* (New York: Bantam Books, 1988), p. 55.

82. *Kidushit Levi, Bereshit.* Reb Levi Yitzhak went on to say that if we do not have this understanding, we are trapped in time and space. But if we are able to connect with the immediacy of ongoing creation, we have the potential to enter the advanced contemplative state called *ayin* (Nothingness). This is the same *ayin* discussed by Isaac the Blind, a level of interconnectedness of all things where there is no separation of space

and no limitation of time. This is the domain of mystical awareness and is one of the foundation points of mystical practice in Judaism.

83. ·Based upon the Hebrew: *Bereshit bara Elohim et ha-shamaim v'et ha-aretz*. The word *"bara"* (created) has an assumed pronoun. Normally, translators presume that *Elohim* is the subject of *bara* (God created); but it could just as easily read "It created," in which case *Elohim* becomes the object rather than the subject. If it were a direct object, it would take the article *et,* but as an indirect object representing something plural, which is its word structure, it does not take an article. The *Zohar* says, "By means of a beginning [it] created *Elohim*" (*Zohar* I:15a).

84. In Jewish mysticism, the potential for Beginning must come out of a creation called Nothing. Thus, the creative force must precede the nothingness that precedes beginningness that precedes the names of God in the creation story.

The first line of the creation story can be represented in mathematical terms as a natural progression. Nothing precedes zero. Zero represents beginning, God is one, heaven and earth are two, and, as we will see, space is three. Thus, *Ein Sof* precedes and must first create Nothingness before the names of God.

85. *Encyclopedia Judaica* 9:35.

86. Clearly, the idea of awareness is not the same as thought. Awareness is an all-penetrating reality; thus there is awareness in Nothingness. Some mystics identify awareness as the central unifying medium of creation, and thus awareness would be another definition of the Divine.

87. Song of Songs 1:2.

88. Ibid., 2:6.

89. Ibid., 5:4–5.

90. Abulafia's commentary to his *Sefer HaYashar,* translated by Moshe Idel, in *Studies in Ecstatic Kabbalah,* p. 10.

91. Sufi tales frequently refer to a magical being called *Khidr,* who is a wise messenger and a kind of prophet.

92. Annemarie Schimmel, *Mystical Dimensions of Islam* (Chapel Hill, NC: University of North Carolina Press, 1975), pp. 165–66.

93. Aryeh Kaplan, *Chassidic Masters* (New York and Jerusalem: Moznaim Publishing, 1984), p. 186; see also Elie Wiesel, *Souls on Fire* (Harmondsworth, Middlesex, England: Penguin, 1972), pp. 175–93.

94. Zalman Schachter-Shalomi, *Paradigm Shift* (Northvale, NJ: Jason Aronson, 1993), pp. 266–68.

95. Psalms 111:10.

96. *Zohar* II:42b.

97. Ibid., I:21a.

98. *Baba Metzia* 59b.

99. Deuteronomy 30:11–14.

100. *Baba Metzia* 59b.

101. *Zohar* I:200a.

102. Idel, *New Perspectives,* p. 248.

103. *Pirkei Avot* 4:1.


Part Two: The Present

1. There are actually only nine mentions of *va-omer Elohim* in the opening section of Genesis, with the tenth being assumed in the opening line *bara Elohim*. This can be read, "and It created God," as the Kabbalists do, or "and God created." Either way, there was a creative activity, implying another emanation—making ten altogether. There are other interpretations regarding the ten sayings. See Aryeh Kaplan, *The Bahir* (New York: Samuel Weiser, 1979), p. 169.

2. Aryeh Kaplan, *Sefer Yetzirah* (York Beach, ME: Samuel Weiser, 1990), pp. 14, 88.

3. An additional *sefirah* often appears on the tree between *binah* and *chesed*. It is called *daat* (knowledge). It is used to balance the tree for those who consider *keter,* at the top, an aspect that is so ephemeral, it actually transcends the tree itself. So there are only ten *sefirot,* even though illustrations often show eleven circles, with *daat* shown in dotted lines to indicate its transient nature.

4. Kaplan, *Sefer Yetzirah,* pp. 199, 219.

5. Kaplan, *The Bahir,* pp. 22, 23, 33, 35, 154–56.

6. See *Zohar* I:3b.

7. *Rosh Hashana* 21b.

8. The *musar* movement was based upon building a greater sense of personal ethics and morals. It was founded by Israel Salanter about 150 years ago out of a concern that ethics, values, and morals were in a serious decline in the Jewish community. The idea was to encourage students to study more written materials which discussed the principles of moral and ethical living, and to require practices that would ingrain these teachings.

9. The fifth day is *hod* of *chesed:* the receptive and acceptance aspect of my generosity. Do I always calculate when generous, or am I sometimes completely spontaneous? Do I question what the recipient will do with what I provide? Do I judge recipients, what they look like, how they present themselves? How far can I separate my self-image from my generosity?

    The sixth day is *yesod* of *chesed:* the harmony of my generosity. Do I feel the balance of the universe in my generosity? Do I sense being nurtured by my recipient as much as I am nurturing her or him? Do I ever give anonymously and feel complete? Do I always pay attention to giving a certain percentage of my income as a way of maintaining harmony?

    The seventh day is *malkhut* of *chesed:* the physical reality of my generosity. I call it the characteristic of surrender. Looking around me, do I have just what I think I need, far more, or far less? Can I do something about this? Do I see a situation where I can do something special that will change someone's life? Can I take on specific exercises to improve my relationship with generosity? Am I able to surrender to really making a change in myself?

Then we would begin the second week: *gevorah*. The first day would be *chesed* of *gevorah*. What is the generous aspect of my restraint? The second day is *gevorah* of *gevorah*: What is the cramped heart of my restraint? The third day is *tiferet* of *gevorah:* What is the compassionate nature of my restraint? And so forth.

10. The five worlds are derived from a sentence in Isaiah (43:7) which says: "All [of existence] that is called in my name, for my glory I have created it, I have formed it, and I have made it." "My name" represents the universe called *adam kadmon;* "my glory" represents the universe of *atzilut.* The other three come from the actual words used in the verse: "created" is *beriyah,* "formed" is *yetzirah,* and "made" is *assiyah.*

11. *Zohar* I:83b.

12. Ibid., I:62b.

13. Ibid., I:206a.

14. Proverbs 20:27. See *Zohar* II:99b, which points out that lamp (*ner*) is spelled *nun-resh.* The *nun* represents *neshama,* while the *resh* represents *ruach. Ner* is also the word for candle. The relationship of *ner* to soul is the esoteric reason why a candle is used to search for *hametz* the day before Passover.

15. *Devekut* is to Judaism as *nirvana, satori,* and other higher states of awareness are to other traditions.

16. The Baal Shem Tov was noted for having three supernatural powers: he could see into the past and future, he knew what was happening in different parts of the world in any particular moment, and he could compact space in a way that would allow him to travel hundreds of miles by horse and carriage in a few hours. Each of these ideas is connected with the essential kabbalistic principle that creation is built upon levels of consciousness.

As everyone knows, our imagination is almost boundless. Our dreams, for example, instantly take us to strange, faraway realms. There are no spacial constraints on consciousness in this sense. Indeed, all of us experience the shortening of the way; we simply do not recognize it. For example, when a close friend or family member is in trouble, needs help, is ill, may be dying, or has just died, many people experience a mysterious inner voice that tells them something is happening. This occurs spontaneously over great distances. We often know that a parent has passed away before we are told, or we sense an ominous quality to a ringing telephone.

Some people experience this once in a lifetime; others get messages at regular intervals. All of these are examples of the shortening of the way. Space disappears; it is as if two people were together in the same moment even though physically they may be thousands of miles apart. This phenomenon remains a mystery to science.

The idea of *kefitzat ha-derekh,* the shortening of the way, is ancient. Three different biblical incidents are explained by it. The Talmud says: "The earth shrank for three [biblical] individuals: Eliezer, the servant of Abraham; our father Jacob; and Avishai the son of Zeruiah." (*Sanhedrin* 95a.)

For more information on *kefitzat ha-derekh,* see Gedalyah Nigel, *Magic, Mysticism, and Hasidism: The Supernatural in Jewish Thought* (Northvale, NJ: Jason Aronson, 1994), pp. 33–50, for an entire chapter on this subject: "*Kefitzat ha-Derekh,* The Shortening of the Way."

17. *Elohai neshama shenetatabi, tehora he.*

18. Our natural inclination is to ask about extremely evil personalities, the Hitlers of history, or modern mass murderers. How could they have pure souls? These are profound questions of good and evil, some of which will be addressed later in this book. But at the core, we must ask ourselves, Could Hitler have existed separate from the source of creation? Questions such as this transcend rationality and can be dealt with only mystically, through faith. But most people are not Hitler, and we must not let our fear of the Hitlers of the world keep us alienated and paranoid. Indeed, the battle of good and evil is won or lost by our decision to embrace good despite the presence of evil, which by its nature tries to keep us separate from divine awareness.

19. *Zohar* I:91b.

20. This is related to the 613 commandments that make up the primary corpus of Jewish law, from which thousands of additional laws are derived.

21. Gershom Scholem, *Kabbalah* (Jerusalem: Keter Publishing, 1974), p. 162; see also *Encyclopedia Judaica,* vol. 10, p. 615.

22. Allen Afterman, *Kabbalah and Consciousness* (New York: Sheep Meadow Press, 1992), p. 48; see also *Encyclopedia Judaica* 7:576.

23. *Zohar* I:137a.

24. See *Zohar* I:208a.

25. Fritjof Capra, *The Tao of Physics* (Boulder, CO: Shambhala, 1975), p. 55. Capra uses a different metaphor, saying that the atoms of an orange blown up to the size of the earth would be the size of cherries.

26. *Zohar* II:13b.

27. Ibid., I:103b.

28. Ibid., I:190b.

29. Homosexuality is an extremely thorny issue in mainstream Judaism. There is no prohibition regarding lesbian relationships, but male homosexuality is clearly proscribed in the Torah. Significant efforts have been made in the Jewish renewal community to revisit this issue and find new ways to understand the laws. People interested in this process should contact the Jewish renewal umbrella organization: Aleph, Alliance for Jewish Renewal, 7318 Germantown Avenue, Philadelphia, PA 19119-1793.

30. Aryeh Kaplan, *Jewish Meditation* (New York: Schocken Books, 1985), p. 157.

31. Ibid., p. 159.

32. Genesis 30:37–38.

33. *Zohar* I:140b.

34. Ibid., I:180b.

35. Ibid., I:235a.

36. Proverbs 5:15.

37. *Zohar* I:235a.

38. The value of the Hebrew letter *lamed* is 30, and *vav* is 6; thus *lamed-vav* is one way

of saying the number 36. A *tzaddik* is a righteous person, often referred to as a saint. Tradition says that thirty-six saints *(lamed-vav tzaddikim)* are hidden in the world at all times to do God's work.

39. *Rosh Hashana* 16b.

40. *Zohar* I:181a.

41. *Betzah* 16a.

42. Ibid.

43. The date is calculated as 165 B.C.E. (before the Common Era). See Scherman and Zlotowitz, *Chanukah* (Brooklyn, NY: Artscroll Mesorah Series, 1981), p. 90.

44. *Midrash Rabbah,* Exodus 21:6.

45. Jeremiah 5:22: "Do you not fear me? asks the Lord. Will you not tremble in my presence, who has placed sand for the bound of the sea by a perpetual decree that you cannot pass it?"

46. *Midrash Rabbah,* Genesis 5:5.

47. A more explicit Midrash brings a proof for this particular incident. A verse says that at the time of the parting of the sea, "the sea returned to its strength *(le-etano)* when morning appeared" (Exodus 14:27). The Hebrew word for "to its strength," *le-etano,* sounds the same as the word *"le-hitano,"* which means "as [previously] stipulated." Thus the phrase could be read, "the sea returned as stipulated [to its preconditioned state]."

  *Le-etano* is spelled *lamed-aleph-yod-tav-nun-vav*; *le-hitano* is spelled *lamed-hey-tav-nun-vav.* The difference between them is that one has a *yod,* the other has a *hey*—the *aleph* is silent. For the Kabbalist, the *yod* and *hey* substitution signals divine intervention, for these are the first two letters of the tetragrammaton.

48. *Encyclopedia Judaica* 12:78.

49. James Gleick, *Chaos: Making a New Science* (New York: Penguin, 1987), p. 23.

50. Louis Ginzberg, *The Legends of the Jews,* 7 vols. (Philadelphia: The Jewish Publication Society of America, 1937), vol. 1, p. 140; vol. 5, p. 71.

51. Ibid., 5:71.

52. Ibid., 1:140–41.

53. Ibid., 1:52.

54. Ibid.

55. Ibid., 1:54.

56. Ibid., 1:55.

57. *Zohar* I:55b.

58. Genesis 1:3.

59. In biblical grammar, the tense is often reversed when "and" precedes a verb. This is called a *"vav* consecutive," and is the reason we normally read this phrase, "and there was light." But if we do not follow these grammatical rules—which is acceptable when hermeneutic rules are applied—the sentence does not change tense.

60. *Zohar* I:46a.

61. *Midrash Tanhuma, Va-yeshev* 4.

62. Exodus 24:18.

63. At the burning bush (Exodus 3:14), Moses learned one of the names of God: *Eheye Asher Eheye* (I will be what I will be). The word *"Eheye"* (I will be), is written *aleph-hey-yod-hey,* which is a variation on the four-letter name of God *yod-hey-vav-hey.* Any four-letter name in which one of the letters repeats can be permutated into twelve combinations: 1232, 1322, 1223, 3231, 3321, 3221, 2132, 2312, 2123, 2321, 2213, and 2231. The pronunciation of these twelve combinations is the kabbalistic key to pass the gate guarded by the angel Kamuel (awakening of God).

64. *Zohar* II:58a.

65. More than 25 million miles. (Each myriad is 10,000 parasangs; each parasang equals approximately 2½ miles.)

66. *Zohar* II:58a.

67. Ginzberg, *Legends,* 3:111; see also *Hagigah* 13b.

68. Ibid., 3:112.

69. Ibid., 3:114.

70. There are ten angelic hierarchies that correspond to the ten emanations of creation. They are *malachim, erelim, seraphim, hayyot* (living beings), *ophanim, chamshalim, elim, elohim, bene elohim* (sons of *elohim*), and *ishim* (supernal "humans") (*Zohar* II:43a).

71. See Ginzberg, *Legends,* 5:96.

72. Ginzberg, *Legends,* 4:151.

73. Ibid., 4:100.

74. *Encyclopedia Judaica* 5:1523–24.

75. *Hagigah* 16a.

76. *Pesahim* 112b.

77. Ibid.

78. Ginzberg, *Legends,* 4:166.

79. The building of the altar could not be done with metal tools. "If you make an altar of stone, it should not be hewn; for if you use a tool on it, you have defiled it" (Exodus 20:22).

80. Ginzberg, *Legends,* 4:150–52.

81. Ibid., 4:168–72.

82. Ibid.

83. Ibid., 7:31–32.

84. *Midrash Rabbah,* Genesis 10:6.

85. *Zohar* I:92b.

86. Ibid., I:189a.

87. Genesis 28:10.

88. Ginzberg, *Legends,* 1:132, 5:159.

89. Ibid., 1:63.

90. One parasang represents approximately 2½ miles. See Adin Steinsaltz, *The Talmud: A Reference Guide* (New York: Random House, 1989), p. 283.

91. *Chullin* 91b.

92. *Midrash Rabbah,* Genesis 68:12.

93. *Zohar* 1:150a.

94. Ginzberg, *Legends,* 5:290–91.

95. *Megillah* 7b.

96. *Baruch Mordecai* is *bet* (2)-*resh* (200)-*vav* (6)-*kaf* (20)-*mem* (40)-*resh* (200)-*dalet* (4)-*kaf* (20)- and *yod*-(10). Total: 502. *Arrur Haman* is *aleph* (1)-*resh* (200)-*vav* (6)-*resh* (200)-*hey* (5), *mem* (40)-*nun* (50). Total: 502.

97. They both equal 358.

98. I first heard of the mobius-strip analogy from Rabbi Joel Baks in Jerusalem.

99. *Yom ha-Kippurim* can be read "the day like Purim."

100. *Zohar* II:69a–b.

101. Reality as we know it will change in the era of messianic consciousness, at which time evil will change into something else.

## PART THREE: HIGHER AWARENESS

1. *Encyclopedia Judaica,* vol. 10, p. 494.

2. *Hagigah* 11b.

3. Ibid., 14b.

4. Aryeh Kaplan, *Sefer Yetzirah* (York Beach, ME: Samuel Weiser, 1990), p. xviii.

5. Some of these have been translated; see Areyh Kaplan, *Meditation and Kabbalah* (York Beach, ME: Samuel Weiser, 1982), pp. 19–54.

6. See Moshe Idel, *Studies in Ecstatic Kabbalah* (New York: State University of New York Press, 1988).

7. Ezekiel 1:16–20.

8. Ibid., 10:15–16.

9. Notice the wordplay in the following verse: "And It rode (*rakav*) upon a cherub (*karuv*) and flew, and soared on the wings of a spirit" (Psalms 18:11).

10. Exodus 25:22.

11. Aryeh Kaplan, *Inner Space* (New York: Moznaim Publishing, 1990), p. 32; Kaplan, *Sefer Yetzirah,* p. 36.

12. The *Zohar* says that there are different levels of positive or negative experience. Whatever actions one does in the positive realm will draw positive influence. Just the opposite occurs if one performs negative acts, for they draw negative influences. Each side will draw the person deeper into it, so we must be careful with every choice we make (*Zohar* I:195b). A way to interpret this in contemporary language is that there are levels of higher consciousness and levels of lower consciousness. A person drawn to higher consciousness is given positive reinforcement and tends to dwell in these higher realms. A person who is drawn to acts of lower consciousness becomes habituated in this behavior and generates negative forces, which ultimately come home for resolution.

13. Martin Buber, *Tales of the Hasidim: Early Masters* (New York: Schocken Books, 1947), p. 66.

14. See Sogyal Rinpoche, *The Tibetan Book of Living and Dying* (San Francisco: HarperSanFrancisco, 1992), pp. 150–69, for an excellent description of the *Dzogchen* practice.

15. A holograph uses a laser to record a diffraction pattern on a photographic plate; then we can project a three-dimensional pattern by shining a laser through this plate. The amazing aspect of the holograph is that if the photographic plate is broken into parts, a laser beamed through any part will still project the whole image.
16. *Shabbat* 127a.
17. *Pesahim* 54a.
18. *Sanhedrin* 98a.
19. Ibid., 97a.
20. Idel, *Studies in Ecstatic Kabbalah,* p. 60.
21. Ibid.
22. Moshe Idel, *Kabbalah: New Perspectives* (New Haven and London: Yale University Press, 1988), p. 259.
23. *Midrash Rabbah,* Song of Songs 5:3.
24. *Avoda Zara* 20b. These twelve points could be compared with the Buddhist path of the *boddhisattva*. They share the similar qualities, but with different emphasis. The path of the *boddhisattva* includes *dana* (selfless giving), *sila* (morality), *kshanti* (patience), *virya* (interest), *dhyana* (meditation), and *prajna* (supreme wisdom). *Dana* connects with *hasiduth* (charity, acts of kindness); *sila* with *zhiruth* (precision), *n'kiuth* (cleanliness) and *tahara* (purity); *kshanti* with *anavah* (modesty, selflessness); *virya* with *zrizuth* (watchfulness); *dhyana* with *prishut* (restraint/separation); and *prajna* with *talmud torah* (wisdom).
25. Moshe Chayim Luzzatto, *The Path of the Just,* trans. Shraga Silverstein (Jerusalem: Feldheim Publishers, 1980).
26. Ibid., chapter 5.
27. Ibid., chapter 9.
28. *Baba Bathra* 10a.
29. The word *"shnorrer"* is sometimes used as a pejorative (panhandler, moocher, cheapskate, bum). That is not my intention. I purposely use the word *"shnorrer"* more frequently than beggar to suggest a different quality to the process. As I point out in this section, the concept of *tzeddakah* is quite different from giving alms, and a person who *shnorrers* is viewed as a dignified soul who has been given this important task in life by God, as discussed.
30. *Baba Batha* 9a.
31. *Zohar* I:104a.
32. Avraham Greenbaum, trans., *Advice: Rabbi Nachman of Breslov* (Jerusalem: Breslov Research Institute, 1983), p. 239; from *Likutey Moharan* II:4,1–2.
33. *Baba Bathra* 10b, regarding the verse "righteousness *(tzeddakah)* exalts a nation, but the kindness of people is sin" (Proverbs 14:34). The general interpretation here is that giving *tzeddakah* from the purity of intentions, no strings attached, is far superior to giving with ulterior motives. In the same section of Talmud, it is agreed that the best way to give is in a charity box so that neither giver nor recipient knows the other. Anonymity is important so that the donor can remain unattached (and the recipient can be free from psychological encumbrances as well).

34. *Baba Bathra* 9b.

35. Helping others must not be at the cost of impoverishing ourselves and thus becoming a burden on society. This teaching of being "anxious" to give charity has more to do with one's frame of mind. It should not be misinterpreted to suggest that we give away everything we have with the expectation that we will be compensated.

36. *Sukkah* 49b.

37. *Berachot* 40a.

38. *Shabbat* 128b.

39. *Encyclopedia Judaica* 3:6.

40. *Hullin* 7b.

41. *Encyclopedia Judaica* 3:7.

42. *Zohar* II:63b.

43. Ibid., II:33b.

44. Ibid., II:42a.

45. Ecclesiastes 1:2.

46. Ibid., 2:17.

47. *Zohar* II:59a.

48. Ibid., I:201a.

49. See Mishnah, *Peah* 1:1; also included in this Mishnah is the amount of produce we leave unharvested "in the corner of the field" for the poor to gather, the amount of "first fruits" we offer to the priests, the amount of times a pilgrim can visit the sanctuary in Jerusalem each year, the value of the offering brought each time, and the amount of Torah study that one can do.

50. Bachya ibn Paquda, *Duties of the Heart,* 2 vols. (New York: Feldheim, 1962), 2:295.

51. Ibid., p. 303.

52. *Nedarim* 62a.

53. Luzzatto, *Path of the Just,* p. 212.

54. Greenbaum, *Advice: Rebbe Nachman,* p. 250.

55. Ibid., p. 251.

56. *Yoma* 86b.

57. Aryeh Kaplan, *Chassidic Masters* (New York and Jerusalem: Moznaim Publishing, 1984), p. 110.

58. Ibid., chapter 23.

59. Ibid.

60. Psalms 111:10.

61. *Berachot* 60a.

62. Luzzatto, *Path of the Just,* chapter 25.

63. *Pirkei Avot* I:17.

64. *Zohar* I:2a.

65. Gershom Scholem, *Major Trends in Jewish Mysticism* (New York: Schocken Books, 1941), p. 136.

66. David A. Cooper, *Silence, Simplicity, and Solitude* (New York: Bell Tower, 1992), pp. 59–73.

67. Ezekiel I:4.

68. *Chagigah* 13b.

69. 1 Kings 19:11–12.

70. *Israel* is a code word for that essence in life that longs to be with its Creator. The word *"Israel"* is composed of two words: *yashar* and *El. Yashar* means "to go straight," and *El* is one of the names of God. The aspect within every being which yearns to go straight to God is called *Israel*. Each person knows the part of themselves that desires to be with God. This is the mystical meaning of the nation of Israel; it is not a geographical location, for it extends throughout the universe.

71. Idel, *Ecstatic Kabbalah,* p. 113; Scholem, *Major Trends,* p. 97.

72. The Maggid of Mezritch, Dov Baer Friedman, who was one of the more important students of the Baal Shem Tov, said: "The desired goal is that one must precede prayer with the act of the divestment of corporeality. Humans are finite and have limits but can make themselves [like] nothingness, without limit. People can do this by directing all their efforts to God alone, not to anything else, or even to themselves. This is impossible unless they make themselves nothing." *Sefer Shemuah Tovah* 79b, quoted by David S. Ariel, *The Mystic Quest* (New York: Schocken Books, 1988), pp. 179–80. (Quote adjusted to neutralize gender reference.)

73. Rabbi Israel Haupstein, *Avodat Israel, Teruma* 31b; quoted in Kaplan, *Chassidic Masters* (New York and Jerusalem: Moznaim Publishing, 1984), p. 139. Italics are mine; I have translated *tzaddik* as "spiritual leader."

74. *Kedushit Levi, Bereshit.*

75. Ibid.

76. Kaplan, *Sefer Yetzirah,* p. 71.

77. Exodus 31:3. This refers to Betzalel, who was the artist/builder of the first *mishkan,* the Ark of the Testimony, which Kabbalists view as the archetype of the cosmic design representing holiness.

78. One of the more famous of these was the Indian teacher Ramana Maharshi, who passed out of his body in 1950. When the students attending him in the dying process anxiously said, "Master, please do not leave us," his reply was, "Where would I go?"


PART FOUR: BEYOND THIS LIFE

1. Honor your father and mother . . . that your days will be prolonged and that it will go well with you" Deuteronomy 5:16; "You shall not take the mother bird together with the young . . . that it may be well with you and that you will prolong your days" Deuteronomy 22:6–7.

2. *Hullin* 142a.

3. Ibid.

4. "The measure in which a person measures, it is given back" *Sotah* 8b (Mishnah).

5. *Pirkei Avot* 5:8–9.

6. Ibid., 1:3.

7. *Shabbat* 32b, based on Job 33:23: "If there be an angel, an interpreter, one among a thousand to declare a person what is right, then It is gracious to this person, and says, 'Deliver this person from going down to the pit.' "

8. Ibid.

9. Ibid.

10. *Baba Bathra* 16a–b.

11. In this example, one could say that divine providence does everything: it influences the mother goat to climb the mountain, to labor, and to give birth at a particular moment. From the perspective of free will, the she-goat is drawn to the mountaintop by instinct. Neither view is correct. Rather, the relational process is continuous: both sides unfold together, and each moment appears to be a spontaneous interaction.

   Also, some would note that it is curious that the sages used an eagle to symbolize this act, when a dove or other benevolent bird would have sufficed. One cannot help but envision what an eagle would do with a newborn goat. Eagles are often viewed in mysticism as saviors, but they can be predators as well. Divine providence saves lives and also takes them.

12. The *Zohar* teaches that when death is near, a person is able to make an accounting of his or her life from a new perspective, so that life events can be seen in ways never before available. *Zohar* I:79a.

13. *Encyclopedia Judaica,* vol. 5, pp. 1425–26.

14. Ibid.

15. Ibid., 15:1188–89.

16. *Zohar* I:226a–b.

17. Ibid., II:225a.

18. The *tzaddik* is actually an entire universe of awareness out of which individual *tzaddikim* (saints) come. According to Lurianic Kabbalah, when the sparks fell and were enclosed in shells in the original Shattering of the Vessels, some sparks did not fall and remained in adamic purity. These sparks are the source for the universe of the *tzaddik*. This *tzaddik* is called "the one who is the real support of the world" *Zohar* I:82a.

19. Ibid., I:225b.

20. Ibid.

21. Ibid., I:56b.

22. *Encyclopedia Judaica* 7:574.

23. The number 236 comes from Psalms 147:5, "Great is our Lord, and of great power." The words "and of great power" *(v'rav koach)* add in gematria to 236. Thus the sentence could be read, "The greatness (height) of our Lord is 236."

24. Simcha Paull Raphael, *Jewish Views of the Afterlife* (Northvale, NJ: Jason Aronson, 1994), p. 319.

25. Ibid., p. 320; quotes *Tikkunei Zohar* 70:132a.

26. *Pirkei Avot* 4:16.

27. Paramahansa Yogananda, *Autobiography of a Yogi* (Los Angeles: Self Realization Fellowship, 1995), pp. 320–21.

28. Richard M. Bucke, *Cosmic Consciousness* (New York: E. P. Dutton, 1901), p. 329.

29. Ibid., p. 152.

30. William Chittick, *The Sufi Path of Love* (Albany, NY: State University of New York Press, 1983), p. 185.

31. Gershom Scholem, *Major Trends in Jewish Mysticism* (New York: Schocken Books, 1941), p. 151.

32. Philip Kapleau, *Three Pillars of Zen* (New York: Doubleday, 1980), p. 167.

33. *Zohar* II:61b.

34. Why did Rabbi Jesse have to hear a heavenly voice before curing the dying man? Why not cure the man without the voice from heaven? The story implies that he used magic, the "special" herb, to save the man's life. This kind of magic was not used indiscriminately by Kabbalists. We have seen that fate can be altered, but that we must at times be resigned to it. Decision making along these lines is subtle. The point of this story is that Rabbi Jesse was alerted that this particular situation required intervention. The operative words in the story are "before its ordained time." Once Rabbi Jesse was alerted to this fact, he could act. He was thus given the opportunity not only to save the man's life, but to reverse the fate that would have come to others in the town. The way in which we tinker with fate is inevitably a source of profound inquiry.

35. *Zohar* II:61b.

36. *Berachot* 8a. The number 903 is derived by gematria from the word *"toza'ot"* in Psalm 68:21, "To God the Lord belongs the issues *(toza'ot)* of death."

37. The rabbis teach that seven things are hidden from us: the day of death, the day of release from trouble, the magnitude of a judgment, what is in our neighbor's heart, where our financial resources will come from, when messianic consciousness will arrive, and when evil will be eliminated. *Pesahim* 54b.

38. Louis Ginzberg, *The Legends of the Jews,* 7 vols. (Philadelphia: The Jewish Publication Society of America, 1937), vol. 4, pp. 113–14.

39. *Ketubot* 77b.

40. Ibid.

41. Eleven in all are enumerated: the five mentioned in our text plus Hiram, the king of Tyre; Eliezer, Abraham's servant; Jabez; Ebedmelech, the Ethiopian; Honadab, the Rechabite; Rabbi Judah ha-Nasi's slave. Ginzberg, *Legends,* 5:96.

42. *Zohar* I:160b.

43. *Moed Katan* 28a.

44. Ibid.

45. *Zohar* I:183a.

46. Ibid., I:200a; also I:83a.

47. Ibid., I:92a.

48. Ibid., I:121b.

49. Ibid., I:183a.

50. Ibid.

51. Ibid., I:183b.

52. Torah and Talmud describe many types of dreams. Almost all give the dreamer access to other realms of reality. The famous dream of Jacob and the ladder reveals his state of mind as he was in a transformational phase of life. Joseph's ability to interpret the dreams of Pharaoh shows how dreams are prophetic (Genesis 41:25–27). Daniel's ability to describe a dream that Nebuchadnezzer could not remember suggests a dream can go far beyond the individual who dreamed it and can be connected with a cosmic reality that will affect the destiny of the entire world (Daniel 2:31–45). See also *Zohar* I:196a.

53. *Eruvin* 13b.

54. *Zohar* I: 217b.

55. Ibid.

56. Hospice nurses have noted the phenomenon that when patients report seeing close relatives who have died, it is frequently a sign that they themselves are soon to make the transition.

57. *Zohar* I:218a.

58. Rebbe Nachman of Breslov, *Likutey Moharan* II:119.

59. *Encyclopedia Judaica* 7:357, 12:997.

60. Jeremiah 7:32.

61. *Sheol* comes from Genesis 37:35, when Jacob was mourning the loss of his son Joseph, and said he would go down to *Sheol*—"thus his father wept for him." In Numbers 16:33, Korach and those rebelling with him are swallowed by the ground and drawn down "alive" to *Sheol*. *Sheol* means "to question," implying that it is a place where our questions are never answered, represented by a parent losing a child. It could also be a place that we end up when we override faith with continuous questioning, as was personified by Korach.

62. *Encyclopedia Judaica* 12:997.

63. *Rosh Hashana* 16b–17a.

64. The actual "crime" is not believing in the potential for resurrection at some point in the future. However, later in this chapter, we will see that there is considerable disagreement as to the meaning of resurrection.

65. Ibid. The house of Hillel said that "God abounds in grace and [thus] inclines [the scales of justice] to grace." The Talmud goes on to debate what this means. Is iniquity forgiven on the one side, or is lovingkindness added to the other? Are there some crimes in which a soul is destroyed before messianic times, or are all souls redeemed? These questions are unresolved.

66. *Nedarim* 8b.

67. *Pesahim* 94a.

68. *Encyclopedia Judaica* 14:100. Some say that there are three distinct ages: the days of the messiah, the resurrection of souls, and finally the world to come. Others say that the world to come precedes the resurrection. These different scenarios are designed to accommodate statements that appear contradictory, but all fall into the same snare of linear thinking, as if time continues in the new reality as we have known it in this reality.

69. *Nedarim* 8b.
70. Ginzberg, *Legends,* 1:18–23.
71. *Pesikta Rabbatai* 52:3, quoted by Raphael, *Afterlife,* p. 150.
72. *Zohar* II:84a.
73. Maimonides, *Helek Sanhedrin,* chapter 10; see Isadore Twersky, *A Maimonides Reader* (New York: Behrman House, 1972), pp. 417–23.
74. "Blessed are you, Hashem, who brings the dead to life."
75. Mishnah, *Sanhedrin* 10:1.
76. The letters in the name Adam *(aleph, dalet,* and *mem)* were viewed as representing three stages of the process of "the sparks of the soul" *(nitzotzot ha-neshamot).* First stage: Adam *(aleph),* when the sparks fell. Second stage: David *(dalet),* the process of redeeming the sparks (the period in which we now live). Third stage: Messiah *(mem),* the full rectification of the fallen sparks—the world to come.
77. *Zohar* I:108a.
78. Ibid., I:124a.
79. Exodus 34:29–35.
80. *Zohar* II:28b.
81. Ibid., I:130b.
82. *Midrash Rabbah,* Ecclesiastes 12:5.
83. Ibid.
84. Allen Afterman, *Kabbalah and Consciousness* (New York: Sheep Meadow Press, 1992), p. 66.
85. *Zohar* II:106b.
86. *Encyclopedia Judaica* 4:360, 7:240–45.
87. Ibid.
88. Ibid., 15:180.

# INDEX

Copartner with God, 75, 98, 286
Cordovero, Moses, 5
Cosmic dance, 12, 143
Creation
    direction/source of, 59, 77
    multitude of stories of, 61
    mysteries of, 108, 217
    story of, 38, 56
    two stories of, 56
    as a verb, 70. *See also* Creation-ing
Creation-ing, 75, 215, 233, 249, 291, 296
Cremation, 295

*Daat* (knowledge), 84, 91, 264, 311
*Dana* (selfless giving), 194
Daniel, 131
David, King, 181, 279
Death, 29, 39, 112, 174, 191, 198, 249, 269,
        276, 280, 288, 294. *See also* Dying;
        *Mavet*
    challenging/influencing, 278–82, 288
    fear of, 281
    feather used at, 260
    first twelve months after, 262
    freedom from, 296
    as friend, 286
    gates of, 278
    nine hundred three types of, 278
    steals free will, 286
Déjà vu, 283
Demons, 37, 134, 135, 140–47
Destiny, 284
Deuteronomy, 49, 74
*Devekut* (attached to), 99, 159, 215, 227,
        231, 312
Dew, 263, 295
*Dhikr* (remembrance), 3
Divine
    attributes of the, 72
    communicating/connecting with the,
        11, 12, 38, 68, 70, 157, 215, 254, 296
    emanations, 51, 83
    essence of the, 99

gift from the, 92
image, 69, 118, 268
inspiration, 231
intention, 74
light of the, 157
presence of the, 51, 53, 62, 68, 69, 144,
        158, 170, 178, 206, 216, 296
Divine Providence, 246, 247, 249
DNA, 84, 85, 89
Dreams, 13, 69, 74, 102, 105, 108, 110, 115,
        139, 146, 182, 188, 241, 256, 269, 270,
        280–87, 322
*Drosh* (examination), 47
Dying
    experience of, 278–81
    process, 257, 280
    rituals, 253–61
    *See also* Death
*Dzogchen* (Buddhist meditation), 178,
        316

Eco-kosher, 14
Ecstasy, 170, 277
Eden, 44, 48, 292
Ego, 91, 213, 214, 224, 296
*Ein Sof* (Limitlessness), 35, 54, 65, 67–72,
        76, 77, 156, 264, 293. *See also* Ohr
        *Ein Sof*
Eleazar (talmudic sage), 121, 216
Electromagnetic force, 112, 134
Eliahu, 12, 24. *See also* Elijah
Eliezer, (talmudic sage) 49, 73, 307
Elijah, 74, 131, 139, 153, 216, 217, 280.
        *See also* Eliahu
Elisha
    our host, 59, 60
    prophet, 216
Elisha ben Abuya, 245
Enlightenment, 1, 9, 215
Enoch, associated with Metatron, 139
Enthusiasm, 191
Equanimity, 185, 214, 222–24, 249,
        257

Sparks, 28, 29, 35, 54
  divine, 155, 156, 179
  fallen, in need of redemption, 108
  raising 29, 126, 174, 180, 182, 189, 198,
    224, 261, 268, 286, 287, 294
  representing souls, 108
  from root souls, 224, 267
Spirit, 95, 97, 98, 113, 117
States, altered, 284
Steinsaltz, Rabbi Adin, 17, 304
Still small voice, 217
*Striemels* (top hats), 23
Sufi, 3, 69, 78
Sukkot, 158, 309
Supernal Mother, 51, 56

*Tahorah* (purification), 260
*Tallit* (prayer shawl), 192
Talmud, 17, 18
Talmud Torah (study), 185
Tanakh (entire Old Testament), 15, 18
Tarshish, 147
*Tashlich* (sending away), 256
TDS (Time Deficiency Syndrome), 166
*Techiat ha-maytim* (life eternal), 231
*Tefilla* (prayer), 129
*Tefillin* (prayer wrappings), 192
*Tehora he* (the soul is pure), 205, 206
Ten, significance of, 83, 84, 130
*Teshuva* (changing conduct), 129
Thirteen principles of faith, 294
Thirty days before death, 287
Thirty-two paths, 86
Thought, 67, 76, 91
  attaching to nothingness, 224
  controlling one's, 174
  negative, 180
Throne, 138, 181, 230
*Tiferet* (beauty), 84, 90, 93, 148, 264,
  312
*Tikkun* (fixing), 29, 30, 140, 179, 262,
  306

*Tikkun ha-nefesh* (mending the soul),
  179
*Tikkun ha-olam* (mending the world),
  180
*Tohu* (chaos), 29
Torah, 15, 47, 181
  as the mind of God, 52
  Oral/Written, 15, 16, 17
  study, 12, 46, 185
  as the Tree of Life, 49
Tree of Knowledge, 44–56, 136, 248
Tree of Life, 44–49, 51, 55, 91, 264
*Treif* (torn), 198
Truth, 14, 282
Tu b'Shevat (festival of trees), 252
Twelve months to purify soul, 262
*Tza'ar ba'alei* (kindness to animals), 198
*Tzaddik* (righteous person), 105, 123–26,
  184, 232, 237–42, 263, 264, 320
*Tzeddakah* (charity), 27, 129, 187, 191, 192,
  194–96, 317
*Tzimtzum* (contraction), 76
*Tzippiyah* (contemplative observation), 37

Understanding, fifty gates of, 92
Unity, 38, 98, 99
Universe, 91, 131, 224
Uriel (archangel), 135, 145

Valley of Ben-Hinnom, 291
*Va-omer Elohim* (and God said), 83,
  311
Vessels, 29, 76
Vital, Chaim, 216, 267

Watchfulness, 184, 191
Water, 50, 84, 121, 131
Western Wall, 3, 192
Will
  divine, 192, 196, 224, 296
  to give, 76, 77
  to receive, 76, 77